Acclaim for Thomas H. Kean and Lee H. Hamilton's

WITHOUT
PRECEDENT

"A devastating indictment of how the Bush administration blocked the Sept. 11 commission at virtually every step." —*Los Angeles Times*

"Kean and Hamilton show us the infighting, the political wrangling, and the Washington conniving. They are not shy about telling the truth as they determined it." —*The Decatur Daily*

"A story simply told, without bravado and posturing. It reveals two authors deeply imbued with an old-fashioned but intensely admirable sense of public service." —*The Globe and Mail* (Toronto)

"Provides us with an incisive overview about how our country makes national security policy, how the president is advised and the dangerous lack of entanglement between some competing bureaucracies. . . . Many of the facts [Kean and Hamilton] uncover will startle the reader. . . . Repeatedly and with terrific thoroughness, shows us how their commission attempted to examine how the systems in place failed to protect us." —*The Denver Post*

"Will give future historians an accurate account of [the 9/11 Commission's] sincere desire to make the nation safer." —*Pittsburgh Post-Gazette*

"Riveting. . . . Provides a behind-the-scenes look at the work of that groundbreaking commission. . . . One is left with is a sense of two public servants performing at the highest level." —*The Times-Picayune* (New Orleans)

"Like other members of their commission, [Kean and Hamilton] vowed to keep the issues before the American public. . . . With the publication of *Without Precedent* [they] are doing just that." —*The Christian Science Monitor*

WITHOUT
PRECEDENT

THOMAS H. KEAN AND LEE H. HAMILTON

Thomas H. Kean was governor of New Jersey from 1982 to 1990, and from 1990 until 2005 he was the president of Drew University. He has served on numerous national committees and commissions, and has worked tirelessly for over a quarter century on behalf of environmental and educational organizations. He lives in Bedminster, New Jersey.

Lee H. Hamilton is president and director of the Woodrow Wilson International Center for Scholars. He was a congressman representing Indiana's Ninth District from 1965 to 1999, during which time he was chairman and ranking member of the House Committee on Foreign Affairs, chairman of the House Permanent Select Committee on Intelligence, and chair of the Joint Economic Committee. He was also co-chair, with James A. Baker, III, of the Iraq Study Group. He lives in Alexandria, Virginia.

WITHOUT
PRECEDENT

THE
INSIDE STORY
OF THE

9/11

COMMISSION

THOMAS H. KEAN and LEE H. HAMILTON

WITH BENJAMIN RHODES

VINTAGE BOOKS

A DIVISION OF RANDOM HOUSE, INC.   NEW YORK

FIRST VINTAGE BOOKS EDITION, MAY 2007

The Library of Congress has cataloged the Knopf edition as follows:
Kean, Thomas H.
Without precedent : the inside story of the 9/11 Commission /
by Thomas H. Kean and Lee H. Hamilton—1st ed.
p.   cm.
1. National Commission on Terrorist Attacks upon the United States.
2. September 11 Terrorist Attacks, 2001.   3. Terrorism—Government
policy—United States.   4. National security—United States.
5. Intelligence service—United States.   6. Terrorism investigation—
United States.   7. Governmental investigations—United States.
I. Hamilton, Lee.   II. Title.
HV6432.7.K43 2006
973.931—dc22   2005056267

Vintage ISBN: 978–0–307–27663–6

Author photograph © David Coleman
Book design by Wesley Gott

www.vintagebooks.com

Printed in the United States of America
10 9 8 7 6 5 4 3 2 1

To the memory of the victims of September 11, 2001,
and to their loved ones

CONTENTS

WITHOUT
PRECEDENT

KEAN

————

SEPTEMBER 11, 2001

On the morning of September 11, 2001, I was at home in Bedminster, New Jersey, recovering from oral surgery. I called my dentist because one of my teeth was doing something strange, and he said, "Turn on the television. Something is happening at the World Trade Center."

When I turned on the set, the first plane had already hit and black smoke was billowing up from the North Tower. Like many Americans, I watched as a second plane, United Airlines Flight 175, crashed into the South Tower at 9:03.

My first impulse was to drive the thirty-five minutes to Drew University in Madison, New Jersey, where I was president. Drew has more than 1,600 undergraduates, and most of them live on campus. There was no precedent for how young people would react to a catastrophe of this scope. Given the school's location, I also worried that many students would have parents, brothers, or sisters working at the World Trade Center. It turned out to be a near miracle that the university was spared such a loss.

When I got to Drew, the phone lines were jammed because so many parents were trying to get in touch with their children. I felt that it was important for students to have someplace to gather, so I sent an e-mail out and we sent runners to all of the dormitories: anyone looking for a place to go would be welcome in the auditorium at around twelve-thirty. I assembled psychological counselors, and Christian and Jewish chaplains. I presented all of the information available about what was going on at the World Trade Center, at the Pentagon, in Pennsylvania, and around the country. Then we did a little praying and some singing. Many of the students had tears in their eyes. Others were numb with shock. At four o'clock, we held a service for prayer.

There was a great impulse to help. Drew is only thirty miles away from New York City and a whole cadre of Drew students, faculty, and staff went to assist with the recovery and treatment operations taking place along the Hudson River, across from Lower Manhattan. Other students were running blood drives. The thought at that point was that there would be many wounded people coming out of Ground Zero, and some would be evacuated across the river. Unfortunately, there was not much to do. Few in the towers survived. Those who did were very badly burned.

In those initial days, I was concerned that Drew's large Muslim population might become a target for people's anger, but my fears were misplaced. On the night of September 11, the students organized a candlelight vigil, and people of all faiths gathered peacefully together. Three days later, the students organized a march through our 200-acre, tree-shrouded grounds. Several hundred young people moved quietly across the campus to honor the lives of the victims, reaffirm their patriotism, and make a statement for peace. The leaders of our Jewish and Muslim student groups walked side by side. At the head of the procession, a young woman sang "Amazing Grace." I was walking well toward the back, but I could hear her beautiful voice echoing off Drew's stone buildings.

This spirit lasted. The Muslim holiday of Ramadan was in November and December of 2001. Drew's Muslim Student Association held a dinner to mark the end of the holiday, and when I stopped by I found Jewish students, along with a rabbi, serving the food.

Those were tough months for New Jersey. You could live anywhere along a corridor in central and northern New Jersey and easily have worked at the World Trade Center: it was the final stop for the PATH commuter train that ran across the Hudson River to Jersey City and Newark; a convenient destination for commuters driving through the Holland Tunnel or taking New Jersey Transit from some of our state's most densely populated areas; and a short trip across the river on a number of ferries. Like many New Jerseyites, I had been in the Twin Towers for countless meetings and engagements—when I was New Jersey's governor from 1982 to 1990, and as a private citizen. For people who approached New York City from New Jersey, those buildings were often their first glimpse of the city in the distance.

All told, nearly seven hundred New Jerseyites perished on 9/11. It seemed that there wasn't a single town that didn't lose somebody. For six months there were funerals across the state. Some families held services right away. Others needed time—days, weeks, or months, as they held out hope for a miracle, or awaited the call notifying them that the remains of a loved one had been found at Ground Zero. Memorials to those who had passed away started to dot the New Jersey landscape.

Don Peterson, who had been my tennis doubles partner for twenty-five years, died with his wife, Jean, when United Airlines Flight 93 crashed into a field in Pennsylvania, forced down by the heroic actions of its passengers.

Fiduciary Trust, a company on whose board of directors I sit, lost eighty-six people in their offices at the World Trade Center that day. One was a friend named John Hartz; John's wife, Ellie, would work as a staff member for the 9/11 Commission, serving as our liaison to the families of the victims of September 11.

On October 16, I spoke at a memorial service held by Fiduciary Trust at the Cathedral of St. John the Divine on Amsterdam Avenue in Upper Manhattan. St. John's is the largest church in the United States and the largest Gothic cathedral in the world. Its history stretches back over a hundred years, and it is projected to be up to another hundred before the building is completed. It is, quite literally, a bridge between the past and the future. That morning, the church was packed with more than 5,000 people. There were prayers, and readings from scripture and from the writings of Abraham Lincoln. When I got up to speak, I was struck when I looked out at the crowd. In the sea of people, I could pick out pregnant women and widows holding newborn babies who would never know a father.

AN APPOINTMENT

THE CALL TOOK ME TOTALLY by surprise. I was at home on a Saturday afternoon, December 14—the day after Henry Kissinger resigned as chairman of the 9/11 Commission—when the phone rang. It was Karl Rove, who was at the time President Bush's senior policy advisor. I did not know Rove very well, though I had met him a couple of times. He said that a great many names had been given to the president as possible members of the commission to investigate the 9/11 attacks, and mine was one of them. They were now calling people on the list to see who was interested and willing to serve. I said I was.

In the years since I served as governor, I have turned down multiple offers to reenter public life—from proposed Cabinet appointments from presidents of both parties, to suggestions that I run for the Senate. But given the impact that 9/11 had had on New Jersey, this was one offer I would not refuse.

The next call came the following afternoon. It was from Andy Card, the White House chief of staff, whom I've known for quite some time, dating back to when he worked for the first President Bush. He said, "Would you do me a personal favor? Would you pretend that I'm the president of the United States?" I said, "What?" He said, "The president has time with his family for the first time in weeks, and we're trying to preserve that time. So would you pretend I'm the president and say yes?"

It took a minute to register what he wanted me to say yes to. I accepted, and the president called me the following day. We spoke briefly. He thanked me for accepting the position of chairman and pledged his administration's cooperation. He offered his judgment that I would probably find structural problems across the government and its intelligence agencies. He was very gracious.

Then I hung up and was alone with this new responsibility, and my mind started to run through the problems. The commission was split, five Republicans and five Democrats, each appointed by their party leadership. Our work would run right into the heat of the presidential election. I didn't know any of the other commissioners well, with the exception of Jim Thompson, whom I knew from when we were both governors. The commission's budget was $3 million, and that would clearly be insufficient.

I thought about how the commission could fail. In my mind, two things could sink us: leaks of classified information, which would destroy our credibility in Washington; and partisanship, which would destroy our credibility with the American people.

I thought about what success would look like. My background is in history: that's what I did graduate work in, and that's what I taught at the beginning of my career. To succeed, *The 9/11 Commission Report* had to be a historical document, not simply a government report with a list of conclusions. We had to present the facts in a story that could be easily understood by the American people, and it had to be clear where those facts were coming from. We could not simply recommend a policy change because it was a good idea: every single recommendation that we made had to spring from the story of 9/11.

Shortly after I was appointed, I went on a long-scheduled vacation to Barbuda, an island off Antigua in the Caribbean, with a local population of only 1,500 people. Barbuda is remote and intentionally underdeveloped; you have to schedule a time in order to use one of the island's few phones. While there, I was receiving daily calls from my vice-chair, Lee Hamilton, and from the White House, which was helping to get the commission set up, so I rented a "global phone," which can be used around the world. The global phone works well, unless a cloud drifts over your head, and on several occasions I found myself standing on an empty beach trying to explain to Lee or Andy Card that I had lost him because of the clouds.

The White House is not accustomed to having problems reaching people, but the respite gave me further time to think. My role as chairman was unique because nearly everyone on the commission had more expertise in national security issues than I did. I'm from New Jersey, not Washington. I was not going to know the documents the best, or bring extensive firsthand experience with counterterrorism to bear. I had to think about how we commissioners were going to conduct ourselves publicly, because I was committed to an open and transparent investigation. I had to think about the publication of our report from day one, because without a successful presentation of our findings and recommendations, they would not be accepted. And I had to think about how to get five Republicans and five Democrats to stop being Republicans and Democrats for the purposes of our work, in the midst of an intensely partisan atmosphere in Washington, D.C.

Where I lacked experience in national security, I brought a lifetime of working with people from different political parties and with different points of view. In the New Jersey legislature, I became the Republican Speaker only by picking up Democratic votes. During my eight years as governor, I always had a Democratic state assembly. I have been on numerous committees and commissions—for instance, a stint chairing the National Wetlands Policy Forum, a group of policy makers, environmentalists, developers, conservationists, and farmers from around the country who somehow had to agree upon a national wetlands policy.

To succeed in a commission, you have to hear one another out and get to know one another as people. We had to get together around the dinner table, not just the conference room table, so that we could laugh together as well as negotiate together. We had to give everyone the opportunity to have his say, so each commissioner would be invested in the process. Throughout our inquiry, every single commissioner was absolutely essential at one point or another—in coming up with an idea, formulating a compromise, or reaching out to a constituency. We could not have succeeded without all of those contributions, and we could not have had those contributions if people had felt alienated or put off.

From the very beginning, I considered Lee Hamilton my co-chair. I knew Lee mostly by reputation, and he more than lived up to that reputation throughout the commission's work. He is one of our nation's finest public servants. From the moment of our first meeting, I knew we could work together. His gentlemanly manner and judicious approach would steer us through partisan disputes, and his vast experience in national security provided a constant source of education for me.

Whereas Lee knew Washington, I knew the region most devastated by 9/11. I cannot say for sure why I was selected as chairman, but my best guess is that it was because I am from New Jersey. This allowed me to work with the families of victims, who were so essential to lobbying the commission, following our work, and seeing that our recommendations were implemented.

I knew them: they had been my neighbors and constituents. I was physically close to them, and they came by Drew for many meetings. We spent incalculable hours talking—on the phone, via e-mail, or in my office. We did not always agree: one time they shouted at me so loudly that reporters could hear the racket from downstairs, and an account of the meeting was printed in the next day's Newark *Star-Ledger*. But none of what the 9/11 Commission accomplished could have happened without them or their determination to see that others not experience a similar loss in future attacks.

From a beach in Barbuda, I could not foresee the multitude of difficulties we would face; nor could I foresee the great moments. On April 29, 2004, all ten of us were ushered into the Oval Office to meet with President Bush and Vice-President Cheney. In the preceding two months alone, we had been through nationally televised hearings; a high-profile dispute between Condoleezza Rice and her former aide, Richard Clarke; attacks on the commission's credibility; the growing drumbeat of the presidential campaign; and the daunting task of considering our report and its recommendations.

President Bush said he would meet with us for as long as we wanted and that he would answer any questions; we had already held a similar meeting with former President Clinton. After the first few exchanges, I realized the magnitude of what was happening: ten independent citizens sitting in the White House and asking questions of the president and vice-president about a national catastrophe. It was without precedent.

I looked out the window at the sun-splashed monuments on the Washington Mall and realized that this was more than simply an interview with the president. This was precisely how democracy is supposed to work.

HAMILTON

SEPTEMBER 11, 2001

On September 11, 2001, I was scheduled to fly on a 9:55 a.m. flight from Washington to Indianapolis. The plane had not yet departed the gate at Ronald Reagan Washington National Airport when a flight attendant rushed up the aisle and told everybody to get off.

My first thought was that there was a fire on the plane. I got my carry-on bag and was off the plane quickly. When we walked through the gate and into the terminal, it was clear that everyone else at the airport was deplaning—the place was crowded and chaotic. Word spread quickly that the airport was being shut down.

I looked out the big glass window at the north end of the terminal and saw clouds of black smoke, but I could not see the source. I started talking with people around me. Several of them said a helicopter had slammed into the Pentagon. I tried to use my cell phone, but it did not work. What I did not know was that American Airlines Flight 77 had taken off at 8:20 a.m. from Dulles Airport, about twenty-five miles away, and crashed into the Pentagon at 9:37, about a mile from where I was standing.

I walked out into the clear and warm September day and found my car in the airport lot. As soon as I turned on the radio, I began to get reports of what was happening—two planes had struck the World Trade Center in New York, another had crashed into the Pentagon, and more planes were unaccounted for. I spent the next three hours making the short drive home as the two towers collapsed in New York City and the scope of the tragedy broadened. Traffic was bumper to bumper; it was the worst grid-lock I had ever seen. People were evacuating Washington.

I realized this was a catastrophic event that would profoundly change both America and American foreign policy for years to come. I had been in the United States Congress for thirty-four years—from 1965 until 1999—serving on the House International Relations Committee for that entire time. When I entered Congress, I had to explain to constituents back home in southern Indiana why American troops were at war in Southeast Asia. When I left Congress, the topic was what role the United States should play as the only superpower in a post–cold war world. In between had been the establishment of relations with China, the hostage crisis in Iran, the endless Middle East peace process, the disintegration of the Soviet Union, the Persian Gulf War, and the U.S. interventions in the former Yugoslavia.

I quickly thought that we had not paid enough attention to terrorism. I remembered numerous briefings on the subject over the years. Terrorism, after all, had been with us—notably the bombing of the U.S. Marine barracks in Beirut in October 1983, and al Qaeda's near-simultaneous attacks on our embassies in Kenya and Tanzania in August 1998. Yet here was an attack on the domestic centers of American economic and military power, with thousands of American civilians lost. Here was a singular event in American history.

It was not possible to see the full implications of 9/11 then, just as we still struggle with them today, but I tried to sort through it all in the days ahead. I am the director of a center for advanced research in Washington, D.C., called the Woodrow Wilson International Center for Scholars, which seeks to bridge the worlds of scholarship and policy. On September 11, our mission altered in ways big and small. Terrorism and the turmoil it represented vaulted to the top of the agenda for many of our programs. The process of obtaining visas became much more difficult for some of our international scholars. Parts of the world that had seemingly slipped from view—notably Afghanistan—were now under a microscope. Security at the Ronald Reagan Federal Building, where we are located, increased dramatically.

I was called to testify at several congressional hearings, including a September 26, 2001, open hearing of the House Permanent Select Committee on Intelligence with the subject "Defining Terrorism and Responding to the Terrorist Threat." Among my fellow panelists was Paul Bremer, who had recently headed up a commission on terrorism, and would go on to be America's envoy in Iraq. Part of the reason I was called to testify was that I had previously chaired the Intelligence Committee. But another was that I had served on the United States Commission on National Security in the 21st Century—better known as the "Hart-Rudman Commission" after its leaders, former Senators Gary Hart and Warren Rudman.

Almost two years before 9/11, that commission issued a report warning of terrorist attacks on the homeland: "America will become increasingly vulnerable to hostile attack on our homeland, and our military superiority will not entirely protect us. . . . Americans will likely die on American soil, possibly in large numbers."

Largely because of this finding, the Hart-Rudman Commission received much attention in the days after 9/11. Its many recommendations—unanimously supported by seven Republicans and seven Democrats, and issued on May 15, 2001—went largely unheeded before 9/11. Foremost among those was the creation of a "National Homeland Security Agency," a recommendation that helped provide a blueprint for the eventual creation of the Department of Homeland Security.

Like many Americans in the months after 9/11, I found myself on a learning curve. I was placed on the president's Homeland Security Advisory Council, and grappled with many questions: Who is the enemy? How much liberty should Americans give up for security? How do we make hard choices about distributing resources for homeland security? How do we pursue foreign policy that goes after the terrorists while also preventing the emergence of new terrorists?

I began reading books on terrorism and Islam. The talks I gave on foreign policy now focused on terrorism and how 9/11 had changed the international environment. From Washington, D.C., to Bloomington, Indiana, I found that Americans were more concerned about their personal security than in any time in my memory.

I thought how wrong much of our national security debate had been over the years. I could not help but go back over decades of U.S. foreign policy. I found myself thinking: What did I know about terrorism? What should I have noticed? In the early 1990s, I was in Congress when we agreed to station U.S. troops in Saudi Arabia. I supported it, and don't remember much debate on it or opposition to it—we needed to contain Saddam Hussein, protect the Gulf States, and ensure the global energy supply. There was virtually no consideration about whether terrorists would be mobilized by the presence of "infidel" armies on sacred soil. Yet here was Usama Bin Ladin saying that that decision had triggered his attack on the United States.

I also thought of the recommendations and reports, such as those of the Hart-Rudman Commission, that had long sat on shelves. In October 2002, I testified before the House and Senate Joint Inquiry into the 9/11 attacks. The subject was the organization of our intelligence agencies; as I had for decades, I argued on behalf of reform.

I also followed closely the debate over the creation of the 9/11 Commission during the summer of 2002. I did not think that I would be a part of it, but I supported it. We had much to learn by looking back, and much to do to protect our people going forward.

APPOINTMENT

I RECEIVED TWO PHONE CALLS from Senator Tom Daschle of South Dakota, the Democratic leader in the Senate—one at the beginning of December, and one on December 12, 2002. In the first call, he asked me if I would serve on the 9/11 Commission, with Henry Kissinger as chairman, and George Mitchell as vice-chairman. I agreed. The next time, he offered an additional surprise. George Mitchell was resigning. Would I consider taking on the job of vice-chair? I immediately said yes. It was not a hard decision. The commission had important work to do; I felt I had an obligation.

The first thought when I hung up the phone was: What do I do now? I turned immediately to the statute for the commission, and was impressed by how broad it was. I was also struck by the reporting date, May 2004, putting us up against the presidential election.

I had run some high-profile investigations before—for instance, the House committee that looked into Iran-Contra in 1987, and the so-called October Surprise Committee, which looked into the release of American hostages in Iran. But in Congress, you have an entire infrastructure on hand to conduct your investigations—congressional staff, security clearances, offices, hearing rooms, and the power to subpoena documents. With a commission, you are starting from scratch. I did not know whom to call.

I thought immediately of the importance of hiring good staff. The commission was mandated to look at a lot of areas—from aviation security to intelligence to emergency response. We would need diverse expertise. I thought about the need for more money—I didn't see any way that the $3 million allotted to us would be adequate for such a monumental task.

I also thought about the incredible responsibility to issue recommendations. People in government are overwhelmed by crises, particularly in wartime. They don't have much time to step back and consider the big picture. We had some political clout with the lineup of commissioners who'd been appointed; we had a mandate that touched upon so many aspects of government; and we would be in the public eye. Here was a chance to effect some dramatic and positive change. From the first day of the commission, I was constantly thinking about what our recommendations would be and how we would go about implementing them so that we could avoid the fate of so many commissions whose counsel had gone unheeded.

I knew we had to be unanimous if the American people were to accept our findings and support the implementation of our recommendations. Luckily, we had an extraordinary chairman in Tom Kean. I had met Tom once or twice before, but did not really know him. Tom has a low-key and patient manner that lends itself to consensus building. He always hears people out. He always shares the spotlight. He cultivates collegiality. It was enormously important that Tom was from New Jersey. He had suffered the tragedy far more immediately than I, as his friends and community had been directly affected. Even living near the Pentagon in northern Virginia, I was struck by how much more traumatic 9/11 had been for the New York area. Everybody knew somebody who'd been affected. Tom appreciated that trauma. He spent scores and scores of hours meeting with the families of the victims—many of whom were from New Jersey. He brought to our investigation that very raw, emotional chord that 9/11 had struck in his region.

In December 2002, before I met with Tom, I went up and talked to some of my former colleagues on Capitol Hill. I was impressed by the interest in Congress—people were tracking this commission; they had high expectations. What I did not fully appreciate was the amount of public interest there would be in our work. Over the next twenty months, you could feel that interest grow: through the prominent coverage of our struggle for access to documents and people, to our public hearings in 2004. There were emotional outbursts in public and private, and more controversies than I could ever have anticipated, but there was also a sense that we had a chance to achieve something special. The nation had come together—Democrats and Republicans—so admirably in the aftermath of 9/11, and that was a source of inspiration to us. We bore that legacy on our shoulders.

1

SET UP TO FAIL

APPROACHING
AN IMPOSSIBLE TASK

[E]xamine and report upon the facts and causes relating to the terrorist attacks of September 11, 2001, occurring at the World Trade
Center in New York, New York, in Somerset County, Pennsylvania,
and at the Pentagon in Virginia.

> — From Public Law 107-306, signed by President
> George W. Bush, November 27, 2002

W E WERE SET UP TO FAIL. The thought occurred to both of us as we
prepared to meet for the first time on a cold day just before the
Christmas season of 2002. The full 9/11 Commission would not meet for
another month; this meeting would be just the two of us.

A thicket of political controversy lay ahead. The legislation creating the
commission had been signed into law by President George W. Bush, after
extended wrangling between Congress and the White House through the
heated and often bitter midterm elections of 2002. We were scheduled to
issue our final report in May 2004, just as the presidential election would
be approaching full boil.

We had an exceedingly broad mandate. The legislation creating the
commission instructed us to examine

(i) intelligence agencies; (ii) law enforcement agencies; (iii) diplomacy; (iv) immigration, nonimmigrant visas, and border control;
(v) the flow of assets to terrorist organizations; (vi) commercial aviation; (vii) the role of congressional oversight and resources alloca-

tion; and (viii) other areas of the public and private sectors determined relevant by the Commission for its inquiry.

In other words, our inquiry would stretch across the entire U.S. government, and even into the private sector, in an attempt to understand an event that was unprecedented in the destruction it had wrought on the American homeland, and appalling even within the catalogue of human brutality.

The breadth of the mandate was exceeded by the emotional weight of 9/11: a singularly shocking, painful, and transformative event in American history that was, in many ways, ongoing. We stepped into moving streams: a congressional inquiry into the attacks was winding down; family members of victims were demanding answers to tough questions; the wounds of regions such as the New York and Washington areas were still fresh; and the nation was fighting a war against terrorism around the world, preparing to go to war in Iraq, and receiving periodic terror alerts at home.

In front of us, we knew, were provocative questions: Was 9/11 preventable? Who was the enemy who had perpetrated this attack? Why did they hate us? What had our government done to fight terrorism before 9/11? How did one assign accountability for 9/11? Were we safer now than we had been on September 11, 2001? What could we do to make the American people safer and more secure?

To answer those questions, we would have to review the most sensitive information in the United States government, talk to top officials in two administrations—one Republican, one Democratic—and conduct an exhaustive review of the facts. We would have to revisit painful events. And when we met for the first time, we were approaching this task with no infrastructure: no offices, no staff, no government security clearances that would allow us to view the necessary information, and a dramatically insufficient budget of $3 million.

Both of us were aware of grumbling around Washington that the 9/11 Commission was doomed—if not designed—to fail: the commission would splinter down partisan lines; lose its credibility by leaking classified information; be denied the necessary access to do its job; or alienate the 9/11 families who had fought on behalf of its creation. Indeed, the scenarios for failure far outnumbered the chances of success. What we could not have anticipated were the remarkable people and circumstances that would coalesce within and around the 9/11 Commission over the coming twenty months to enable our success.

But on December 18, 2002, we were starting without any blueprint for how to go forward. The clock had started ticking almost a month earlier, when President Bush signed the bill creating a 9/11 Commission. So we were, in fact, already running behind.

FALSE STARTS

THE STORY OF HOW THE 9/11 COMMISSION was created and began its work is one of false starts.

The idea of forming an independent commission to look into the 9/11 attacks was first voiced in the Senate by Senators Joe Lieberman (D-Conn.), John McCain (R-Ariz.), and Robert Torricelli (D-N.J.) in October of 2001. Strong support emerged in the House, led by Representative Tim Roemer (D-Ind.), who was joined by Representatives Chris Shays (R-Conn.) and Nancy Pelosi (D-Calif.). But it would be more than a year before legislation creating the commission was passed by Congress and signed into law by President Bush.

Part of the reason for this lapse in time was the work of a congressional inquiry into the 9/11 attacks that was conducted jointly by the House and Senate Intelligence Committees, and led by Senator Bob Graham (D-Fla.) and Congressman Porter Goss (R-Fla.). From February to December 2002—and particularly in public hearings in September and October— the Joint Inquiry of the Intelligence Committees shed light on some of the intelligence lapses that had preceded 9/11. Americans learned about how the FBI and CIA were hampered by an inability and a reluctance to share information; how two 9/11 hijackers known to the CIA had lived openly under their own names for a period of months in Southern California; how a memo originating from the FBI's Phoenix field office had suggested that the issue of Arab men receiving training at flight schools needed to be looked into; and how Zacarias Moussaoui had been arrested in Minnesota weeks before September 11 and described as a terrorist suspect with an interest in flight training.

The Joint Inquiry did excellent work, but it was clear that the 9/11 story went well beyond the performance of the intelligence agencies under the jurisdiction of the Intelligence Committees. How do you tell the story of 9/11 without assessing the borders that the hijackers penetrated, the aviation security that they foiled, the military and diplomatic policies that the United States used to pursue Usama Bin Ladin and al Qaeda in the months and years preceding September 11, 2001, or the emergency response in New York and northern Virginia on that horrible day? Revelations of disturbing problems in our intelligence agencies also suggested the need for further investigation. The clock was set to run out on the Joint Inquiry at the end of 2002, and the inquiry was uncovering more leads than it had the time to track down. If there were such systemic problems, then there clearly needed to be further inquiry into what went wrong and how to protect the American people better.

These two shortcomings—the need for a more comprehensive telling of the 9/11 story, and the need to contemplate further how to keep the American people safer—were complemented by other thorny issues. One was access. Because the Joint Inquiry was a congressional committee, the White House cited the constitutional separation of powers, and refused to turn over a slew of documents sought by the Intelligence Committees—for instance, records from the National Security Council, which coordinates counterterrorism policy for the government, and the president's daily intelligence briefings. For similar reasons, key White House officials such as then National Security Advisor Condoleezza Rice did not testify before the Joint Inquiry.

Another problem was partisanship. If an inquiry were to be broadened from examining the performance of intelligence agencies to include an examination of the wider policy choices of the Bush and Clinton administrations, then it would be far more difficult for Republican and Democratic members of Congress to work in a nonpartisan manner as the 2004 elections loomed.

All of these factors pointed toward the need for an independent, bipartisan commission with complete access to government documents and officials. Senator Lieberman introduced legislation on this in the spring of 2002, while the Joint Inquiry was still at work, and there was extended debate through the summer about the need for an independent commission. The chief obstacle was the White House, which argued that the congressional inquiry was continuing, and that an independent investigation would distract the government from waging the ongoing war on terrorism. At several points, it appeared that the proposal to create a 9/11 Commission was dead.

This is when the 9/11 families made their voices heard. In the aftermath of the attacks, many of the families who had lost loved ones found themselves alone in their grief, and at the same time presented with baffling and heartbreaking responsibilities. Imagine having to fill out detailed forms for 9/11 charity funds only weeks after you have lost a husband or wife; or attending meetings for one of the many memorials being built in the middle of Pennsylvania, northern Virginia, and New York, and in the smaller communities so hard hit in the greater New York area. In confronting these new and unique responsibilities, many families formed strong bonds. Some founded support groups, which connected them with other survivors or with family members of victims, and served as clearinghouses for information.

Take the experience of just one family member, Mary Fetchet. Mary is a social worker from New Canaan, Connecticut, who lost her twenty-four-year-old son, Brad, in World Trade Center 2. Through the initial excruciating days of checking hospitals for Brad, Mary and her husband started opening their house to other families, sometimes hosting hundreds of people. Mary then received a 600-page booklet from her congressman, Chris Shays, about how to navigate the various scholarship funds and other compensation vehicles that were being put together for survivors and the families of victims. Congressman Shays and other members of Congress from the region helped the families through the process of understanding these issues—including the heartbreaking task of recounting on dry, impersonal forms the details about a deceased loved one, ranging from how much money that person earned to his or her day-to-day expenses.

Soon Mary found herself traveling to New York with a handful of other families for a meeting at Senator Hillary Clinton's (D-N.Y.) office, at which they discussed the calculation of "economic and non-economic damages." Attending this meeting qualified Mary as an expert, and before she knew it she found herself behind a microphone explaining economic and noneconomic damages to an auditorium full of 9/11 families and reporters, even though she had avoided public speaking for much of her life. Her attendance at these meetings landed her on a Family Advisory Board, whose job was to sort through issues for a 9/11 memorial.

Like many other family members, Mary was moving from one issue to the next, all the while dealing with the grief of losing a loved one and the horror of waiting for his remains to be found in the rubble of New York City's Ground Zero. Some of these families began to ask questions: What was the government doing to protect my loved one before 9/11? Why weren't there better evacuation procedures at the World Trade Center? What happened on those four flights? Why wasn't the memo from the FBI's field office about Arab men training in flight schools acted upon?

Soon these families turned their grief—and the connections they had made with one another and their members of Congress—into advocacy. Learning about the proposal for an independent 9/11 Commission, they used their unique standing to push for a commission that could provide answers to some of their questions and issue recommendations to help ensure that others would not perish in future terrorist attacks. In June 2002, the families held a large rally in Washington, D.C.—where their interest in a commission converged with the efforts of certain members of Congress. Immediately, the issue of the 9/11 Commission gained prominence.

The families refused to take no for an answer. Some would come down to Washington to be told that Congress and the White House were trying to work something out on creating a 9/11 Commission, and to please be patient. Then, when these family members returned home, they would be notified that some remains of their loved ones had just been found— perhaps only a body part. This injected more than a little urgency into the process. And there were thousands of stories like this, many of which all ten commissioners would hear in the months ahead.

Over the summer of 2002, 9/11 families met with members of Congress and White House officials. Senators Lieberman and McCain, and Congressmen Roemer, Shays, and Chris Smith (R-N.J.) worked hard on Capitol Hill. Meanwhile, the American people showed a powerful interest in the information about the 9/11 attacks coming out in the Joint Inquiry and in press reports. In September, the White House ended its opposition and announced that it would back the creation of a commission—with Press Secretary Ari Fleischer directly crediting the 9/11 families by saying, "The administration has met with some of the families of the 9/11 groups, who have talked about the need for a commission to look into a host of issues, and they have made compelling arguments."

There was much to be done, though. Over the next two months, detailed negotiations were undertaken about how to set up a ten-member commission. The main questions were about whether the president—or the congressional leadership—would appoint the chairman; what the breadth of the commission's mandate would be; how long the commission would have to complete its investigation; what the commission would be permitted to see; and what kind of subpoena power the commission would have. These may seem like highly technical issues, but each ended up having an enormous impact on how we did our work.

The issue of subpoena power was hugely important. Having the power to issue a subpoena would give the commission greater leverage in negotiations for access to people and sensitive government documents, and could—if need be—compel access to something when it was denied or slow in coming. The question was whether it would take five or six votes to issue a subpoena. On a commission with five Republicans and five Democrats, this slight mathematical difference was crucial. Ultimately, the commission did get subpoena power, and it was determined that the issuing of a subpoena would require either the concurrence of both the chair and vice-chair, or at least six votes in favor—meaning that bipartisan agreement would be needed. The question of whether or not to subpoena documents, particularly from the White House, became one of the most vigorously debated issues within the commission, almost causing us to split apart at certain junctures.

Another issue that would affect our work was the time allotted for the commission's investigation. Republicans wanted the inquiry to last one year—placing the reporting date sometime in late 2003; Democrats wanted the inquiry to last two years—placing the reporting date shortly after the 2004 presidential election. The two sides decided to split the difference, allowing eighteen months for the inquiry—a period of time that proved insufficient.

The final decisions on these issues were not yet made when Americans went to the polls in November 2002. The Republicans did well—taking back control of the Senate and holding their majority in the House. In this new political reality, the final issues were worked out—with the president getting the power to appoint the chairman of the commission, and the appointment of the other nine members going to the congressional leadership: Trent Lott (R-Miss.), the Republican leader in the Senate, would appoint two members; Dennis Hastert (R-Ill.), the Republican Speaker of the House, would appoint two members; Tom Daschle (D-S.D.), the Democratic leader in the Senate, would appoint two members; Richard Gephardt (D-Mo.), the Democratic leader in the House, would appoint two members; and Daschle and Gephardt would together choose the vice-chair.

It would be hard to design a more partisan way to appoint a commission. President Bush was gearing up for his reelection campaign. Congressman Gephardt was launching his own presidential campaign, and Senator Daschle was facing a tough fight for reelection in South Dakota. Senator Lott made his appointments while immersed in a brewing controversy over whether he would remain Republican leader, after he made comments praising the segregationist 1948 presidential campaign of outgoing senator Strom Thurmond. Complicating matters was an informal agreement that Senator McCain, a chief backer of the commission, could essentially veto one of Lott's choices—an arrangement made in part to reassure 9/11 family members, who were concerned that the commission would be deadlocked by the requirement of six votes for a subpoena, and would never be able to flex its muscle.

On the day before Thanksgiving—November 27, 2002—before an audience that included many of the 9/11 families, President Bush signed the bill creating the 9/11 Commission. The president used the White House's stately Roosevelt Room to announce his choice for chairman. It certainly had the feel of a momentous occasion; by his side was a figure well known to the American people and the world: Dr. Henry Kissinger, the former national security advisor and secretary of state under Presidents Nixon and Ford. President Bush instructed Kissinger to "follow all the facts, wherever they lead." Senator Daschle appointed George Mitchell, the former Senate majority leader and a chief negotiator of the Northern Ireland Peace Accords, to be vice-chair.

Many people applauded the seriousness of the appointments. Two men could not be better qualified to conduct a broad study of American policies. But controversy soon surfaced. Because the commission was created by an act of Congress, the Senate Ethics Committee determined that the commissioners had to abide by congressional rules on the disclosure of possible conflicts of interest. Kissinger ran a consulting firm well known to advise foreign governments and multinational corporations. To follow the rules of disclosure, he would have had to divulge any client that had paid him more than $5,000 over the preceding two years—in other words, his entire client list.

Kissinger is a lightning rod just as he is a towering figure in American life. Some see him as a leading American foreign policy maker of a generation; others see him as closely aligned with the government secrecy of the Nixon administration, or the still-debated foreign policy decisions of the early 1970s. In 2002, editorial pages and political pundits weighed in on both sides. *The New York Times* ran editorials with headlines such as "Henry Kissinger's Entangling Ties" and "The Kissinger Dodge," while *The Wall Street Journal* ran an editorial with the headline "Borking Henry Kissinger." Senator John Kerry (D-Mass.) called for Kissinger to step aside, while the White House argued that he was a presidential appointee, and thus not bound by the same rules of disclosure as the commissioners appointed by Congress.

It was an inauspicious beginning for a commission that would have to avoid partisanship in order to succeed. The 9/11 families weighed in largely on the side of disclosure; their chief concern was that the commission be independent of conflicting interests. On December 11, George Mitchell took the surprising step of resigning; he, too, was beginning to face questions about disclosures involving the client list of his law firm.

On December 13, more than two weeks after the clock started ticking on the commission, its chairman, Henry Kissinger, stepped aside.

In retrospect, there are important questions raised by the Kissinger-Mitchell controversy—chiefly, how do you get people for these types of inquiries who have the requisite expertise to probe the inner workings of government, while also insisting upon a level of independence from the very agencies and entities you are asking them to evaluate? Do you excessively limit the pool of potential commissioners by eliminating those with connections to certain private interests?

We had little time to contemplate such things. The appointments of Kissinger and Mitchell had been rolled out with great fanfare, followed by both men's high-profile appearances on Sunday television talk shows; our appointments came by press release. We, the substitutes, had to get out of the wake of this storm and get going with an investigation that had known little but tumult.

HOW TO SUCCEED

In december, shortly after his appointment, Tom came down to Washington for a series of White House meetings. Chief of Staff Andy Card was the only senior White House official whom Tom knew well, and in the early days of the commission, Card's aide for domestic policy, Jay Lefkowitz, was the commission's point person at the White House. On his first trip to Washington as chairman, Tom met with Card and Lefkowitz, and was then taken from office to office in the West Wing and introduced to many people who would be key figures in the coming months, including White House Counsel Alberto Gonzales and National Security Advisor Condoleezza Rice.

There was a good deal of wariness in the White House about the commission. People there were friendly and cordial, and pledged their cooperation. But many voiced concern that we not become a "runaway commission," in which Democrats or 9/11 families opposed to the Bush administration used the platform of the commission to bash the president. In those initial meetings, the White House also made clear to Tom that the commission should not expect extra time or money—"Live within your budget" was an oft-repeated phrase.

The White House also suggested some candidates for executive director for our staff. The importance of this position cannot be overstated. While the two of us and the other commissioners were guiding the investigation and handling the politics, we needed an exceptional individual to lead the staff and somehow organize the enormous and eclectic set of issues within our mandate. Tom met with one of the White House's suggested candidates—a former high-ranking military official—during his initial meetings; the man was well qualified, but he did not share the same vision for the commission as Tom.

Lee's earliest meetings were with Senator Daschle and the Democratic leadership office. If the White House was wary of a runaway commission, congressional Democrats were wary of a commission that was overly controlled by the White House—either through commissioners, staffing, or limitations placed on access to documents and people. Just as the White House proposed its own candidates for staff positions, the Democratic leadership also offered to help locate staff.

We both appreciated the early assistance from our party leadership. However, we knew the most important meeting was the first one between the two of us, and this took place on December 18 in Lee's office at the Woodrow Wilson International Center for Scholars, five days after the Kissinger resignation, for a lunch of soup and turkey sandwiches. Nearly the entire commission had been appointed, but we would not meet for another month. The holidays were approaching, people were clearing their schedules and adjusting to this new responsibility, and the two of us needed to figure out how to proceed.

We got along immediately. This proved extremely important—both for the sake of the commission, and because we would go through long stretches of time when we spoke to each other more than we spoke to our own wives. Tom made the first decision, which was that we would effectively be co-chairmen—meaning we would have to agree on key decisions—because he wanted to set a tone of collegiality and bipartisanship.

This was unusual; the chairman runs most commissions and congressional committees. But the truth is we disagreed on only one major issue throughout the tenure of the commission. Indeed, our tendency to agree led our fellow commissioners to refer to us as "the twins." We wanted this unified leadership to provide a model for the other commissioners and the commission staff. Unanimity on the commission was a must if the American people were to accept our findings as authoritative and support our recommendations. Otherwise, the commission's work would be chalked up as another partisan blame game.

We also decided to have an integrated—meaning nonpartisan—staff. In congressional committees, there is usually a Republican staff, which works for the Republican members of the committee; a Democratic staff, which works for the Democratic members; and staff aides assigned to individual members. This model could have bred division within the commission, with essentially two separate inquiries—one Republican, one Democratic—proceeding at the same time. By having an integrated staff, we wanted to send the message that we were going to be nonpartisan. We also took a subtle step to prevent the issuance of the dissenting reports that are often filed in congressional and independent inquiries—with the entire staff working toward one final report, it would be harder to prepare a separate, partisan document.

This unified front served as the commission's public face. We decided that in all press conferences and television interviews, the two of us would appear together. If a television station called Tom and asked for an interview, the answer was: "Not without Lee." This was a matter of some annoyance to television producers in the early going, but it served us well: the face of the commission that reached the American people was almost always bipartisan, even as the issues that sprang up were often infected with partisanship.

The most controversial decision was our determination to be as open as possible: we would hold hearings in public, and commissioners would speak freely about the progress of the investigation. Over the course of the commission, some people accused us of grandstanding; others said we were presenting preliminary findings and stoking the very partisanship we had hoped to avoid. One Op-Ed in *The New York Times* went as far as the headline "From One Commission to Another: Shut Up."

We felt that openness was a must. Part of the commission's function was to educate the public about 9/11, and to prepare them for our report and recommendations. Public hearings allow a commission to build credibility with the media and the American people by demonstrating the seriousness of the inquiry. Some commissions have done excellent work very quietly—going dark upon creation, and then emerging on the other side with a report. Usually that report, no matter how good, gets little notice from a media and public that is neither familiar with the commission nor conditioned for its findings. Then the report sits on a shelf, gathering dust.

We also felt an obligation to be public because we were dealing with 9/11. This was an event that had happened to all of us, so working in the light of day was appropriate. Indeed, there was a real hunger in America for greater openness—at the same time that we were getting started, *Time* magazine named as its "Person of the Year" three whistle-blowers, including Colleen Rowley, the FBI agent who wrote a memo shedding light on pre-9/11 failures within the Bureau. Americans would not have tolerated a commission that kept the public in the dark and refused to ask officials to testify in the open. People were entitled to answers about what happened before 9/11, and what the government was doing to keep them safe. Part of our reason for being was to perform that role, even though it upset some people at times—particularly during our more politically inflammatory hearings in 2004.

History also gave us a powerful incentive to be open about what level of access—to people and government documents—we were being given. This was a lesson we could take from the Warren Commission, which had looked at the John F. Kennedy assassination. For decades, the Warren Commission's findings have been poked and prodded by conspiracy theorists, in large measure because the commission is not perceived as having had full access to the most secretive materials in the government. Lee Harvey Oswald may have acted alone, but over the years people could point in different directions and say to the commission, "You didn't look at this document about U.S. policy toward Cuba; you didn't talk to so-and-so; you didn't turn over this stone." To avoid such accusations, we had to be able to stand up in front of the American people and say, "We have asked for everything that has to do with the 9/11 story, and have seen everything that we asked for."

In general, secrecy is a precursor to cynicism and conspiracy theories. Later in 2003, when pages of the Joint Inquiry report were deemed classified and were redacted from public view, this suggested to many that the role of Saudi Arabia in the 9/11 attacks was being covered up. When NORAD—the part of the military that protects America's airspace—was not forthright or accurate in its official statements about what transpired on 9/11, it provided room for alternative theories to emerge about what happened in America's skies on September 11, 2001—theories that ranged from the inaccurate to the bizarre. We wanted to give an authoritative account of 9/11; we did not want to give fodder to conspiracy theorists who could question why we were undertaking our investigation in secret.

Being public helped us stay in touch with the emotions of 9/11. Our hearings were passionate and heated at times, but if we had performed a dry policy study, we would have lost touch with the magnitude of our undertaking: a full airing of how nearly 3,000 people—with 3,000 sets of families and friends—were murdered. It was painful. But when we played tapes from that day—for instance, the voice of Betty Ong, the heroic flight attendant who called to calmly notify her dispatcher about the details of the hijacking—it brought home the responsibility that rested on all of us to get this right. In a small way, it was cathartic for the nation to confront publicly the horrors, and to learn the lessons, of a terrible moment in our history.

The 9/11 families kept us in closest touch with the emotions of the tragedy, and insisted the loudest that the commission not hide behind closed doors. We both met with representatives of the families shortly after our appointments, and quickly understood that we needed some mechanism to stay in touch with the families. The family representatives with whom we had the most contact—at the outset, and through the commission—formed a group called the Family Steering Committee (FSC). The FSC was made up of individuals who had lobbied for the commission, and who held leadership positions in four organizations— Families of September 11, Voices of September 11th, the Skyscraper Safety Campaign, and September 11th Advocates. There were other 9/11 family groups, but most of our contacts were with the individuals particularly active in lobbying the commission. Neither the broader universe of families nor the FSC was a monolith—they differed with us, and with one another, throughout our investigation.

Our initial family meetings were intense. Each family member had a painful story to relate. Many passed on pictures, keepsakes, or tributes to their husbands, wives, sons, daughters, brothers, and sisters who had perished. In Tom's first meeting with the FSC, he went around a conference room table and had each family member tell him something about their experience. Kristen Breitweiser, who was one of the most visible family advocates, took off a ring from her finger and passed it to Tom. She told him to put it on his finger and, choking up, said, "That's my husband Ron's wedding ring. I lost him on 9/11. That was found about six weeks later in the rubble with a part of his finger still in it. That's all I have left. Hold that ring, do your job, get the answers, and do what needs to be done to prevent future attacks."

That was the kind of emotional impact that the families brought to bear before, during, and after the commission: when holding a vigil in front of the Capitol or the White House, talking to the press, or lobbying a member of Congress. That emotion was connected to huge and specific expectations for what the commission should accomplish. Many families expected faster progress than we could deliver, believing that we could take the baton from the Joint Inquiry running at full speed. They were distressed by the fact that we had to act methodically: first hire a staff, draw up a budget, and get security clearances. Almost without fail, at the beginning of the commission and throughout, the families pressed us to move faster and be more aggressive.

One of the remarkable aspects of those first meetings was the amount of research the families had done. Tim Roemer recalls that when he first came into contact with one of the family members while he was on the Joint Inquiry, he was asked which body had more members, the House or the Senate. That inexperience faded fast: by the time we met with the families in December 2002, they knew how to get things done in Washington, and they had focused on particular issues.

The families gave both of us a document entitled "September 11 Inquiry: Questions to Be Answered," a list of fifty-seven questions and follow-up questions about 9/11 divided into eight categories. The level of detail on most of these questions was highly impressive—for example: "Why was the CIPRIS [the Coordinated Interagency Partnership Regulating International Students, created by Congress in 1996] system not used to track foreign students after it was recommended by the National Commission on Terrorism in 1998 and was so effective in trials?"

The families also had other demands. Initially, they had pressed for one of their own representatives to be named as a commissioner. After our appointments, they voiced some displeasure that the commission was made up of politicians, having wanted people from outside of the Washington establishment. In place of being on the commission, some of the family members advocated that one of them be hired to the commission's staff—something that we would consider in the coming months. They also had a long list of people they wanted us to call as witnesses at public hearings, going all the way up to Presidents Clinton and Bush.

Over the next twenty months, we had our ups and downs with the families, whose list of questions would grow. Often they were our closest allies, supporting our requests for more funding or more time on Capitol Hill. Sometimes, they were aggressive critics, issuing press releases blasting our approach. But there was no question that the families would be essential validators for our report. They had pushed for the commission, they were the public face of the most extreme form of suffering and loss that took place on 9/11, and they were watching us like hawks. If they were unsatisfied with our work, the impact of our findings would be greatly diminished.

The other item that had to be acted on right away was hiring an executive director. We needed someone quickly so we could start hiring other staff and setting up an infrastructure. Recommendations came from many sources, but we seriously considered only one candidate: Philip Zelikow. About fifty years old with a boyish face and carefully parted brown hair, Zelikow is a leading presidential historian, has worked on the National Security Council for George Herbert Walker Bush, has published a number of highly acclaimed policy books, and has directed the Miller Center of Public Affairs at the University of Virginia. He is equally at home discussing the origins of Islam, technological fixes for bureaucratic information sharing, or the details of how visas are processed. He expects a lot out of people, including himself, and is not afraid to break a little china trying to get something done. Throughout the tenure of the commission, it was not uncommon to receive e-mails from him sent well after midnight.

We found Zelikow on the recommendation of our fellow commissioner Slade Gorton, who had worked with him on the commission headed by Gerald Ford and Jimmy Carter on federal election reform (which Zelikow directed), and on the Markle Task Force on National Security in the Information Age. Lee called Zelikow first to gauge his interest, and then Tom followed up, reaching him in meetings with information technology leaders in Silicon Valley. Their conversation was extensive, and continued in a meeting at Drew University a few days later, in early January.

Zelikow had nearly the exact same conception of the commission as we did. Like Tom, he viewed it as a historian would—as telling the authoritative story of what had happened on September 11, 2001, so that our recommendations would emerge directly from the facts of the 9/11 story. Like Lee, he saw a chance to reform government to better face the threats of the twenty-first century. From the very beginning, he saw the need for a report prepared as a chronological history, written clearly for publication, and distribution in bookstores around the country, with notes and appendixes so that a reader could find where each conclusion had come from— an unusual format for a government report. He also stressed the need to look closely at the enemy. Because he had worked at the National Security Council, he had a quick grasp of the access—to documents and people— that we would need to get all of this done.

Zelikow was a controversial choice. In the 1990s, as an academic, he had co-authored, with Condoleezza Rice, a book about German unification, and he later assisted Stephen Hadley in running the National Security Council transition for the incoming Bush administration in 2000–2001. Democratic commissioners other than Lee were wary of Zelikow's appointment. The 9/11 families questioned his ability to lead a tough investigation. He was also known to be a somewhat combative manager—there was a view that he had stepped on a few too many toes in running the NSC transition.

But we had full confidence in Zelikow's independence and ability—and, frankly, we wanted somebody who was unafraid to roil the waters from time to time. He recused himself from anything involving his work on the NSC transition. He made clear his determination to conduct an aggressive investigation. And he was above all a historian dedicated to a full airing of the facts. It was clear from people who knew and worked with him that Zelikow would not lead a staff inquiry that did anything less than uncover the most detailed and accurate history of 9/11.

As historians, Tom and Zelikow also looked closely at the precedents of other commissions. The only real examples of commissions with mandates of the same size and import as ours were the Warren Commission, in 1963–1964, and the Roberts Commission, in 1941–1942, which investigated the attack on Pearl Harbor. Both provided cautionary tales.

In addition to demonstrating the need for a level of access—and a public conception of the level of access—that was unquestionable and complete, the Warren Commission convinced us of the need to clearly reference our sources. The Warren Commission—and the Lockerbie Commission on the bombing of Pan Am Flight 103—had this problem: probably good conclusions, but the reader couldn't tell where they were coming from. If we were going to write a definitive historical account, every fact and conclusion in the report had to be easily referenced to its source—which is why we ended up with two hundred pages of endnotes.

Neither the Roberts Commission nor a subsequent congressional inquiry into Pearl Harbor in 1946 provided an authoritative account of the Japanese attack on Hawaii, for these reasons and others. For one thing, the Pearl Harbor inquiries were perceived as partisan—intent upon finding individuals to blame, and not looking at the flaws across the government that had enabled the attack to take place. The Pearl Harbor inquiries also looked at the attack from only one side: ours. The other half of the story—the Japanese intent, planning, and execution of the strike—was ignored.

We could not repeat these mistakes. To avoid them, we had to create a new model for how to conduct a high-profile commission. We would be nonpartisan and independent. We would be public instead of secretive. We would stay in touch with the families who had a unique interest in our work, while also staying in touch with the American people. We would seek a level of access that was necessary to do our job and that could dispel claims that we had not seen everything. We would not miss the forest for the trees in the 9/11 story by looking solely for individuals to blame. And we would not neglect the enemy in telling the story.

THE MAKEUP OF THE COMMISSION

OF COURSE, THE MOST IMPORTANT FACTOR in whether or not we would succeed was the makeup of the commission. Any successful commission needs commissioners with political clout, broad expertise, and a willingness to work toward consensus. We had that—though consensus would not always be easy in coming.

On the Democratic side, the Senate leadership appointed Max Cleland and Richard Ben-Veniste, and the House leadership appointed Tim Roemer and Jamie Gorelick. On the Republican side, the House leadership appointed Fred Fielding and Jim Thompson, while the Senate leadership appointed Slade Gorton and John Lehman.

When he was appointed, Max Cleland was in the process of transitioning out of the U.S. Senate. A Vietnam veteran who lost both of his legs and one of his arms to a grenade, Max has relentlessly overcome huge odds over the years. He served as a Georgia state senator, as director of Veterans Affairs for President Jimmy Carter, and for more than a decade, as Georgia secretary of state, and he was elected to the Senate in 1996. In 2002, Max lost a hard-fought campaign against Saxby Chambliss—a campaign that left Max and many around him embittered by attack ads that suggested he was weak on national security. Max served with us for a year before he was appointed to the board of the Export-Import Bank (he was replaced on the commission by former Senator Bob Kerrey), and went on to take a prominent role in John Kerry's presidential campaign. While he was with us, Max always advocated taking a tough approach with the White House on access questions.

Richard Ben-Veniste is one of the most tenacious lawyers in Washington. He came to national attention at a young age as chief of the Watergate Task Force of the Watergate Special Prosecutor's Office, where he was a familiar sight at the side of Leon Jaworski. Over the years, he has held a variety of government posts, including chief counsel to the minority for the Senate Whitewater Committee. Richard was probably our toughest questioner at public hearings, challenging witnesses in a studied and even tone. With Richard on the commission, no one could accuse us of soft-balling witnesses.

When he was appointed to the commission, Tim Roemer was leaving the House, where he had represented the Third District of Indiana for twelve years, serving on the Intelligence Committee and the Joint Inquiry, and sponsoring legislation to create the 9/11 Commission. Tim has a sharp intellect, with both an M.A. and a Ph.D. from Notre Dame and several years' experience as a Capitol Hill staffer. During the struggle to create the commission, he forged close bonds with the 9/11 families, staying in touch to the point where he was attending their graduation ceremonies and other celebratory events, and he was the commissioner closest to the families throughout our inquiry.

Jamie Gorelick is an extraordinarily hardworking and able lawyer. The only woman on the commission, Jamie had pressed the Democratic leadership to appoint her, pointing out that their alternative choices—including former New York governor Mario Cuomo—would have left the commission with all men. When she was appointed, Jamie was vice-chair of Fannie Mae. She previously served as general counsel to the Department of Defense and was deputy attorney general in the Clinton administration. She came under fire toward the end of our work when Attorney General John Ashcroft confronted her at one of our hearings—an incident that prompted an ugly firestorm that even provoked a threat on Jamie's life. She was collegial and committed—as willing to open her home for a commission dinner as she was likely to send a steady stream of e-mails to us from her BlackBerry.

Fred Fielding provided invaluable and pragmatic legal counsel. Fred served as Richard Nixon's deputy White House counsel and then as Ronald Reagan's White House counsel. When we got bogged down in our negotiations with Judge Alberto Gonzales, President Bush's then White House counsel, Fred could weigh in as an authority on the separation-of-powers issues that were often in dispute, and serve as a useful contact to the White House legal staff. A widely connected figure in Washington who is extremely popular in the Republican Party, Fred has an affable manner that makes it a pleasure to be around him.

Jim Thompson brought a vital outside-the-Beltway perspective. He was Illinois's longest-serving governor, spending fourteen years in the statehouse. A tall former prosecutor who came to be known as "Big Jim" to Illinois political observers, Jim brought a sharp legal mind to our work. He also proved crucial at certain junctures because of his close relationship to Speaker Dennis Hastert, a fellow Illinoisan. This was particularly helpful, as the commission had to struggle against skepticism about our inquiry within the House Republican caucus. Jim also weighed in publicly at well-chosen moments—the opening comments he made at our first public hearing and his closing comments at the rollout of our report were among the most dramatic words spoken throughout our inquiry.

Slade Gorton brought a gift for consensus building that comes from a pleasant personality and eighteen years in the U.S. Senate. Slade served three terms representing the state of Washington, and remains a popular figure in the Senate Republican caucus, a fact that was certainly helpful to the commission. Slade is also an experienced and skilled lawyer, having served as Washington's attorney general. Time and again, he was able to bridge disagreements and divisions within the commission by proposing changes in language or a compromise on a complex issue, usually working with Jamie Gorelick. Often, he would take out a piece of paper in the middle of a particularly difficult commission meeting and quickly jot down language that ended up serving as our compromise position.

John Lehman was the Trent Lott appointee who met with the approval of John McCain. John was a National Security Council staffer under Henry Kissinger, and currently runs a private equity investment firm in New York. As secretary of the navy under President Reagan, he was a colorful and noteworthy reformer with a restless and powerful intellect, and in the years since, he has written several books about military history and the U.S. Navy. He took a particular interest in our recommendations on intelligence reform, and worked on that issue often throughout the commission. He was also very important to us in reaching out to the Department of Defense, and in staying in touch with Senator McCain, who was among our closest allies in the Senate.

Most of us were not well acquainted when we were appointed. We spoke by phone and some of us met informally, but it was well into January before we held our first meeting. It is Tom's style for people to get to know one another socially, as individuals, not just as Republicans or Democrats, so our first meeting was a dinner at the Wilson Center. It was January 26, 2003, Super Bowl Sunday. As the Tampa Bay Buccaneers ran up the score on the Oakland Raiders, we met over dinner. There was some wariness. While the event was largely social, there was already some rumbling about the two issues that would put some strains on the commission in the coming months—staffing, and whether or not to use our subpoena power.

After the dinner, Richard Ben-Veniste offered Tom a ride back to his hotel. It was a chance for each to scope the other out. In the days after Richard's appointment, Republicans had noted to Tom that Ben-Veniste was likely to be one of the tougher Democrats—the others had served either in Congress or in high-level executive branch positions, whereas Richard was more of a prosecutorial figure known for being a staunch partisan. On the drive back to the hotel, though, the ice broke a bit. As Richard dropped him off, Tom thought to himself, If we can laugh together, then we can work together.

The following day we met formally as a commission for the first time. The two of us made some opening remarks about the historic significance of the 9/11 Commission and the need for a bipartisan tone, and we welcomed Philip Zelikow as our choice for executive director. Each commissioner then spoke about the magnitude of the task that lay ahead and offered his or her personal reflections on 9/11. The tone was solemn. We all agreed that this was as important a task as any of us would have in public life.

Zelikow presented a conception of how the commission could do its work—with an emphasis on a report prepared for general public consumption and a staff organized around subjects of inquiry. Much of our initial discussion dealt with how to gain access to the House and Senate Joint Inquiry report, which we were mandated to look at as a starting point. We also discussed how to hire and organize a staff—a topic that would preoccupy, and at times divide, the commission for the next two months.

After the meeting, commissioners fanned out and met with 9/11 families, who had been invited to the Wilson Center. Each of us assured them of our seriousness, listened to their goals for our inquiry, and agreed to recuse ourselves from any area of the investigation where we might have a conflict of interest—for instance, several commissioners worked for law firms that represented American and United Airlines, and thus recused themselves from parts of the investigation that dealt with airline security. The families' tone was constructive, though skeptical. It was a full two months into our existence and we still had no office space, no schedule for our work, and no government security clearances. We had a total of one employee.

We issued a single press release announcing that we had met and hired Philip Zelikow as executive director. With the departure of the outsize personalities of Kissinger and Mitchell, public attention on the commission had dwindled. The following day, President Bush delivered his State of the Union Address and further laid out his case for war against Saddam Hussein. The commission that had managed to attract controversy before it even got started was now just a blip on the Washington radar screen.

2

A START-UP

I am one of the handful of lucky ones. Just blocks away from here
lay the unrecovered remains of many friends and colleagues, some
dear friends. They can no longer speak for themselves and I am left
with the unchosen, unhappy task of trying to speak for them.

> — Harry Waizer, Cantor Fitzgerald employee and
> 9/11 survivor, testifying at the 9/11 Commission's
> first public hearing, March 31, 2003

THERE IS NO ROAD MAP for how to set up a commission. We spent the
first few months of 2003 jumping over logistical and administrative
hurdles so we could get to work. Meanwhile, pressure to get going
increased. Families of victims who had waited more than a year for
answers did not understand why they had to wait longer. Members of Congress who had supported our creation asked what we were doing. Commissioners and staff were frustrated.

To understand our dilemma, it is helpful to think of the commission as
a start-up business. We had to hire and organize a staff, which grew to
nearly eighty people; plan how to organize our inquiry; locate and equip
office space; and like any start-up, we had to form a budget and seek
financing. Add to this, though, the fact that this start-up was being created
within the U.S. government: our office space and employees had to be
cleared by the FBI and CIA to handle top-secret information; we had to
seek financing from Congress and the White House; and we had to be
wary both of political concerns and of bureaucratic red tape.

The initial task was to hire a staff. Our agreement was that as chair and vice-chair, we had to concur on every person hired. After Philip Zelikow came on board as executive director, he began recruiting and interviewing candidates. Finding applicants was no chore—each commissioner had received hundreds of résumés; the chore was choosing people for the top jobs.

Zelikow was selected with little consultation with the rest of the commission, but several commissioners had concerns about the kind of inquiry he would lead. Since he was an academic, they worried that he would conduct a professorial study of U.S. policy. To balance that approach, they wanted a more prosecutorial investigator as the commission's general counsel—a lawyer who would chase down the facts, serve subpoenas, and interrogate witnesses; someone with experience running major litigations or congressional inquiries. Under this model, two people would effectively be in charge of the staff: Zelikow, driving policy analysis, and a general counsel, getting to the bottom of the 9/11 story.

The choice of a general counsel had strong political undertones. Because Zelikow had credentials as a Republican—indeed, one who had collaborated with Condoleezza Rice and aided the Bush transition—Democratic commissioners pressed for a powerful general counsel who could assure them and the American people that the commission wasn't soft-pedaling aspects of the investigation that might embarrass the Bush administration. Zelikow had recused himself from dealing with issues that involved Rice and the National Security Council transition of 2000–2001. But many people inside and outside of the commission still felt strongly that since the executive director was a Republican, other top staff positions had to be reserved for Democrats.

This understandable concern was somewhat assuaged when we hired Chris Kojm as deputy director. Chris was Lee's call. He had worked for Lee for fifteen years on the House International Relations Committee, including assisting with the Iran-Contra investigation, and had spent 1999–2002 serving as deputy assistant secretary of state at the Bureau of Intelligence and Research.

Chris is an unflappable professional, and an extraordinary organizer and editor, skills that would be invaluable in setting up public hearings and preparing the final report. With a patient manner, a sympathetic ear, and an understated style, Chris was a perfect complement to Zelikow—if Philip could roil the waters a bit, Chris could smooth them over. As deputy director, Chris took on much of the day-to-day management of the commission's staff, and helped recruit new talent when the commission was in need of different expertise. For commissioners and congressional staff, Chris was often the go-to guy when you needed to get something done.

But the fact that Kojm was a Democrat did not smooth the waters within the commission. He was not a lawyer, and thus did not have attributes that Democratic commissioners were looking for to balance Zelikow. So, for a few weeks, as the rest of the staff filled out, the controversy over the general counsel position persisted. Throughout this process, general counsel candidates were introduced by individual commissioners and vetted by the full commission. On a few occasions, a very able lawyer supported by one side of the commission was deemed unacceptable by others—usually because the lawyer in question had done high-profile work for the Democratic Party or for Democratic political campaigns, or had worked on the Watergate Task Force. This provoked accusations on both sides—that the White House was vetoing Democrats through the Republican commissioners, or that the Democrats were putting forward highly partisan lawyers.

At one point, Republicans within and around the commission suggested that a partisan Democratic general counsel would necessitate the hiring of a Republican general counsel, and even provided us a list of candidates that could be considered for this position. This would have caused precisely the kind of division within the commission and the staff that we were determined to avoid. Two lawyers looking out for the interests of their respective political parties would have guaranteed a divided commission.

This stalemate began to prompt whispers around Washington. The skepticism that had surrounded the 9/11 Commission's creation reemerged, with Republicans grumbling that the commission was out to get the president, and Democrats countering that the Republicans wanted the work of the commission to be a whitewash.

Uncertainty lasted well into March as candidates came and went. Above all, we became focused on temperament—finding a lawyer who would be tough and persistent, but not overly confrontational or partisan. Matters were complicated when Zelikow met with Judge Alberto Gonzales, President Bush's White House counsel, to discuss the kind of access he envisioned for the commission. The meeting did not go particularly well, as Gonzales found Zelikow aggressive and overly expansive in laying out his expectations for access, and from that point on Gonzales refused to meet with Zelikow. So the very executive director whose ties to the White House some on the commission were looking to balance with a general counsel had already strained his own relations at the counsel's office—our primary point of contact with the White House.

In mid-March, we found the right man for general counsel. Daniel Marcus was well recommended by several people we trusted, particularly Lloyd Cutler, the former White House counsel for Presidents Carter and Clinton. Dan had spent many years at a prominent Washington law firm and had served in senior positions in the White House counsel's office and the Justice Department in the latter years of the Clinton administration. He was viewed as a Democrat, which was certainly helpful in calming Democratic concerns. But Dan is more a professional than he is a partisan—the work he had done for Democrats was in government, not in politics.

Dan's personal manner is very lawyerly. His inclination is to talk and work things out. But his agreeable nature is buttressed by toughness: he was not afraid to take people on, including some commissioners who were experienced lawyers. Off the bat, it helped that the one commissioner whom Dan did know was Jamie Gorelick, who was able to assure the other Democratic commissioners that Dan was a good choice.

Dan recruited an extraordinarily able deputy, Steve Dunne, an experienced prosecutor at the Justice Department. Later on, Dan and Steve would continue trying to work things out with executive agencies even after we had served them with subpoenas.

The divisions that emerged over the hiring of the counsel did not go away. Instead, they reappeared in questions about how to negotiate with the White House and whether to use the power of subpoena to get access to documents and people. Always there was tension between those in the commission who wanted to push harder—often backed by the 9/11 families—and those who thought we were pushing too hard; this division was often split down partisan lines. Ultimately, though, this tension served us well. To succeed, we had to be both conciliatory and confrontational at times, and these two approaches helped us steer an effective middle course that got us the access we needed without drawn-out legal battles or partisan fights—though there were some close calls.

Several commissioners also disagreed with our decision not to hire an individual aide on the staff for each commissioner. Most commissioners assumed that the commission would follow the model of congressional committees, in which each member tends to have an aide who reports to him or her. Several commissioners came to us and said, "This is who I want to work for me on the commission staff." We had to explain that this was not how the commission was going to do business. It helped, in those early days, that we were so underfunded. A tight budget made a good excuse for disabusing commissioners of the idea that they were going to have personal assistants.

We did not want any staff organization that would create competing centers of power: we wanted one nonpartisan staff working for the whole commission. Our basic organizational structure comprised a front-office triumvirate: Zelikow drove and organized the staff's work; Kojm worked closely with Zelikow, while handling much of the hands-on daily management of the staff; and Marcus, working closely with Dunne, pursued the documents and interviews we needed, weighing in often on policy questions. Working with this front office were a special assistant, a deputy for administration, and a deputy for communications.

The rest of the staff hiring was less political, though no less important. Underneath the front office were nine staff teams organized around the areas specified in our congressional mandate. We started with teams looking at al Qaeda; intelligence; counterterrorism policy; terrorist financing; border security; law enforcement; aviation and transportation security; national response on 9/11; and the emergency response in New York and northern Virginia on 9/11. These last two teams eventually merged into one, whose job it was to assess the local and national response on the day of 9/11, and the first team split into two, with one assessing al Qaeda and the other focused specifically on the 9/11 plot. Each staff team had a leader who supervised several staffers, setting up something of a pyramid structure: team members reported to team leaders; team leaders reported to the staff front office; the staff front office reported to the chair and vice-chair.

To staff these teams, we looked for the best experts in the United States. We wanted to hire eclectically: people from inside and outside of government; people who had immersed themselves in these issues on the congressional Joint Inquiry into 9/11; and people who could bring a fresh perspective. We hired lawyers and historians, government workers and congressional aides. We did not ask about the candidates' politics. Indeed, when staff came on board, they got a set speech about how the commission was going to be run on a nonpartisan basis. Disagreement and debate were welcome on issues of fact and interpretation, but we wanted the staff to leave their politics at the door. Fierce arguments about how to proceed did occur—it was not unusual for one of us to receive a phone call from Kojm that began with the words "We've got a problem." This was indicative of the strong personalities we had on staff, and foreshadowed some of the tension we had to manage throughout the commission.

We ended up with an extraordinary breadth of expertise: John Farmer, a former attorney general of New Jersey; Dietrich Snell, a sitting deputy attorney general of New York; Douglas MacEachin, a former deputy director for intelligence at the CIA; Mike Hurley, a CIA officer who had run major operations in the war in Afghanistan; John Roth, a former chief of the Asset Forfeiture and Money Laundering division at the Justice Department; Sam Brinkley, a former air marshal; Ernest May, a professor at Harvard University; and a long list of specialists with experience in the areas under our mandate.

We also had a close connection to 9/11 on the staff: Kevin Shaeffer. On the morning of September 11, Kevin was working as a lieutenant in the Naval Command Center at the Pentagon, and was tracking and reporting on the attacks at the World Trade Center. When American Airlines Flight 77 crashed into the Pentagon and sent flames and jet fuel in all directions, twenty-nine people in the command center were killed, including all of those in Kevin's section. Having ingested jet fuel and inhaled smoke, Kevin pulled himself out of the Pentagon, his body on fire, and was taken to the burn facility at the Washington Hospital Center with burns over 40 percent of his body. His final memory of that day, just before he went under, is insisting that the doctor remove his wedding and navy class rings from his finger instead of cutting them off.

Weeks of excruciating pain ensued. On October 4, 2001, Kevin suffered two heart attacks, and his doctors were not certain he would make it through the night. His wife, Blanca, signed his military retirement papers to increase the benefits that would go to his family. Kevin did survive but endured months of rehabilitation and many skin grafts, while relearning basic skills such as how to tie his shoes and button his shirts. Over the summer of 2002, he recovered at home, where he closely tracked the news about the creation of the Department of Homeland Security and the 9/11 Commission. The idea of looking back and learning lessons through something of an after-action report suited Kevin's military disposition. That fall, he attended the ceremony marking the signing of the legislation creating the Department of Homeland Security.

In mid-December, soon after the commission was appointed, Lee and several other commissioners received e-mails from Kevin, in which he recounted his personal story and to which he attached news articles that had been written about him. Max Cleland, who knew firsthand about overcoming traumatic injuries, had met with Kevin for lunch, and he recommended him to the commission highly. Lee had his own meeting with Kevin, at the Wilson Center, and was impressed by Kevin's calm and persistent focus on rebuilding his professional life by working with the commission, even as the scars of his burns and skin grafts were still visible on his neck and face. Lee referred him to Zelikow and Kojm, who were running the hiring.

But Kevin's hiring did not come easy. He had been in the navy since age nineteen, and had never had a job interview until he met with Zelikow and Kojm about working on the commission. He told his story, and Zelikow's response was that he wasn't going to give him a free ride. He asked, "Why should I hire you? The commission does not really have a role for you." Kevin answered persuasively: he was young, with military experience and a particular determination to review the response to the attacks. His references from the Pentagon were exceptional.

After all the uncertainty Kevin was finally hired to work with the commission on the review of the emergency response in New York, and the emergency response at the Pentagon that had saved his life. He ended all of his e-mails with "Never Forget."

AN INFRASTRUCTURE

At the same time that we were hiring people, we had to set up a physical infrastructure to accommodate our work. This was no small matter.

Before we acquired office space in early February, staff interviews took place in Philip Zelikow's hotel room and, later, at an apartment he rented in downtown Washington, D.C. At that point, the commission did not even have a phone number, which made communication difficult for prospective staff, press, and 9/11 family members. Zelikow had hired an extraordinarily able special assistant, Stephanie Kaplan, whose cell phone served as the commission's initial point of contact.

That February saw some of the largest snowstorms in recent memory shut down the government and much of the Washington area. On one of the first days that Zelikow conducted staff interviews, Washington's Metro was barely running and many roads were unplowed. Zelikow and Kaplan sat amid piles of résumés, thinking that applicants would be calling to cancel. Yet people came trudging in, one after another.

Finding offices was difficult because we needed a space that could accommodate highly classified information. In government terminology, this is called an SCIF: a Sensitive Compartmented Information Facility. Nobody is permitted inside an SCIF without a government security clearance, unless accompanied by a security officer. You cannot bring unauthorized electronic devices inside an SCIF, either—for instance, all cell phones must remain outside. You cannot use computers there without a security clearance, or take in and bring out disks or CDs without the approval of a security officer.

With the CIA's help, we found an SCIF in an unassuming office building in downtown Washington that could accommodate up to about forty people. The office had one main conference room that served as the commission's meeting place. It was a plain room, with shades drawn, bare walls, a long table, and chairs for staff lining the walls. One day, somebody brought in a picture of the Statue of Liberty in front of the World Trade Center, and that was our only wall decoration.

This unassuming conference room was our hub of activity: with commission meetings, witness interviews, and long editing sessions for our staff reports and the final report. There were often complaints that the office lacked a coffee machine, particularly during some of our longer sessions and interviews—during our day-long interview with Sandy Berger, President Clinton's national security advisor, staff members had to make near-constant trips to the nearest coffeehouse to keep up with Berger's penchant for coffee drinking.

As a commission, we held frequent conference calls, and met in person about once a month, with meetings increasing in frequency as we moved through our work. In our initial meetings in February and March, commissioners were getting to know one another, and there was a natural inclination to be wary of those in the other political party. In these early months, Democrats—all of whom, unlike the Republicans, were located in Washington—occasionally met as a group, assembling once in December in Lee's office at the Wilson Center, and speaking a number of times during conference calls about staffing and getting the commission up and running. Republican commissioners repeatedly suggested to Tom that they hold meetings as a Republican caucus, in addition to commission meetings, but Tom said no: they would meet only as a commission. As the weeks went by, the requests dwindled, and so did the meetings and conference calls of the Democratic commissioners.

Tom's determination to be bipartisan spread to the seating chart. Republicans tend to enter meetings and sit next to Republicans; Democrats do the same. At our second meeting, Tom announced a rule: at the commission's conference room table, there would be no Republicans sitting next to Republicans, no Democrats sitting next to Democrats. There was some grumbling over this. A few people muttered that being told where to sit was like being back in kindergarten. But everybody moved, and that was the way we sat—in private and in public—until we disbanded.

The location of the office building had to be kept secret, which was at times a challenge, particularly since we were in the middle of one of the busiest areas of Washington, D.C. On one occasion, a camera crew from NBC filmed commissioners leaving the building, and wanted to use the footage as part of a story on the commission. We had to plead with them not to do so, or at least to use it in a way that would not reveal the address of our building.

For several weeks after we acquired the office space, only a few of our staff were allowed to work there because the others lacked the necessary security clearances, even though the SCIF did not yet have classified documents in it. So in February, we had an SCIF without classified material in it, and staff without the security clearance that would have enabled them to work there. Meanwhile, we had to set up a computer system, build a Web site, acquire telephones and fax machines, and make sure we were stocked with the needed supplies. It was an incredibly busy and difficult period; time was already becoming an issue.

Getting security clearances for staff and commissioners dragged into April and May. Occasionally, this became a cause of public concern, in part because the families were impatient. It is hard to understand why former senators, congressmen, and other public officials need to be carefully investigated before they are entrusted with classified material. Yet our dilemma was that it can take up to six months or even a year for the FBI and CIA to do the kind of rigorous background checks required to give somebody a top-secret security clearance. Such checks involve interviews with friends, acquaintances, and colleagues, and a detailed review of documents, from financial records to residency and travel history. At several points, we called the White House, and they were helpful in expediting clearances. One FBI agent who interviewed Tom as part of his background investigation complained that the Bureau was being asked to rush the process. But we didn't have time to spare: without clearances, we couldn't do our job.

The time-consuming burden of handling classified information came up again and again throughout our inquiry. We ended up with three offices: our original SCIF in downtown Washington; a second D.C. office near Capitol Hill; and an office in New York City. Each of these locations was set up to handle different levels of classified material: the first D.C. office had computers with access to "top-secret" information; the second D.C. office and the New York City office had access to only "secret" information, a lower level of classification.

We were handicapped because the classified documents could not leave the offices—a huge inconvenience for Tom and the other commissioners who did not live in Washington. We also couldn't transfer material among the offices because each office was set up to handle a different level of classification. Certain highly sensitive material could not even come to our offices; instead, it had to be reviewed on the premises of the CIA or the White House's New Executive Office Building. Some of our most tiresome and extended negotiations with the White House had to do with whether or not we could even take our notes back to our offices after these sessions.

While the process of getting security clearances was bothersome, we were principally concerned about our budget. In December and January, we received some advice from Michael Bayer, who was staff director for the commission that investigated the bombing of Pan Am Flight 103 by Libyan-backed terrorists. Bayer was helpful in explaining administrative issues to us, and he did not think that $3 million was realistic for an inquiry of our scope. He drew up an initial budget estimate in January that suggested that our inquiry would cost $12 million.

When we started asking around Congress, it was apparent that the $3 million had been established as a marker: nobody knew what an investigation like this was going to cost, so the authors of our mandate put in a figure comparable to what past commissions had received. We directed our staff to put together an estimate of how much the inquiry would cost. This task was led by our extremely efficient manager of operations, Dianna Campagna. We wanted a figure that was high enough that we wouldn't have to go back to Congress to get more money, but low enough that it wouldn't give anybody sticker shock. The result was a draft budget of $14 million, necessitating an increase of $11 million from what we had been given. More than half of that $14 million would go toward paying staff. The rest would go toward rent for offices, travel by staff and commissioners, and various equipment and supplies. We then took this number to the full commission to get their go-ahead before negotiating with Congress and the White House.

Asking for more money is not the best way to get off on the right foot. We were already on unsteady ground with Congress. Particularly in the House, many Republican members had opposed our creation, and were not inclined to help the commission succeed. Holding the budget at $3 million was one way to ensure that we did not. When Tom started calling around to different members, several told him that we had to live with the $3 million. But we had no choice: our estimates indicated that without an increase, the commission would go broke by August 2003, almost a year before our May 2004 reporting date.

Whereas some members of Congress opposed the commission, others were simply not tuned in to our work. Several weeks after the commission got started, Tom received a call from a top staffer for Senator Bill Frist (R-Tenn.), who had become majority leader at the beginning of January. The staffer asked Tom who was on the commission. Tom, assuming that a Republican staffer would be unfamiliar with the Democrats, started to list the Democratic commissioners. The staffer cut in: "No. I want to know who the Republican commissioners are." Trent Lott, who was unhappy at being ousted as Republican leader in the Senate, had neglected to provide Frist's office with a record of whom he had appointed to the commission.

As if the political context was not difficult enough, we were also making our request within a volatile budgetary environment. This was in February and March 2003, when the White House was busy working with Congress on an emergency supplemental spending bill to provide more than $80 billion for combat operations in Iraq. Money was tight; attention was focused on the Persian Gulf.

We met with key congressional leaders and supporters of the commission through February and early March. Among our most important congressional supporters was Senator John McCain, who fought hard for the extra money, and whose help was critical at many junctures. McCain was adamant that there be a robust inquiry into the 9/11 attacks, and was skillful at exerting pressure both within Congress and in public, often working with Senator Joe Lieberman. In both the Senate and the House, we could also count on strong support from a long list of members, principally those from the areas most affected by the attacks: New York, New Jersey, and Connecticut. For the purposes of getting our money, this congressional support had to turn into action by the appropriations committees.

The second track we worked on was with the executive branch, where our chief point of contact in the early going was Jay Lefkowitz at the White House. We asked that the necessary increase be obtained through the transfer of funds within the National Foreign Intelligence Program—the same portion of the federal budget that funded our initial $3 million; or, alternatively, that it be included in the Iraq war supplemental. The tone of these negotiations was constructive, but it was not always clear that we would get the additional funds.

It was touch-and-go through March. The White House was saying supportive things, but the commission's request did not turn up in the Iraq supplemental. The House Republican caucus and Speaker Dennis

Hastert's office remained the most difficult obstacles. Throughout the life of the commission, and indeed through the passage of intelligence reform legislation based upon our recommendations, the strongest congressional wariness came from House Republicans. In the case of the budget, the stated concern was that we would become a "runaway commission"—the same phrase used by the White House in Tom's initial meetings. It did not help that we didn't have a single commissioner who had served as a Republican in the House, or that four of our Republican commissioners lived outside of Washington, and were thus less visible on Capitol Hill than the Democratic commissioners.

Yet that March, we also had a first inkling of the public support we could garner. Without being asked, the 9/11 families mobilized on our behalf, lobbying members of Congress and making statements in the media. The press picked up on the issue, and we were soon in news stories, editorials, and the cable news cycle for the first time since the Kissinger and Mitchell controversies. Commissioners called members of Congress, and our congressional supporters issued strong statements on our behalf. The power of the 9/11 families to draw public attention to such a mundane issue as the budgeting for an independent commission was remarkable.

We were playing a game of chicken. We had gone about our business of hiring staff and setting up offices under the assumption that we would get more money. We made clear, privately and publicly, that we were not going to preside over a failure—which suggested to some that, without the budget increase, we might resign. Another factor on our side was that the $3 million was so absurdly low for an inquiry of the magnitude of ours that the principal discussion had to be about how much of an increase to give us, rather than whether to give us an increase at all. We pointed out that the commission investigating the recent space shuttle tragedy was set to spend in the neighborhood of $40 million. Why, then, should the commission looking into 9/11 live with a budget of $3 million?

Ultimately, the White House and Congress were not willing to let the commission derail before it got started. The commission had a public hearing scheduled for March 31 and April 1, in New York City, with family members and survivors of 9/11 scheduled to testify. To make these people revisit painful memories of personal loss in front of a commission that was going broke would have been a travesty.

The White House agreed to provide an additional $9 million for the commission in the National Foreign Intelligence Program. Then Congress stepped in and insisted that it would provide the increase of $11 million. What had been a struggle to withhold money had become a virtuous competition over who could give it to us first. Ultimately, we received the funding from Congress, and it proved sufficient to cover the entire life of the commission—we even ended up giving $1.4 million back at the end of our work.

We went into our first public hearing with confidence that we had the budget to do our job, just as we were slowly acquiring staff and infrastructure. We had also learned an important lesson about the kind of support we could draw upon when we hit a bottleneck. The commission made politicians nervous. They were afraid that they might be singled out for blame by our work, but they were also afraid to be accused of stonewalling our work. This made for some terse exchanges. But we had learned for the first time that we had some clout.

TO NEW YORK

STAYING IN TOUCH WITH THE REGION most affected by 9/11 was a principal concern for Tom, and from the outset he wanted to have an office in Manhattan. We needed people in New York who knew their way around the bureaucracies of the emergency response units and the management of the World Trade Center, which had been operated by the Port Authority of New York and New Jersey. We also needed a presence that was closer to many of the 9/11 families who were following our work so closely. Holding our initial hearing in New York, rather than in Washington, was critical—both to illustrate for commissioners and staff the magnitude of our responsibility, and to show the country, and the New York region, that we did not intend to be just an inside-the-Beltway entity.

Yet as we approached our inaugural public hearing, we did not yet have a New York office space in operation, and the 9/11 families were not happy with us. Though they had fought for a budget increase, many were frustrated with our progress. Initially, the Family Steering Committee (FSC) had lobbied for one of their prominent representatives to be hired onto the commission's staff. Then they were miffed that we had not immediately delved into material and planned for public hearings with high-profile witnesses. When they heard about our problems in hiring a general counsel or the difficulty in getting security clearances and a budget increase, they felt that the White House was undercutting the commission. When we explained that many of the things we were doing—

getting offices, assembling a staff, awaiting security clearances—took time, they thought we were being passive.

The inaugural hearing was an opportunity to make a public statement that we were up and running, and also to define the nature of our inquiry. Yet our New York City investigation got off to an inauspicious beginning. In advance of our hearing, Zelikow and several staff went up to Manhattan to meet with the top staff for Mayor Michael Bloomberg at City Hall. The purpose of the meeting was to make contact and discuss how the city and the commission could cooperate.

The first words from the mayor's staff were "What are you doing here?"—albeit said in somewhat more colorful language. Our staff then received an extended outburst from the mayor's office about how the commission had no mandate to investigate New York, and should stick to Washington. Of course, the commission had every intention to include New York in our investigation, as we were mandated to look at the "immediate response" to the attacks. But from the outset, we learned we would face resistance from New York City.

Putting together the hearing itself was not easy. Commissioners traveling up to New York had been well briefed, but we were also more than a bit understaffed, and the personnel we did have, who were just coming on board, were based in Washington, not New York, and were dealing with the inconvenience of not being able to work in our office space because of security clearances. Some staff members had worked in Congress and knew how to put together public hearings, but for many others this was their first experience with one.

The agenda for the hearing revealed several objectives. We would hear from survivors of the attacks and families of the victims, in order to establish for commissioners and the public the commission's purpose and the expectations of people with an intensely personal interest in our work. We would hear from New York officials—Mayor Bloomberg and Governor Pataki—and from members of Congress from the region. And we would make available panels of experts on several of the policy areas covered by our mandate—counterterrorism policy, border security, law enforcement and domestic intelligence, and emergency response.

Our hotel accommodation fit with our determination to connect with the events of 9/11. The Millenium Hotel, on Church Street in Lower Manhattan, had been seriously damaged by the collapse of the World Trade Center, which showered the hotel with debris and blew out its windows. The hotel runs along the east side of Ground Zero, with its rebuilt windows offering panoramic views of the site. When Lee walked into his hotel room the night before the hearing and opened the curtains, he had to sit down and pause for several moments.

Nothing can prepare you for your first encounter with Ground Zero. It was Lee's first glimpse of the site, and he was struck immediately by the enormity of the emptiness, which does not fully come across on television or in photographs: including the two towers, six buildings collapsed as a result of the attack, leaving sixteen acres of empty space in the middle of one of the most densely populated areas on earth. Gazing down at the space, a year and a half after 9/11, Lee had a new understanding of and appreciation for the magnitude of the tragedy.

On the eve of the hearing, though, we found that part of our agenda had been upended. Several days before the hearing, former Senator Daniel Patrick Moynihan of New York died. At the time, Senator Moynihan was keeping an office at the Wilson Center, which Lee directed. All of our congressional witnesses—including Senators Charles Schumer and Hillary Clinton of New York—attended the Moynihan memorial service in Washington, D.C., which was scheduled for the same day as our hearing, so we lost a panel of witnesses.

The hearing venue was the old Alexander Hamilton Customs House, a stately building erected in 1902 and located only blocks from Ground Zero. Ironically, the building bore the mark of Senator Moynihan. While in the Senate, he had taken a long-standing interest in preserving great buildings—among them, the customs house. It was Moynihan who saved the building from destruction in the late 1970s, and who prompted its restoration under the New York City Landmarks Preservation Commission in the 1980s. As we took our seats in the auditorium of a great New York City building on the morning of March 31, we were part of Pat Moynihan's living legacy.

It felt good finally to sit on a dais more than four months after the creation of the commission. But there were signs that we were not yet running smoothly. The pitchers of water and the glasses in front of us were rented. Minutes before Tom called the hearing to order, we realized that the commission had no gavel. Our staff had to find a judge's chambers and borrow one for the hearing.

We had not yet hired staff members to be liaisons to the 9/11 families, so our outreach to family members, while we were planning for the hearing, was lacking. Thinking there would be a big turnout, we had advised 9/11 families to arrive very early. Perhaps this dissuaded some of them from coming—as we looked out on the 350-seat auditorium, we saw more empty seats than we had expected. However, we also saw a trend that would continue throughout our work: many of the family members who did come brought placards with pictures of their loved ones, which they held in their laps or placed on the seats next to them.

We started with opening statements by the commissioners. Tom began by summarizing our charge: "To find out why things happened, how they could have happened, and what we can do to prevent their ever happening again. We will be following paths and we will follow those individual paths wherever they lead. We may end up holding individual agencies, people and procedures to account. But our fundamental purpose will not be to point fingers."

At the mention of not "pointing fingers" there was a stir in the room, as many of the families were outraged: to some, the whole reason to have a commission was to point fingers. They had been deeply dissatisfied that the congressional hearings into 9/11 had not focused on accountability, and they expected us to name names of people who were responsible for the failure to prevent 9/11. Several said to us that the commission was about achieving "justice" for the loss of their loved ones. We approached accountability more carefully: we would be unyielding and comprehensive in uncovering facts, but our purpose was not to assign blame to individuals for 9/11. Tom's comment launched a debate that lasted throughout the commission; for some families, the issue was never settled to their satisfaction.

Tom also articulated our view of partisanship: "Five of us happen to be registered as Republicans, five of us as Democrats, but we're not going to operate as party members, and the staff is not partisan." Lee echoed these thoughts in his statement, saying, "In all we do as a Commission, we will strive to be independent, impartial, thorough, and nonpartisan." These may have been just words, but they represented our initial decisions on the structure of the staff and the tone of our inquiry. Our task would include repeating those words in the months ahead, and buttressing them with deeds.

Some of the initial disagreements and concerns within the commission came to the surface. Fred Fielding referred to how leaks of sensitive information could destroy the commission's credibility—a concern among Republicans who felt that leaks of selective information could be used to try to damage the president. Richard Ben-Veniste expressed his frustration with the difficulties we were beginning to have in obtaining the report of the congressional Joint Inquiry, and the slow process of obtaining security clearances. Tim Roemer voiced concern about the White House's slowness in acceding to our budget request.

As commissioner statements went on, Lee became nervous. He was shuttling back and forth from the dais to the greenroom, where some of our witnesses were arriving. Governor Pataki was on a tight schedule, and could not wait for the commissioners to finish their opening remarks, so we had to interrupt their statements to make time for the governor to make a brief statement. He recounted memories from the day of 9/11, and concluded that "New York State government and I'm sure the people of New York stand ready to cooperate in any way we possibly can to help you on this important mission."

We then resumed commissioner comments, coming to the statement that received the best audience response. Jim Thompson has a way of summarizing the core of an issue, and on the matter of accountability he did just that, saying:

> Here is the American bargain. Each of us, as individual citizens, take a portion of our liberties and our lives and pass them to those whom we elect or appoint as our guardians. And their task is to hold our liberties and our lives in their hands, secure. That is an appropriate bargain. But on September 11th, that bargain was not kept. Our government, all governments, somehow failed in their duty that day. We need to know why.

His remarks were punctuated by loud applause from the family members in attendance.

Once again Lee found himself in the awkward position of shuttling back and forth from the dais to the greenroom, where Mayor Bloomberg was getting increasingly impatient waiting through commissioner statements. Bloomberg also had a surprise. When we had initially asked him to appear, he refused, saying that he would issue a statement but would not deliver it personally. When pressed, he agreed to appear but said that he would take no questions. Finally, he agreed to questioning but specified that his police and fire commissioners—Ray Kelly and Nicholas Scopetta—would not be coming. However, when he arrived, he was accompanied by Kelly and Scopetta, which caught us off guard: they were important witnesses, but we were not prepared to question them.

When the mayor took his seat to make his statement, he had grown frustrated by the wait, and slammed a stack of papers down in front of him. As Bloomberg began his testimony, Zelikow leaned over and whispered something to Tom about the plans for questioning, given the unexpected presence of the police and fire commissioners—not an unusual occurrence during a public hearing. Bloomberg stopped speaking and, addressing Tom, asked if he should wait for Tom's conference to conclude before he continued.

In his statement, Bloomberg excoriated the federal government for short-changing New York in its homeland security appropriations, saying at one point, "If we distributed monies to the military this way, our troops in Iraq would have bows and arrows to fight with."

This was not the last time that a witness would use a public appearance before the commission to make a political point; indeed, it was a sign that we were being viewed as a prominent vehicle for public exposure, even within the rough-and-tumble world of New York City politics. But commissioners were irked by the testimony. We had not prepared to question the police and fire commissioners, and did not know that the mayor was going to go into this policy detail.

This incident further cooled our relationship with the city, which was weakened even more by a legal confrontation later in 2003. Still, the two of us were impressed at the level of questioning from our fellow commissioners, who probed the mayor and his commissioners about preparedness and the counterterrorism coordination among local, state, and federal governments.

The mayor was followed at the witness table by our panel of 9/11 survivors, who gave the most emotional and dramatic testimony of the day. The first witness was Harry Waizer, an employee of Cantor Fitzgerald, which lost 658 employees on September 11, 2001. Waizer sat before us in a dark suit, white shirt, and red tie, dressed not unlike the thousands of people bustling along the sidewalks outside the doors of our hearing venue in Manhattan's financial district. Yet another aspect of Waizer's appearance intimated his unique personal story: his face was badly scarred and discolored from burns and skin grafts, and when he opened his mouth to speak, his voice was low and hoarse.

His 9/11 story began on an elevator in World Trade Center 1 that filled with fire upon the impact of American Airlines Flight 11. Waizer described getting out of the elevator somehow and walking down seventy-eight flights of stairs, and noticing the shocked expressions on the people he encountered along the way: "I saw the look on many of those faces turn to sympathy or horror as they saw me. At one point I noticed a large flap of skin hanging on my arm. I did not look any further."

He described the toll on his family when he endured nearly seven weeks in an induced coma, with what was estimated as a 5 percent chance of survival. And then he described the responsibility of speaking for others, and how that responsibility now rested with us, the commission, saying:

I have no political experience, but I do have experience as an informed citizen. It tells me that commissions such as this are usually formed by men and women of good will, have committed, intelligent members and staff possessed of good will, and eventually produce reports that are read carefully and seriously by others of good will. Yet the findings of such commissions are often ignored in the end. Compassion and concern are often spread thin, and other important issues become priorities after the glare of the public spotlight fades. My fear is that the work of this Commission will have a similar fate.

Here was a man with extraordinary moral authority challenging us not to fail. It was one of countless moments throughout the commission when remarkable people expressed an eloquent and personal interest in our success. The cumulative effect of these expressions always propelled us forward.

Four other survivors followed. David Lim, a Port Authority police officer, who broke down repeatedly in describing how he had somehow managed to survive Tower 1's collapse, and believed himself to be dead, only to find himself standing on top of what immediately became known as Ground Zero.

Lee Ielpi, a firefighter who lost his son in the attacks and worked for months in the recovery effort on the smoldering remains, and who described the discovery of his son's whole body—one of only 292 intact bodies to be discovered among the 2,792 who perished in New York.

From the Pentagon, Kevin Shaeffer had helped put us in touch with Brian Birdwell, a uniformed lieutenant colonel in the army, who described sustaining burns over 60 percent of his body. Lieutenant Colonel Birdwell summed up his experience bluntly: "When an 80-ton airliner traveling at over 300 miles an hour with over 10,000 gallons of petroleum jet-A slams into a building 15 to 20 yards from you, you may also discern that I sit here at the miraculous hand of Christ."

Our last witness on the panel of survivors was Craig Sincock, a retired army officer who had worked in the Pentagon along with his wife, who died on September 11. He gave us an idea of the kind of bonds that formed out of the ashes of 9/11 when he began by gesturing to Lieutenant Colonel Birdwell next to him and saying, "This gentleman right beside me, Brian Birdwell, is the only survivor out of my wife's office. He is now my dearest friend. He's like a brother to me."

Looking around the dais, we saw few dry eyes. In the period preceding the hearing, we had not had the same kind of interaction with survivors as we had with the families of victims. Part of the reason for this was that many survivors had different concerns and reactions from the families who had lost loved ones. Whereas family members had been left with an enormous void to fill in their lives, survivors were enduring an arduous process of physical rehabilitation, rebuilding their own lives, and trying to move past this terrible thing that had happened to them. Now, before us, was the firsthand experience of terrorism. We had little to ask them—all we could do was marvel at their stories.

The next panel—made up of 9/11 family members—had been the most difficult to put together. The problem was that so many family representatives had wanted to testify. By this point, some of the unity of the family groups was beginning to crack, as family members differed on a variety of issues—some political, some practical, and some personal. We ended up with four family leaders: Steve Push, who had lost his wife, Lisa Raines, on American Airlines Flight 77; Mary Fetchet, who had lost her son, Brad, in the World Trade Center; Mindy Kleinberg, who had lost her husband in the World Trade Center; and Allison Vadhan, who had lost her mother on United Airlines Flight 93, which crashed in Pennsylvania. We also promised several other family representatives that they would get the opportunity to testify at later hearings.

There were notable emotional differences between the survivor panel and that of the families. For instance, Harry Waizer had said:

> I have no rage about what happened on 9/11, only a deep sadness for the many innocent, worthy lives lost and the loved ones who lost so much that day. . . . Neither do I feel anger at those who arguably could have foreseen, and thereby prevented, the tragedies. If there were mistakes, they were mistakes of complacency, a complacency we all shared.

The families, however, expressed grief that was noticeably laced with anger. Steve Push put this most succinctly when he said:

> Within two weeks, however, my strongest emotion was anger. And I think I probably differ substantially from Mr. Waizer and Dr. Sincock in that. In fact, actually, anger is an inadequate word to describe what I felt. What I felt was a rage so intense it was like no emotion I had ever felt before. But I haven't let go of this anger. I've tried to pour it into working to see that something like this never happens again.

This anger translated into a desire for answers to very specific questions about the nation's preparedness on 9/11. As Mary Fetchet put it, "We deserve answers to the long list of questions we have. . . . I am frustrated to have suffered the loss of a son and yet to be required to spend time away from my family and fight for the establishment of a commission that should have been in place on the day of the tragic events."

We heard a great deal of those questions in the family testimony. Just a brief sample would include: How did the hijackers get into the country? What steps did the aviation community take amid the growing threat of terrorism? What were the breakdowns in communication between control towers, the FAA, NORAD, and other government agencies? Were there evacuation policies in place at the World Trade Center and were they followed? Why was President Bush permitted by the Secret Service to remain in the Sarasota elementary school where he was reading to children? Can the FBI, an agency steeped in a law enforcement culture, transform itself into a counterterrorism agency, or do we need a new domestic intelligence agency like Britain's MI5? Is the Department of Homeland Security making America safer?

There were also tough comments directed at the commission. Steve Push spoke for many families when he pointedly disagreed with Tom's opening statement, saying: "I think this Commission should point fingers. . . . [T]here were people, people in responsible positions, who failed us on 9/11." Mary Fetchet said: "I want to express to all of you my very deep concern about the slow progress of the Commission and stress the urgency we feel as precious time is being wasted." And in the questioning period, Mr. Push expressed the view of many when he said: "We want to see lots of subpoenas."

The families were as willing to be public critics of the commission as they were to be our public partners. In fact, the hearing—which was held in New York in part to facilitate family member attendance and testimony—may have caused us problems with the 9/11 families rather than engendering goodwill. There was anger and frustration over our stated approach to accountability, and our reluctance to haul government witnesses before us right off the bat to testify about their failures. After a month of lobbying Congress on behalf of our budget request, the families now shifted to prodding us to be more aggressive. This was a pattern that continued throughout our work—with family members supporting us with Congress and the White House, but pushing us when their attention was focused squarely on our conduct of the investigation.

The evening in between our two days of hearings, the commission ate dinner at yet another Lower Manhattan landmark—Fraunces Tavern, the 350-year-old establishment that was a favorite of General George Washington when he was in New York following the American Revolution. Indeed, just a few hundred yards from the site of the World Trade Center, General Washington once bade an emotional farewell to his staff, among them Alexander Hamilton, before boarding a boat back to his home in Mount Vernon, where he thought he would be retiring.

Over dinner, commissioners reflected on our first public day. The 9/11 survivors and families had made an indelible impact. Most commissioners had not met extensively with the families, and some had not spent significant time in New York since the attacks. The dramatic survivor testimony, the family photographs of the victims scattered throughout the auditorium, the often audible sobs of the family members throughout the proceedings, had all impressed upon us the uniqueness and importance of our endeavor.

We wound up the hearing the next day with our series of expert panels. That morning our hearing had managed to attract attention in the press. We had come to New York as a public entity with little public profile, but like the commissioners, the media had been moved by the voices of the survivors and family members. Several reporters remarked to us that we were not an ordinary commission—we were something different, and more interesting. This was reflected in how we referred to ourselves, and how the public referred to us: commissions are usually known by the names of their chair or co-chairs; but we did not want to be known as the "Kean Commission" or the "Kean-Hamilton Commission." In all public statements, we called ourselves the "9/11 Commission."

We left New York satisfied that we had made a good first public impression, and had established the personal impact of the day of September 11, 2001, as an appropriate emotional starting point for our work. Yet the reality was the commission was up but not fully running. A general counsel had only recently been hired, we had yet to submit requests for documents to executive branch agencies, and we were still having problems getting access to the congressional Joint Inquiry report that was supposed to serve as a foundation and starting point for our own inquiry. Most of our staff still lacked security clearances.

Steve Push's comment—"We want to see lots of subpoenas"—was a backdrop for much of what happened over the rest of 2003. We would have trouble getting access to documents, and we would have trouble holding the commission together—particularly on the question of whether to act on Push's demand. We would, after all, be asking to see documents that no commission or independent body had ever seen before. But, as the survivors reminded us in New York, we were looking into an event the likes of which the United States had never seen before.

3

COOPERATE OR CON~~FRONT~~

WHAT TO ASK FOR AND
HOW TO GET IT

If there's pressure, good.

— Tom Kean, July 8, 2003, speaking after the
release of the commission's first interim report

W HAT DO YOU ASK for and how do you get it? Those two questions
dominated our work through 2003, dividing the commission,
straining our relations with the 9/11 families, complicating our dealings
with the White House, and making the commission front-page news.

We knew certain information would be particularly hard to get—for
instance, the daily intelligence briefings given to Presidents Clinton and
Bush, memos and e-mails written within the White House, and reports of
interrogations of al Qaeda detainees. To get that kind of access, we had to
build our credibility as we went along: through the thoroughness and professionalism of our document requests and interviews; through our ability
to handle, and not leak to the press, classified information; and by how we
presented ourselves in public. That is how it works in Washington; people
are wary of an unknown entity.

It is the rare commission that is equally interested in interviewing air
traffic controllers, CIA officers, and NYPD officers, or reviewing transcripts of 911 calls made from within the World Trade Center, intelligence
briefings of senior officials, and records of covert actions in Afghanistan.
We dealt with the White House; the huge range of executive branch agencies with a role in the 9/11 story; Congress; state and local governments in

ork, Virginia, and elsewhere; FBI field offices; FAA and NORAD command centers; and far-flung State Department embassies, CIA stations, and military bases. We also dealt with the corporate sector, such as United and American airlines (whose flights were hijacked), and private companies with offices in the World Trade Center.

We had to decide: How deep and how far do the roots of 9/11 run? That is a difficult question to answer. We were mandated to examine the "facts and circumstances surrounding 9/11." In an ideal world, we could just have turned to the U.S. government and asked for all information relevant to the 9/11 attacks. But such a request could have been interpreted in infinite ways. We had to sort through what information was part of the 9/11 story and what was not. In a way, we would define what information was relevant to 9/11 by asking for it.

Do you ask for all materials pertaining to American foreign policy and intelligence reporting in the Middle East over the last two decades? If fulfilled, such a request would leave you with millions of pages of files to sort through. To focus our work and have any chance of finishing on time, we needed to give some structure to the process of asking for information. A starting point was the time frame for our investigation.

There were compelling arguments about the need to reach back into history. The question was how far back? Certainly, we were interested in the watershed August 1998 al Qaeda bombing of American embassies in Kenya and Tanzania, and the Clinton administration's response of launching cruise missile attacks on al Qaeda training camps in Afghanistan and a factory in Sudan suspected of producing chemical weapons. But what about the "Black Hawk Down" incident in 1993, when seventeen Americans were killed in Somalia, and American bodies were dragged by mobs through the streets of Mogadishu—an image that was televised around the globe? What did not become widely known for some time was the involvement of a Saudi extremist named Usama Bin Ladin, who was just beginning to move onto the radar screen of international terrorism, and who had helped train and equip the forces who killed the Americans in Somalia.

Or what about the attack in 1983, when the terrorist group Hizbollah killed 242 Americans in a suicide truck bombing of a marine barracks in Lebanon? In both Somalia and Lebanon, U.S. administrations responded by withdrawing troops. Were there not lessons about the terrorist threat, and the consequences of U.S. policies, from these atrocities and our response to them?

Similar cases could be made in other areas of our investigation. To understand the development of Islamic extremism, you could ask for documents on Bin Ladin's fatwas against the United States; the development of extremist, anti-American Islamic madrasahs in Pakistan in the 1980s and 1990s; the mujahedin fighters—among them Bin Ladin—who resisted the Soviet invasion of Afghanistan in the 1980s, some of whom formed the core of what became the Taliban and al Qaeda; or the Iranian revolution of 1979, which destabilized the Middle East and triggered religiously motivated violence across the region. The list goes on and on.

Our staff teams with highly focused mandates also made compelling cases for reaching back several years. The team working on border security looked at how the nineteen hijackers had gotten into the United States. But they also wanted to look at how Islamic extremists had been crossing our borders for years. For instance, how had Omar Abdul Rahman, the notorious "Blind Sheik" who was the spiritual leader of the group that bombed the World Trade Center in 1993, gotten into the country despite his ties to Islamic extremists?

We decided that our full-scale documentary investigation would begin at January 1, 1998. Several factors influenced the choice of 1998. At that point, Bin Ladin had decamped to Afghanistan from Sudan, and the Clinton administration had adopted the approach it would use to combat terrorism in the coming years. Over the course of the year, Bin Ladin issued his notorious fatwa, publicly declaring war on the United States; the 9/11 plot was hatched; the simultaneous embassy bombings took place; and the United States launched military, intelligence, and diplomatic efforts to kill or capture Bin Ladin. In short, 1998 was the year that terrorism—and al Qaeda specifically—moved to the front burner for American policy makers.

The 1998 date was not binding; it was a guide to frame our approach toward requesting documents. When teams found investigatory leads further back in the past, they were encouraged to follow them. So the team looking at the development of al Qaeda studied information on Bin Ladin's time in Sudan in the mid-1990s, and the team looking at transportation security reviewed the findings of a commission on aviation security headed by Vice-President Al Gore, which released its report in 1997.

An equally complicated question was where to cut off our investigation. The law instructed us to "make a full and complete accounting" of "the extent of the United States' preparedness for, and immediate response to, the attacks." But what is the "immediate response" to 9/11? Is it the emergency response effort at the Pentagon and the World Trade Center? The initial decisions made by President Bush and the national leadership in the days after September 11, 2001? The invasion of Afghanistan and the targeting of al Qaeda's leadership? The passage of laws such as the USA PATRIOT Act and the creation of the Department of Homeland Security? What about the decision to go to war in Iraq, which was often explained by the Bush administration as being motivated by the experience of 9/11?

The Bush administration told us that they interpreted "immediate response" as the day of 9/11. We took a somewhat different view. Although we possessed neither the time nor the staff to detail and evaluate all that had taken place since 9/11, we saw our primary investigatory responsibility as telling the authoritative story of the lead-up to and the day of September 11, 2001, and while we also did not have the mandate for a broader investigation—for instance, there is no mention of the PATRIOT Act or the Iraq war in the law creating the commission—we did believe that "immediate" could and should be defined more broadly than strictly the day of 9/11. The date we settled on as a cut-off, therefore, was September 20, 2001, the day President Bush addressed a joint session of Congress, identified al Qaeda as America's enemy, declared a war on terrorists that would have a "global reach," and issued an ultimatum to the Taliban. That way, we would be able to achieve a fuller understanding of how the government absorbed the attack and made the key decisions that shaped the declaration and commencement of what would be known as the war on terror.

However, in addition to our fact-finding investigation we were supposed to issue recommendations based upon "lessons learned from the attacks of September 11, 2001." In order to be relevant, our recommendations had to reflect both the pre-9/11 failures of the government and the changes made since 9/11. Take aviation security. A recommendation that looked only at the state of aviation security on September 20, 2001, would be useless in light of all that has taken place since. Anybody who has flown an airplane in the last few years knows that the federal government has increased aviation security in notable ways, so we needed access to information about how these and other post-9/11 policy changes were functioning. We worked out an agreement that permitted us to look at materials evaluating current policies—for instance, if the Department of Transportation or the Department of Homeland Security had a study assessing tightened aviation security since 9/11, we were entitled to see that study.

Some wanted us to take a more expansive approach. On the question of Iraq, for instance, Max Cleland and others outside the commission argued that the invasion of Iraq was the key post-9/11 policy decision about how to wage the war on terror. While that may or may not be correct, we saw no way to approach the question of the Iraq war within our mandate. The war started after the commission came into being; our fact-finding efforts were focused on al Qaeda and its extensive history in countries such as Afghanistan, Pakistan, and Saudi Arabia.

We did assess Iraq's ties to al Qaeda and the question of whether Iraq had had a hand in the 9/11 attacks, but we did not look at topics such as Iraq's weapons of mass destruction capability, or Saddam Hussein's impact on the greater Middle East. Thus we were in no position—legally or factually—to assess the decision to go to war in Iraq. We were the 9/11 Commission, not the Iraq War Commission. Even so, the subject came up repeatedly throughout our hearings and our work, as the war in Iraq cast a longer shadow over the nation's foreign policy and politics.

While we shaped a framework for our investigation, our staff teams were formulating work plans through the spring of 2003, and presenting them to the commission. These work plans contained the key questions that the teams sought to answer. So for the border security team, the broad question would be: How did the nineteen hijackers get into the country and why did our border systems fail? More specific questions would delve into areas such as budgeting for border security, information sharing between agencies, or how visas were issued at U.S. embassies and consulates abroad.

The team work plans followed these questions with lists of the material needed to get the answers: unclassified readings for the commissioners, including the best books on the various subjects; the government documents, classified and unclassified, that the teams would be requesting; and the people whom the teams wanted to interview. For the border security team, the list of people to be interviewed ran the gamut from border guards and consular officers to the former commissioner of the Immigration and Naturalization Services, and top officials at the Departments of Justice and State.

As with the time frame, requests had to be narrow enough topically so that the teams could complete their investigations. Thus instead of asking an agency for all documents related to "terrorism"—which might include information on the Irish Republican Army or the FARC in Colombia—a team would narrow its request to Usama Bin Ladin, al Qaeda, or known al Qaeda affiliates. If, in the course of a team's investigation, it became apparent that the team needed more information, it could follow up those leads with further document requests. We wanted the teams to see everything that was directly relevant to 9/11; we did not want them to get overwhelmed by the sheer volume of information available within the federal government.

We instructed the teams to place no limits on the type of information they asked for—and they did not. Our team investigating counterterrorism policy submitted a list of officials to interview. The first six names on the list were:

1. President George W. Bush
2. Former President William J. Clinton
3. Vice-President Richard Cheney
4. Former Vice-President Al Gore
5. Condoleezza Rice, National Security Advisor
6. Samuel Berger, Former National Security Advisor

Teams also asked for documents that are not usually turned over to commissions or even to congressional committees—internal memos and e-mails from the National Security Council and the president's daily intelligence briefings.

The teams funneled their requests through Dan Marcus and Steve Dunne, our general counsel and deputy general counsel. Part of the reasoning for this was procedural—not all of the teams included lawyers, so the language had to be recalibrated to suit the format of an official request for documents. But a larger issue was cohesiveness. We had nine staff teams, but we did not want to have nine separate investigations. If our report was going to be coherent and unified, we had to join together the story of pre-9/11 aviation security failings with pre-9/11 intelligence failings, and so on. Just as our staff was integrated, rather than divided along partisan lines, we wanted our inquiries into separate policy areas to be integrated through our staff front office of Philip Zelikow, Chris Kojm, Dan Marcus, and Steve Dunne.

To facilitate the handling of our document requests, the Bush administration set up a system of naming points of contact for the commission at each agency. Zelikow helped conceptualize the framework for this arrangement by drawing on the precedent of President Harry S. Truman's directives to executive branch agencies to cooperate with the inquiry into Pearl Harbor. The idea was to have a single official at each agency responsible, and accountable, for cooperating with the commission.

This agreement was formalized on March 19, 2003—before any of our document requests had gone out—when White House Chief of Staff Andy Card sent a memo to the secretaries of state, the treasury, defense, the interior, transportation, energy, and homeland security, and to the attorney general, the director of central intelligence, and the archivist of the United States. The memo stated President Bush's "clear policy of support for the Commission's work"; instructed the department heads to "designate an appropriate senior official" to serve as their point of contact for commission requests for information or witnesses; and designated a single official, Adam Ciongoli, as the primary liaison between the executive branch and the 9/11 Commission.

At the time, Ciongoli was serving as the counselor to Attorney General John Ashcroft at the Justice Department. He was a bright and brash young lawyer who negotiated a number of key initial understandings with Zelikow, Kojm, and Marcus, all of whom had good relations with him. But he was continually pulled away by other assignments for Ashcroft, and he did not develop good relations with some other commission staff.

Our document requests were going out to Ciongoli and the other agency points of contact in May and June, just as we were making our first requests of the White House, which was handling all of its dealings with the commission through the office of White House counsel Alberto Gonzales. We soon encountered problems, both in obtaining information and with the laborious conditions placed on our access to some information. But first we encountered divisions within the commission about how to ask for documents and witnesses—divisions that were never bridged.

TO SUBPOENA OR NOT TO SUBPOENA?

To be credible, we knew the commission had to see every document we requested. Anything less would have invited criticism of our report, left room for conspiracy theories, and tarnished the weight of our findings and recommendations with the public. The question was how to achieve that access, and within the commission this question usually boiled down to whether or not to use our power of subpoena.

The issue of the commission and subpoena power was controversial even before we came into existence. The 9/11 families fought hard for it, but they and some congressional Democrats were disappointed that the law required six votes within the commission to issue a subpoena, rather than five. Time and again, the families reminded us that they wanted to see lots of subpoenas. Right or wrong, they equated the commission's strength and resolve with its willingness to issue a subpoena for documents.

Democrats on the commission, other than Lee, generally favored a robust use of the subpoena power. Jamie Gorelick argued that subpoenas could accompany every document request, and Richard Ben-Veniste concurred that it would not be unusual to issue blanket subpoenas in an investigation such as ours. Tim Roemer had fought for the inclusion of a subpoena power when he helped create the commission in Congress, and he felt that the commission should use that power to compel cooperation. In general, those in favor of using the subpoena power felt that subpoenas would preclude the need for extensive negotiations over acquiring documents, while sending a message to the government and the public that we were determined to uncover all relevant information.

We decided against an aggressive use of subpoenas for several reasons. First, the executive branch was required by statute to cooperate with us, and President Bush had a stated policy of cooperation with the commission. Given this context, we thought that issuing document requests, rather than subpoenas, would be the natural starting point, with subpoenas reserved for use if an agency was unresponsive or evasive. This is the procedure that most congressional committees use when seeking information from a government agency.

If we had issued subpoenas, litigation could have ensued as the subpoenas were contested in the courts. After all, subpoenas are not self-enforcing. A court has to decide to issue an order to enforce one. In our case, federal agencies could have taken us to court and litigated the matter. Since we had a limited amount of time and staff, the last thing we needed was to get bogged down in a court case about whether or not we were entitled to certain documents—better to have those discussions in a cooperative negotiation.

Furthermore, we knew that many of the most important documents we sought were potentially the subject of an executive privilege claim—meaning that the president might not be legally compelled to share that material with another branch of government, even with a subpoena. Dan Marcus advised us that if it came to a legal battle, the courts might very well side with the president, or—more important—even if the courts eventually sided with us, they might not enforce the subpoenas and get us the documents in time for us to do our work. So we actually had a better chance of seeing what we wanted to see in time without issuing a subpoena for it.

There was a political side as well. Subpoenas of the White House or executive branch agencies from the 9/11 Commission would have appeared adversarial. It was neither our charge nor our intention to be an adversary to the White House; to do so would have led half the country, and possibly several of the Republican commissioners, to question our motives. We were supposed to be independent, not necessarily confrontational. We were investigating a national catastrophe, not a White House transgression; this was 9/11, not Watergate.

What made the commission unique was not the fact that we could subpoena the White House, but the fact that we were investigating 9/11. Thus when we did feel that documents we needed to see were being withheld, the trump card we could play was to go public with our concern, because the public had a strong interest in learning the full truth about 9/11. Our restraint served us well when we actually did vote to issue subpoenas, in the fall of 2003. By withholding subpoenas until we thought an agency was being unresponsive or evasive, we strengthened the impact of the subpoena in the eyes of the agencies, the media, and the public. To receive a 9/11 Commission subpoena then became a mark of public shame. This led other agencies to get their act in order, and buttressed our position with the White House, which certainly did not want to receive a subpoena from the 9/11 Commission going into an election year.

Since we were not issuing subpoenas, we did want to put in place a process that verified that we were seeing everything we'd requested. To that end, we asked that the heads of the agencies sign a letter of certification saying that they had delivered to the commission every document that we'd requested, thus making senior officials accountable for the successful fulfilling of our document requests. Still, our initial choice to negotiate rather than to issue subpoenas put a tremendous amount of pressure on the two of us. We would be the ones leading negotiations with the White House. We had to produce. We were staking our credibility on the decision to be cooperative rather than confrontational.

The divisions within the commission were exacerbated when information was slow in coming. The first point of tension was the report of the congressional Joint Inquiry into 9/11, which had concluded its investigation at the end of 2002 but had not yet published its findings. We were required by statute to "first review the information compiled by, and the findings, conclusions, and recommendations of, the Joint Inquiry." The Joint Inquiry report, which was being reviewed for declassification and publication, contained a wealth of material about the 9/11 attacks and the performance of our intelligence agencies before 9/11. The "information compiled by the Joint Inquiry" included transcriptions of congressional hearings, and voluminous documentary evidence obtained from the CIA, FBI, and other agencies. For our teams looking at intelligence, it was the only such body of evidence.

The problem was we couldn't get our hands on it. The Joint Inquiry report and supporting materials were in the possession of the House Intelligence Committee. The report was classified, and the committee leadership was worried about showing it to others because they had experienced terrible problems with leaks to the press throughout their investigation. The materials compiled by the Joint Inquiry were stored away in boxes interspersed with internal congressional documents, such as deliberations of members of Congress and memos from congressional staff. The Joint Inquiry did not have enough staff remaining to go through those boxes to remove the congressional documents, so they claimed "congressional privilege" over all of the boxes of documents. So even though the boxes were full mostly of CIA and FBI documents, we could not review any of their contents because they also contained congressional documents.

This was frustrating enough, particularly since we were a creation of Congress, but matters were made worse by the fact that Joint Inquiry materials also had to be reviewed by the executive branch before they could be turned over to us, since they contained information that had originated there. So we were hung up with both Congress and the Bush administration over the documents that were mandated to be the starting point of our investigation.

We made some progress between February and April of 2003, in part because we personally reached out to Porter Goss, the chairman of the House Intelligence Committee. But seeking access to sensitive information can be maddening, even if you have security clearances, a secure facility, and assurances of cooperation from a committee chairman. We were initially permitted to review the Joint Inquiry report, but only the report (not the supporting documents compiled by the Joint Inquiry), and only at the Ford Building on Capitol Hill, where the remaining Joint Inquiry staff was going over the report in advance of its declassification and publication. At that point, the Joint Inquiry had only two employees and the building was open only at their convenience—normally 9:00 a.m. to 5:30 p.m. So, every time they wanted to review the report, commissioners or staff had to take the Washington Metro over to the Joint Inquiry offices during these limited hours. Even so, we were still negotiating for access to the supporting materials, which included transcripts of the Joint Inquiry's twenty-two hearings, nine of which had been public and televised.

The issue became a flash point within the commission on April 25, when Tim Roemer went to the Ford Building to review transcripts of closed Joint Inquiry hearings. Roemer, who had served as a member of the Joint Inquiry before being appointed to the 9/11 Commission, was denied access to the transcripts and was told that possible executive privilege questions relating to the transcripts were still being worked out between Adam Ciongoli and the Joint Inquiry. This led to some heated discussions in the commission, as those who thought we should be more aggressive in seeking documents felt that the commission was not being accommodated. Roemer was upset that Philip Zelikow was agreeing to restrictions on access; Zelikow was upset because he thought he was working through the problem; everyone was frustrated.

The 9/11 families were outraged. The notion that Roemer could not review Joint Inquiry materials almost six months after the 9/11 Commission's creation fed their mistrust of the Bush administration and their belief that we were not being tough enough in pursuing information. Both they and Roemer aired their concerns to the press, and news stories appeared detailing our difficulties. This made only small waves, but it hinted at the media interest in our struggle for access, just as it irked some in the commission and the executive branch when 9/11 Commission negotiations showed up in the newspaper.

Whatever honeymoon we had been having with the 9/11 families was certainly over. We were meeting with them regularly and explaining our positions, but they were impatient. At the beginning of May, we received a letter from the Family Steering Committee asking a number of questions about our progress: whether we had access to Joint Inquiry materials, how many of us had read the Joint Inquiry report, and how we were planning to conduct our investigation. Like their initial questions in December and their testimony in March, they were highly specific in their demands—for instance, asking to "receive a list of all staff and Commissioner assignments." Their letter concluded: "We continue to be frustrated with the slow progress of this Commission. . . . One of our greatest concerns is that the Commission will run out of time."

By this point, we had hired two "family liaisons," who worked out of the New York office: Ellie Hartz, whose husband, John—a friend of Tom's— died in the World Trade Center; and Emily Walker, who escaped from World Trade Center 7, where she worked for Citigroup Global Investment Management. These liaisons provided a daily contact point for the families, and maintained what would be a constant dialogue between family representatives and the 9/11 Commission. But some of the families were still upset that we had not hired a member of the FSC to serve on the commission staff.

Discussions were difficult. When the families were together in a room, they fed off one another's emotions, and there was, of course, considerable passion behind their arguments. We stayed in consistent contact with the FSC, which totaled just above ten members. We also made efforts to reach out to other family groups, but we were not always successful. Some family members who had been involved in lobbying for the commission became less engaged in tracking our work as time went on—either because they were willing to take a more hands-off approach, or because their approach differed from that of the FSC. A variety of 9/11 families turned up at our public hearings, but the FSC was the one unit that stayed engaged throughout.

We tried different arrangements. To facilitate the interest of the FSC members, we "assigned" a commissioner to be a contact point with some of the more engaged family members. Mostly, we listened—particularly Tom and Tim Roemer. Some commissioners were skeptical that we could ever satisfy the families' expectations. Tom was determined, though, that the 9/11 families' point of view be absorbed by the commission. Occasionally, they yelled at us; but they had a right to yell.

The nature of our relationship over the coming months was push and pull—meeting and talking with the FSC on a regular basis, benefiting from their support when problems went public, responding to their questions or demands as best we could when they were unhappy. Our interest was the same: a strong commission with the access and resources necessary to get the job done. But on the question of how to achieve that goal, we often disagreed.

It was a fine line. We knew we owed our creation in large part to their hard work. We also knew they had the most compelling personal interest in the commission's findings, and that their views were taken seriously by the press and the public. If there was a story about the commission in the media, a member of the FSC was likely to be quoted. If there was a controversy involving the 9/11 Commission on Capitol Hill, members of the FSC were likely to be there, lobbying on our behalf. If we prepared a report that the FSC did not like, it would undercut our credibility. Yet we were not preparing a report for the 9/11 families—we were preparing it for the American people. We could listen, answer questions, and take suggestions, but we could not structure our work around the specific expectations of the FSC. At times, we simply could not satisfy their demands.

The question of access to the Joint Inquiry was one of those cases, and it was one of the more puzzling access problems we faced. Through the publication of its report in late July, the Joint Inquiry continued to claim congressional privilege over some of the documents it had compiled from the CIA. Fortunately, the FBI had duplicates of the files it had turned over to the Joint Inquiry, though extended negotiations with the Bureau were required to get those files. The CIA had not made duplicates of many of the documents it had given to the Joint Inquiry, so we needed to request that it reproduce and then provide them to us. The whole process was unnecessarily laborious, particularly since we certainly had a "need to know."

Problems with access to the Joint Inquiry report were not unique to the 9/11 Commission—they became an issue for the American people as well. When the Joint Inquiry report was released, there were twenty-eight blank pages where information had been "redacted" from public view. This led to rampant speculation about what was in those twenty-eight pages that homed in on the possible involvement of Saudi Arabia in the 9/11 attacks. By being secretive, the government opened the door to cynicism and conspiracy theories. The Joint Inquiry did much good work, but the media coverage of its report focused on those twenty-eight blank pages. It was a further lesson to us about the need to avoid those kinds of redactions, as we faced the same challenge as the Joint Inquiry: writing a report for publication based largely on classified information.

The problem of over-classification is apparent to nearly everyone who reviews classified information, and it was certainly apparent to us. The core of the problem is the fact that people in government can get in trouble for revealing something that is secret, but they cannot get in trouble for stamping SECRET on a document. Thus the default rule becomes: when in doubt, classify. Particularly in our early days, the 9/11 Commission faced this problem.

When we brought this issue up with top officials, cooperation almost always accelerated. For instance, at the FBI, Director Robert Mueller made it clear that the Bureau was to cooperate with the 9/11 Commission, and people there quickly took action to be more responsive to our requests. As our public profile and political clout grew, there was more incentive for agencies to cooperate. Agency officials did not want to be seen as "stonewalling" the 9/11 Commission. However, we lacked that clout when we were getting started and negotiating for access to the Joint Inquiry materials.

Even when classified material did come through, the problem of over-classification was clear. Many commissioners complained about it. People wanted to be able to take documents back to their offices or home with them to read. Day in and day out, it becomes extraordinarily restricting to have to do all of your work in a secure facility.

Before serving on the 9/11 Commission, Tom had not dealt with the world of classified Washington. When he got his security clearance, he took the train down from New Jersey for his first experience reviewing classified material. Philip handed him a several-hundred-page FBI document with SECRET and TOP SECRET stamped all over it. He dove into it, as any curious citizen would.

When you review highly classified material, there is almost always a security officer in the room—someone who stands by silently and watches you as you read. Tom carefully made his way through the classified FBI report, absorbing the secrets of the U.S. government. When he finished, he looked up at the security officer and said, "I knew all of this. There's almost nothing in here that I couldn't have known from reading the newspapers."

The security officer looked at him and said, "Yeah. But you didn't know it was true."

NEGOTIATING WITH THE WHITE HOUSE

OUR MOST IMPORTANT NEGOTIATIONS were with the White House. The White House was where policy was set for the rest of the executive branch, where the most sensitive information resided, and where the most political interest was focused.

For the first few months of the 9/11 Commission, our contact with the White House was largely through the political or policy staff. At a certain point, though, we were turned over to the legal staff, and that was the way it stayed throughout the rest of our inquiry. Our negotiations ran through the White House counsel's office, though on occasion we reached out to Andy Card on matters of particular importance.

These negotiations essentially ran on two tracks: our staff—Zelikow, Marcus, and Dunne—met with lawyers from the counsel's office and the National Security Council; then, when issues needed resolution, Gonzales met with the two of us. We never struck broad agreements with the White House on access—issues were handled in an ad hoc manner, so we had many meetings. Often, we would go back to the 9/11 Commission with a White House offer on access to something, and it would be decided that we should go back and negotiate for more. Suffice it to say, we spent a lot of time with Alberto Gonzales.

Our relations were amicable. Alberto Gonzales is a courteous man. We met in his corner office on the second floor of the White House's West

Wing. He never sat behind his desk; instead, we met around his coffee table, often with Gonzales in shirtsleeves. He never referred to the president by name or title, but rather always said "client"—"Let me take this back to my client," or "I've got to protect my client." He never raised his voice a decibel, and his approach was formal—it was always "Governor Kean" and "Congressman Hamilton." We in turn asked his staff what he liked to be called, and they said, "Judge Gonzales." We got the sense that the 9/11 Commission was a priority responsibility for Gonzales, and that he discussed the issue on a fairly regular basis with his "client."

Our most difficult issues involved executive privilege. Executive privilege is a long-claimed right of presidents to resist requests for certain information from Congress and the courts—usually information that involves communication between the president and his advisors, or certain highly sensitive military or diplomatic information. The core concept is that the executive—the president—must have unimpeded access to the opinions of his staff. The reasoning in large part is that if the White House staff knows that their internal deliberations or advice to the president will one day be turned over to a congressional inquiry—or to a commission such as ours—they will be less inclined to be forthright and more inclined to hedge their conclusions and protect themselves.

Gonzales did not want to set any precedents that could erode executive privilege—he wanted to protect his client's and the presidency's rights of executive privilege. Precedent was his main concern. It is well known that the Bush administration feels that the powers of the presidency eroded during the Clinton administration, and that the Bush administration feels compelled to enhance the power of the executive. Gonzales did not want to turn over internal White House documents to the 9/11 Commission—which was a creation of Congress—and thus set a precedent that future commissions or congressional committees might cite when demanding to see internal White House documents.

Much of the information we requested could have fit that description because it was unprecedented for a commission like ours to see it. We asked for extensive documents from the National Security Council. We did not just want to see a policy directive on counterterrorism, al Qaeda, or Afghanistan; we wanted to see the deliberations that had led to that directive—memos, e-mails, minutes of meetings. We asked for the president's daily intelligence briefings—the "PDBs"—viewed by many as the "Holy Grail" of confidential communications to the president. Lee had chaired the House Intelligence Committee in Congress for several years, and he had never seen a PDB.

We knew from the beginning, as did the White House, that we would want this access, as the PDBs clearly represented key intelligence conclusions and policy decisions regarding terrorism before 9/11. The Joint Inquiry had been denied it. To avoid the same fate, we decided to build up from less controversial material. Our first document request to the White House was for a number of interview transcripts—for instance, the extensive interviews that President Bush and other top officials did with *The Washington Post*'s Bob Woodward when Woodward was writing his book *Bush at War,* about 9/11 and the war in Afghanistan. This material addressed topics under our consideration, but involved someone who did not work for the White House—Woodward or some other journalist—and was thus not privileged to the executive. We wanted to lay the groundwork for getting to the internal documents that we really coveted. This approach worked for our staff as well, which wanted to review documents from the various government agencies before reaching the top of the policy-making pyramid.

In June, the 9/11 Commission submitted a request for the NSC documents and a slew of other highly sensitive materials. We persuaded the White House lawyers that allowing us to see these documents, and to take notes on them, would not constitute a waiver of executive privilege on their part because the commission was a government agency, and there would be no disclosure of these documents in the commission's final report without prepublication review by the White House for classification purposes. But the White House wanted to retain physical possession of the documents, so we had to review them in the Executive Office of the President, in a reading room located in the New Executive Office Building. We could not make copies.

This compromise did not settle the issue. The next hurdles became which commissioners and staff could review the documents, and whether they could take their notes back to the 9/11 Commission offices. Every commissioner wanted access to every document. The White House wanted strict limitations on both of these fronts—limiting staff with access to White House documents to just two or three people, limiting the commissioners with access to certain materials to just the chair and vice-chair, and restricting the amount of notes the staff could bring back to the 9/11 Commission's office. We argued that we needed more staff with access; that all commissioners should be allowed access; and that we would need our notes in order to write our report.

In addition to the executive privilege issues, the White House was concerned about leaks—the more people who saw these materials, the more likely it was that information would leak out to the press. The matter of leaks came up time and again. The concern was really twofold. First and foremost, you do not want a leak of classified information that could harm the national security of the United States—for instance, information that could indicate to the enemy what sources and methods are used to gather intelligence. Throughout the 9/11 Commission, we do not think any commissioners leaked information like this.

There were, however, leaks of a second kind: internal commission deliberations, particularly those that touched upon our dealings with the White House. For instance, the two of us reported back to the full commission about the status of our negotiations with the White House. Sometimes, those reports found their way into the press in a way that put pressure on the White House: by identifying a document we were seeking or by hinting that the commission was considering a certain course of action, such as the issuance of a subpoena.

Without fail, the White House reacted strongly against these leaks. The Bush administration's view of what constituted an inappropriate communication to the press included nearly all of these references to unresolved negotiations between the 9/11 Commission and the White House; conversely, several commissioners felt entitled and even obliged to be forthcoming about those negotiations.

We made the point to commissioners that leaks were not helpful, and that internal commission information should not be disclosed, particularly with regard to the White House negotiations. We also made the point to the White House that the fact that some commissioners spoke to the press about commission matters was not a sign that they would leak highly sensitive information that could affect the security of the United States. But in the White House's view, some of the Democrats on the commission were highly partisan, spoke too often to the press, and might be tempted to leak classified information in a manner that was designed to embarrass the White House.

The White House had a precedent for limiting access to documents to the two of us—with the congressional Intelligence Committees, certain sensitive material is shared with only the chair and ranking member. In our view, it was difficult to go back to the full commission and say that information was being kept from them, or that the chair's and vice-chair's notes were being kept in the possession of the White House.

Another issue that came up in June was the question of agency representatives sitting in on our interviews with federal employees. The White House argued that the executive branch agencies had the right to send a representative to all our interviews—so, for instance, when our staff interviewed an FBI agent, there would be a representative of the FBI sitting in on the interview. We thought that essentially having a minder monitoring the interview would have a chilling effect on the witness, causing him or her to be less forthcoming with our staff.

This made for tedious negotiations. As with the question of notes, we were very much stuck on "rules of the road" issues—how we would view documents, how we would conduct interviews. Commissioners were frustrated, and some Democrats continued to argue—along with the 9/11 families—on behalf of issuing a subpoena. But we thought the use of a subpoena could trigger the very claim of executive privilege—which would have sent the matter into the courts—that we were trying to avoid. Irksome though the process was, we felt these issues could be worked out amicably, though time concerns also necessitated that they be worked out promptly.

Meanwhile, documents from executive branch agencies were starting to flow into our offices in the tens of thousands; so many, in fact, that there was concern as to whether staff could get through all of them. Some agencies were being more responsive than others. The CIA was cooperating, but we were having trouble getting some of their internal documents on the pre-9/11 war on terrorism. The FBI had improved its cooperation after Director Mueller assigned additional Bureau staff to work with the 9/11 Commission, but some records were past due, and we were having trouble getting access to information related to the trial of suspected al Qaeda operative Zacarias Moussaoui. We also experienced troubling delays with our requests to the Department of Defense, particularly with regard to documents from NORAD and some pre-9/11 military policy issues.

The 9/11 Commission received an important boost at the beginning of July, when Dan Levin was appointed by the Justice Department as the executive branch's point of contact for the 9/11 Commission, replacing Adam Ciongoli. Levin is extremely efficient. Good-humored and practical, he was also experienced, having served as chief of staff to the attorney general in the George Herbert Walker Bush administration, and, before his assignment as our point of contact, chief of staff to Director Mueller. As a former lawyer at the NSC, Levin brought a firm understanding of some key documents in question. He was assigned to the 9/11 Commission full-time, and brought on a number of deputies. His appointment indicated that the Bush administration was gaining a better understanding of the breadth of material we were seeking. When problems arose,

Levin was able to get things done—the commission could not have done its work without him.

Still, the situation was not satisfactory at the beginning of July. We were more than a third of the way through the time allotted for our investigation, and there were troubling bottlenecks in the delivery of documents: cooperation was uneven across the executive branch, and we were hung up with the White House on conditions for access. Our patient approach was paying some dividends, but not enough. Tensions within the commission, and with the 9/11 families, were becoming harder to manage. We did not issue subpoenas. Instead, we decided to go public.

GOING PUBLIC

THE LAW CREATING THE 9/11 COMMISSION allowed us to issue "interim reports" before our final report. In one of our early meetings, Richard Ben-Veniste suggested issuing a progress report, or "report card," detailing our efforts to obtain information. At our June 26 meeting, we revisited the idea, and the commissioners embraced it. For the commission, it was an effective compromise—it satisfied those who wanted to put more pressure on the White House, while not going as far as the issuance of subpoenas.

It was an unusual step for a government commission to issue such a report. We wanted to build public support for our work, and use that support to strengthen our position in negotiations with the Bush administration, but we had to achieve the right balance. If there were no criticisms in the interim report, it would look like a whitewash. If we came out and excoriated the executive branch, it would look like a witch hunt, and the agencies whose cooperation we needed might recoil. We needed to demonstrate our professionalism, seriousness, and nonpartisanship. Where we did make criticisms, we needed to substantiate them, and stress that the problems could be corrected. We were not out to score political points; we were out to get the information we needed to do our job.

The three-page interim report went through a dozen drafts. Our staff relayed the status of their document requests to the front office, where Dan Marcus and Steve Dunne brought everything together. Commissioners reviewed the report to make sure they were comfortable with the language, and Dunne coordinated its final drafting. Differences came down mainly to language: Democrats wanted adjectives that were a little tougher in highlighting the lack of cooperation; some Republicans were skeptical of finger-pointing. Several commissioners wanted to highlight the point that delays were endangering our ability to complete our inquiry on time; others were concerned that the report not overlook the substantial progress being made in acquiring documents. On all of these issues, we opted for a "just the facts" approach—we would dispassionately present the status of our work, and let the reader draw conclusions.

This was our first significant press event, and we did not have an elaborate press operation. Al Felzenberg was our deputy for communications. A presidential historian and Princeton Ph.D., Al worked for Tom when he was governor of New Jersey, as an assistant secretary of state. He went on to hold a number of jobs on Capitol Hill and for the Department of Defense, and is a former Heritage Foundation fellow. Al was originally slated to work on one of our staff teams, but took over our press relations in March 2003. For a full year, he was our only full-time employee devoted to communications—putting out statements and press releases, getting to know the beat reporters covering the 9/11 Commission for various publications and networks, and handling a growing pile of media inquiries.

On July 8, the commission's chair and vice-chair presented the interim report at a press conference in an auditorium at the Wilson Center. Our public hearings had drawn some media interest, but nothing like this. A line of more than a dozen television cameras faced us from the back of the room. It was our first time together in a high-profile setting in Washington, and we faced a number of skeptical audiences. The seats were crowded with the Washington press corps, including the reporters who would be covering the "9/11 Commission beat" in the coming months. Family members, particularly the most engaged FSC members, had made the trip down. Richard Ben-Veniste sat in the front row. Months of quiet negotiation were now thrown under a spotlight.

We read the interim report aloud, alternating between the two of us, which served us well for two reasons. First, it reaffirmed our bipartisanship. Just as we went together to media interviews, we wanted to make clear that the public face of the 9/11 Commission was undivided. Second, it focused attention on what we were saying. Often at Washington events, statements are handed out to the press and you skip right to questions. This was the first 9/11 Commission event for many members of the media in attendance. We wanted them to digest what we were reporting before they asked their questions.

Tom read first, stressing the historic nature of our endeavor: "In the last six months, the Commission has launched the most wide-ranging outside investigation of American national security in the history of the

United States. We make this point so that the public will understand that the issues we are addressing have few, if any, precedents." This was the key point we were making in our negotiations with the White House: we understood that we were asking for unprecedented access to government documents, but we were doing so because we had been charged to explain an unprecedented event. Now, we were making our argument to the American people.

We were careful to credit the executive branch for its cooperation, yet also to be blunt about the problems. Lee went through the status of cooperation with different agencies. For the White House, we referenced our extensive document requests and ongoing discussions on conditions for access. For the FBI, we noted the "slow start" in answering requests, but the increased attention that Director Mueller had given to the commission. For the Justice Department, we noted some overdue document requests and the problems in obtaining access to materials related to the Moussaoui case. For the Defense Department, we noted that problems "are becoming particularly serious. . . . Delays are lengthening, and agency points of contact have so far been unable to resolve them." It was our most pointed criticism.

Lee went through the generally positive responses from the Departments of State, Treasury, and Transportation, and the more mixed responses of the Department of Homeland Security and Congress—including the problems obtaining materials from the Joint Inquiry. Tom closed by putting the onus on the administration:

> We believe the President when he says he is committed to assisting the Commission. The White House has demonstrated that commitment in some vital ways, but the next few weeks will be crucial. We will need strong support from the White House to insure that we are able to receive the materials we require in sufficient time to meet the statutory deadline. . . . We plan to provide a number of these interim reports as we proceed with our task. We believe we will issue the next one in the month of September.

The first question, from CNN's Bob Franken, framed the issue as the media saw it: "The person who's been in Washington awhile *might* construe this as an effort to put pressure on a recalcitrant administration." Tom responded by citing the unprecedented access we were seeking and in some cases getting. As we said throughout the press conference, it was often more a matter of the Bush administration being overwhelmed by our requests than it was a matter of "recalcitrance." But Tom made the point that delays, for any reason, were not acceptable: "Now, as you read this report, [you will see that] some agencies have done pretty well; some agencies have become problems. . . . So if there's pressure, good."

The rest of the questions tracked closely issues that would dominate media coverage of the 9/11 Commission in the months ahead: whether we needed an extension; whether we were seeking access to the president's daily intelligence briefings; whether we would ask to interview the president; whether we would ask to interrogate al Qaeda detainees; and whether we were concerned about the presence of agency "minders" in our interviews. Some of these questions we had dealt with; some lay just ahead. This was our first time speaking to the press about most of these issues.

We did not want to get boxed into attacking the White House. For instance, when James Rosen of McClatchy newspapers asked us, "Do you agree that the administration is stonewalling?" Tom was circumspect: "Well, no, the White House is not stonewalling. We've got a number of documents already. . . . We expect to get a lot more. We do need speed and we do need to get [the] documents we need in a timely fashion. But 'stonewalling' is the wrong expression." Our position was that we were simply asking the administration to live up to its stated policy of cooperation. We knew that whatever criticism we made would be picked up and, to a certain degree, hyped by the news media. And it was.

We had an idea that there would be media and public interest in our interim report, but we had no idea how much. Interview requests poured in; for the first time, evening newscasts led with the 9/11 Commission; the headline on the front page of *The New York Times* the next day read "9/11 Commission Says U.S. Agencies Slow Its Inquiry"; and the 9/11 families were pleased with us for the first time in months. Overnight, our work seized the attention of a much broader audience; reporters began to call us on a routine basis, and the issues of what we would get access to, and how we would get that access, became matters for public debate and concern.

Cooperation from the executive branch accelerated, and documents flooded into our offices. We had not lashed out at agencies, but we had drawn their attention to negotiations that were previously farther down on their priority lists. Now there was an interest not only in cooperating with the 9/11 Commission, but in cooperating quickly. Everyone had been put on notice that we had the tool of public disclosure at our disposal. Nobody wanted to turn up in the next interim report.

The interim report changed the landscape of our investigation. Our initial public hearing had failed to break through and capture the public's imagination, but our interim report had woken people up. With that report, we set a tone and demeanor that was bipartisan, judicious, and dogged, without being inflammatory. As we moved into the fall, our negotiations for access—particularly to the president's daily intelligence briefings, or PDBs—became matters of national concern. Our first subpoenas were yet to be issued and our steepest climbs lay ahead, but our work and our intentions were now in the public domain.

Just as important, the interim report improved relations within the commission and with the 9/11 families. Democratic commissioners who were unsure about our approach of negotiating for documents were now satisfied that we were willing to take public risks to get the access we needed. Instead of heading into our most sensitive access negotiations with a commission drifting apart and the families voicing their public displeasure, we had managed to circle our wagons in a show of public unity.

For the two of us, it was a successful completion of our first test together in the public eye. Several reporters had approached us after the press conference and commented that we had "done a good job." And they weren't the only ones. After the last reporters trickled out of the Wilson Center auditorium, Ben-Veniste approached Tom. It was nearly six months after that first car ride back to Tom's hotel following our first commission meeting. He looked at Tom and said, "Well, you're better than I thought you were."

4

FINDING THE FACTS

[W]e want to work with Chairman Kean and Vice-Chairman Hamilton. And I believe we can reach a proper accord to protect the integrity of the daily briefing process and, at the same time, allow them a chance to look and see what was in the—certain—the daily briefings that they would like to see.

— President George W. Bush, October 27, 2003

IN THE FALL OF 2003, the nation's attention was turning to politics. Due to record levels of fund-raising, a sense of frustration within the Democratic Party electorate, and concern about the unstable situation in Iraq, the presidential primary season was drawing unusual early attention. When Washington emerged from its characteristic August downtime, people were gearing up for an aggressive and divisive year running up to the 2004 election. At the same time, we were moving toward the more substantive and high-profile period of our work, and drawing public attention of our own.

On September 23, we issued our second interim report. We explained that enormous progress had been made over the previous two months, as two million pages of documents were made available to the 9/11 Commission—four times what was provided to the congressional Joint Inquiry into 9/11. We noted pending document requests and outstanding problems, but said that "executive branch agencies have significantly improved their performance in responding to our document requests."

We also tried to shift some attention from these questions about document access to questions about the substance of our work and prospective recommendations. We highlighted key questions for our investigation and indicated the direction of our thinking. For instance: "Is the Intelligence Community organized properly to carry out the war on terrorism?" and "Do we have a government-wide, unified strategy for counterterrorism with the best balance of diplomacy, law enforcement, financial measures, military action, covert action, and public diplomacy?" and "Has the FBI carried out enough reform and the right reforms? Or do we need a new domestic intelligence agency?"

This attempt to shift the conversation from process to substance was, perhaps, wishful thinking. We were discussing substantive matters within the commission, and our staff was plowing through documents and conducting interviews. But several access questions remained unresolved, and trailed us into 2004. Our most difficult negotiations remained ahead, as did the most hard-fought intracommission debates. Access questions, after all, were essential—if our substantive conclusions and recommendations were to have any credibility, we needed to see everything we'd asked for. The question remained how aggressive to be in seeking that access.

Within and outside the commission, we paid a price for the tone of our second interim report. The Family Steering Committee grew more critical. They issued their own interim report in the form of a "Report Card for the 9/11 Commission," grading our performance in several areas. Suffice it to say, our average was somewhere around a D+. Even as documents were flowing in, commissioners who favored the use of subpoenas grew increasingly impatient.

Our standard for issuing a subpoena went beyond slow document release—a problem that could have been symptomatic of large bureaucracies or the enormous scope of our requests. We reserved our subpoena power for when people were unwilling or unable to produce what we asked for. It became a question of trust: Could we trust an agency to fully provide the materials without being legally compelled to do so? The Federal Aviation Administration (FAA) was the first agency for whom the answer to that question was no.

On September 11, 2001, the FAA was responsible for regulating the safety of civil aviation in the United States. Telling the story of what happened to the four hijacked flights depended on getting extensive evidence from the agency. This responsibility was initially assigned to staff teams 7 and 8—staff team 7 was responsible for aviation security and learning what had taken place on the four affected flights; staff team 8 was responsible for the national and air traffic control response on 9/11.

Team 7's document requests went largely through the newly created Transportation Security Administration (TSA), which is a part of the Department of Homeland Security. In the wake of 9/11, the TSA took over responsibility for civil aviation security from the FAA. From the TSA's point of view, there was no reason not to share as much documentation as possible—after all, any information about pre-9/11 failings in aviation security only further demonstrated the need for the TSA's creation.

Our problems with the FAA came out of team 8's work. Staff team 8 had combined with the team doing emergency response, under the leadership of John Farmer. Farmer was one of our most important hires. On September 11, 2001, Farmer was attorney general of the state of New Jersey. As the state's chief law enforcement officer, he set up a victims' assistance center on the New Jersey side of the Hudson River; worked with the FBI to look for clues, finding significant evidence in the garbage at Newark International Airport, where one of the flights took off; and coordinated New Jersey law enforcement with the federal, state, and local agencies working together in those initial weeks. The ensuing anthrax letters were mailed from a post office in Hamilton Township, New Jersey, so Farmer's workload only escalated.

Four months after September 11, Farmer's term as state attorney general expired, and he went from knowing everything to being out of the loop. A year later, Farmer responded enthusiastically to Tom's invitation to join the commission staff, but he did not want to uproot his family to Washington. It was only after we opened our office in Lower Manhattan that Farmer was able to come on board. Farmer and John Azzarello, another highly able member of our emergency response staff, took on the leadership of the investigation into what had happened in the air on 9/11, as well as what had happened on the ground—thus we ended up with one large team responsible for telling the story of September 11, 2001.

The staff dealt both with FAA headquarters in Washington and with the various air traffic control command centers scattered around the nation. The national Air Traffic Control System Command Center is based in Herndon, Virginia, from where it oversees all American airspace. FAA control centers around the nation monitor different chunks of airspace, and are required to notify the national command center if there is a suspected hijacking. The four hijacked flights on September 11 were monitored by several of these control centers, principally Boston, New York, Cleveland, and Indianapolis.

Telling the 9/11 "story in the skies" required a detailed account of the FAA's cooperation with the North American Aerospace Defense Command (NORAD), the joint command of the United States and Canada that defends the airspace of North America. When military jets appeared in the sky over New York and Washington on 9/11, they were under NORAD command. To understand how the FAA and NORAD worked together to protect America's skies that day, we had to find out when the FAA notified NORAD about the hijacked aircraft, and what NORAD did with that information. Regrettably, neither the FAA nor NORAD was forthcoming or comprehensive in answering our document requests.

Our staff issued document requests to the FAA on May 7 and July 2, 2003. This included requests for tapes of air traffic controllers speaking with the hijacked flights; records of what time the FAA contacted NORAD about the suspected hijackings; statements made by FAA personnel after the attacks; FAA reports and internal assessments of its actions on 9/11; and a range of other materials. By the end of August, the FAA had assured us that the documents they had delivered constituted a complete response to our requests.

Our investigation then proceeded from procuring and examining FAA documents to conducting interviews with agency personnel about those documents. After the FAA said that their document release was complete, several members of our staff interviewed FAA personnel—in Washington and Virginia, and at the command centers in Boston, New York, Cleveland, and Indianapolis. What we discovered was troubling.

Our staff in each of the four cities began by asking what kinds of records the FAA offices had kept of the day of 9/11. They found that there was substantially more material than the FAA had delivered, including tapes and transcripts that our staff had asked for and not received. On several occasions, a witness even went to retrieve documents that were in the FAA field office but had not been delivered to the commission. And these were significant materials: for instance, tapes of FAA personnel responding on 9/11 and records of FAA notification to NORAD.

Members of our staff stayed in touch with one another and realized they were having the same experience in each of the FAA locations. They took their concerns to some of the FAA personnel in the field, who explained the problem: FAA headquarters had provided our staff with the "accident package" but had neglected to provide the "accident file"— meaning that the FAA had turned over to us the distilled product of their own internal investigation into 9/11, but had failed to turn over the extensive raw materials that had gone into that investigation, even though that is precisely what our staff had asked for.

We did not issue a subpoena immediately. Instead, we went to our point of contact at the FAA with this information. The FAA acknowledged its error and went to work to correct the problem; soon, boxes and boxes of new material came into our office. But Farmer and his team were still upset.

On October 14, the commission held a public hearing in Washington looking at intelligence policy. Farmer asked the commission staff front office if he could brief the commissioners during our lunch break. Farmer is a highly effective lawyer, and he had prepared for the briefing as if he were preparing to go to court. He laid out what he had asked the FAA for, what he had received, how significant the gaps in access were, and how substantially his team had been set back in its investigation. The FAA had produced more documents, he reported, but his team had not yet reviewed them, and they had lost confidence in the FAA's willingness or ability to fulfill the commission's document request without the legal compulsion of a subpoena.

Farmer's briefing lit up the commissioners. Those who had advocated for subpoenas all along argued strongly that the FAA's intransigence illustrated the need to immediately subpoena every executive branch agency, lest we uncover similar problems in their document release. The frustration was acute. It was nearly a year into our work—more than halfway through the time allotted for our investigation—and one of our staff teams' work schedule had been upended. Still, neither the two of us nor the majority of the Republican commissioners felt it necessary to issue blanket subpoenas because of the FAA's failure. We ended our lunch break and went back to the hearing with the situation unresolved.

After the hearing concluded, Slade Gorton proposed a compromise: we would refrain from issuing subpoenas to every agency, but we would subpoena the FAA, and accompany that subpoena with a warning to the rest of the executive branch. There was some disagreement on this, but after extended discussion the commissioners acceded to Gorton's proposal. It was one of many occasions throughout our work when Gorton bridged divisions within the commission, often by proposing the language for an agreement that found the center of an issue.

The next day we put out a statement announcing our intention to subpoena the FAA. We also leveled a warning, saying:

> This disturbing development at one agency has led the Commission
> to re-examine its general policy of relying on document requests
> rather than subpoenas. We have voted to issue a subpoena to the

FAA for the documents we have already requested. This will not only underline our specific concerns about the serious problem created for the Commission by the FAA's failure to respond fully to our document requests, but will also put other agencies on notice that our document requests must be taken as seriously as a subpoena, and that they must review the efforts they have made so far to assure full compliance. In the absence of such assurances, additional subpoenas will be issued.

We were demonstrating—to the White House, the executive branch agencies, the 9/11 families, and the public—that if we were pushed sufficiently, we would push back.

Like our first interim report, the FAA subpoena had an effect more powerful than we had imagined. Because we had withheld issuing subpoenas up until this point, the issuing of this one resonated strongly. It was an enormous blow to an agency's credibility to receive one—more so than being named and shamed in an interim report—and the White House correctly saw it as a shot across the bow to them and the rest of the executive branch. The same day as our statement, Judge Gonzales issued a memo to all of the department and agency heads that had received 9/11 Commission document requests, saying, "The Chief of Staff [Andrew Card] expects departments and agencies to take document requests as seriously as a subpoena and to avoid such problems in the future."

Dan Marcus held a meeting with our staff team leaders and asked them to report any problems or delays that might merit a subpoena. He specified in a follow-up e-mail that he meant any "instances in which an agency, despite having been put on notice by us that their production is (or is suspected to be) deficient in a significant respect, has failed to come forward with responsive documents or has responded inadequately." We wanted, once and for all, to remove any obstacles to document release.

The Department of Defense, and specifically NORAD, fit Marcus's description of an agency responding inadequately. Farmer and his team were facing problems with NORAD similar to those we faced with the FAA. As with the FAA, an investigation of NORAD dealt with multiple sites. The four hijacked flights on 9/11 were in NORAD's Northeast Air Defense Sector—known as NEADS and headquartered in Rome, New York. On the morning of September 11, NEADS called on two bases with fighter aircraft—Otis National Guard Base, in Cape Cod, Massachusetts, and Langley Air Force Base, in Hampton, Virginia—to scramble military aircraft to respond to the hijackings.

In late October, our staff went to Rome to tour the NEADS facility. In response to their document request, our staff had received from NORAD, which runs NEADS, one generally garbled transcript of what had taken place on September 11. But when Farmer and his staff received a tour of the facility in Rome, they found a room crowded with more than twenty banks of operators: some weapons controllers and some flight controllers. In asking questions, our staff found that the conversations conducted by each of these twenty operators were tape-recorded, yet we had received no transcripts or tape recordings of what took place at these phone banks on September 11. There were also discrepancies between things NORAD was telling us about their performance on the morning of September 11— things that the agency had stated publicly after 9/11—and the story told by the limited tapes and documents the commission had received.

Farmer immediately suspended the tour of NEADS and the interviews our staff had scheduled and flew back to New Jersey. He met with Tom, alerting him to the severity of NORAD's failure to comply with the document request, and to some of the troubling differences between NORAD's official account of 9/11 and what our staff was uncovering. These were puzzling and disturbing developments, and they account in part for some of the more bizarre and inaccurate conspiracy theories about 9/11. At the core of several prominent conspiracy theories is the notion that the military had foreknowledge or warning of the attacks, and had issued a "stand down" order on 9/11, thus permitting the attacks to occur. Part of the reasoning behind these theories is that people went over what NORAD said after 9/11 and realized that things did not add up— planes were not where NORAD said they were at specific times, or could not have done what NORAD said they did within a plausible time frame.

Where there is inconsistency or incompleteness in government accounts, there is room for doubt; where there is room for doubt, there is room for conspiracy theories, which attempt to fill that space by creating a hypothetical version of events that captures people's imaginations. The uncertainty surrounding the military's response on 9/11 heightened the commission's responsibility to provide an authoritative factual record of the day. But questions about the FAA and NORAD were not unique to the notions of fringe conspiracy theorists. The 9/11 families had also seized on the holes in the 9/11 story in the skies—how the FAA and NORAD communicated that day, and how NORAD had responded—and had given us detailed questions based on their own research.

On November 5, Lee and Slade Gorton met with Secretary of Defense Donald Rumsfeld, Deputy Secretary Paul Wolfowitz, Under Secretary of

Defense for Intelligence Stephen Cambone, and other senior officials at the Pentagon. Throughout the commission, Rumsfeld sought to be cooperative. He invited each of the commissioners to meet with him. Often these meetings took the form of breakfasts or lunches in a room next to Rumsfeld's office at the Pentagon.

Secretary Rumsfeld is inquisitive and engaged in meetings. Most of the time is spent with him asking detailed questions. He was interested in our work and recommendations, and had previously led his own commission on missile defense in the late 1990s. One criticism that he offered was that he did not think interim reports were a good idea, as they suggested preliminary judgments before issues could be fully considered. But he was personally cooperative, and able to clear up issues upon which we had reached an impasse with the Department of Defense.

When we met on November 5, NORAD was not our only problem within the Department of Defense. We were also waiting on reports of interrogations with al Qaeda detainees, which were vital to our understanding of the 9/11 plot, and some high-level documents about military policy toward terrorism before 9/11. Rumsfeld pledged to give the commission everything it had asked for, and offered to establish a timeline for the delivery of outstanding documents and materials. He said he had only recently learned about the problems in fulfilling our requests—particularly from NORAD—and he was clearly distressed by NORAD's conduct. He instructed Cambone—the commission's point of contact at the Department of Defense—to "get these people what they need."

Despite this constructive tone, at a full commission meeting the following day, our staff recommended the issuing of a subpoena, particularly with regard to NORAD. The staff front office suggested that the NORAD situation bordered on willful concealment. As with the FAA, the staff had lost confidence in NORAD's willingness or ability to fulfill the document request. Farmer believed that NORAD was delivering incomplete records with the knowledge that the commission had a fixed end date that could be waited out. Dan Marcus and Steve Dunne also recommended a subpoena—pointing out that, unlike the FAA, NORAD had not acted immediately to correct problems in document release.

Lee said he could not support issuing a subpoena to NORAD because of the personal assurances he had received from the secretary of defense the previous day. Rumsfeld had agreed to every point Lee had raised, setting deadlines to fulfill Lee's requests. Lee felt that responding to such a constructive meeting by issuing a subpoena could pollute relations with the secretary and the Department of Defense at a time when they had pledged to cooperate. It was Lee's style to give people an opportunity to live up to their word.

Several commissioners disagreed, including Slade Gorton, who had also attended the meeting. NORAD had withheld documents for months, delaying the work of the staff and losing their confidence. To ensure the full delivery of documents and to be credible, the commissioners argued, the commission had to issue a subpoena for all NORAD-related materials.

It came to a vote. This was the only matter on which the two of us disagreed throughout the entire 9/11 commission. The vote was 6 to 4 in favor of issuing the subpoena, with Tom voting for and Lee voting against. So on our only division between chair and vice-chair, the chair and Slade Gorton sided with the Democrats, and the vice-chair sided with three Republicans. This was unusual. In a way, by voting as we did, we each boosted our stature with our opposing parties, while conversely raising doubts within our own parties.

The next day, Lee called Secretary Rumsfeld to alert him to the subpoena. Rumsfeld was not happy, but he pledged his continued cooperation in resolving the matter. We issued a public statement, this time focusing on NORAD. We said, "In several cases, we were assured that all requested records had been produced but we then discovered, through investigation, that these assurances were mistaken and that records of importance to our investigation had not been produced." Once again, the work of our staff team on the day of 9/11 had led to a subpoena. The grist for conspiracy theorists looking into 9/11 was in the mill. The pressure was intense to get that part of our investigation right, and the staff had lost so much time that our hearing on the 9/11 story in the skies was postponed for months. Indeed, the delays from NORAD and the FAA made it highly unlikely that the team could complete its work as scheduled by our May 2004 reporting date.

Subpoenas were now regarded as a public demand for accountability on the part of an agency, in addition to being a legal tool. Our second subpoena had nearly evenly divided the commission and split the two of us. But our most sensitive access matter lay ahead, as was indicated by *The Washington Post* headline describing our subpoena of the Department of Defense: "9/11 White House Subpoena Omits Classified Briefings." The headline was not exactly accurate—we had subpoenaed the Pentagon, not the White House—but the headline writer put the focus squarely where the public's was: on our struggle to gain access to the president's daily intelligence briefings.

THE PRESIDENT'S DAILY BRIEFINGS

Six days per week, the president of the United States receives an intelligence briefing from a senior CIA officer, usually accompanied by the director or deputy director of central intelligence. The briefing is generally made up of a few short points—less than a page in length—that the intelligence community feels the president should know, and a somewhat longer piece that describes a particular issue in depth. This briefing—known as the president's daily briefing, or PDB—is also delivered to a number of other senior national security officials inside and outside the White House. Before the recent intelligence reform, the PDB was prepared by the CIA, hand-delivered to the assigned recipients by CIA officers who remained with the officials while they read it, and afterward returned to CIA headquarters, in Langley, Virginia.

Getting access to the PDBs was not the purpose of our investigation, though in the fall of 2003 it often seemed that way. In fact, the range of White House documents that we received access to in July, August, September, and October of 2003 provided far more substance for our final report—internal National Security Council documents on al Qaeda, presidential directives on terrorism, covert action reports, records of meetings and deliberations, and so on. A glance through the notes of our final report bears this out: look for the number of references to "NSC memo," "NSC note," "NSC e-mail," or "White House cable."

This access was unprecedented, even with the restrictions imposed. What were these restrictions? The documents were literally under lock and key in a safe in a reading room at the New Executive Office Building. To get access to the documents, you had to be escorted into the room by a White House official; the files were sorted by the name of the commissioner or commission staff member, because each of us had different levels of access. You reviewed the documents at a simple table, and depending on your level of classification, you often had to leave your notes—or portions of your notes—in the reading room as well.

Laborious though this process was, it was crucial that we go through it. These documents constituted a treasure trove of information spanning the Clinton and Bush administrations. Through the fall, we continued detailed negotiations with the White House on these access conditions. But people following the commission knew the access we were getting, and were impressed that we were seeing material that nobody outside of the executive branch was usually permitted to see.

Still, the PDBs were of immense importance. They represented what the intelligence community told our most senior officials about the threat of terrorism before 9/11. Reviewing them would enable us to evaluate the quality of the information funneled up to the president, and to evaluate what the president did with that information—what changes in policy the PDBs provoked, or what requests for clarification or further study they precipitated. The PDBs were also, in many people's minds, the answer to the question most famously asked by Senator Howard Baker about Richard Nixon during the Watergate hearings: "What did he know, and when did he know it?" Even if there were no stunning revelations, it was necessary to answer this question for the public record.

It was also an issue of credibility. To put it bluntly, the PDBs are important because people believe they are important. These are the most secretive, high-level national security documents delivered to the president in writing. The congressional Joint Inquiry into the 9/11 attacks had not seen them, thus their leadership could not stand before the American people and say, "We have seen every high-level document that pertains to 9/11." In the minds of the families, the press, and some commissioners, the PDB issue became a litmus test: anything less than direct access to the PDBs would seriously diminish the public's confidence in our report, because people could say, "Well, you didn't look at the PDBs." Our commission could be doubted as the Warren Commission was doubted.

Lurking in the background was speculation about one particular PDB received by President Bush at his ranch in Crawford, Texas, on August 6, 2001. This is the now-famous PDB entitled "Bin Ladin Determined to Strike in US." Through 2002, rumors about this PDB, including aspects of its provocative title, leaked out in the press. The Bush administration acknowledged the existence of the August 6, 2001, PDB, but refused to make its contents public. At a press conference in the spring of 2002, Condoleezza Rice discussed the PDB in generalities, but refused to offer much in the way of specific information, and declined to testify in front of the congressional Joint Inquiry. This fed the rumor mill.

Many people, including the 9/11 families, speculated that the PDB contained warnings—"smoking guns"—that al Qaeda intended to fly planes into tall buildings, warnings that would have directly refuted a statement made by Condoleezza Rice shortly after 9/11 that "no one could ever have imagined that terrorists would fly planes into buildings." Thus the 9/11 families were adamant that we have access to the PDBs—for some of them, this was the commission's single most important responsibility.

But just as many people saw the PDBs as keystones of the 9/11 story, the White House saw them as keystones of executive privilege. If the 9/11

Commission—a creation of Congress—got to see the PDBs, then congressional committees might cite us as a precedent, and seek PDBs in the future. The Bush White House was not simply withholding their own PDBs; they were also withholding the Clinton administration PDBs. They argued that the PDB is the president's vehicle to get the best assessments of his intelligence agencies. Those assessments must be free and unfettered. If somebody preparing a PDB knows that it will be looked at years later by people outside the executive branch, in a totally different context, they might pull a punch to protect themselves. The quality of the work would suffer, harming the president and the national security of the United States.

We did not ask for the PDBs right away. Just as we worked our way up to asking the White House for the NSC documents, we also worked our way up to the PDBs. We wanted to have an established relationship with the White House first, and we wanted to build our credibility that we would not leak information to the press to damage the president. When we filed a document request for the PDBs, we did so through the CIA, which prepared the PDBs and kept possession of them. If it came to litigation, it might be easier to sue the CIA for the documents than the White House.

Our request was specific. We did not ask to see all PDBs from 1998 to September 20, 2001. Instead, we asked for PDBs, or portions of PDBs, that addressed Usama Bin Ladin, al Qaeda, terrorist threats inside the United States, the possibility of airplanes being used as weapons, and issues involving terrorism and Afghanistan, Pakistan, Saudi Arabia, Sudan, Yemen, and Germany.

The White House responded in early September by proposing a briefing—the commission would not see the PDBs, but would be briefed on their contents. It was unlikely, if not impossible, that this would satisfy all of the commissioners. But we agreed to the briefing with the understanding that we reserved the right to negotiate for further access. We expected to be briefed on the substance of the PDBs; the White House had a different expectation.

The briefing was held in our document reading room at the New Executive Office Building, on October 16, 2003, the same day we held a hearing on intelligence policy and decided to subpoena the FAA. We were ushered in along with a few of our senior staff; several lawyers from the White House, the NSC, and the CIA were on hand. There was a detailed presentation by the White House and NSC lawyers, with PowerPoint documents breaking down the number of PDBs responsive to our document request—for instance, we were told how many PDBs mentioned al Qaeda, or how many mentioned the possibility of attacks inside the United States, or how many dealt with terrorism in Afghanistan. Other process matters were included, such as how many officials in the Clinton and Bush administrations had received the briefings—but the substance of the briefings was excluded. So we were told there were X number of PDBs about al Qaeda, but we were not told what those PDBs said.

The atmosphere in the room was not good. As the PowerPoint presentation dragged on, Lee had a sense that the briefing was going to be unsatisfactory. As a member of Congress, he had experienced these kinds of briefings before, from several White Houses: briefings that offered insights into questions of process, but withheld details about substance. Looking around the room at the faces of our fellow commissioners, we could tell that this was not what they had in mind.

After the briefing, we asked some questions, some of which the briefers refused to answer, adding to the strain in the room. Then we asked to be left alone to hold a commission meeting, which was unusual, given that we were in the executive branch SCIF and not in our own space. None of the commissioners was happy. Knowing the number of PDBs on a given subject was not going to help us write a credible report. If anything, the briefing had been so unsatisfactory that it had heightened our determination to get access to the substance of the PDBs.

The next series of offers and counteroffers dealt with how many PDBs we could see, and who could see them. There were more than three hundred PDBs from the Clinton and Bush administrations that the White House identified as responsive to our document request—meaning that they addressed one of the topics we had identified as pertinent to our mandate. Of those PDBs, a core group of approximately twenty dealt with subjects that the White House deemed critically relevant to our mandate and the 9/11 attacks. In the White House's view, the larger group of more than three hundred PDBs contained information that we had access to through other documents, such as the Senior Executive Intelligence Briefing—a daily intelligence report that went to a larger group of officials within the executive branch than the PDB did.

The White House wanted to limit access to the PDBs to the chair and vice-chair by permitting the two of us to review the small group of approximately twenty, and by providing some sort of briefing on what was in the larger group of three-hundred-plus PDBs. This proposal was not without precedent. Again, Judge Gonzales was drawing on the model of congressional Intelligence Committees, where the chair and ranking member saw highly classified materials that the rest of the committee did not. The question, from our point of view, was whether this arrangement—and the various iterations it took—would provide us with sufficient access to do our job and hold the commission together. Would the commission accept something less than access for all ten commissioners? Would the public and the 9/11 families accept this as a credible level of access? Would we be able to review these documents in a manner that permitted us to give a credible and authoritative account of the lead-up to 9/11? We decided that the answer was no.

Our trump card was a subpoena. We did not know if we could win a legal battle to obtain access to the PDBs. The president could claim executive privilege, and we would have to fight it out in the courts. But the White House certainly did not want a court battle to protect pre-9/11 PDBs with warnings about terrorism going into an election year. Thus the threat of a subpoena was as much a tool of political leverage as of legal leverage.

We had been ambiguous in our negotiations about whether or not we would subpoena the PDBs or executive branch agencies. We did not negotiate by threatening. We did say to Judge Gonzales, "Look. There are ten commissioners. We cannot guarantee which way people will vote if it came to a vote on a subpoena." At times, the White House was concerned about the possibility of a 5 to 5 vote, splitting the commission along partisan lines. This was wishful thinking. At some of our moments of higher tension, there might have been seven or eight votes for a subpoena, though probably not for the PDBs. Still, the White House could not assume that we would not vote to subpoena.

Beyond the executive privilege issues, Gonzales remained concerned about leaks to the media. Frankly, the White House did not trust the full commission. To begin with, they did not know us very well. Tom was the only one appointed by the president, and he had not been the president's first choice for chairman. Slade Gorton and John Lehman had been appointed by Senator Trent Lott at a time of turmoil, when Lott was being replaced as Senate majority leader, in part because the White House did not support him. Above all, the White House felt that some Democratic commissioners were highly partisan, and would leak information, perhaps inaccurately, to embarrass the president.

Several times through the summer and fall of 2003, Gonzales had reacted strongly to what he considered to be damaging leaks. These leaks dealt with process issues: what documents the commission was seeking, or the state of negotiations between the commission and the White House. Whenever one of these news stories appeared, it set back our negotiations, so we repeatedly warned commissioners that leaks could undermine our negotiating position—the White House had to trust us not to leak the contents of sensitive documents such as the PDBs if we were to see them.

After two months of negotiating, we approached a stalemate in late October. We did not want to go to court, but Tom did go to the court of public opinion. He invited Phil Shenon, the reporter covering the 9/11 Commission for *The New York Times,* to Drew University for an interview. On Sunday, October 26, the account of that interview was the lead story in the *Times,* with the headline "9/11 Commission Could Subpoena Oval Office Files."

In the interview, Tom laid down a marker for the kind of access the commission needed: "Anything that has to do with 9/11, we have to see it—anything. There are a lot of theories about 9/11, and as long as there is any document out there that bears on any of those theories, we're going to leave questions unanswered. And we cannot leave questions unanswered." We had made these arguments to Judge Gonzales in private; now we were making them in public.

Speaking of the commission's inability to get certain documents, Tom said, "I will not stand for it. . . . That means we will use every tool at our command to get hold of every document." When asked explicitly about the possibility of a subpoena, he said, "It's always on the table, because they [the White House] know that Congress in their wisdom gave us the power to subpoena, to use it if necessary." Again, the commission's access negotiations were thrust to the forefront. The exasperation Tom expressed was heightened by growing time pressure. To get our work done and have any reasonable chance of meeting our deadline, we needed to get these access questions behind us.

The White House was not happy that Tom had made the issue public. The following day, President Bush was asked about Tom's comments in a meeting with reporters in the Oval Office. The president replied:

> You're talking about the presidential daily briefing. It's important for the writers of the presidential briefing to feel comfortable that the documents will never be politicized and/or unnecessarily exposed for public purview. I—and so, therefore, the kind of statements out of this administration were very protective of the presidential prerogatives of the past and to protect the right for other presidents, future presidents, to have a good presidential daily brief.
>
> Now having said that, I am—we want to work with Chairman Kean and Vice-Chairman Hamilton. And I believe we can reach a

proper accord to protect the integrity of the daily brief process and, at the same time, allow them a chance to take a look and see what was in the—certain—the daily briefs that they would like to see.

The president's comments changed the equation. First, he explicitly referred to the "presidential daily briefing"—before, we were not even permitted to publicly cite the documents by name. This is a unique quirk of Washington: items can be declassified the moment a president references them in public. Second, he committed his administration to reaching a deal; he was now personally invested in an outcome where the commission got access to the PDBs, though he had not gone beyond the White House offer of having only the two of us look at them.

The political stakes were raised. Democratic candidates in the presidential primary seized on the PDB issue to attack the president. Governor Howard Dean issued a statement saying, "I am very concerned by the President's foot-dragging on cooperation with the bipartisan 9/11 commission. The administration's current stonewalling suggests that there is more that they knew and want to hide from the American public." Senator Joe Lieberman weighed in, saying, "President Bush may want to withhold the truth about September 11, but the American people, and especially the victims' families, demand and deserve it." Such responses were an indication of how the commission could—and would continue to—be caught up in the presidential campaign.

The White House offered to let the two of us, along with two commission staff members, review the core group of approximately twenty PDBs, and then brief the other commissioners on their contents. One of us—either Tom, Lee, or one of the staff members—could then review the larger group of more than three hundred PDBs to determine if any of them was demonstrably critical to our investigation. If so, that one designee could make the case to the White House for enlarging the core group of PDBs, which would be the subject of a report back to the full commission.

We presented this offer at a commission meeting on November 6—the same meeting at which we decided to subpoena the Department of Defense for NORAD documents. There was strong opposition to it. Democrats felt that all ten commissioners, or at least a larger subset of commissioners, needed to see the PDBs. A vote to accept the deal failed; a vote on whether to subpoena the PDBs failed, but received the support of the four Democratic commissioners other than Lee.

The next day we met with Judge Gonzales and White House chief of staff Andrew Card. Card's presence indicated that the issue was now a top priority for the White House—several times throughout our investigation he was engaged on matters of urgent or extreme importance. Both Gonzales and Card made clear that the final decision was to be made by the president. Card also voiced his displeasure at an article in that morning's *New York Times,* headlined "9/11 Panel May Reject Offer of Limited Access to Briefings." Again, the White House was distressed that internal commission deliberations were being aired in the press.

We presented our counterproposal: in addition to the two of us, two commissioners, one Republican and one Democrat, would review the core group of PDBs. Out of this four-person "review team," two representatives of our choosing would review the more than three hundred PDBs to see if any of them needed to be added to the core group. This way, the commission would control who got access to the PDBs, and one of the other Democratic commissioners would see them. If this deal were rejected, we could accept the original deal only grudgingly: the commission would then be divided, our statements would express disappointment, and there would likely be problems with the public, the 9/11 families, and the press.

This compromise moved us forward. Over the next few days, we hammered out the details of how this review team would operate. On November 11, we received a letter from Judge Gonzales outlining the White House's conditions for viewing the PDBs, stating that no precedent was being set, and warning us that leaks of information from the PDBs would end our access to them. The conditions allowed for a four-person commission review team who could look at the core group. That review team could then prepare a statement reporting to the rest of the commission on the contents of the core group. Two members of this review team would be allowed to view the larger group of PDBs, and could recommend that items within the larger group be added to the core group if they were felt to be "demonstrably critical" to the commission's work, though Judge Gonzales had to approve an expansion of the core group.

We accepted. In our statement announcing the agreement, we wrote, "We expect the terms of this agreement will provide the Commission the access it needs to prepare the report mandated by our statute, in a manner that respects the independence and integrity of the Commission. We remain committed to obtaining the access we need to fulfill our mandate." The process was not over—we had yet to achieve "access." If the review process was not sufficient, we reserved the right to reconsider the agreement, and possibly issue a subpoena.

Not everyone was happy. At a volatile commission meeting, eight commissioners supported the agreement, but Tim Roemer and Max Cleland openly dissented, arguing that all ten commissioners needed access to the PDBs. The Family Steering Committee put out a statement blasting the agreement, arguing that all ten commissioners needed access, and saying, "As it now stands a limited number of Commissioners will have restricted access to a limited number of PDB documents. This will prevent a full uncovering of the truth and is unacceptable."

The two of us wrote an Op-Ed for the November 16 edition of *The Washington Post,* explaining the agreement. We stressed that the White House would not be editing any of the material we would review, we would have access to every document we'd asked to see (documents that the Joint Inquiry had not seen), and we could use that material to inform all ten commissioners and draft our final report. We pointed out that "under this agreement, the Commission has gained a degree of access to sensitive information unequaled in the history of the United States." We also acknowledged our political balancing act: "Some have suggested we have impinged too far on the prerogatives of the presidency; others say that we have not gone far enough. The bottom line is that this agreement allows us to see everything we have requested."

This assuaged some concerns, but the FSC remained unconvinced. In a follow-up statement, they said, "The Commission has seriously compromised its ability to conduct an independent, full, and unfettered investigation." In conversations with our 9/11 family liaisons and with commissioners, some FSC members complained that we had backed down—it was while discussing the PDBs that a meeting in Tom's office became so loud, with family members yelling about the need for full commission access, that reporters outside heard the commotion and reported it in the next day's Newark *Star-Ledger.* We were approaching the anniversary of the creation of the 9/11 Commission, and were charting a delicate course through turbulent legal, political, and emotional waters. We had reached an agreement on PDBs. Unfortunately, we had not reached the end of the PDB controversy.

THE REVIEW TEAM

WE DISCUSSED THE COMPOSITION of the review team at a dinner in Mead Hall at Drew University, the building where Tom's office is located. It was a tense meeting. Democratic commissioners were not happy that the agreement excluded most of them from viewing the PDBs. Tim Roemer continued to oppose the agreement, even when he was suggested as a member for the review team.

We settled on a review team composed of the two of us, Jamie Gorelick, and Philip Zelikow. As a former deputy attorney general, Gorelick was familiar with PDBs, and was thus a good choice for assessing their contents; the same held true for Zelikow, who had worked in the NSC. The four of us looked at the core group, and Gorelick and Zelikow reviewed the larger group of more than three hundred PDBs.

Originally, we planned that the fourth member of the review team would be a Republican commissioner. However, upon reflection, we felt it was vital for a member of our staff to participate. Substantively, Zelikow was the logical selection. But this choice further upset the Family Steering Committee. Through the summer, they became increasingly distrustful of him because of his past ties to Condoleezza Rice, and even suggested that he resign. As soon as we named him to the review team, they asked that he be replaced. This was an instance where all we could do was explain our reasoning and move on.

We started our review of the PDBs on December 2, and immediately ran into problems. When Gorelick and Zelikow reviewed the larger group of PDBs, they recommended that approximately fifty of them were "demonstrably critical" to the commission's mandate, and needed to be moved into the core group. Their standard for a PDB's being demonstrably critical was that it contain information needed to inform our final report that was not available to the commission from other sources. Moving these extra fifty or so PDBs into the core group would allow the two of us to view them, and permit us to address their contents in the review team's report to the rest of the commission.

The White House balked at this. There was clearly a disconnect between their expectations for the commission's review team and ours. We felt entitled to make a substantive case for why a PDB could be moved from the larger group to the core group—for instance, if it addressed activities involving Taliban sponsorship of Usama Bin Ladin, we needed to include that information in our final report. In the White House's view, the only reason to move an item from the larger group to the core group was if it were a PDB that had escaped their notice as fitting their own criteria for what was demonstrably critical to a review of the 9/11 attacks. When the November agreement was reached, they had thought this might apply to only one or two PDBs from the larger group; even when they sought to compromise during the review process, they agreed to move first eleven, and then fifteen PDBs into the core group—far fewer than the number identified by Gorelick and Zelikow.

The divide was similarly great on the report that we prepared for the full commission about the core group of now approximately twenty PDBs. The November agreement gave the commission "wide latitude" in preparing this statement, but it also described it as "a concise statement of the results of their review." Our draft statement ran well over ten pages, and included the titles of different PDBs and a nearly complete re-creation of the August 6 PDB. Gorelick also thought it was important for the commission to know the rough context of what was in the larger group of more than three hundred PDBs, so she included language describing the nature of the larger group of PDBs.

Again, the White House balked. Their view was that *concise* meant brief—perhaps one or two pages characterizing what was in the core group. They objected to the near re-creation of the August 6 PDB, the inclusion of PDB titles in the report, and the references to PDBs that were not in the core group.

The process was extremely frustrating. Zelikow and Gorelick spent hundreds of hours reviewing the larger group of PDBs: going to the reading room at the New Executive Office Building, taking notes on each PDB, and having those notes stored at the reading room. Whereas we had had three months of negotiation on obtaining access to the PDBs, we now had another three months of negotiation on implementing that agreement. There were drafts and redrafts of the two documents—with Gorelick and Zelikow's memo arguing for the transfer of more than fifty PDBs to the core group, and about the nature of the report on the core group that would go to the full commission. Common ground between our position and that of the White House was hard to find.

For legal advice, we reached out to a prominent Washington lawyer with expertise on executive privilege, Robert Weiner, asking him what our chances were if it came to a subpoena and litigation with the White House on a matter of executive privilege. Ironically, our legal case on the PDBs would be better than if we had had to subpoena internal NSC documents. Because the CIA produced the PDBs and distributed them to officials other than the president, the claim of executive privilege was weaker than it would have been for documents that were prepared within the Executive Office of the President and that offered advice exclusively to the president.

The problem, from our standpoint, was time and cooperation. In arguing for a subpoena, the 9/11 families often assumed that it would be self-enforcing. But the reality was we would have to go to the courts to enforce the subpoena; the courts would have to make a judgment on whether or not to enforce the subpoena; and the White House would appeal any subpoena all the way up to the Supreme Court. Legally, there was almost no chance that the matter would be resolved by our reporting date, so the clock would run out before we obtained access. A subpoena would also destroy our relationship with the White House. We still needed cooperation on a range of issues—access to the president and vice-president, public testimony from Condoleezza Rice, and declassification of materials for our hearings and for the final report. That cooperation would be unlikely under the cloud of a court case.

Still, the mere prospect of a subpoena remained a potent option. Politically, it would bring huge pressure to bear on the White House, and they might relent without a court battle. As the review team process dragged into January, we considered two different types of subpoenas. First, we could simply subpoena all the PDBs, or a specific number of the PDBs. Alternatively, we could subpoena the notes and reports prepared by Gorelick and Zelikow, which were being held at the New Executive Office Building.

The fact that we considered issuing a subpoena for our own notes illustrates how cumbersome the process was. We had more difficult and contentious commission meetings on this issue. Tim Roemer, who had dissented from the original agreement and was close to the Family Steering Committee position, felt the White House was exerting too much authority over what we could and could not see. We had a vote on whether to subpoena the PDBs that drew three Democratic yeas. Gorelick and Zelikow were tired of splitting hairs with the White House lawyers. We asked them to make one more effort to settle the issue—if a compromise could not be reached, we would subpoena our notes.

The logjam was broken when Zelikow and Gorelick gave up their effort to be allowed to transfer PDBs to the core group, and simply drafted a report to the commission that went beyond what was in the core group. The report provided an itemized summary and discussion of nearly one hundred PDB items; gave detailed context for the PDBs, conveying the type of intelligence that presidents had received in the PDBs; re-created, word for word, the August 6 PDB; and allowed Zelikow and Gorelick to brief the commission to explain some of the specifics in the report. This was less than we wanted, and more than the White House wanted us to reveal, but on February 9, Judge Gonzales agreed to permit the release of the Gorelick-Zelikow report to the full commission.

We presented this agreement at a 9/11 Commission meeting on February 12. First, Gorelick and Zelikow explained the agreement, and then they presented their report in a briefing to the commission that lasted for nearly three hours. There was still some dissent, but not enough to justify our issuing a subpoena. After all, in Gorelick and Zelikow's report, we had gone well beyond the parameters of the original agreement, as understood by the White House. Later that day we put out a statement announcing the successful implementation of our PDB review.

The issue had reemerged publicly. Earlier, on February 8, President Bush had appeared on NBC's *Meet the Press with Tim Russert,* in an interview from the Oval Office. It was a sensitive time for the president. Things in Iraq were not going well, his State of the Union Address had received mixed reviews, and Senator John Kerry had momentum in the Democratic primaries. This unusual Oval Office interview was widely seen as an attempt to seize the initiative and lay out some of the themes for his reelection campaign. Russert questioned him aggressively about the lack of weapons of mass destruction in Iraq. The president defended the decision to go to war and cited the centrality of 9/11 to his presidency, referring to himself as a "war president."

In response to a question from Russert, President Bush addressed the 9/11 Commission's access to the PDBs, saying, "We have given extraordinary cooperation with Chairmen Kean and Hamilton. As you know, we made an agreement on what's called Presidential Daily Briefs, and they could see the info the CIA provided me. . . . We have shared this information with both those gentlemen, gentlemen I trust, so they could get a better picture of what took place prior to September eleventh." The gentlemen he was referring to were the two of us, but the statement was not entirely accurate—we had seen only the core group of PDBs, not the larger group. The two who had seen all of the PDBs were Gorelick and Zelikow.

Given the president's statement, the controversial nature of the process, and the fact that we were the public face of the 9/11 Commission, we asked Gonzales to allow the two of us access to the larger group of more than three hundred PDBs. It was a difficult request. The White House was not entirely happy with us. Once again, they were upset about some articles detailing the commission's consideration of a subpoena, particularly since Democratic candidates continued to make the administration's "stonewalling" an issue in the campaign. Still, the White House accepted.

When the two of us finally did view the PDBs, Tom nearly upended the conditions. The minder ushering us into the reading room asked Tom if he was going to take any notes. Tom replied, "I don't need to. I have a photographic memory." The minder's face went white in horror and confusion. How were they going to maintain possession of the chair's memory?

Ultimately we got the access we needed. Three commissioners—Jamie Gorelick and the two of us—saw every PDB responsive to our document request. The rest of the commission received an account of all PDBs that related to al Qaeda and the events of September 11. Unfortunately, the process had been bumpy. The PDB question opened sharp divisions within the commission that broke down roughly along partisan lines, and hurt our relations with the 9/11 families. It also helped convince us that we needed more time for our inquiry, which led to a difficult struggle to agree upon and obtain an extension for the commission's reporting date.

The process was also not beneficial to the White House. Because negotiations for access to the PDBs were so difficult, increasing numbers of Americans believed that the White House was stonewalling us—either to cover up information or to undercut the commission by sapping our time. But the White House's belief in executive privilege is deeply held, and in fact they guarded more Clinton administration PDBs than Bush administration PDBs. But they would have saved themselves a lot of time and political trouble if the process had not been so laborious. Later on, we successfully made the argument that they needed to go even further in debunking conspiracy theories by declassifying the August 6 PDB and, later on, a PDB from the Clinton administration.

The truth is PDBs are not very impressive. You might imagine that they contain incredibly secretive, precise, and accurate information about anything under the sun. The reality is quite different—and, frankly, disappointing. Most of the PDBs we saw were not very helpful to President Clinton or Bush. Snippets of intelligence are relayed with little context. Conclusions are heavily qualified, and there is little information that a president can actually act upon. If there is something that you take away from reviewing the PDBs, it is that the president should be better served in his daily intelligence briefing.

In seeing these documents—along with the millions of other pieces of paper that came to the commission—we achieved the kind of unprecedented and comprehensive access that was necessary to write an authoritative report. But that access brought with it a responsibility: nobody else was going to be able to review this wealth of materials for many years to come. We had an obligation—to the 9/11 families, to the American people, and to history—to get our report right. We were the eyes for all of these other parties.

5

GETTING THE STORY

Assessing the truth of statements by these witnesses—sworn enemies of the United States—is challenging. Our access to them has
been limited to the review of intelligence reports based on communications received from the locations where the actual interrogations take place.

> — From text box at the beginning of chapter 5,
> *The 9/11 Commission Report*

THROUGHOUT 2003, MUCH OF THE PUBLIC focus on the 9/11 Commission was on our struggle for documents. Would we see every
piece of paper that detailed what people in government knew about terrorism, when they knew it, and what they did about it? But paper trails
were only part of our inquiry. We were also talking to hundreds of people,
in public and private, from inside and outside government. Their stories
provided depth and color, giving a human face to the story. Reading hundreds of memos gives you only part of the picture—you also have to talk
to the people who wrote and received those memos.

In the spring and summer of 2003, our staff teams put together extensive lists of people they wanted to interview. Just as our document requests
built up to the top of the pyramid—the president's daily intelligence
briefing—so, too, did our interviews build up: from scholars and journalists, to agents in FBI field offices and airport security checkpoints, to the

most senior officials in two U.S. administrations, including two presidents. We encountered strong personalities, personal and bureaucratic rivalries, and people making vigorous cases on behalf of their actions and opinions. Many of the intense feelings and differences that surfaced in our 2004 public hearings first became evident behind the closed doors of our interviews.

As with our document requests, we had differences with the White House regarding interviews. The most notable disagreement involved the presence of agency representatives at our interviews. Judge Gonzales took the position that all government witnesses, both current and former officials, would be providing us with government information; therefore, the agency that the witness worked for had a right to send a representative along to observe the interview. We objected, feeling that this amounted to agencies sending a "minder" to track what was being said, and that this minder would have a chilling effect on the interviewee. We wanted our witnesses to be candid and, when appropriate, critical about their agency's performance. A minder might cause somebody to think twice before speaking candidly.

We worked out a number of compromises. First, we insisted that the government not have the right to send a representative to an interview with a *former* government official, unless that former official specifically asked for one (something that happened very rarely). Second, an agency representative could not directly interfere with the conduct of the interview—for instance, by answering questions or supplementing a witness's answers. Third, we could request a different representative if we thought a particular minder was having a chilling effect on the witness. Finally, we reserved the right to request an interview without an agency representative in certain circumstances—a right that we acted upon only in the very few cases when an individual witness requested it.

Over the summer of 2003, the issue of agency representatives at interviews was a contentious one within the commission, and in our negotiations with the White House. Many commissioners felt that the presence of a representative would compromise the independence of our inquiry, and none of us was particularly happy about it. But we were pressed for time. The White House's position was not unusual; it is common practice, for instance, for agency representatives to attend staff interviews during congressional inquiries. Our priority was to keep the investigation moving, rather than having another drawn-out argument with the White House. The matter received public attention, and came up at the press conferences after the release of both of our interim reports. In September, when asked if minders were still present at interviews, Tom summed up our stance: "Still got minders, still don't like them."

One reason we did not push the point was that our staff reported back that the minders did not seem to be having an intimidating effect. On only a handful of occasions did complaints surface. For the most part, witnesses were candid. One anecdote that drove this point home involves an interview with an FBI employee at a field office with a minder present. Our staff asked the FBI witness what he thought of reforms implemented since 9/11 by FBI Director Mueller; the witness replied, "F—— the director."

The commission also debated the question of whether or not to place witnesses under oath. Some commissioners argued that this would be necessary to ensure that witnesses were telling the truth. But our staff—particularly the prosecutors—argued that witnesses speak more openly when not under oath, whereas people under oath are guarded, weighing every word against the fear that they will violate an oath and subject themselves to legal challenges.

Commissioner attendance was another concern. Under our statute, a commissioner had to be on hand to administer an oath—something that was logistically impossible for the more than 1,000 interviews we conducted. Therefore, we decided that there would be only two circumstances when we would place witnesses under oath: first, if there was likely to be a specific factual dispute between two accounts; second, if we had good reason to suspect that a particular witness had not been truthful.

Our desire to interview officials from the Executive Office of the President (EOP)—i.e., White House or National Security Council staff—sparked another trying negotiation. Once again, the issue was executive privilege. Presidential staff members do not testify in front of congressional committees because their actions on behalf of and advice to the president are privileged. But since the NSC coordinates policy among the different agencies responsible for counterterrorism, and is closely involved in operations—especially covert operations—we needed to interview NSC personnel. Our staff team responsible for counterterrorism policy had about twenty current and former NSC officials listed as prospective witnesses. We also knew that we wanted to interview top officials: Chief of Staff Andrew Card, National Security Advisor Condoleezza Rice, Deputy National Security Advisor Stephen Hadley, Vice-President Dick Cheney, and President George W. Bush.

The White House imposed strict conditions on EOP interviews. To begin with, the interviews would be considered voluntary, to avoid setting a precedent. They would be referred to as "meetings" instead of "interviews." These "meetings" would be time limited; the EOP officials could not be placed under oath; and there were limitations on the number of commission staff or commissioners who could be present for an interview. (This led to some unfair criticism of the commission: when less than the full commission showed up to meet with Condoleezza Rice, some people, including the White House press secretary, lambasted the commission for demanding that she testify in public yet not showing up in full to meet with her in private. In fact, we were abiding by the White House's originally expressed preference.) There was also a list of proposed "guidelines" about planned areas of inquiry, and detailed procedures for "pre-meetings," where we would brief the White House or (for witnesses at or above the "assistant secretary" level) a Cabinet department or agency about the questions we planned to ask.

At a commission meeting on December 8, 2003, some commissioners voiced strong objections to these guidelines. They felt that it was reasonable to have some conditions on Executive Office of the President interviews, which were, after all, extraordinary. It was also considered worthwhile, albeit cumbersome, to have pre-meetings, since it would be useful for the witnesses to go over the material to be covered in the areas we wanted to address. But the commission wanted to pursue different lines of questioning with different witnesses, and thus we felt we should not have to restrict ourselves to uniform procedures for all witnesses. We were happy to supply topic areas in advance, but we would not submit questions: we wanted prepared witnesses, not prepared answers.

Despite the limitations on us, we did not encounter White House officials who had been rehearsed. One of our key interviews was with then Deputy National Security Advisor Stephen Hadley. Hadley had overseen the White House's effort to develop a new strategy to combat al Qaeda in the months leading up to 9/11. When we were questioning him about what information about al Qaeda had been briefed to President Bush before 9/11, he cut in: "You know, you should really take a look at the PDBs." The NSC and White House lawyers in the room, many of whom had been involved in our protracted negotiations over the PDBs, looked ready to faint.

Preparing for interviews was time-consuming. Letters were written to witnesses to indicate what topics would be covered: this was no small task, what with the hundreds of witnesses to be interviewed. Many witnesses were of interest to multiple staff teams; for instance, a particular CIA or NSC official could be of interest to the teams investigating intelligence, terrorist financing, and al Qaeda, so we had to coordinate schedules to be certain that the right people attended each interview. And we continued to be pressed for time. It was not until the end of the summer of 2003 that we had enough documents to be prepared for our most important interviews. We wanted to hold public hearings in 2004, and needed our interviews to be largely completed before these hearings took place; we had a long list of high-level officials to work through in December, January, and February.

There were also extraordinarily important interviews with mid-level officials who, before 9/11, had as their primary focus the issues of al Qaeda and terrorism. Among these were the analysts assigned to the CIA's "Usama Bin Ladin unit," such as Michael Scheuer, who has written two best-selling books about the war on terrorism under the pseudonym "Anonymous," and who had recently resigned from the CIA; the former director of central intelligence's Counterterrorism Center, Cofer Black, who moved to the State Department after 9/11; the former coordinator for counterterrorism at the State Department, Michael Sheehan, who has since moved to New York City, where he is deputy police commissioner for counterterrorism; and the former national coordinator for counterterrorism at the NSC for Presidents Clinton and Bush, Richard Clarke.

These witnesses were the most active officials in the U.S. government who understood the threat from al Qaeda before 9/11, and their prescience was borne out by a catastrophic strike on the American homeland. Before 9/11, they worked countless hours trying to prevent such an attack: they pushed their agencies and the government to take terrorism more seriously, while much of the government, and most of the country, did not even know what "al Qaeda" was. Now the enemy they had fought out of sight for years was at last the focus of a fully mobilized U.S. government and of the American public. In Clarke's case, mixed emotions—about having been right about al Qaeda but having failed to prevent an attack—came forth when he became the first U.S. official to apologize for the government's failure to prevent the attacks in one of the more remarkable moments of the commission's public hearings.

There was a phenomenal amount of information to cover. The questions for Clarke alone ran to thirty pages, and our staff spent parts of three days with him. As testimony poured in from Clarke, Scheuer, Black, Sheehan, and numerous other officials who worked on terrorism before 9/11, certain policy story lines and questions emerged: Why did we fail to capture or kill Usama Bin Ladin after the 1998 embassy bombings? How did the government respond to the surge in terrorist threats before the millennium? Why didn't we respond to the al Qaeda attack on the USS

Cole, in 2000, which killed eighteen Americans in uniform? Could America's newly developed Predator unmanned aerial vehicle have been deployed to locate or even kill Bin Ladin before 9/11? How did the government respond to the surge in terrorist threats over the summer of 2001?

Our staff had to organize this flood of incoming information, and make sure it was available to the commissioners, staff, and teams who could not attend certain interviews. The documents that had flowed into the commission were scanned into computers so that they would be immediately available to a variety of staff and commissioners, and so that search words could yield different documents in the commission's database. We needed a similar way to make the interviews widely accessible.

Many interviews were recorded, though we were not permitted to record those conducted with current officials from the Executive Office of the President. All of the recordings were digital and could be put on the commission's computers so that others could listen to them. Not all the recorded interviews were transcribed, since the conversations dealt with highly classified information: you can count on one hand the number of people in Washington who have the necessary skills and security clearances to do that kind of work, and some of these transcriptions can run on for hundreds of pages, so we ordered transcriptions for only extremely important interviews.

Our staff produced a remarkable amount of Memoranda for the Record (MFRs): written summaries of these interviews. Of 1,200 or so interviews, there were nearly 900 MFRs. Accuracy was important. Some testimony involved very specific language—for instance, whether the legal authority for a covert action was phrased to allow for the killing or capture of Usama Bin Ladin—so our MFRs replicated that testimony with a high degree of specificity. It often took several days to prepare an MFR, which had to be checked for accuracy against the notes of several participants in an interview. An MFR could run to twenty or thirty pages, and would be read by commissioners and staff members as building blocks for the public hearings and final report.

These digital recordings, transcriptions, and MFRs are important historical documents in their own right. Today, they sit classified in the National Archives. For future scholars interested in 9/11 and the roots of the war on terrorism, the tape or transcription of an interview with Samuel Berger, President Clinton's national security advisor, or a thirty-page MFR of an interview with Richard Clarke, or simply a summary of an interview with a particular FBI agent, will be invaluable; taken together, they form an oral history of 9/11.

All of this data needed to be pulled together. In late November, right before our interviews with top policy makers, Philip Zelikow asked the staff team working on counterterrorism policy to put their work into a chronological timeline leading up to 9/11. The timeline was highly detailed: for February 1998, the staffer working on diplomacy could say what was going on at the State Department, or the staffer working on the military could say what was going on at the Department of Defense. The work of different teams was also added, so if something particularly important happened in terrorist financing on a certain date, this was reflected in the timeline. This chronological document expanded to well over a hundred pages.

By putting the information we had collected from documents and interviews into this one document, we began to get a sense of the story: we could put ourselves back to October 17, 1999, or March 11, 2001, and determine what threats were being reported by the intelligence community, what meetings were being held at the State Department, or what directives were going out from the NSC. This could be used for witness questioning. For Berger, for instance, you could say, "On such and such a date, a memo saying this went to the president. What do you remember about it?" Or for Condoleezza Rice, you could say, "On such and such a date, there was an interagency meeting on this subject. What do you remember about that meeting?" By the end of 2003, the amount of information we had compiled was unique within the government: nobody else had pulled together such disparate evidence on 9/11.

While our work with documents generally informed the questioning of witnesses, at times our staff would learn in interviews of documents we had not reviewed. For instance, in one of our later interviews, a witness asked our staff if they were familiar with an exercise in 1998 in which Richard Clarke worked with a group of officials from the Department of Defense, the FAA, and the Secret Service to plan a response to a scenario in which terrorists commandeered a jet in Atlanta, loaded it with explosives, and flew toward Washington. Upon hearing of that exercise, our staff had to circle back and try to locate a document trail.

From December 2003 to February 2004, we interviewed senior officials from the Clinton and Bush administrations: Secretaries of State Madeleine Albright and Colin Powell; Secretaries of Defense William Cohen and Donald Rumsfeld; National Security Advisors Samuel Berger and Condoleezza Rice; Attorneys General Janet Reno and John Ashcroft; and Chairmen of the Joint Chiefs of Staff Hugh Shelton and Richard Myers. All told, we had an interview "A List" of more than fifty people, and a "Super A List" of the fifteen or so current Cabinet secretaries or top assistants to the president (including Rice), at whose interviews the White House required the chair or vice-chair to be present (usually Lee, because he lives in the Washington area).

Witnesses were generally accommodating and cooperative—Cabinet officials are often more comfortable in the surroundings of their own offices. These interviews were not for show; they were extended and highly substantive. We did not simply ask, "So, what do you think about terrorism?" or "What do you remember about 9/11?" A designated staff member would lead the questioning, and a commissioner would supplement this with questions in his or her particular area of interest. Our general approach was chronological: working off our timeline, we walked the witness through the events of their time in office. For the Bush administration officials, we walked them up to 9/11, recounted the events of the day and the immediate aftermath, and then asked for their assessment of current policies.

One of our most important interviews was with National Security Advisor Condoleezza Rice—on February 7, in the Situation Room at the White House. (The 9/11 families were very upset that Rice had not talked to the congressional Joint Inquiry, given that she had played a vital role in coordinating counterterrorism policy before 9/11.) The interview was on a Saturday, and we spent several hours with her. Rice was well prepared and lucid. Because of the centrality of her role, the fact that Berger was testifying in public, the insistence of the 9/11 families, and the differences that emerged between her and Richard Clarke, we urged the White House to allow her to testify in public; they resisted for several months, citing executive privilege.

As we moved through our interviews, witnesses were impressed with the information compiled by the commission. They saw that this was a serious investigation: that our staff had compiled a remarkable amount of information; that we weren't simply looking for people to blame. They also saw that the commission was poised to write a thorough account of 9/11; that being the case, they wanted to be sure to get their own stories across.

We wanted to talk to Vice-Presidents Gore and Cheney, and Presidents Clinton and Bush. We knew this request was unusual: President Lyndon Johnson, for instance, refused to testify in front of the Warren Commission, sending instead a three-page letter. If we had asked for access to President Bush and Vice-President Cheney at the beginning of our work, they probably would have said no, and few people would have noticed. That is one reason we waited until the commission had enough clout and credibility, so that when we asked them, they would not want to say no.

ABROAD

MANY IMPORTANT WITNESSES LIVED outside the United States. Traveling to countries such as Afghanistan and Pakistan allowed our staff to see firsthand where al Qaeda had taken hold and where they trained and operated. Our recommendations needed to draw upon the experiences of men and women on the front lines of the war on terrorism. That is why many commissioners supported the idea of international travel by our staff. For some time, there was even talk of commissioner trips. The two of us considered traveling to the Gulf States, but commissioner travel was never fully pursued.

The most extensive staff trip took place in October 2003, with a small delegation visiting Saudi Arabia, Yemen, the United Arab Emirates, Afghanistan, Pakistan, and the United Kingdom. Philip Zelikow planned most of the trip with the State Department, which coordinated the interviews we wanted to conduct and kept tabs on our meetings with foreign officials. The deputy secretary of state, Richard Armitage, was particularly helpful in expediting what could have been a laborious process. Zelikow also worked with points of contact at the FBI, which had legal attachés in each of the countries we visited; the CIA, which had several major stations we wanted to visit; and the Department of Defense, which was engaged in ongoing combat operations in Afghanistan.

The trip took place at an inopportune juncture. October brought several key moments for the commission, including our subpoena of the FAA and our negotiations with the White House over the PDBs. Having the executive director and several senior staff halfway around the world at that point was less than ideal, which was part of the reason our deputy director, Chris Kojm, canceled his participation in the trip. Still, we thought the benefits of travel outweighed the drawbacks.

The White House counsel's office was the designated contact point between the 9/11 Commission and the Bush administration. In planning the trip, Zelikow often went directly to the State Department, the FBI, the Department of Defense, or the CIA; it was characteristic of his style at times to bypass formalized procedures. When the White House lawyers responsible for dealing with the commission began picking up rumors about a major overseas trip planned by commission staff, they were not pleased. They also insisted on sending a White House representative to sit in on interviews.

Logistically, this kind of trip is hard to arrange. We sent a very small del-egation: Zelikow; Kevin Scheid, the head of our staff team looking at intel-ligence; Mike Hurley, the head of our team looking at counterterrorism policy, as well as team member Dan Byman; and Dietrich Snell, the head of our team investigating the 9/11 plot. Afghanistan is a war zone, and Saudi Arabia and Pakistan are dangerous for Westerners, particularly U.S. officials. Our staff needed armed guards at times, but we wanted to keep these details small. Travel was by military or CIA aircraft, and to facilitate a busy itinerary the delegation needed to be small enough to travel by helicopter.

The host countries were helpful and clearly conscious of the 9/11 Com-mission. They knew we were going to help shape U.S. government and public opinion about foreign actions before and after 9/11, so they were quite solicitous. A country such as Saudi Arabia or Pakistan wanted to make a case that it did not have ties to al Qaeda before 9/11, and had been a strong ally in combating terrorism since 9/11. A country such as Afghanistan wanted to demonstrate its importance as a U.S. ally, and argue that it deserved and depended upon American aid. One of our staff remarked that these foreign governments were more eager to cooperate with the commission than some U.S. government agencies.

After a short stop in Qatar, Saudi Arabia was the first destination. After 9/11, there was rampant speculation about Saudi involvement in the attacks. Fifteen of the nineteen hijackers were Saudi nationals, as is Usama Bin Ladin. It was well documented that money from wealthy indi-viduals and charities in Saudi Arabia flowed to al Qaeda before 9/11, and rumors circulated about the possibility that al Qaeda had been funded by the Saudi royal family. The twenty-eight redacted pages in the congres-sional Joint Inquiry report into 9/11 were widely reported to link Saudi Arabia to the attacks. Conspiracy theories were floating around regarding the departure of more than one hundred Saudi nationals from the United States in the days shortly after 9/11, including several members of the Bin Ladin family. Public opinion—including among many in the U.S. Congress—was turning sharply against a country that had been a key U.S. ally for many years, even though most Americans realized that the U.S. economy could not function without oil from the Gulf States.

Sorting out fact from fiction about Saudi Arabia, while assessing our complex relationship with this key country, was among our most impor-tant and anticipated tasks. The Saudis realized this, and took a tremen-dous interest in our work. Prince Bandar, the longtime and highly influential Saudi ambassador to the United States, made some phone calls to help facilitate our staff's trip. His intervention, and cooperation between the State Department and the Saudi government, opened many doors. While in Saudi Arabia, our staff worked closely with FBI officials, who noted that the commission was being granted interviews in Saudi Arabia that the FBI had been seeking for months.

In addition to tracking down leads specific to the 9/11 investigation, our staff in Saudi Arabia looked at the history of al Qaeda, terrorist financing, and the current state of Saudi-American counterterrorism cooperation. Staff members met with U.S. officials in the country—diplomats, military, law enforcement, and intelligence liaisons—while also meeting a wide range of Saudi government officials.

Our staff also sought perspective on the dilemmas facing a country governed by a large and wealthy royal family allied with the West, with a huge young, unemployed, and often radical population. At one particular gathering, they met with about thirty or forty Saudi civilians, all young to middle-age males, who were educated, articulate, and part of the so-called moderates within Saudi society. Almost unanimously, they were harshly critical of the United States and its policies. They did not defend crashing planes into buildings, but they believed strongly that the United States was unfair in its approach to the Middle East, particularly in its support for Israel. These feelings were not surprising, but hearing them firsthand from so-called moderates drove home the enormous gap between how we see ourselves and our actions in the Middle East, and how others perceive us. It was an experience that Americans don't often get.

In Afghanistan, our delegation started in Kabul, meeting with the Afghan ministers of Defense and the Interior, the Afghan intelligence chief, and a number of other government officials. Their message was explicit: don't leave us again. Many of these men had fought in the mujahedin resistance against the Soviet Union in the 1980s, only to see the United States lose interest in Afghanistan after the Soviets withdrew. Through the 1990s, the country was plagued by civil war, with most of it eventually falling under the control of the Taliban, who gave sanctuary to their al Qaeda allies. The new government warned that a similar scenario could play out without sustained help from the United States and our allies.

One of our staff meetings was with an Afghan vice-president who had served as an interpreter for Ahmed Massoud—the charismatic military commander of the Northern Alliance, the armies from northern Afghanistan that fought an extended civil war against the Taliban and al Qaeda. Massoud had collaborated sporadically with the CIA in the years leading up to 9/11, as Usama Bin Ladin was a common enemy. Through 2001, the United States was considering a program of increased aid to Massoud and the Northern Alliance. On September 9, 2001, al Qaeda terrorists posing as journalists assassinated Massoud. Like many people whom our staff interviewed in Afghanistan, Massoud's interpreter was in a position to speak of the current situation and of the history that had led up to 9/11. He offered an insider's view, one impossible to get in Washington, on the complex and constrained efforts by the CIA to kill or capture Bin Ladin between 1998 and 9/11.

Our staff also got a look at the situation on the ground. In Kandahar, the former Taliban stronghold in southern Afghanistan, and at Bagram Airbase, the U.S. base north of Kabul, our staff spoke with top U.S. commanders and with Special Operations teams that had recently been in combat against al Qaeda and Taliban forces. They met also with the Dutch head of the International Security Assistance Force, the multinational military force trying to keep the peace in a war-ravaged nation. They met with U.S. military advisors training the new Afghan National Army, and watched nighttime training exercises as Americans trained Afghans to carry a heavier burden in the war on terrorism.

One meeting that has since drawn attention regarded a pre-9/11 Department of Defense program. On October 21, at Bagram Airbase, Zelikow and two of our staff met with three intelligence officials from the U.S. Defense Department; an executive branch minder was present. One of these witnesses referred to a pre-9/11 program known as Able Danger, which was used to develop information about al Qaeda.

In August 2005, a year after our report came out, Congressman Curt Weldon publicly alleged that the Department of Defense intelligence officer had told our staff that Mohammed Atta—a 9/11 pilot and the attack ringleader—had been under surveillance before 9/11 as part of the Able Danger program. Yet none of our staff at that meeting recalled Mohammed Atta's name being mentioned; nor did the executive branch minder. The MFR prepared shortly after that meeting makes no mention of Atta. As each of our staff members has said to us, if Mohammed Atta's name had come up as being under surveillance, they certainly would have remembered it. Immediately after the Bagram Airbase interview, we made requests to the Department of Defense for Able Danger documents. None of those documents made any mention of Mohammed Atta or any other future 9/11 hijackers.

As in Saudi Arabia, the commission staff made a concerted effort to meet with Afghani civilians. At roundtables with regional warlords, religious leaders, and ordinary Afghans, we discussed the current war on terrorism and the history of the Taliban and al Qaeda. And the staff sought out the places we would write about in our report. They visited the former compound of Mullah Omar, the Taliban's reclusive leader, who provided indispensable sanctuary to Bin Ladin and his cohorts. They took helicopter rides over the camps where Bin Ladin evaluated and trained recruits, and where he had selected operatives for the 9/11 attacks.

After Afghanistan, it was on to Karachi, the teeming Pakistani metropolis of more than fifteen million. Like Saudi Arabia, Pakistan is trailed by questions about its pre-9/11 actions. The Taliban and al Qaeda grew and developed within its borders. Pakistan's intelligence agency maintained close ties to the Taliban before 9/11; some radical Islamist madrasah schools within Pakistan became recruiting bases for terrorism; and radical militias fighting in Kashmir were known to have ties both to the Pakistani military and to al Qaeda. Since 9/11, the Pakistani government has been perhaps America's most important counterterrorism ally—helping to facilitate our operations in Afghanistan, and arresting hundreds of al Qaeda terrorists—yet it has also drawn complaints, particularly since Usama Bin Ladin is widely believed to be at large within Pakistan's borders.

Karachi has long been an incubator of radical Islamist thought and al Qaeda planning. Khalid Sheikh Mohammed, the mastermind of the 9/11 plot, was captured in an early 2003 raid on a Karachi apartment orchestrated by the CIA, the FBI, and Pakistani security services. While in Karachi, our staff met with U.S. officials in the American consulate—which has itself been a terrorist target—and with senior police officials, including one who had served as a conduit for messages from the Pakistani government to Mullah Omar. As in Afghanistan, the interviewees in Pakistan combined a personal perspective on current developments and an historical legacy of spending more than a decade among the burgeoning movement of radical Islam.

Karachi was followed by a trip to Peshawar, a city located in the Afghan-Pakistani border region where Bin Ladin is reportedly hiding; then Islamabad, Pakistan's capital. The large official U.S. presence in Islamabad offered mixed assessments of Pakistani cooperation. Our staff also met with Pakistani officials from the country's Foreign, Defense, and Intelligence ministries. Again, our staff sought perspectives outside of government. One U.S. diplomat hosted a dinner at her home for commission staff and for Ahmed Rashid, a Pakistani journalist who has long tracked the growth of the Taliban and al Qaeda in Central and South Asia.

On the way home, our staff delegation visited the United Kingdom. No ally works with the United States as closely and on so many fronts as the United Kingdom. Among the recommendations we were considering was the creation of a domestic intelligence agency, modeled somewhat on Britain's MI5. Our staff met with several MI5 officials. Later in November, the director-general of MI5, Elizabeth Manningham-Buller, attended a 9/11 Commission meeting in Washington and offered an extensive description of her agency and its mission.

From the more than one hundred interviews commission staff conducted on this trip, as from our interviews at home, themes and recommendations emerged for our report. Repeatedly, the staff asked American personnel from the military, the diplomatic corps, and intelligence and law enforcement: Who is in charge of the hunt for Usama Bin Ladin? Who is coordinating the fight against terrorism? These men and women were doing extraordinary and dangerous work, and making notable progress in rolling back al Qaeda. But in all our interviews, nobody could answer these two questions.

THE 9/11 PLOT

WHEN WE SET UP OUR STAFF TEAMS, we assigned the subject of "al Qaeda" to staff team 1. But we quickly realized that our attempt to understand al Qaeda was twofold. First, we needed to offer a comprehensive portrait of the organization: its history, leadership, motives, and methods. Second, we needed to tell the story of al Qaeda's most successful operation—the 9/11 attacks—so we created staff team 1A, charged with providing a definitive account of the 9/11 plot.

After 9/11, many facts—and fictions—about the plot reached the public. We all learned that nineteen men armed with knives and possibly box cutters took control of passenger airplanes and turned them into guided missiles. We subsequently learned a smattering of details: about the hijackers' time passed in the United States, their flight training, and some of their history in places such as Afghanistan, Saudi Arabia, and Germany. Theories proliferated about connections to foreign governments, the hijackers having guns, the so-called twentieth hijacker. In the run-up to the invasion of Iraq a majority of Americans believed Saddam Hussein was involved in the 9/11 attacks. Still more far-fetched ideas flew around the Internet: the U.S. government was involved; the CIA or Israel's intelligence agency, the Mossad, was responsible; or the planes that struck the Pentagon and World Trade Center towers had actually been missiles.

Often, the truth about a criminal conspiracy comes out in the trial of the conspirators, where the public is presented with evidence and witness testimony. This time, though, there would be no trial: the nineteen perpetrators were dead, victims of their own atrocities. So we directed our team 1A to approach their task as if putting together the case against the conspirators. What would a prosecution of these nineteen men look like? How would prosecutors lay out the case before a jury?

We recruited Dietrich Snell to lead this team. Snell is a deputy attorney general in the office of Eliot Spitzer, the attorney general of the state of New York. He had experience prosecuting terrorists. While at the U.S. Attorney's Office for the Southern District of New York, he prosecuted Ramzi Yousef, the mastermind of the 1993 bombing of the World Trade Center that killed six and wounded hundreds. Later in the 1990s, he issued a sealed indictment for another terrorist mastermind—Ramzi Yousef's uncle—who had planned to blow up twelve airplanes over the Pacific Ocean: Khalid Sheikh Mohammed.

Snell and his investigators had a lot of material to work with. The FBI was well into the largest criminal investigation in its history, entitled Pentagon/Twin Towers Bombing Investigation, or PENTTBOM. The PENTTBOM team had conducted tens of thousands of interviews and collected a wide variety of physical evidence, which had been analyzed by FBI labs. We could never replicate this work, but we could draw upon it through document requests and interviews with the FBI agents assigned to PENTTBOM.

At the beginning, cooperation was spotty. The FBI viewed the 9/11 Commission warily. What benefit—to individual FBI agents, or to the Bureau as an institution—would there be in cooperating with the commission? But FBI Director Robert Mueller soon saw the commission as hugely important to the future of the Bureau. During the Joint Inquiry, the FBI had come under intense scrutiny and criticism for its failure to prevent 9/11. The Joint Inquiry had recommended further study on the question of whether to create a new domestic intelligence agency, and thus take that responsibility away from the FBI. Mueller recognized that a 9/11 Commission recommendation to create a new domestic intelligence agency could derail his efforts to reform the Bureau into a counterterrorism agency, and take away a large chunk of the Bureau's responsibility.

Throughout our work, Mueller was the most cooperative Bush administration official. He was always available. He called every commissioner, and probably had lunch with every one of us, usually going out of his way to come to us—atypical for a high-ranking member of government. Whereas some officials could be defensive with regard to their agency's pre-9/11 performance, Mueller's approach was to acknowledge pre-9/11 shortcomings, and to focus on what was being done to remedy the problems. He gave the commission an extended briefing on his counterterrorism reforms, and supplied carefully prepared charts and booklets detailing all that the FBI had done since 9/11.

Mueller's approach toward the commission rippled down to the FBI's senior leadership. An FBI team was set up to facilitate the commission's requests. On occasion, certain sensitive material had to be carefully screened before we received it—for instance, to protect the identities of confidential FBI informants. But by the summer of 2003, our staff was receiving information that the FBI would ordinarily never release to another agency, even another law enforcement agency.

One particularly complex legal issue involved information related to the government's prosecution of Zacarias Moussaoui. Moussaoui had been arrested in August 2001 as he was taking flight lessons in Minnesota, and was later tied to al Qaeda. The government was in the process of prosecuting Moussaoui. Since many of the government's witnesses and evidence in the Moussaoui case related to the 9/11 attacks, it was also of interest to us. But the Moussaoui prosecution team was concerned that if witnesses and evidence relevant to their prosecution were turned over to us, their ability to use that information in the Moussaoui trial might be compromised. To obtain access, we had to agree that we would not disclose that information prior to the release of our final report, and that— if the Moussaoui trial had not yet taken place—we would consult the government's lawyers before publishing the information in our report.

The investigation of the 9/11 plot also led us abroad. The two major locations of interest to our staff were Saudi Arabia, where fifteen of the nineteen hijackers came from, and Germany, where an al Qaeda cell in Hamburg produced three of the four 9/11 pilots, including the ringleader, Mohammed Atta. Another location of interest was Spain, where Atta traveled shortly before 9/11, meeting with co-conspirator Ramzi Binalshibh, and where a prosecuting judge had alleged that some people in his custody were part of the 9/11 conspiracy.

Yet the most difficult access question was not tracking down leads in Germany, or even Saudi Arabia—it was obtaining access to star witnesses in custody. The nineteen perpetrators were dead. Their leader, Usama Bin Ladin, remained at large. But several key witnesses for the 9/11 plot were in custody, most notably Khalid Sheikh Mohammed, a mastermind of the attacks, and Binalshibh, who had helped coordinate the attacks from Europe. These and other detainees were the only possible source for inside information about the plot. If the commission was mandated to provide an authoritative account of the 9/11 attacks, it followed that our mandate afforded us the right to learn what these detainees had to say about 9/11.

In June 2003, we put in a request to the FBI, CIA, and Department of Defense for "all reports of intelligence information" obtained from a list of detainees that ended up totaling 111—in other words, access to the reports of interrogations of these detainees. The idea was that we would not start with a controversial request such as asking to interrogate the detainees directly, but would instead begin by accumulating information from the records of the government's interrogations. We did not seek the full interrogation reports; our only concern was obtaining information relating to the 9/11 plot or to the actions taken by al Qaeda before 9/11.

Problems emerged over the summer. The FBI and CIA were fairly responsive; the Department of Defense was less so. But it was clear that the government's interrogators were not asking the detainees the kinds of questions we wanted answered. We wanted to know about the 9/11 plot; the government understandably was more interested in current threats. We wanted to know about the history of al Qaeda before 9/11; the government wanted to know about al Qaeda today and its future plans. We wanted to learn more about Mohammed Atta; the government wanted to know where living al Qaeda operatives were hiding.

We also had no way of evaluating the credibility of detainee information. How could we tell if someone such as Khalid Sheikh Mohammed, a sworn enemy of the United States, was telling the truth? Usually, a prosecutor can question a witness directly. In this case, we were receiving information thirdhand—passed from the detainee, to the interrogator, to the person who writes up the interrogation report, and finally to our staff in the form of reports, not even transcripts. Often, it took six weeks for a report of an interrogation to be produced. In some cases, we could corroborate the truthfulness of what a detainee was reported to have said by comparing that information with other evidence. But in some cases we couldn't; and in others, detainees offered contradicting accounts. There was still confusion about key events: How did the idea for the 9/11 attacks get translated into an operation? What steps did al Qaeda take after Usama Bin Ladin approved the operation? How were operatives selected to be a part of the 9/11 attacks?

By the fall of 2003, our staff was frustrated—at the speed with which they were getting information from detainees, and with the quality of that information. The matter came to high-level attention for the first time on

November 5, at Lee's meeting with Secretary Rumsfeld. Lee recounted the history of our pursuit of access to detainee information, and voiced concern over the slowness of the Department of Defense's response. Rumsfeld pledged his cooperation and set a deadline for the delivery of additional information. We were not yet asking for direct access to detainees, but that request was soon to be made.

On December 22, the two of us had a lunch meeting with the director of central intelligence, George Tenet. Like Secretary Rumsfeld, Tenet was hospitable and cooperative. On several occasions, commissioners went out to his office at CIA headquarters, a massive complex tucked off the George Washington Parkway in Langley, Virginia.

To get into the CIA, you have to go through very tight security. At the first checkpoint, at the CIA's entrance, you would not know that the road amid lush, green surroundings leads to a sprawling, labyrinthine complex with tens of thousands of employees. To reach Tenet's office, you have to go through more security checkpoints until you reach the inner sanctum of the CIA complex.

On this occasion, the two of us were having a breakfast meeting with Tenet and some of his aides. We had a long agenda to work through, but before we could get into it, Tenet opened by saying, "You're not going to get access to these detainees." Tenet likes to be accommodating—he is a skilled politician just as he is a skilled intelligence officer. But Lee, who has known Tenet for twenty-five years, could tell from Tenet's demeanor that there would be no give in his position on the matter.

We countered that we wanted direct access to only certain detainees who had critical knowledge of the formation and execution of the 9/11 plot. Though our request for interrogation reports involved more than one hundred detainees, we narrowed our request for direct access for interviews to only seven key detainees. We also voiced our concern that CIA interrogators were more focused on current and future threats; that we could not evaluate the credibility of the detainees' accounts without interrogating them directly; and that our staff—with their focus on the 9/11 plot and al Qaeda's pre-9/11 history—had more expertise than the CIA's interrogators in the areas we were interested in, and were thus better qualified to interrogate the detainees on these matters.

Tenet's argument, which was echoed by others in the government, came down to three points. First, the location of the detainees was secret. A high-profile detainee such as Khalid Sheikh Mohammed was not being held at the U.S. base in Guantanamo Bay, Cuba, where many of our alleged al Qaeda prisoners were held. At one point, we were told that even the president of the United States did not know where these top al Qaeda detainees were. That may or may not have been true. But it was clear that the location was known to an extraordinarily small group of people, and that the detainees were being held in places that were logistically difficult to reach—it would not be as simple as going to northern Virginia or even Cuba if our staff were to interrogate them.

Second, Tenet and others were adamant that if we had direct access to the detainees, we would interrupt and compromise the interrogation process. We were told that there was a careful flow to interrogation. An interrogator would meet with a detainee scores, if not hundreds, of times, establish a relationship, and pursue sensitive lines of questioning to elicit information vital to the security of the United States. Breaking into that process with a new interrogator could upset the flow of questioning that had taken months, or even years, to establish. It could also interrupt efforts to obtain intelligence on current terrorist threats and activity that was vital to counterterrorism.

The third issue was the ongoing Moussaoui case. Moussaoui had demanded the right to interrogate detainees such as Khalid Sheikh Mohammed and Ramzi Binalshibh as part of his legal defense, arguing that they were potential witnesses for his trial. This, he maintained, was part of his constitutional right to mount a defense. Thus far, the government had successfully resisted Moussaoui's efforts in the courts, though not without difficulty, arguing that the detainees were "enemy combatants" and that the terms of their detention fell under the exclusive authority of the president. The executive branch worried that if the 9/11 Commission set a precedent as an independent entity—even one that was part of the government—achieving access to these witnesses for something other than intelligence purposes, such a precedent might bolster Moussaoui's case that he had a right to interview the detainees. In that case, the designation of the detainees as "enemy combatants" rather than "prisoners of war," and thus protected by the rules of the Geneva Convention, would be in jeopardy.

We offered several compromises. On the issue of location, we said that our staff interrogators could be blindfolded on their way to the interrogation point so that they would not know where they were when they arrived at the location. On the issue of interrupting interrogations, we agreed that our staff would not have to interrogate the detainees themselves. Instead, we said that our staff could observe the interrogation through one-way glass so that the detainee would not know they were there; that way, our staff could at least observe the detainee's demeanor and evaluate his credibility. Or our staff could listen to an interrogation telephonically, and offer questions or follow-up questions to the CIA interrogator through an earpiece.

These compromises were rejected. What Tenet did offer, however, was the opportunity for the commission to submit questions and follow-up questions for the detainees to the CIA interrogators. We presented this offer to the full commission at a meeting on January 5, 2004. Dietrich Snell argued that the commission needed to push for direct access to the detainees. He made a compelling argument that it was his responsibility to evaluate the credibility of these witnesses. Reading reports does not give you nearly as much information as talking with people directly, and without corroborating evidence, it gives you little or no chance to evaluate the credibility of a witness's statements.

The commission decided to push the issue. We drafted a letter to Secretary Rumsfeld and Director Tenet—the two officials with authority over the detainee process—knowing that they would share the draft with Judge Gonzales. We acknowledged their concerns, but argued that we could agree to procedures that would not upset the current interrogation process—for instance, the use of one-way glass. We argued that our staff had expertise on the 9/11 plot that might exceed that of the current CIA interrogators, that the current process was working too slowly to get us the information we needed by our reporting deadline, and that we needed a way to evaluate the credibility of the detainee information we received.

We never formally sent the letter or released it publicly, though Tenet and Rumsfeld reviewed it in draft form. On January 21, Lee and Fred Fielding met with Tenet, Rumsfeld, Gonzales, and a representative of the Department of Justice in Gonzales's office in the West Wing. The meeting was cordial, with Tenet and Gonzales taking the lead. Once again, we were presented with the administration's core arguments for denying us direct or real-time access to the detainees—even through one-way glass or over the telephone. Tenet offered a proposal to provide the best arrangement short of direct access: the CIA would appoint a "project manager" to be a focal point for ensuring that we got the information we needed. Working through him, we could submit questions and follow-up questions, and in this way, interrogation reports would get to our staff much faster.

Tenet's offer was the best we would receive. Legally, we did not have solid grounds to seek anything further. The possibility of issuing a subpoena for the detainees came up. But our general counsel, Dan Marcus, advised us that the commission's mandate did not easily encompass a subpoena of the detainees. The law creating the 9/11 Commission allowed for us to "ascertain, evaluate, and report on the evidence developed by all relevant governmental agencies regarding the facts and circumstances surrounding the attacks." Interrogation reports fit that description; physical interrogations with detained enemies of the United States did not. Nor was it clear whether or how a court would enforce such a subpoena.

The other possibility was going public. This strategy had worked before in getting us access that we might otherwise have been denied—most notably with the PDBs. The Bush administration pleaded with us not to take the issue public. They said it was a matter of national security. If we went public with our concerns, it could trigger an avalanche of inquiries about access to detainees. Foreign governments might follow suit, seeking access to or expedited trials for foreign nationals in U.S. custody—a scenario that has, in many ways, played out anyway in the aftermath of revelations and allegations of detainee abuse by U.S. soldiers and CIA interrogators.

We decided not to take the issue public. We simply did not think we could win the argument—in public or private—in the time available to us. The administration's position was firm, and they were on more solid legal ground than they had been on the issue of the PDBs. Their concerns were also legitimate. We felt it was vital both to our mission and to national security to get answers to our questions: by learning about 9/11, our government would learn a great deal of useful information about al Qaeda. But we did not want to risk interrupting the interrogation of these detainees, which was important to U.S. efforts to obtain intelligence to thwart attacks, capture terrorists, and save American lives.

Interestingly, there was no pressure from some of the usual sources for us to push for access. For instance, the 9/11 families never pressed us to seek access to detainees, and the media was never engaged on this issue. We were prepared to talk about the detainee question in all of our 2004 press conferences, but we were almost never asked about it. This may be because it lacked the intrigue of searching for pre-9/11 documents. For whatever reason, when it comes to "What did he know, and when did he know it?" the public's imagination was more focused on President Bush or President Clinton than on Khalid Sheikh Mohammed. To the families, the press, and the public, the commission's role was getting to the bottom of the government's role in allowing 9/11 to happen, not necessarily getting to the bottom of how al Qaeda planned 9/11.

We decided to give Director Tenet's offer a chance to work. And it did, to a degree. We were able to submit hundreds of questions and follow-up questions to be asked in interrogations. Our questions were asked faster, and information flowed back faster. The situation was not ideal—we never even got to meet with the people conducting the interrogations—but we did get access to information we needed; our report, particularly chapters 4 and 6, draws heavily on information from detainees, notably Khalid Sheikh Mohammed and Ramzi Binalshibh.

In drafting our report, we inserted a text box explaining how we had obtained detainee information, and how we were presenting the information in the report. Part of the text box reads:

> Assessing the truth of statements by these witnesses—sworn enemies of the United States—is challenging. Our access to them has been limited to the review of intelligence reports based on communications received from the locations where the actual interrogations take place. We submitted questions for use in the interrogations, but had no control over whether, when, or how questions of particular interest would be asked. Nor were we allowed to talk to the interrogators so that we could better judge the credibility of the detainees and clarify ambiguities in the reporting. We were told that our requests might disrupt the sensitive interrogation process.

Where we drew on detainee information, we attributed statements, pieces of information, or parts of the story to different witnesses—for instance, by saying, "KSM [Khalid Sheikh Mohammed] acknowledges formally joining al Qaeda, in late 1998 or 1999, and states that soon afterward, Bin Ladin also made the decision to support his proposal to attack the United States using commercial airplanes as weapons." The qualification "KSM acknowledges" lets the reader know where the information came from. Where we could corroborate these detainee reports from other witnesses or evidence, we did. Where we could not, it was left to the reader to consider the credibility of the source—we had no opportunity to do so.

By the time we wrote the text box and put out our report, the issue of how the government managed the detainee process was in the public eye. The Abu Ghraib prisoner abuse scandal broke in March 2004, revealing widespread humiliation of and brutality toward Iraqi detainees in American custody. Further allegations followed concerning abuse in Afghanistan and Guantanamo Bay. In retrospect, this may suggest why detainee access was such a sensitive issue for the executive branch in December, January, and February.

While we could not interview the detainees, their stories reached us, albeit through intermediate channels. Their voices are joined with the thousand other voices that we heard from inside and outside the government. We planned to write a report populated by characters: human beings who struggled, and continue to struggle, on both sides of the war on terror.

6

FINDING A VOICE

Okay, my name is Betty Ong. I'm number three on Flight Eleven.

— Betty Ong, flight attendant on board American
Airlines Flight 11, on September 11, 2001

DOCUMENT REVIEW AND INTERVIEWS were the first two tracks of our approach; the third was public hearings. We were not required to hold hearings in public—some commissions do not. For instance, the Silberman-Robb Commission on prewar estimates of weapons of mass destruction in Iraq conducted its business in private. But our intention was to conduct a transparent inquiry. The principal debate within the commission concerned whether or not hearings were the best use of our staff's time, particularly as we were still acquiring and reviewing information in 2003.

Every hour that our staff spent preparing for a hearing—contacting witnesses, organizing panels, and preparing commissioners—was an hour they were not reviewing documents and conducting interviews. Since every hour of public hearing took about fifty hours of staff preparation, some commissioners thought it made little sense to have staff spend valuable hours organizing hearings in 2003 before we had findings to present to the public.

Yet there were compelling arguments for having hearings in 2003. One benefit was educational. We had plenty of time to hear directly from the government—in the form of documents, interviews, and the hearings we would hold with Clinton and Bush administration officials in 2004. The 2003 hearings—which we referred to as "policy hearings"—gave us a chance to hear from scholars, journalists, former government officials, and the private sector. Their diverse perspectives framed the issues, offering historical context, pointing out deficiencies in America's counterterrorism policies, and suggesting recommendations. As outsiders, they could also offer more candid judgments of the successes and failures of government.

After our inaugural hearing in New York City, our second hearing was held in Washington, in the main Senate hearing room located in the Hart Senate Office Building, on May 22–23. We began with Senators John McCain and Joe Lieberman, and Congresswoman Nancy Pelosi, the Democratic leader in the House. We then heard from a panel of the chairmen and ranking members of the House and Senate Intelligence Committees, and a panel of representatives from the communities affected by 9/11 in New York, New Jersey, and Connecticut. Their statements offered expectations for the 9/11 Commission's work, and provided pledges of support from congressional leaders.

That afternoon and the next morning we focused on civil aviation security. Here we encountered our first problems with the FAA and NORAD. Senior officials from the FAA and NORAD—Jane Garvey and Craig McKinley—made statements about the timeline of 9/11 that were later proven to be inaccurate. At this point, we did not have the full body of evidence pertaining to what happened in the skies on September 11, 2001, nor were we putting our witnesses at public hearings under oath. But later, we uncovered factual inaccuracies in what Administrator Garvey and General McKinley told us—a matter we discuss later in this book.

Our next hearing was held on July 9, the morning after we issued our first interim report. We heard from three panels comprising experts from academia. The first panel provided an overview of al Qaeda; the second focused on the question of state sponsorship of terrorism; the third addressed broader challenges within the Islamic world. These experts depicted the evolution of a shadowy terrorist network, stretching from the Middle East to Indonesia, with a deeply rooted history in Afghanistan and Pakistan. As it did periodically throughout our work, the topic of Iraq flared up. One of our witnesses, Laurie Mylroie, was a leading supporter of the theory that Saddam Hussein had ties to al Qaeda, and possibly the 9/11 attacks. She argued, among other things, that Khalid Sheikh Mohammed, the mastermind of 9/11, was an operative of Iraqi intelligence. This sparked disagreement. While our statutory mandate did not instruct us to evaluate the Iraq war, we had to address the question of whether Iraq was involved in 9/11.

Over the summer, these hearings put us at a low point with the 9/11 families. Wide-ranging discussions with experts were not what the families had envisioned when they lobbied for a 9/11 commission. Before each hearing, our staff held a conference call with the families. Increasingly, these calls became opportunities for the families to vent their frustration. They didn't like that we were interviewing academics and not government officials; they didn't like that we weren't asking tougher questions; they didn't like that we weren't placing witnesses under oath. Our 2003 hearings rarely attracted much media attention, which also concerned the families. They had fought for an investigation of 9/11 so that questions about why and how their loved ones had died would be answered. To them, it was the most important task imaginable. That it was playing out in public in the form of background policy hearings in front of a C-SPAN audience was not acceptable, even though we continued to explain to them that we were not yet ready to present findings and answers, and that government witnesses and public scrutiny would come.

On September 10, just before the second anniversary of 9/11, the Family Steering Committee put out a statement saying, "We appreciate that the Commission staff is working very hard on this complex probe. However, no findings from the Commission's investigation have been released. A lot of frustration stems from the fact that we have not heard anything of substance." They demanded that witnesses be sworn in under oath, that subpoenas be issued, and that

> hard hitting hearings be held in which government officials from the Bush and Clinton administrations are publicly questioned. . . . If the Independent Commission's open hearings are evidence of the Commission's understanding of their mandate, then the Independent Commission's obligation as required under law will not have been met. This failure will not only be for the 9/11 victims' families, it will be a failure for all of the American people.

We were at a difficult juncture. We were caught between competing forces: our staff wanted more time to investigate so that we would have findings to present; the 9/11 families wanted more findings to be presented at more public hearings. Meanwhile, with our strategy of pursuing access to documents and people through cooperative negotiation under strain, we were worried about meeting our May 2004 deadline.

In tracking down the 9/11 story, we also needed to spend time on policy recommendations, the forward-looking part of our mandate. One vital area that we had to make a recommendation on was intelligence reform. As the most successful surprise attack ever on American soil, 9/11 had also been the most catastrophic intelligence failure in recent American history. While we were doing our work, it was also becoming clear that there had been another massive failure in assessing Iraq's prewar weapons of mass destruction, as American forces occupying Iraq found none of the predicted stockpiles of chemical or biological weapons.

Intelligence was the topic of our fourth public hearing, held on October 14. We heard from a number of former senior officials, including James Schlesinger, a former director of central intelligence and secretary of defense, and John Deutch, a former director of central intelligence. Our witnesses offered a range of opinions—from preserving the status quo, to extensive and detailed proposals for restructuring how our intelligence agencies worked, and worked with one another. As we prepared to delve in the coming months into the intelligence failures embedded in the 9/11 story, this hearing helped lay out for us the kinds of recommendations we would be considering as fixes.

Our fifth public hearing was held on November 18 at Drew University, whose campus provided a bucolic late-November setting. The topic of the hearing was emergency preparedness and the private sector. Eighty-five percent of our nation's critical infrastructure is in private hands. How the private sector protects that infrastructure—and its employees—may help determine the success and casualty rate of future attacks. Two problems became clear: there were no accepted standards for how companies must prepare for terrorist attacks; and even with standards, there were no incentives for the private sector to improve preparedness. Out of that hearing, we turned to the American National Standards Institute (ANSI) to prepare a set of private-sector standards.

The New Jersey venue also gave us a chance to make a tour of Ground Zero. The tour was arranged with the help of Kevin Shaeffer, the member of our staff who survived the attack on the Pentagon. Shaeffer had become friendly with Captain Lee Ielpi, one of the witnesses from our first public hearing in New York City. While working to uncover the remains of his son and other victims at Ground Zero, Ielpi had developed close relations with some 9/11 families and the various city and state agencies working in Lower Manhattan. He arranged for the supervisors from the Port Authority of New York and New Jersey and the Lower Manhattan Development Corporation (LMDC) to give us a tour of the site the morning after our hearing at Drew.

The representatives from the Port Authority and the LMDC walked us around the site, explaining in detail the harrowing events of 9/11: pointing out where bodies of people jumping from the towers had landed, and how the huge structures had collapsed. A somber mood came over the commissioners. All spoke in hushed tones. Many had tears in their eyes. Among the powerful visual symbols at the site were the family memorials comprising countless pictures of those who had lost their lives. In many cases, family and friends had attached to the memorial messages to and about their loved ones. Tom had to step back from the tour to comfort Ellie Hartz, our staff family liaison, who had lost her husband, John, on 9/11.

The last of our policy hearings, held on December 8, dealt with security and liberty. Those in government were focusing aggressively on the goal of preventing attacks. We wanted to consider what liberties Americans were giving up to obtain better security—a question related to whether or not to recommend the creation of a new domestic intelligence agency. We heard from experts on the law and civil liberties on domestic intelligence collection, privacy rights, the detention of terrorist suspects, and the future of the FBI. Opinions ranged from proposals to create a new domestic spying unit within the FBI, to the implementation of new privacy safeguards, to arguments for more robust legal authorities to track down terrorists in the United States.

The day after our December 8 hearing, we had our only change on the commission. Over the summer, Senator Tom Daschle had nominated Max Cleland to serve on the board of the Export-Import Bank. Since the Ex-Im job was a government post—confirmed by the Senate—Cleland could not serve on both it and the commission, so he had to step down as a commissioner. Cleland had emerged as the Bush administration's most vocal critic on the 9/11 Commission. An opponent of the Iraq war, he was distressed that we were not assessing the government's decision to go to war in Iraq, and he often referenced Iraq at our public hearings. Over the summer, he gave a well-publicized interview in which he explained the commission's delay in obtaining access to the Joint Inquiry report as a case in which "the 9/11 Commission was deliberately slow walked because the administration's policy was, and its priority was, we're going to take Saddam Hussein out."

Cleland had also joined on as a high-profile surrogate with John Kerry's presidential campaign, and would eventually introduce Kerry at the Democratic National Convention. Max has extensive experience on national security and an enjoyable demeanor; yet his views on Iraq and his opposition to the Bush administration may have made it difficult, if not impossible, for him to sign on to a unanimous report that did not take President Bush to task over Iraq.

In early December, Daschle called Lee and told him that he was inclined to fill Cleland's slot with Bob Kerrey, the former two-term senator and governor from Nebraska. Like Cleland, Kerrey is a Vietnam veteran who was severely wounded, having lost a leg in battle. He now lives in New York City, where he is president of the New School University. Kerrey had wide-ranging experience on national security, having served on the Intelligence Committee in the Senate, so it was not hard for him to pick up on the issues we were reviewing. He brought charisma and a rapid-fire speaking style to the commission's public hearings, often drawing the approval of the audience and the 9/11 families for his hard questions and combative approach. He has a curious, sharp, and unpredictable mind, and he threw himself into our work. Zelikow went up to the New School and briefed Kerrey for hours; then Kerrey came down to the commission offices over the Christmas holiday to read documents and get caught up. For his first commission meeting, he rode down to Washington on the train with Tom.

As Kerrey was coming on board, the commission was on precarious ground. We had yet to present substantive information, our policy hearings had drawn little attention, and we were known mostly for clashes with the Bush administration over access to documents. These stories often left out the cooperation provided by the White House in granting us documents and interviews. But conflict, not cooperation, sells newspapers and draws ratings. And, quite frankly, the occasional reports of conflict between the commission and the White House helped us get more access to documents and witnesses.

But conflict stories also created unnecessary and unhelpful controversy. One prominent example took place in December 2003, just after our policy hearings concluded and Kerrey was named to the commission. After our hearing at Drew, Randall Pinkston, a CBS news reporter, asked to do a profile of Tom for *60 Minutes II*. Tom agreed, and on December 3, a CBS camera crew came to Drew for several hours, filming Tom walking around campus and talking to students and Drew staff, and taping an hour-long interview about the work of the commission.

Two weeks later, our deputy for communications, Al Felzenberg, got a call from CBS: the interview was going to be the lead story on the *CBS Evening News,* not a profile on *60 Minutes II.* It was 6:15; Dan Rather was scheduled to start his newscast with the story at 6:30. The headline was

"9/11 Chair: Attack Was Preventable." To buttress the headline, CBS had lifted a few sentences out of an hour-long interview, among them one of Tom saying, "I mean, this was not something that had to happen," and "there are obviously people who made major mistakes, there are people that—certainly if I was doing the job—who would certainly not be in the position they were in at that time because they failed." Footage of then National Security Advisor Condoleezza Rice saying that no one could have foreseen the attacks was juxtaposed with Tom's comments. The suggestion was that we had uncovered evidence that the attacks should have been averted, that Rice was to blame, and that she should be fired.

Having quotations taken out of context is part of public life. But even by that standard, the CBS report was a stretch. What Tom had said was:

> To say we're going to point fingers is probably not accurate. But as you read the report, you're going to have a pretty clear idea what wasn't done and what should have been done. And what we're looking for, how could this have been prevented? I mean, this was not something that had to happen. How could this have been prevented? What actions could have been taken by the government? Federal, local, state? What could have happened that would have prevented this from happening and once we look at that, what mechanisms can we put in place to prevent this from happening in the future that might help to disrupt a future 9/11?

With regard to officials losing their jobs, Tom had earlier referenced people who had permitted the hijackers to get into the country illegally, let them onto airplanes, or failed to act on information within the FBI and CIA. Yet the CBS report appeared to affix the accountability for all of these failures on Rice.

The story was picked up around the country. The White House and congressional Republicans were upset that the Republican chairman of the commission had taken such a position in the middle of the inquiry. Secretary Rumsfeld wrote the commission asking us to advise him if any members of his staff needed to be fired. We were flooded with inquiries and interview requests from American news outlets, and from countries as far flung as Pakistan, Israel, Egypt, and India. Certainly 9/11 did not have to happen; it was not a preordained act of nature, and our investigation detailed a number of missed opportunities to prevent the attacks. But we were not going to lay the blame at the feet of Rice or any other single official: to do so would have been inaccurate and irresponsible. Tom sifted through the pile of interview requests and went on ABC's *Nightline* to explain his comments, with the understanding that his appearance would be live and unedited.

This incident was just one of many controversies that flared up in the press during our work, but it indicated the sensitivity of words and 9/11, and presaged difficulties for our hearings in 2004. To many in the media, the natural extension of asking whether 9/11 could have been prevented was asking who was to blame for not having prevented it. Since we would be holding hearings with senior officials from two administrations, one Democratic and one Republican, the question was distilled further: Who was to blame, Clinton or Bush? Our task, as 2003 turned to 2004, was not to assign blame; it was to distill the massive amount of information we had gathered, and to make the facts public.

PERMEABLE BORDERS, VULNERABLE SKIES

FEW TASKS APPEAR MORE MUNDANE than stamping passports or monitoring airline passengers passing through metal detectors. But the men and women who perform these duties are as important to counterterrorism as CIA officers or Special Forces units. Most people following our work were anxious to hear about decisions made in the White House or the CIA. But part of our responsibility was to show that decisions made at a border checkpoint or an airport metal detector are equally essential. Each time a 9/11 hijacker passed one of those points, an opportunity was missed to foil the plot. This was the topic of our hearing on January 26–27, 2004.

For the first time, the commission was prepared to present findings to the public; the question was how to do so. We drew upon a model from the congressional Joint Inquiry into the 9/11 attacks, in which Eleanor Hill, the inquiry's staff director, opened the hearing by summarizing what the staff had learned on a particular subject. These staff statements functioned like opening statements at a trial, where the prosecution lays out its case. Our staff would read aloud their findings to date on a given subject; the witness testimony and questioning would then support, refute, or elaborate on those findings, like a cross-examination. This was particularly helpful since we would be seeking information from some witnesses who did not want to be forthcoming.

Commissioners did not get involved in preparing staff statements, beyond giving broad direction. One point that we made time and again dealt with style and tone. Some reports out of Washington are littered with acronyms and highly legal language that cannot be understood by anyone who hasn't attended law school or worked twenty years on Capitol Hill. Others are so weighted by opinion that the facts get lost. We insisted upon simple language and factual judgments—no acronyms and no adjectives.

The staff teams drafted the statements and submitted them to the staff front office for editing. We were particularly fortunate to have Chris Kojm, our deputy director, who had worked as an editor and had set up countless congressional hearings. Kojm had to be an enforcer in terms of report length. There is a tendency for writers of a jointly prepared report to become convinced of the overwhelming importance of the aspect of the story they are working on. In staff statements, bits and pieces of the story had to be put in the right context of relative importance to other aspects of the story. Since these staff statements had to be short enough to be read, every word needed to be justified.

Staff statements also gave us a chance to work out a process for clearing material for publication by the White House. We were determined to avoid the fate of the Joint Inquiry and its redacted pages. To achieve that goal, Philip Zelikow recalibrated the arrangement—instead of submitting staff statements for declassification, we submitted them for pre-publication review. This meant that the statements were drafted to be unclassified, but since they were written from classified information, the administration had an opportunity to flag something as classified. To use an analogy, we wanted the staff statements to be treated more like the memoirs of former national security officials that touched upon classified information than like government documents running through a laborious declassification process.

This is a somewhat simplified way of characterizing the situation, but it worked. Zelikow pushed the envelope in other ways. Often, the administration had little time to disseminate the statements for extensive review by the agencies. On an occasion where the administration wanted to classify a large segment of a statement, Zelikow insisted that the statement be published with the deleted segment appearing as a bracketed box within the text, thus drawing attention to what we felt was unnecessary redaction. Of course, at the end of the day the executive branch controlled these decisions, and our staff had a legal obligation to abide by them. But the commission was determined to push as much information about 9/11 as possible into the public domain.

Who would actually read the statements aloud at the hearings became a cause of contention. Zelikow wanted to read all of the statements, as was done by Eleanor Hill with the Joint Inquiry. Part of this was because he felt embattled. The 9/11 families, and the FSC in particular, had accused him of a conflict of interest because of his past relations with Condoleezza Rice. They and other critics pointed to our 2003 hearings as proof that he was leading a staff investigation that was overly academic and that was unwilling to ask tough questions. Now that we were prepared to put out findings that were quite critical of the performance of the U.S. government, Zelikow wanted to be front and center.

Staff in Washington is often in the shadows. Having seventy high-quality people working for us also meant that we had seventy egos; the notion that a rare spotlight on the staff's work would focus solely on Zelikow did not go over very well. At this point, the morale of our staff was not particularly high. They had been overworked and operating under extraordinary time pressure. Zelikow's hard-charging style, effective in getting a lot out of people, also alienated some. Commissioners, too, were wary of Zelikow's taking the spotlight alone, which could have created the impression that he had been alone in directing the commission's work.

We worked out a compromise. Zelikow would sit at the table with other staff members responsible for the topic—usually, the leader of a particular staff team and some members of that team. Zelikow would introduce the statement. In a few cases, he read most or all of it; in most cases, he turned it over to a staff team member to read. To those watching a hearing, this was an insignificant detail—three or four anonymous staffers sitting at a table facing a dais and reading their findings to the commission. But to those doing the reading, it was the culmination of a huge amount of work, and an important moment in their careers. This was the situation on the morning of January 26, 2004, when, instead of witnesses, our hearing began with a staff statement entitled "Entry of the 9/11 Hijackers into the United States." Zelikow opened the statement and turned it over to Susan Ginsburg, the leader of the staff team responsible for borders and immigration.

It was widely believed that all of the hijackers had been in the country legally. FBI Director Mueller had previously supported that view, saying, "Each of the hijackers . . . came easily and lawfully from abroad." Our investigation drew on extensive and new information. For instance, Ginsburg and her staff examined the four hijacker passports that were recovered—two from the wreckage of United Airlines Flight 93, in Pennsylvania, one that was picked up at the World Trade Center before the towers collapsed, and one from a piece of luggage that did not make it from the hijackers' connecting flight and onto American Airlines Flight

11. They also looked at all of the hijackers' visa applications and pre-9/11 terrorist "watch lists," and interviewed scores of people.

The evidence showed that some of the hijackers had been here unlawfully, and had not obeyed immigration laws in the United States. Two of the surviving passports had been doctored, and the other two had what our staff referred to as "suspicious indicators." Three hijackers had made false statements on visa applications that could have been detected—for instance, saying they had not previously applied for a U.S. visa when they had. Five hijackers had entered the United States more than once, and three of those five had violated immigration laws that could have led to their being barred from reentry, for instance, by entering the United States on a tourist visa and then enrolling in a flight school. On several occasions, hijackers entering the United States had received greater scrutiny from border officials, and on a number of those occasions the hijackers made false statements. In total, at least six of the nineteen hijackers had violated immigration laws while in the United States.

The statement presented a succinct portrait of missed opportunities. Every time a hijacker offered up a doctored passport, made a false statement on a visa application or in an interview, or violated an immigration law, there was an opportunity to foil the plot, or at least to remove one of the potential perpetrators. We missed nearly all of those opportunities.

In our first witness panel, we heard from the former head of the Immigration and Naturalization Services (INS) and the former assistant secretary of state for consular affairs—two of the key agencies that had failed to seize these opportunities. They spoke about the lack of attention to and lack of resources for counterterrorism in travel and immigration before 9/11. But the most powerful statement came from someone much farther down the chain of command, who had a personal example of how to exploit the terrorists' vulnerability while traveling.

Jose Melendez-Perez, an immigration inspector at Orlando International Airport, whom our staff found via a CIA tip, had kept a potential hijacker out of the country. He testified before us about this encounter, which took place on August 4, 2001, when he interviewed a Saudi named Mohamed al Katani, who was attempting to come into the United States. Melendez-Perez recalled how "upon establishing eye contact he exhibited body language that was arrogant. . . . I had the impression of the subject that he had knowledge of interview techniques and military training." Because Katani didn't have a return ticket or hotel reservation and did not speak English, Melendez-Perez was suspicious and questioned him further with an Arabic interpreter. Katani claimed to be meeting a friend who would not be arriving in the United States for another three or four days, even though Katani claimed that his own visit in the United States was going to be only six days long.

Melendez-Perez thought that Katani's story and demeanor didn't add up. He tried to put Katani under oath, but Katani refused to answer any more questions. At this point, Melendez-Perez went to his supervisor and detailed the holes and problems in Katani's story; then he offered a judgment: "I further explained to the AAPD [assistant airport director] that when the subject looked at me I felt bone chilling cold effect—the bottom line, he gave me the chills." Because Katani would not answer questions under oath, he could be denied entry, and was subsequently put on a plane back to Saudi Arabia.

Our staff had judged from its investigation—much of which remains classified—that at the time that Melendez-Perez was interviewing Katani, Mohammed Atta was waiting to pick him up at the Orlando Airport. Mohamed al Katani was likely the twentieth hijacker. The flights that crashed into the World Trade Center and the Pentagon each had five hijackers; the flight that crashed in Pennsylvania had only four, perhaps making it easier for the heroic passengers on that flight to force the plane down. Katani may have been slated to be the fifth hijacker on Flight 93.

Richard Ben-Veniste had met with Melendez-Perez, and was very impressed—his story illustrated the difference an individual could make in defending his country. In his questioning of Melendez-Perez at the hearing, Ben-Veniste made this point:

> [I]t is extremely possible and perhaps probable that Mohamed al Kahtani [*sic*] was to be the 20th hijacker. Based on that premise, and taking into account that the only plane commandeered by four hijackers, rather than five, crashed before reaching its target, it is entirely plausible to suggest that your actions in doing your job efficiently and competently may well have contributed to saving the Capitol or the White House, and all the people who were in those buildings, those monuments to our democracy, from being included in the catastrophe of 9/11, and for that we all owe you a debt of thanks and gratitude.

At that point, the entire room broke into sustained applause. John Lehman later told Melendez-Perez, "If everyone up and down the chain had been as professional as you, the attacks would not have happened." Yet Melendez-Perez had not been contacted by any government agency after 9/11—not even the intelligence agencies that knew who Mohamed al Katani was. As Melendez-Perez said in his statement, "The only government contact I have had about this incident came from the September 11th Commission this past fall when the border team investigating [*sic*] the incident."

The second day, we shifted to aviation security and the four flights. Again, our staff presented new revelations about 9/11. We learned that the FAA did have information before 9/11 warning about the possibility of a hijacking by terrorists affiliated with Usama Bin Ladin and al Qaeda—including suicide hijackings in which an aircraft would be used as a weapon. Yet none of the intelligence was specific. Furthermore, a list of suspected terrorists barred from flying on commercial airplanes before 9/11 ran to only twenty names, whereas a State Department watch list of potential terrorists had more than 60,000 names, including those of two of the hijackers.

Nine of the nineteen hijackers were actually selected by the FAA's computer-assisted passenger pre-screening (CAPPS) program, which checks the list of passengers against certain risk factors in order to identify potential terrorists. However, the only action prompted by that selection was additional scrutiny of the hijackers' checked baggage for explosives—not further screening of their personal possessions or their carry-on bags. This was emblematic of an aviation security system that—like our borders—was permeable: even when the FAA's tool for pre-screening potential terrorists succeeded in identifying nine of the hijackers, it was irrelevant to stopping the attacks, because pre-9/11 security measures were aimed at keeping bombs out of baggage, not at keeping planes from being turned into guided missiles. The hijackers were nineteen for twenty in getting into the country; they were nineteen for nineteen in getting onto the four flights with lethal knives, box cutters, and—in some cases—probably Mace or pepper spray (which were banned items).

Our morning panel of witnesses reinforced these findings. Jane Garvey, the former administrator of the FAA, confirmed that the FAA's security directives before 9/11 were geared toward combating the threat of explosives on planes. Claudio Manno, a former intelligence director at the FAA, said that before 9/11 the CIA was reluctant to reveal the names of suspected terrorists to the FAA because that information was classified. Cathal Flynn, a former security chief at the FAA, said he was not aware of the State Department's watch list of suspected terrorists until the week of our hearing, more than two years after 9/11. In short, nothing the FAA was doing before 9/11 had seriously threatened to stop the hijackers; meanwhile, information that could have helped the FAA keep two of the hijackers off a plane was elsewhere within the U.S. government.

That afternoon, we learned about the last line of defense against the 9/11 plot, which had been similarly ineffective. As our staff reported,

"The anti-hijacking training for civil aviation crews in place on 9/11 was based on previous experiences with domestic and international hijacking. It was aimed at getting passengers, crew, and hijackers safely landed. It offered little guidance for confronting a suicide hijacking." Thus pilots, flight attendants, and passengers were not instructed to resist hijackers; instead, they were explicitly directed: "Do not try to overpower hijacker(s)." Only after learning of the catastrophe at the World Trade Center did the passengers on United Airlines Flight 93 initiate a new protocol by overpowering the hijackers and preventing further death and destruction in Washington, D.C.

Our staff also addressed a number of questions that the 9/11 families had asked about the four flights. For instance, our staff reported that the hijackers had not purchased blocks of tickets on each of the flights in order to ensure that there would be a smaller number of passengers on board; that the hijackers did not use pilots' credentials to gain access to the cockpits of the planes; and, as an interim judgment, that there was no evidence that a gun was used on board any of the flights.

The gun issue demonstrated the difficulty of dealing with the "fog of war" from the day of 9/11: sorting through memories from a day of enormous shock with an extremely fast pace of events. One of the FAA's after-action memos had made mention of a gun on one of the flights, but our staff found that they could not corroborate where that claim originated. The same held true for accounts from the flights themselves. For instance, one of the family members who received a phone call from one of the flights reported hearing a loved one say something like, "He may have a gun," but the actual recordings of communications from the flights and the vast majority of secondhand accounts specified only knives and box cutters.

There were literally thousands of people connected to the four flights on that day who had heard from friends and families on board, or who had worked in some capacity for the FAA or at one of the airports on 9/11. Our staff team working on the four flights began by relying on accounts from these witnesses from closer to the day—for instance, transcripts of the FBI's extensive interviews in the days and weeks after 9/11 were regarded as more reliable than repeating these interviews more than two years after the day. Where there was uncertainty or the need for further information—as with the gun issue—our staff would conduct an interview. This was tough: in most cases, you would be asking the witness to recall what was likely one of the worst moments of his or her life; many were still struggling to get past the pain of their experience.

The most wrenching pieces of evidence were the tapes of passengers and flight attendants calling friends and families to let them know what was happening on board the flights, and the thirty-two-minute flight voice recorder from Flight 93, in which the hijackers can be heard commandeering the plane, and then panicking as the passengers attempt to take the plane back. Together, these recordings comprise an oral record of some of the most terrible minutes in American history. From them, we learned how the hijackers sealed off the front sections of the planes after the seat belt sign was turned off, threatened the use of explosives and killed or severely injured passengers and crew members, and pushed their way into the cockpits. This evidence also suggests that on two of the flights, Mace or pepper spray was used to subdue passengers and crew in the front of the plane.

After hearing from our staff, we decided to provide an unfiltered glimpse of this evidence. Our witness was Nydia Gonzalez, an operations specialist at American Airlines Southeastern Reservations Office in Cary, North Carolina. Gonzalez's office received a phone call at 8:19 on the morning of September 11, from Betty Ong, one of the flight attendants on board American Airlines Flight 11. In the aftermath of 9/11, news reports described Ong as frenzied and hysterical on the phone. This was highly inaccurate. For nearly twenty-five minutes, Ong calmly relayed information about the events on board Flight 11, setting an example of professionalism in the face of danger.

As part of Gonzalez's testimony, we decided to play an audio recording of four and a half minutes of Betty Ong's telephone call. Our staff had found Ong's closest relatives through American Airlines, and they granted us permission to play the tape, understanding that it was important to put information into the public record and to make public Betty Ong's bravery. We flew Ong's sister and brother—Cathie Ong-Herrera and Harry Ong—to Washington for the hearing, and our staff met them at the airport and made sure that they were seated in the first row of the audience.

Before playing the tape, we introduced the Ongs, who were greeted with warm applause. As soon as the tape came on, complete silence overtook the hearing room. The voices were at times caught in static, but the initial words were clear: "Number three in the back. The cockpit's not answering. Somebody's stabbed in business class and . . . I think there's Mace . . . that we can't breathe. I don't know, I think we're getting hijacked."

All of us have seen pictures of the two planes crashing into the World Trade Center towers. Suddenly, though, we were taken inside one of those flights, both by the presence of the voices from that day and by Ong's lucid description of the events taking place:

> BETTY ONG: Our number one has been stabbed and our five has been stabbed. Can anybody get up to the cockpit? Can anybody get up to the cockpit? Okay. We can't even get into the cockpit. We don't know who's up there.
>
> MALE VOICE [from Reservations Office]: Well, if they were shrewd they would keep the doors closed and—
>
> BETTY ONG: I'm sorry?
>
> MALE VOICE: Would they not maintain a sterile cockpit?
>
> BETTY ONG: I think the guys are up there. They might have gone there—jammed their way up there, or something. Nobody can call the cockpit. We can't even get inside. Is anybody still there?
>
> MALE VOICE: Yes, we're still here.
>
> FEMALE VOICE: Okay.
>
> BETTY ONG: I'm staying on the line as well.

At this point, Nydia Gonzalez gets on the phone. The second recording we played was Gonzalez's call to the American Airlines operations center, when she reports her conversation with Ong. Throughout this call, Gonzalez stayed on another line with Ong, though that exchange was not recorded. The man at the operations center reports back to Gonzalez that Flight 11 is being treated as a confirmed hijacking; that other air traffic has been moved out of its way; and, most ominously, that Flight 11 has turned its transponder off and moved to a lower altitude. At times, you can overhear Gonzalez talking to Ong. The recording concludes when Gonzalez loses the connection to Ong:

> NYDIA GONZALEZ: She doesn't have any idea who the other passengers might be in first. Apparently they might have spread something so it's—they're having a hard time breathing or getting in that area.
>
> What's going on, Betty? Betty, talk to me. Betty, are you there? Betty? [Inaudible.]
>
> Okay, so we'll like . . . we'll stay open. We, I think we might have lost her.

Gonzalez lost contact with Betty Ong at 8:44. American Airlines Flight 11 crashed into the North Tower of the World Trade Center just over two minutes later. Betty Ong, who was forty-five years old and known to her friends as "Bee," died along with the other passengers on the plane, but not before demonstrating her heroism, and enabling air traffic controllers to get other flights out of the way, law enforcement to identify the hijackers through her careful reporting of their seating, and the world to know what took place on board her flight. Other crew members from the four flights displayed similar heroism.

Hearing those voices brought back the unique emotions we felt on September 11. The catastrophe, which had gradually begun to fade from America's memory as the country and the world moved on, was again present and raw. The implications of the policy failures we had identified were now horrifyingly illustrated. The reason why the ten of us were sitting on a dais in a hearing room in Washington, D.C., was no longer remote.

The hearing was not without problems. The second staff statement—which dealt with the failure to adequately track three terrorists on government watch lists—drew interpretive conclusions instead of merely laying out facts: for instance, saying, "Therefore, in thinking about the question of accountability, that potential list tends to expand to everyone. In effect, though, this means no one." This prompted a rebuke from Commissioner Bob Kerrey, who followed the staff statement by saying:

> I just want to publicly make it clear that I think it's a very good statement but there are many conclusions in here that I could not sign off on. And I don't want the public to presume that because staff has presented it to the Commission that the Commission embraces the conclusions that have been reached fully.

Kerrey's statement pointed to the delicate balance between fact and opinion that the staff had to respect in drafting these statements.

We also did not do enough to brief the news media beforehand. In later hearings, we preceded the release of the staff statements with briefings for the press. Still, we did manage to focus public attention on substantive matters within our inquiry. As *The Christian Science Monitor* reported, we also "challenge[d] widely held assumptions about 9/11, especially the view that the attackers entered the country legally and violated no laws while they were here." Attention was drawn to those corrected assumptions about 9/11 in part by the drama of the Betty Ong tape. On January 26, the evening newscasts featured those tapes, and we learned that unbeknownst to us, CNN had carried that portion of our hearing live. We were struck by the extent of the public's interest, which went well beyond the human interest in the heart-wrenching tapes. People started downloading our staff reports off the Internet in huge numbers, and in some cases the reports were reprinted in newspapers.

That January hearing was the beginning of an extended revisitation of 9/11 by the American people that continued for the following six months. It was sometimes painful and often controversial, as we tried to color in the rough outlines of 9/11 that many people had stored away in their memories. The unresolved question at the end of January was just how long our work would go on.

AN EXTENSION

WHEN THE TWO OF US HELD a press conference at the end of the second day of our January 26–27 hearing, we concluded with a statement:

> All of you know the Commission has been considering whether to seek an extension of its statutory deadline. The good news is that most of our documentary and interview work is done. . . . The bad news is that much work remains, and some hard work in finalizing our report. We are aware of the political arguments back and forth about whether an extension is a good thing. We have decided that the right course is simply this: Put aside the politics and just ask for the time we really need. The Commission therefore requests that the Congress amend our statute to extend the lines for completing our report by at least 60 days.

The commission did not arrive at that conclusion easily, nor did we easily convince the president and Congress to accede to our request.

The extension question was an unwelcome presence throughout our inquiry. The commission had lost time at its beginning with the resignations of Kissinger and Mitchell. We had lost more time as the lengthy process of getting secure offices and security clearances prevented us from digging into our work until the spring of 2003—nearly six months after the clock started ticking. And we had lost time as we struggled to obtain access to the documents we needed to see. The good news was that the public was aware of these delays in our work, and was thus conditioned to understand our request for more time. The bad news was that we were running right into the tempest of the presidential election.

Even when the commission was created, people worried about our deadline and the 2004 election. Original proposals suggested a commission that ran for two years, but that was scaled back to eighteen months to place the reporting date in May. The Democratic Convention was scheduled for the end of July, and the Republican Convention for the beginning of September. A May reporting date allowed time before the heat of the campaign picked up; the White House, unaware of what would be in the report, wanted time to answer any potential criticisms of the president. Democratic candidates hammered President Bush throughout the primary campaign, in part for "stonewalling" the 9/11 Commission's requests for access to documents and people. These charges did not help us in our negotiations; instead, they suggested to the White House that our work was already being politicized, and fed their suspicion that leaks to the press from Democratic commissioners were being used to score points against the president.

Like any public proceeding in Washington, the commission was also the subject of swirling rumors, which were often cause for unnecessary concern, even paranoia, within a White House gearing up for reelection. Early in 2004, Tom received a call from Andy Card, the White House chief of staff. Card said that he had heard that the commission was going to publicly call for the firing of George Tenet the following day, and would Tom please reconsider. The president likes Tenet, Card said, and would be in a nearly impossible position if the commission went forward with its announcement.

It took a few moments for Tom to realize that Card was serious. The commission had no plans at all to call for the dismissal or resignation of George Tenet. Somehow, the White House chief of staff had been misinformed. Tom gave Card assurances that the commission was not in the business of calling for personnel changes in the middle of its inquiry. But the incident indicated the extent to which the commission was viewed warily as both unpredictable and capable of inflicting harm on the administration.

Fate dictated that interest in the commission increased just as interest in the political campaign was picking up. The same day that we requested an extension, Democratic voters were going to the polls in the New Hampshire primary. Senator John Kerry had won the Iowa caucuses a week earlier, and looked primed to lock up the Democratic nomination by March. President Bush's reelection team had made it clear that their campaign would focus directly on the issue of 9/11 and President Bush's leadership in combating terrorism. Because of the money raised by the two parties and the partisan differences in the country, it was apparent that the general election campaign in 2004 would start earlier than ever before.

The campaign was discussed as we considered our extension request. We took up the question at a commission meeting on December 8, 2003. Commissioners, including the two of us, had been privately polling staff about whether or not they needed more time to prepare for hearings and write a report, but the issue had not yet been discussed in the full commission. Most of the staff was strongly in favor of our being granted more time—the time pressure had become so acute that the running joke on the staff was that they were lucky it was not a leap year, so there was an extra day. The commissioners were split, and not necessarily along partisan lines. Some commissioners were wary of any kind of extension, fearing it would politicize our work. Several commissioners—chiefly Democrat Tim Roemer and Republican Slade Gorton—were adamant that an extension be six months, putting the reporting date past the November elections.

There were several problems with a six-month extension. Above all, there was a concern, particularly from the White House, about leaks. The White House view, which we shared, was that you would not be able to hold a lid on *The 9/11 Commission Report* through a presidential campaign. There would be too many people—in and around the commission—with access to our work. It was nearly inevitable that bits and pieces would leak out—Democrats would leak fragments to tarnish President Bush, and Republicans would leak fragments to blame President Clinton. This view was held more strongly by the Republicans, as it was a Republican president running for reelection, who would thus be more vulnerable to a barrage of negative leaks, or "death by a thousand cuts," as one commissioner put it.

Both of us came to the view that it was better to get the report out in full before the election. Any one piece of information lifted out of the report and leaked to the press might have the ability to score political points, but would be almost meaningless taken out of context. The American people needed to get the full picture or no picture at all. If their view of 9/11 was funneled through selective bits and pieces scattered into the political winds, their already flawed understanding of 9/11 might be irreparably impaired.

Tom was also strongly in favor of releasing the report before the Democratic and Republican conventions. Commissions don't often see their recommendations become law, particularly when those recommendations deal with reforming entrenched bureaucracies. Tom argued that if we did a good job with our report and released it in the run-up to the conventions, we could set off a bidding war between the two parties to embrace our recommendations, prompting the Congress to act, and act quickly.

There were also practical reasons why six months might be too long.

Many of our staff had other commitments—they had agreed to work for us on the supposition that their work would be done by the summer of 2004. To ask them to stay on for six more months would be unfair, and some key staff told us they had unbreakable commitments for the fall. Furthermore, there was merit in setting a deadline. With something like 9/11, you could always use more time—we could have gotten an additional five years and filled all of that time with work. At some point, we had to force ourselves to get a report done—the question was how much extra time was needed to complete our document review, interviews, and public hearings, and to write a credible report.

We asked our staff: What is the minimum amount of extra time you need? The answer was two months, though several commissioners continued to argue for six. The next step was determining how to get that extra time. We began with quiet inquiries to the White House, the Senate leadership, and the House leadership about whether they would support an extension. Through January 2004, the answers came back: no, no, and no, though the Democratic leadership in the Senate and House was supportive, as were key congressional allies, such as Senator McCain.

It was risky to take the issue public. If we asked for an extension and did not get one, it would have a devastating impact on the credibility of our findings: people could correctly argue that our work must be incomplete since we did not have the time we'd asked for. But there were advantages to asking for the extension right after our hearing. Through our findings on border and transportation security, we had demonstrated the value and quality of our work. Opposing the extension would put people in the awkward position of opposing a full airing of the facts about 9/11.

Our friends in the Congress took up the issue, though they were originally inclined to support a six-month extension: Senators McCain and Lieberman, working with Senator Daschle, moved to introduce a bill calling for a six-month extension. In the House, several voices were raised in support of a six-month extension, including Democratic leader Nancy Pelosi, and Republican representatives Chris Smith and Rob Simmons. Like Commissioners Roemer and Gorton, they were convinced that taking the commission past the election was the right thing to do. We disagreed, and knew from our negotiations with Judge Gonzales that the White House would not sign off on six months.

It was a sign of both the intensity of feeling about 9/11 and the intensity of the political year that the rather technical issue of a two-month extension for an independent commission became the subject of vociferous debate. Supporters weighed in strongly. We were pleased that some had seized upon the quality of our staff statements in arguing for extra time. On January 30, a *Washington Post* editorial headlined "Lift the Deadline" argued:

> This week the commission released—in connection with a round of public hearings—four staff reports with some preliminary findings. The work seems likely, in some respects, to alter the public's understanding of the attacks. . . . There is simply no good reason to prevent such work from continuing to completion—whether that means before, during, or after election season.

Others were not so kind. Our detractors on the political right saw the extension as proof that the commission was out to defeat President Bush's reelection. This view was apparent in a *Wall Street Journal* editorial headlined "The 9/11 Ambush," which ran the same day as the *Post* editorial:

> The membership and behavior of the current 9/11 commission have always looked like a political crackup waiting to happen. Now the commission—which was supposed to report in May—is asking for still more time. . . . Our sources tell us the real problem is that Democrats have held up drafting the final report with the excuse that some document might materialize that changes the entire picture.

We were once again walking a tightrope. We had no choice but to be cognizant of the sensitive political reality within which we were operating, yet we had to make our case absent any politics. We did so repeatedly in meetings and phone calls with Gonzales and Andy Card. Card's position was "Do you really need this?" And our answer was a firm yes—without the extra time, we would not be able to follow the leads we had uncovered, and our conclusions and recommendations would not be as informed as they might be.

The White House did not want to block a full investigation, nor did it want to be lambasted for running out the clock on the commission. On February 2, we worked out our compromise. In the statute creating the commission, we were directed to report in May and close down on July 26, 2004—allowing two months to close our offices and file our records. The White House agreed to allow the commission until July 26 to issue our report, and August 25 to close down—thus we would receive a two-month extension on our reporting date, and a one-month extension on the life of the commission.

The extension still needed to get through Congress. We made progress in the Senate, as Majority Leader Bill Frist seconded the White House compromise. But we ran into a roadblock in the House. Speaker Dennis Hastert continued his staunch opposition to any extension for the commission. He said, time and again, that he feared that an extended deadline would turn the commission report into a "political football." Support for the commission within the ranks of the House Republican caucus remained thin.

Throughout February, we quietly pressed the Speaker. Jim Thompson was our best point of contact, as he knew Hastert well from Illinois. Thompson gave assurances that our need for an extension was legitimate, and that we would work in a bipartisan manner to ensure that our report was not politicized. But even as legislation for an extension came up in the Senate at the end of February, Hastert continued to voice his opposition, vowing to block a House vote on whether or not to pass an extension. Meanwhile, time pressure was building—staff members had to know whether or not they could allow for an extra two months. Without an extension, we would have to cancel hearings, stop some investigatory work, and go right into drafting the report.

Outside pressure on the Speaker grew as commissioners publicly argued for more time and the 9/11 families made their voices heard. On February 26, Lee went on CNN with host Aaron Brown. Introducing the segment on the commission's request for an extension, Brown said:

> We admit we don't do "causes" very well on the program, and I don't do "outrage" well at all, yet tonight, a cause, and an outrage. The decision by the Speaker of the House to deny the independent commission investigating the 9/11 attack on America a sixty-day extension, that's all, sixty days, is unconscionable and indefensible, which no doubt explains why neither the Speaker nor any member of the House leadership nor any of their press secretaries would come on the program to talk about it, despite repeated requests.

Brown's view, echoed by many commentators and editorial pages, was emblematic of the difficulty of the Speaker's position—it was hard to argue against a full inquiry into 9/11.

On Friday, February 27, Senators McCain and Lieberman made a deft parliamentary maneuver. The House and Senate were trying to work out differences on legislation providing for spending on federal highway projects. While they worked out these differences, a two-month extension was proposed to continue federal spending on highways. In the Senate, any one senator can put a "hold" on a piece of legislation. McCain and Lieberman pledged to hold up the highway bill unless they received assurances from Hastert that he would hold a vote in the House on our extension.

Holding up money for highway projects is a good way to get Congress's attention. Without an extension of the highway bill, five thousand workers from the Department of Transportation would be on furlough the following Monday. Members of Congress would face questions from constituents about why the spigot of federal money for highway projects had been turned off—and they would have to answer that it was because the 9/11 Commission was not being given two extra months to complete its work. Senator McCain put it bluntly: "We all have a choice here to make," between the disruptions in the highway projects and "telling the families of those who died on 9/11 that the commission will not be able to complete its work." McCain faced the potential wrath of every highway worker in America and officials in every state, but his gamble paid off. That afternoon, Hastert gave us assurances that he would support the extension. The following Tuesday, we met him and reiterated that our report would not be a "political football."

We now had the time we needed to hold our hearings and write a credible report. Our next hearings, on March 23–24, promised to garner even more attention, with a list of witnesses that included two secretaries of state, two secretaries of defense, a former national security advisor, the director of central intelligence, and one former staff member on the National Security Council, Richard Clarke. What we could not anticipate was that circumstances would coalesce to make that attention overwhelming.

7

THE PERFECT STORM

A BOOK, A CHARGE,
AND AN APOLOGY

I also welcome the hearings because it is finally a forum where I can apologize to the loved ones of the victims of 9/11; to them who are here in the room, to those who are watching on television, your government failed you. Those entrusted with protecting you failed you. And I failed you. We tried hard, but that doesn't matter because we failed. And for that failure, I would ask, once all the facts are out, for your understanding and for your forgiveness.

> — Richard Clarke, former national coordinator
> for counterterrorism, testifying before the
> 9/11 Commission, March 24, 2004

THE EXTENSION GAVE US A BOOST at the beginning of March 2004. Because of our high-profile witness list, the public spotlight would be on us during our March 23–24 hearings. That spotlight was brightened by a perfect storm of outsize personalities, disputed facts, global events, and partisan politics that swelled the media coverage of our work, and nearly swamped the 9/11 Commission just as it was making us a household name.

The congressional Joint Inquiry into 9/11 featured testimony from the director of the FBI, Robert Mueller, and the director of central intelligence, George Tenet. But their focus was on intelligence, not policy-making. Since our mandate included diplomacy, military policy, intelligence policy, and the coordination of counterterrorism across the government, we invited the top policy makers in these areas from 1998 to

September 11, 2001, to appear at our hearing: Secretaries of State Madeleine Albright and Colin Powell for diplomacy; Secretaries of Defense William Cohen and Donald Rumsfeld for military policy; Director Tenet for intelligence policy; National Security Advisors Samuel Berger and Condoleezza Rice for national policy coordination; and former National Coordinator for Counterterrorism Richard Clarke.

Having this number of top-level officials crowded into a two-day period had its advantages. The hearing showed the tools that the government uses to fight terrorism. And there was a resonance to having these leading national security officials—nearly all of them household names—appear one after another. No single public hearing had featured such a prominent list of witnesses. In how many countries do the leading figures of government have to testify publicly, under oath, about their actions leading up to a national catastrophe?

We did not, however, succeed in getting Condoleezza Rice to testify at the hearing. On February 20, 2004, we invited her to appear, and three days later, Judge Gonzales declined on her behalf. This was not a surprise. We had already discussed Rice's appearance at length with Gonzales, and it continued to be a point of negotiation for another month. We felt that the hearing would be incomplete without Rice, as she was essential to the story. As national security advisor, she advised President Bush and oversaw the Bush administration's efforts to combat terrorism before 9/11. She was in charge of coordinating policy among the various national security agencies of the government. Moreover, her public testimony was, along with access to the PDBs, one of the two top priorities for the 9/11 families who had fought for the creation of the 9/11 Commission.

The Bush administration based its refusal to allow her to appear on executive privilege. As a member of the White House staff, the national security advisor does not testify before congressional committees or commissions created by Congress ("legislative bodies" was the term used by the White House). The White House felt that allowing Rice to testify would break this precedent, possibly leading future national security advisors to be compelled to testify and eroding the principle of executive privilege. Legally, we would have been on uncertain ground had we attempted to compel Rice to testify, as such testimony would have been unprecedented.

Tom called Henry Kissinger, who had served as both national security advisor and secretary of state for President Nixon. Kissinger told Tom that he had testified as secretary, but never as national security advisor. Lee checked with Sandy Berger, who said that he had appeared at policy briefings before Congress as national security advisor, but never as a witness—

thus he had not appeared at a witness table and had not testified under oath; no transcript had been made of his appearance; and there had been no public presence at the briefings. The one exception was an appearance in front of a committee investigating the allegation that President Clinton had exchanged stays in the Lincoln Bedroom for campaign contributions, but in that instance his testimony had had nothing to do with his responsibilities as national security advisor.

There was also the fact that Rice had already been interviewed in private for several hours, answering all of the questions we put to her. We could not argue that we needed her public testimony to fulfill our mandate, because we had already gotten the information from her that we needed to write our report; all we could argue was that her appearance was necessary to inform the public of what she had already told us, and that she should do so under oath.

The point we made, over and over again, was that the White House would be better off letting her testify, as their refusal to allow her to do so gave the impression that they had something to hide, even if that wasn't the case. Instead of Rice, though, the White House asked if they could send Richard Armitage, the deputy secretary of state, to testify. We agreed, even though Armitage did not play the role in coordinating policy that Rice did.

Several commissioners were unhappy about this. They pointed out that Armitage would already be sitting next to Colin Powell, his boss, during Powell's testimony, and that adding Armitage after Richard Clarke would take time away that would be better spent questioning Clarke.

While commissioners dealt with the sensitive issue of lobbying for Rice's public testimony, our staff was drafting statements that covered the top decision-makers in the Clinton and Bush administrations. Our previous staff statements had been hard-hitting and revelatory in their detailed findings on border and aviation security. But their findings involved and implicated largely mid-level officials and the leadership of agencies such as the INS and the FAA. The statement on counterterrorism policy summarized the actions and decisions of the top foreign policy makers in the two administrations, including two presidents.

All four staff statements detailed failures in policy. The staff statement on diplomacy recounted the government's inability to persuade the Taliban to expel Bin Ladin, and Pakistan to apply more pressure on the Taliban to do so. The staff statement on the military detailed three instances in which possible opportunities to kill Bin Ladin were not taken. The staff statement on intelligence outlined a strategy including various covert actions that had failed to harm Bin Ladin or seriously undermine al Qaeda. And the staff statement on national policy coordination detailed the formulation of policies that had failed to meet the urgency or gravity of the threat posed by al Qaeda.

Getting the staff statements cleared for publication was difficult. These statements dealt with matters that were almost never discussed publicly—negotiations with foreign leaders, the consideration of different kinds of military strikes, covert actions to capture or kill Usama Bin Ladin, covert support for the Northern Alliance combating the Taliban in northern Afghanistan, the deployment of the Predator unmanned aerial vehicle to spy on, and potentially kill, Bin Ladin and top al Qaeda commanders. Undoubtedly, this constituted a public airing of "sources and methods" used by the U.S. government in combating terrorism.

The Bush administration established a high-level group composed of senior officials from different departments and agencies to review the staff statements. We made several arguments on behalf of declassification. First, we were mandated by Congress to tell the 9/11 story and lay out the facts. Second, we needed to show, in some detail, how these policies had failed so we could make the case for new and better policies; when we issued recommendations, we wanted the American people to understand the facts that had led us to make those recommendations. Third, nearly all of the sensitive matters related to events several years in the past—for example, addressing a reality within Afghanistan that no longer existed—so we were not compromising any ongoing operations by discussing these now-dated sources and methods of fighting terrorism.

Another argument was that a number of these stories were already in the public domain. The managing editor of *The Washington Post*, Steve Coll, had recently published an excellent book entitled *Ghost Wars*, about the U.S. government's covert war against al Qaeda before 9/11. *Ghost Wars* goes into great detail in describing the methods used or contemplated by the CIA in trying to get Bin Ladin. If a covert action program could be discussed in Coll's published book, we argued, then certainly the 9/11 Commission could discuss it.

Several commissioners also pointed to *Bush at War,* Bob Woodward's account of the Bush administration's response to 9/11. *Bush at War* clearly draws upon classified materials, including accounts of meetings of the most senior officials in government, and planning for war against al Qaeda—including clandestine action and the invasion of Afghanistan. Why could the White House permit publication of such sensitive information in Woodward's book, but not in the staff reports of the 9/11 Commission?

The administration ultimately allowed the publication of nearly everything that we wanted included in the staff statements. By the middle of March we were primed to hold a hearing that featured an unprecedented line-up of witnesses, accompanied by an unprecedented level of openness about how the government used various tools of counterterrorism. But this hearing was eclipsed by the publication of yet another book dealing with the run-up to 9/11 and the government's initial response: Richard Clarke's *Against All Enemies.*

For our other witnesses, counterterrorism was a part (usually a small part) of their jobs; for Clarke, as national coordinator for counterterrorism from 1998 through 9/11, it was his entire job. This made him a hugely important figure to our inquiry. Yet while Clarke was well known in Washington, particularly within the national security bureaucracy, he was not well known to the public. Through our hearings, we thought we would be introducing him to the nation. But Clarke introduced himself first.

Our staff interviewed Clarke in mid-December and January. In those interviews, they learned that he was highly critical of the Bush administration. His basic charge was that President Bush and his top advisors had not taken terrorism seriously before 9/11: a strategy Clarke developed to combat al Qaeda was ignored; his own position as national coordinator was downgraded; high-level meetings to discuss counterterrorism were not held; and urgent warnings about potential al Qaeda attacks over the summer of 2001 were not acted upon with urgency.

Clarke told our staff that he was writing a book. The original publication date was set for the summer of 2004, but in late February, Stephanie Kaplan, the commission's special assistant, was looking on Amazon.com and found out that either Clarke or his publisher had moved the publication date of the book up to March 22, to coincide with the hearings. From a publishing standpoint, it was an ingenious move. Clarke was going to receive a huge platform, sitting at the same hearing table as Cabinet secretaries from two administrations; the interest in the hearings was guaranteed to promote interest in his book.

We often told our staff that we did not want any big surprises from our hearing witnesses. All were interviewed in private in advance of the public hearing. We wanted to use the public hearings to present our findings, and to force our witnesses to answer the same questions in public—in a way, to ensure accountability. Just as a lawyer does not want to be surprised by the witnesses he or she calls to the stand, we did not want witnesses at our hearings presenting information that we were not prepared for. When we learned that the publication of Clarke's book was being moved up, we wanted to review a copy. But Clarke's publisher knew it was sitting on a bombshell and thus kept a tight hold on the manuscript. We tried ordering advance or review copies, but nothing worked.

Dan Marcus, our general counsel, explored legal avenues, considered the possibility of issuing a subpoena for the book, and entered into discussions with the publishers. We ended up reaching a deal that got our staff limited access to the book so that we could be prepared for the hearing. Under the terms of the deal, three staff members who worked on the counterterrorism policy team that had interviewed Clarke privately would be permitted to review the book: Mike Hurley, Alexis Albion, and Warren Bass. These three staffers were specified by name by Clarke's representatives, and had to sign forms pledging not to disclose the contents of the book to anybody until 7:00 p.m. on the Sunday before the hearing, when Clarke was slated to appear on *60 Minutes*. The agreement specified that our executive director (Philip Zelikow) could not review the book—Clarke and Zelikow had apparently not gotten along when Zelikow worked on the NSC's transition from the Clinton administration to the Bush administration in December 2000 and January 2001.

Hurley, Albion, and Bass received one copy of the book on the Friday before the hearing. Each took turns reading it in the confines of our crowded office space. Because they shared offices with others, they hid the book in a drawer or locked it in a safe when they left the office. The book mirrored almost exactly what Clarke had told them in private, down to the phrasing he used and the anecdotes he recalled. But on top of that, the book included a blistering critique of the war in Iraq and President Bush's leadership in the war on terror. The concluding paragraph pretty well sums up Clarke's outlook:

> The nation needed thoughtful leadership to deal with the underlying problems September 11 reflected: a radical deviant Islamist ideology on the rise, real security vulnerabilities in the highly integrated global civilization. Instead, America got unthinking reactions, ham-handed responses, and a rejection of analysis in favor of received wisdom. It has left us less secure. We will pay the price for a long time.

It was a devastating charge to make, particularly with the country heading into a presidential election in which terrorism would be a leading issue.

Clarke went public with his views on *60 Minutes* on March 21, three days before he was scheduled to appear before the 9/11 Commission. He expanded his critique, saying, "Frankly, I find it outrageous that the president is running for reelection on the grounds that he's done such great things about terrorism. He ignored it. He ignored it for months, when maybe we could have done something to stop 9/11. Maybe. We'll never know." He also expanded on a charge in his book that President Bush, in the days after 9/11, pushed him to tie Iraq to the attacks:

> The president dragged me into a room with a couple of other people, shut the door, and said, "I want you to find whether Iraq did this." Now he never said, "Make it up." But the entire conversation left me in absolutely no doubt that George Bush wanted me to come back with a report that said Iraq did this.

Clarke stressed that his charges were not politically motivated; he was simply "putting out facts that I think people ought to know."

This was the tipping point in an already volatile political atmosphere. In the beginning of March, Senator John Kerry had locked up the Democratic nomination for president, and was telling Republicans to "bring it on" if they wanted a national security debate. The Bush-Cheney campaign had already rolled out ads tying President Bush's case for reelection to his leadership in the war against terrorism. The situation in Iraq was deteriorating, and weapons inspector David Kay had reported in January that he had found no weapons of mass destruction in Iraq. Clarke's charges made headlines around the globe, and his book shot to the top of best-seller lists.

Republicans hit back. The White House accused Clarke of grandstanding, and launched a vigorous assault on his character and credibility, calling him a disgruntled former employee, citing his close friendship to a top advisor for John Kerry named Randy Beers, and dubbing his book *Dick Clarke's American Grandstand*. Conservative commentators tied Clarke's actions to our work. *The Wall Street Journal*, in an editorial entitled "Sins of Commission," opined:

> It was always a terrible idea for the September 11 commission to drop its report in the middle of a Presidential election campaign, and we are now seeing why. That body is turning into a fiasco of partisanship and political score settling. To be precise, Democrats are using the commission as a platform to assail the Bush Administration for fumbling the war on terror, implicitly blaming it even for 9/11.

This editorial ran on March 22, a day before our hearing took place.

For many Republicans, Clarke's media blitz was proof that we had become what they feared all along: a "runaway commission." As disagreements with the White House mounted, Republicans saw Democratic commissioners criticizing the Bush administration in the press, and a 9/11 Family Steering Committee that was increasingly focusing its ire on President Bush and his top advisors, and was skillful at getting its views in print and on television. Despite our efforts to present a unified and nonpartisan front, many Republicans felt that partisan Democrats and their allies among the 9/11 families had commandeered the 9/11 Commission. Now they were accusing us of providing a forum for Richard Clarke to bash the president.

The good news for us was that the commission was now being seen as the definitive arbiter of 9/11. We had a high public profile, people were widely aware of the extraordinary access we had received to documents and people, and the findings released at our January hearing had made it clear that we were piecing together the authoritative account of 9/11. Because of that prestige, our witnesses took the commission very seriously; they knew that in giving their account to us they were giving their account to history.

The bad news was that politics now threatened to overtake our mission. The more partisan voices on both sides were ready to lay the blame for 9/11 at the feet of the other side. These voices had generally been drowned out by the aura of national unity that surrounded 9/11, but now—given the imminent election, the increasingly divisive atmosphere in the country, and Clarke's charge and some of the countercharges it had provoked—assigning blame for 9/11 was the name of the game.

It was a perfect storm: the White House's refusal to permit Rice to testify, Clarke's book release, the beginning of the presidential general election campaign, the reemergence of Iraq as an issue in our proceedings, and the increasingly bare-knuckle, partisan approach toward 9/11. Now the eyes of the country would be on our witness stand, not simply to learn the facts about 9/11, but also to watch the next installment of an escalating political drama.

PRE-9/11 FRUSTRATIONS AND A POST-9/11 APOLOGY

ONE WAY OF MEASURING THE INTENSITY in a hearing room is by the number of photographers between the dais and the witness table. On ordinary days, with the Senate conducting its business, two or three photographers will be crawling around there, snapping pictures of witnesses or of the senators posing questions. When we took our seats on the dais on the morning of March 23, nearly the entire area between us and the small, red witness table was filled in with people wielding cameras, waiting to capture a signature moment. Every seat in the hearing room was taken, and a crowd of curious congressional staff waited outside for seats to open up; the press tables that lined the sides of the room could not hold all of the reporters; in addition to C-SPAN, the cable news networks planned to hold large segments of the proceedings live.

For each of our hearings, we reserved large sections of seats for the 9/11 families. Looking out, we saw the familiar faces of those who had sat through some of our less attended hearings, accompanied by the pictures of loved ones that they carried or hung around their necks. One man had propped up in the seat next to him a poster with faces of 9/11 victims filled in over a picture of the Twin Towers. Family members applauded often over the two days of hearings, and we occasionally had to ask them to refrain from outbursts of emotion. But they continued, the crackling of applause punctuating dramatic moments.

The hearing commenced with our staff reading a statement on diplomatic efforts to counter al Qaeda before 9/11. The story was one of frustration. The government had applied pressure on the Taliban to turn over Usama Bin Ladin and cease providing sanctuary to al Qaeda, but these efforts had failed, as the United States underestimated the commitment of Taliban leader Mullah Omar to Bin Ladin. Efforts to persuade Pakistan to use its considerable clout over neighboring Afghanistan to get the Taliban to turn over Bin Ladin had also failed, in part because U.S. policy toward Pakistan before 9/11 had other priorities, such as dealing with Pakistan's nuclear weapons capability and its conflict with India. Pressure on Saudi Arabia and the United Arab Emirates, the other countries with suasiveness over the Taliban, had also been inadequate: we never achieved full sharing of intelligence or tracking of terrorist financing with the Saudis, and the UAE maintained its own travel and financial ties with the Taliban.

Our first witness was former Secretary of State Madeleine Albright, who was accompanied at the witness table by her former under secretary of state, Thomas Pickering. She was followed by then Secretary of State Colin Powell, who was accompanied by his deputy secretary, Richard Armitage. Upon standing and raising their right hands to take an oath to tell the truth, the witnesses were greeted with a barrage of clicking cameras that was so loud that it provoked a stir in the audience.

Albright and Powell both offered vigorous defenses of their administrations. Albright said, "I can say with confidence that President Clinton and his team did everything we could, everything that we could think of, based on the knowledge we had, to protect our people and disrupt and defeat al Qaeda." Powell nearly echoed this sentiment with regard to the Bush administration, saying, "From the start, the president, by word and deed, made clear his interests and his intense desire to protect the nation from terrorism." Each of their statements, and those of the witnesses who followed, were the products of intense preparation by both the secretaries and their considerable staff. Words were carefully chosen, and showed their actions and the actions of their administrations in the most positive light.

Yet the picture that emerged, in testimony and in questioning, was that the policies pursued by both administrations before 9/11 had been limited in their effectiveness, and that more robust policies to pursue al Qaeda had generally been considered unfeasible. Both former secretaries of state commented that intelligence about Bin Ladin's and al Qaeda's whereabouts in Afghanistan had not been "actionable"—meaning it had not been precise enough to enable a successful military strike. Yet both said that a full-scale invasion of Afghanistan before 9/11 would have been rejected by the American people, the U.S. Congress, and the international community. Furthermore, both allowed that other priorities had prevented the government from acting more vigorously.

Similar frustration was expressed in our afternoon panels on military policy. Again, we began with a staff report, this one detailing the military's pre-9/11 efforts against al Qaeda. On August 20, 1998, the Clinton administration responded to bombings of American embassies in Kenya and Tanzania with cruise missile strikes on al Qaeda camps in Afghanistan, and on a chemical plant in Sudan. Bin Ladin eluded these strikes, and that was our last attempt to strike him militarily before 9/11—though it was not the last opportunity. Our staff presented details about three occasions during which intelligence about Bin Ladin's whereabouts was sufficient to prompt plans for military strikes: in December 1998, February 1999, and May 1999. However, in each case, action was not taken because the intelligence was not sufficiently "actionable"—policy makers worried that the strike might miss Bin Ladin, and kill large numbers of innocent civilians or, in one case, members of the UAE royal family. As the staff statement says, "The challenge of providing actionable intelligence could not be overcome before 9/11."

Actionable intelligence was also lacking in another way after the al Qaeda bombing of the USS *Cole* in October 2000. This time the problem was in assigning responsibility for the attack. The intelligence community immediately suspected al Qaeda, but they could not come to a firm conclusion; without a definitive finding pointing to Bin Ladin or al Qaeda, the Clinton administration felt constrained from taking action, and a finding was not reached until the summer of 2001. The staff report also detailed frustration with the pre-9/11 military options. Short of invasion, possibilities such as the use of cruise missiles, air strikes, or the deployment of Special Forces were also limited by the lack of actionable intelligence, and the difficulty of operating in and around Afghanistan. Frustration with these limitations led to consideration of other options, such as arming the unmanned aircraft Predator with missiles that could be used to target Bin Ladin and the al Qaeda leadership.

Our next witness was former Secretary of Defense William Cohen. Cohen echoed some of the points made in the staff statement that intelligence for military strikes had not been actionable. In response to a question from Fred Fielding about developing other military options, such as the use of small units of Special Forces to pursue Bin Ladin, Cohen said, "We have 13,500 troops in Afghanistan right now, not to mention [how many] the Pakistanis [have there], and we can't find Bin Ladin to date. So, the notion that you're going to put a small unit, however good, on the ground, or a large unit, and put them into Afghanistan and track down Bin Ladin, I think is folly." Another intriguing element of Cohen's testimony was the reemergence of political controversy from the late 1990s. Many people concluded that the Clinton administration's bombing of the factory in Sudan had been misguided. But Cohen remained adamant that the intelligence he saw convinced him that al Qaeda had ties to that facility, arguing, "I would do it again based on that intelligence."

Cohen also revisited charges that President Clinton had bombed Iraq in 1998 to divert attention from the impeachment proceedings in Washington, the so-called wag the dog charge. Cohen remembered getting called into a closed session of Congress by then Speaker Newt Gingrich and speaking for three hours in defense of President Clinton's actions:

> I was prepared at that time and today to say I put my entire public career on the line to say that the President always acted specifically upon the recommendation of those of us who held the positions for responsibility to take military action, and at no time did he ever try to use it or manipulate it to serve his personal ends. And I think it's important to be clear because that "Wag the Dog" cynicism that was so virulent there I am afraid is coming back again, and I think we've

got to do everything we can to stop engaging in the kind of self-flagellation and criticism, and challenging of motives of our respective presidents.

It is a statement that Cohen clearly felt strongly about making, and it reflected the unique vantage point of a Republican who had served as a member of a Democratic administration.

Secretary Rumsfeld appeared with his deputy, Paul Wolfowitz, and the chairman of the Joint Chiefs of Staff, General Richard Myers. In advance of the hearing, we had learned the unusual fact that while Cabinet secretaries were put under oath when appearing before Congress, the secretaries of state and defense were not. Nonetheless, we asked Powell and Rumsfeld to appear under oath, and Powell quickly accepted. But Rumsfeld wouldn't give us an answer either way, even though we contacted his office six times. So when Rumsfeld sat at the witness table, we had no idea whether or not he would take an oath—we found out only when Tom asked to swear him in, and he stood and raised his right hand.

Rumsfeld acknowledged the spike in reports of possible al Qaeda attacks in the spring and summer of 2001, saying, "There was a good deal of concern. It was certainly not business as usual." In response, he said the Bush administration was putting together a more "comprehensive policy" to go after al Qaeda than the Clinton administration's, a process that did not conclude until September 10, 2001. Like Cohen, Rumsfeld spoke of the limitations of the pre-9/11 military options. In his view, even killing Bin Ladin before 9/11 might not have prevented the attacks, as the plot was already well in motion by 2001.

There was tough questioning of both Cohen and Rumsfeld. Throughout the hearing, Bob Kerrey expressed his frustration that the United States had not taken al Qaeda seriously enough before 9/11. Speaking in articulate bursts, Kerrey made the most of his allotted time, often continuing on through loud applause from the audience. To Secretary Rumsfeld, he said:

> It wasn't just that we were attacked on the 11th of September, Mr. Secretary; it's the same group of people that hit the *Cole* on the 12th of October [2000], the same group of people that tried to hit the *Sullivan* [sic] a few months before that, the same group of people that were responsible for the Millennium attacks against the United States that we had interrupted—and in Jordan, the same group of people that hit our East African embassy bombings [sic] on the 7th of August, and we now believe the same group of people who were

responsible for other attacks against the United States. This was an army led by Osama Bin Ladin who declared war on us on the 23rd of February, 1998. . . . It seems to me that a declaration of war, either by President Clinton or by President Bush, prior to 9/11 would have mobilized the government in a way that at least would have reduced substantially the possibility that 9/11 would have happened. Do you agree or not?

Kerrey's view, which he repeated to each witness, was that either president could and should have rallied public opinion and government action to go after al Qaeda as robustly as al Qaeda was going after us. In different ways, each witness expressed the view that the government was doing all it could. Rumsfeld argued that declaring war against al Qaeda would have been meaningless without the policies and capabilities to back up the declaration.

Differing critiques of both administrations emerged, as well as different issues that prompted witnesses to be defensive. The critique of the Clinton administration was that it had been too tentative in going after al Qaeda before 9/11: as al Qaeda launched attacks and issued fatwas against the United States, there was not a robust strategy to check the increasing threat, and it was unclear whether the CIA was authorized to kill Bin Ladin, or whether they had to try to capture him. The critique of the Bush administration was that it had not taken terrorism seriously before 9/11: as threat reports spiked in the spring and summer of 2001, there were no senior-level policy meetings about al Qaeda, and the policy produced on September 10, 2001, was nearly the same as that of the Clinton administration. Defenders of the Clinton administration said that the administration had come to grips with the terrorist threat by 2000, as evidenced by its intense efforts to prevent attacks around the millennium. Defenders of the Bush administration said that it had been developing a more comprehensive strategy to roll back al Qaeda, but that it had simply run out of time.

It was a surreal day. One secretary of state would be testifying, and another would be waiting in the greenroom behind our dais. As we ran slightly over time, Lee would go to check on the next witness and often find him or her relaxed and confident, reviewing testimony or ready to speak casually about other things. On the dais, we maintained a delicate balance. We had to keep on schedule but we wanted to give commissioners the time to ask their questions.

A unique element of our approach was that we deferred to other commissioners to ask questions at public hearings. The two of us spent enough time in front of the public. The hearings were a chance for the other commissioners to be in the spotlight and ask questions based upon their own interests and expertise. After coming on board, Bob Kerrey remarked to Tom that he had never been on a congressional committee in which the chair and ranking member spoke so little and deferred so much to other members in public hearings. Indeed, in some congressional hearings, the chairman and ranking member speak for the majority of time. We wanted the public to get a sense that the commission reflected the work of individuals from a broad spectrum of experience, and we wanted our fellow commissioners to feel invested in the process. Still, the higher profile the hearing, the less happy commissioners were to adhere to time limits for questioning; for Tom that first day, it was a full-time job just managing the flow of the hearing.

For our staff, the first day also held complications. During the hearing, the White House let us know that some key National Security Council documents about the formulation of Bush counterterrorism policy had just been made available to us. Since the documents were relevant to the testimony we would hear the following day, we had staff reviewing these newly available documents well into the night between our two days of hearings.

The following morning, many of the major newspapers reported extensively on our findings, going as far as to reprint sections of the staff statements. But as we retook our seats for the second day of the hearing, tension was building toward the appearance of Richard Clarke. His criticism was driving the public discussion of the hearings. As a former national coordinator for counterterrorism, he appeared in each of our staff statements. In short, before his public appearance before us, Clarke cast something of a shadow over the testimony of people who were far more prominent in public life than he was—people who were now compelled to agree with or refute his charges.

The hearing room was more crowded and abuzz with anticipation than it had been the day before. Our first witness was George Tenet, the director of central intelligence under both Clinton and Bush. In advance of the hearing, Tenet had informed us that he would refuse to discuss covert operations in public. This presented some difficulty, because so much of what the CIA had been doing to go after al Qaeda before 9/11 involved covert action in Afghanistan. In preparing for the hearing, our staff gave us a PowerPoint presentation on what we could ask in public, with "red lines" that we could not cross. Often, we had to figure out how to ask questions in an unclassified way—for instance, by discussing strategy broadly without going into detail about specific operations. This was frustrating, particularly since covert operations were discussed at length in the book *Ghost Wars*, and were mentioned in our own staff statement.

The staff statement on intelligence policy provided an overview of the various things the CIA had been doing to combat al Qaeda before 9/11. These included working with foreign intelligence services to disrupt terrorist activity; using proxies in Afghanistan to try to capture or kill Bin Ladin and al Qaeda leadership; and using the Predator to spy on Bin Ladin. The CIA had been involved in efforts to develop a new strategy under the Bush administration, which was difficult given the escalating reports of threats from al Qaeda. The commission staff statement observed: "Although Tenet said he thought the policy machinery was working in what he called a rather orderly fashion, Deputy DCI John E. McLaughlin told us he felt a great tension—especially in June and July 2001—between the new administration's need to understand these issues and his sense that this was a matter of great urgency."

Because so many CIA agents had worked so hard to fight al Qaeda before 9/11, we knew they were sensitive to charges that they had not done enough—after all, they had done more than anyone else. Our statement made this point: "Before 9/11 no agency did more to attack al Qaeda, working day and night, than did the CIA. But there were limits to what the CIA was able to achieve by disrupting terrorist activities abroad and using proxies to try to capture Bin Ladin and his lieutenants in Afghanistan." Just as our staff praised the CIA's efforts, it also questioned why the CIA had directed those efforts toward a strategy that was not succeeding, and concluded: "But if officers at all levels questioned the effectiveness of the most active strategy that policymakers were employing to defeat the terrorist enemy, the Commission needs to ask why that strategy remained largely unchanged throughout the period leading up to 9/11."

Tenet is expressive in public appearances, at turns humorous, passionate, agitated, and exasperated. He gave a strong defense of the CIA's pre-9/11 performance, saying, "The idea that [the CIA's clandestine officers] are risk-averse, couldn't get the job done, weren't forward-leaning—I'm sorry. I've heard those comments, and I just categorically reject them." Tenet made the case that covert actions were not a "silver bullet." But he was equally willing to acknowledge the shortcomings of pre-9/11 efforts.

In posing a comprehensive question, Lee summed up the basis of our inquiry: "I don't believe there's any high-level public official that I've ever met that would not act to protect the American people. But the overarching fact, of course, is that we did not do it. And we lost a lot of people. So the question that we have to address—and here I need some help from you—is why were we unable to do it?"

Tenet responded candidly:

> We didn't steal the secret that told us what the plot was. We didn't recruit the right people or technically collect the data, notwithstanding enormous effort to do so. . . . We didn't integrate all the data we had properly, and probably we had a lot of data that we didn't know about that, if everybody had known about, maybe we would have had a chance. . . . Visa policies, watch list policies. We didn't watch-list [the hijackers]; the FBI didn't find them.

This answer—with its focus on failures of spying, information sharing, and cooperation among intelligence agencies—was helpful to us for looking both back at 9/11 and forward to our recommendations, which would have to suggest how to correct these problems.

The next witness was President Clinton's national security advisor, Samuel Berger, a similarly charismatic personality. A staff statement on national policy coordination preceded Berger's testimony. The statement catalogued the various strategies used or considered between 1998 and 9/11—diplomatic pressure, military strikes, stepping up support for the Northern Alliance, arming the Predator, spending more money on counterterrorism. It covered many of Clarke's complaints, just as it told of the Bush administration's defense that it wanted to form a more comprehensive counterterrorism strategy. The statement concluded by recounting a memo Clarke had written to Rice before a September 4, 2001, meeting: "He urged policymakers to imagine a day after a terrorist attack, with hundreds of Americans dead at home and abroad, and ask themselves what they could have done earlier."

Berger defended the Clinton administration's record. In response to the charge that there had been ambiguity about the CIA's authorization to kill Bin Ladin, Berger said, "We gave the CIA every inch of authorization it asked for." Citing the attempt to kill Bin Ladin with the 1998 cruise missile strike, he said, "There could not have been any doubt about what President Clinton's intent was after he fired 60 Tomahawk cruise missiles at Bin Ladin in August '98." Like previous witnesses, Berger lamented the absence of "actionable intelligence"—in targeting Bin Ladin with missile strikes and in assigning responsibility for the bombing of the *Cole*.

After Berger, we broke for lunch. Because of the number of people going in and out of the hearing room, the beginning of the first witness's testimony after lunch can be a bit chaotic. When Richard Clarke took his seat at the witness table and raised his right hand to be sworn in, many people were still taking their seats, and some of the more vocal 9/11 family members were still outside the hearing room giving interviews to the press about the morning's proceedings. Still, two dozen cameras went off at once, creating their own clamor.

Every witness who appeared before us submitted an extended written statement for the record, and then usually summarized or read portions of that statement before taking questions. In the days leading up to the hearing, Clarke had spoken to our staff about the detailed testimony he was preparing, including what portions might be useful for him to read or paraphrase. However, he did not read any part of his statement, and spoke for only a minute or so. His words provided one of the most dramatic moments of the commission:

> Thank you, Mr. Chairman. Because I have submitted a written statement today, and I have previously testified before this commission for 15 hours, and before the Senate-House Joint Inquiry Committee for six hours, I have only a very brief opening statement.
>
> I welcome these hearings because of the opportunity that they provide to the American people to better understand why the tragedy of 9/11 happened, and what we must do to prevent a reoccurrence. I also welcome the hearings because it is finally a forum where I can apologize to the loved ones of the victims of 9/11; to them who are here in the room, to those who are watching on television, your government failed you. Those entrusted with protecting you failed you. And I failed you. We tried hard, but that doesn't matter because we failed. And for that failure, I would ask, once all the facts are out, for your understanding and for your forgiveness. With that, Mr. Chairman, I would be glad to take your questions.

It was a stunning moment. No other government official—former or current, in public or in private—had used the venue of the commission to apologize for failing to prevent the attacks. Whereas 9/11 family members in the audience often applauded the slightest hint of an apology, Clarke's statement was greeted with silence—perhaps because some of the family members were still getting situated after the lunch break, perhaps because they were shocked to finally hear what they had been waiting for. Clarke's apology was controversial. Some saw it as a moment of political theater—a way of inoculating himself against criticism while putting the spotlight on the Bush administration's failure to apologize. Others saw it as a heartfelt gesture from a man who had worked long and hard against terrorism, and who deeply regretted the fact that this work had not succeeded in averting catastrophe.

More than in the questioning of any previous witnesses, with Clarke's testimony, commissioners split down partisan lines, with Democrats praising Clarke, and Republicans attacking him. Tim Roemer began by asking Clarke to assess how much of a priority terrorism had been for the Clinton and Bush administrations. Clarke responded: "My impression was that fighting terrorism in general, and fighting al Qaeda in particular, were an extraordinarily high priority in the Clinton administration, certainly no higher priority. . . . I believe the Bush administration in the first eight months considered terrorism an important issue but not an urgent issue." Other Democrats praised Clarke. Richard Ben-Veniste said, "I want to express my appreciation for the fact that you have come before this Commission and stated in front of the world your apology to what went wrong. To my knowledge, you're the first to do that." Bob Kerrey began his questioning by saying, "You really in many ways are an example of a single individual coming to government and demonstrating that you can make a difference over a long period of time."

Meanwhile, each of the four Republican commissioners other than Tom sought to poke holes in Clarke's argument. Slade Gorton was first, asking Clarke to detail the strategy that he had presented to the incoming Bush administration in January 2001: "Assuming that the recommendations that you made on January 25th of 2001 . . . assuming that that had all been adopted, say, on January 26, year 2001, is there the remotest chance that it would have prevented 9/11?" Clarke's response was, "No." Even Clarke's more robust recommendations for action against al Qaeda— including arming the Predator, supporting the Northern Alliance, and bombing some al Qaeda camps—shared the inherent limitations of other pre-9/11 policies; they were forecasted to roll back al Qaeda over the course of three to five years, not by September 11, 2001.

Jim Thompson took aim at Clarke's credibility, citing a press briefing that Clarke had provided in August 2002, when he still worked for the Bush administration. (The Fox News Channel had taken the unusual step of making that briefing public, though it had been intended for background purposes only.) Thompson began by asking, "Mr. Clarke, as we sit here this afternoon we have your book and we have your press briefing of August 2002. Which is true?" Clarke responded that he had not lied in August 2002; he had simply emphasized the positive actions taken by the Bush administration, while downplaying the negatives. Standard practice, he said, for a "special assistant to the President." He and Thompson went back and forth on the matter for some time, culminating with Thompson saying, "But what it suggests to me is that there is one standard—one standard of candor or morality for White House special assistants and another standard of candor and morality for the rest of America." Clarke replied, "I don't think it's a question of morality at all. I think it's a question of politics."

John Lehman suggested that Clarke was using his platform to sell books, and cited the same inconsistencies as Thompson in concluding, "You've got a real credibility problem. . . . I'd hate to see you become totally shoved to one side during a presidential campaign as an active partisan selling a book." Clarke responded by pointing out that he had worked for President Reagan and both Presidents Bush, and had voted as a Republican in the 2000 presidential primaries. He added: "The White House has said that my book is an audition for a high-level position in the Kerry campaign. So let me say here, as I am under oath, that I will not accept any position in the Kerry administration, should there be one."

Fred Fielding challenged Clarke about his six hours of testimony in front of the congressional Joint Inquiry into 9/11, citing discrepancies between what he said then and what he said in his book. Clarke responded that he had not been asked by the Joint Inquiry his opinion about the Bush administration's focus on Iraq, and—as in the press briefing—had not said anything that was inaccurate, but had simply stressed positive aspects of the Bush administration's record.

Most of the 9/11 families in the audience were very much on Clarke's side, applauding his answers. Some of the Democratic commissioners were upset that Republican commissioners were asking questions that emanated from the White House. Some of the Republican commissioners were upset that Democrats were using Clarke's appearance to score points against the president. But there was nothing the two of us could do except wait it out. The partisanship was not surprising. It was a top-level hearing, with passions running high. Clarke's charge was serious, and promised to become a major issue in the 2004 campaign.

Whether you agreed with him or not, Clarke was compelling. He was an embattled figure, but that was a result not only of the seriousness of his charges but also of his own decision to release his book on the eve of our hearings. He was composed, and spoke in a level tone even while being aggressively challenged. Generally, we avoided the second part of his charge—that the war in Iraq was a massive diversion from the war on terrorism—because that area was not part of our mandate. The first part of his charge—that the Bush administration ignored terrorism before 9/11—was central to our mandate. Unfortunately, the person who could offer the other side was Condoleezza Rice, and she was not testifying before us that day. After Clarke's appearance, much of the hearing room emptied out. Many of the 9/11 families surrounded Clarke, embracing him and thanking him for his apology, some with tears in their eyes. Many of the reporters rushed off to file stories about the dramatic moments in his testimony.

There was a sense of exhaustion in the room. Secretary Armitage concluded the hearing. He has an affable manner, and managed to make light of the controversy, saying that he gave *Against All Enemies* the "Washington read"—meaning that he checked for his own name in the index. Despite the divisions that had emerged throughout our hearing, Armitage cited a "stunning continuity" between the Clinton and Bush administrations' efforts to combat terrorism—a candid remark that seemed to be reflected in the bulk of the testimony we had received. But Armitage's vantage point was limited to the State Department, a point made by several commissioners—particularly Richard Ben-Veniste, who cited precedents that national security advisors had appeared in open session before Congress. Ben-Veniste said to Armitage, "My point is that if the White House wanted to fully cooperate and make Rice available, there would be no impediment for their doing so."

After the hearing was over, the two of us held a press conference. We were both tired, and Tom was looking forward to getting on the train back to New Jersey. In our statement, we returned to the factual findings contained in our staff reports, and the consensus among our witnesses about the limitations of pre-9/11 counterterrorism policies. Understandably, the focus of the questioning was on the differences that had emerged, including the partisan tenor of the commissioner questioning.

Tom voiced his belief that it was an understandable partisan spell that would pass: "Occasionally a bit of partisanship breaks out, but I think that overall, this is a commission that is—this is a commission who's struggling to be nonpartisan or bipartisan at a very difficult time in this country's history."

Lee echoed the sentiment:

> We certainly did have in the last two days some questions and comments that had more of a partisan tinge to them than they—we've had in the past. But just keep in mind when this hearing occurred. I mean—it occurred right at the point of Dick Clarke's book coming

out. It occurred right after a weekend in which the partisan guns were firing at full blaze here. And this commission does not operate in a sterile vacuum. We're part of the process that goes on here in Washington.

It was difficult. The hearings were a success in many ways. Our staff presented the most detailed account yet about what had transpired in the years and months leading up to 9/11. The American people had the opportunity to learn about how their government combated terrorism, and how and why we could not prevent 9/11. Yet just as the commission was getting its maximum public exposure, we appeared to be at our moment of maximum partisanship.

We were proceeding on two tracks at once: a factual track and a political track. On the factual track, we were making progress in getting to the bottom of the 9/11 story. On the political track, we were being pulled apart by the divisions that mirrored the nation's bitter partisanship. September 11 was now a high-stakes issue in the 2004 campaign. We had made a decision to be public and transparent—now we were experiencing both the up- and downside of that decision. Having a national conversation about 9/11 was painful. Having that conversation in the run-up to the most divisive presidential election in recent history was even more painful.

Politics or book sales aside, a very serious charge had been leveled by Richard Clarke. We would have to deal with that charge. But we could not air the facts, or get past the politics, without hearing from Clarke's former boss, Condoleezza Rice.

THE COMMISSION

Richard Ben-Veniste is a skilled and tenacious lawyer and was one of our toughest questioners at the hearings.

Fred Fielding is one of the most able and likeable lawyers to pass through Washington, D.C., in recent years.

Jamie Gorelick was an extraordinarily capable and hard-working member of the commission.

Bob Kerrey brought charisma, experience, and independent thought to the commission when he replaced Max Cleland in December 2003.

John Lehman was a dynamic presence and contributed a wealth of knowledge about intelligence and military issues.

Slade Gorton has an amiable manner, a senator's knack for consensus building, and a lawyer's eye for detail.

Philip Zelikow, our incomparable executive director, combined a scholar's appreciation of history with a policy advisor's understanding of the U.S. bureaucracy.

Tim Roemer's focus on 9/11 stemmed from his tenure on the congressional Joint Inquiry into 9/11, his close relationships with the families, and his expertise on national security.

Tom Kean (LEFT) and Lee Hamilton preside over the final hearing of the commission.

Jim Thompson brought an outside-the-Beltway perspective and a keen ability to weigh in ably and articulately at key junctures.

The staff of the 9/11 Commission comes together for a group photograph. Their unique assortment of talent, experience, and dedication made them, in one commissioner's words, "a national treasure."

WITNESSES AND HEARINGS

Secretary of Defense Donald Rumsfeld (RIGHT) appeared before us, along with his deputy, Paul Wolfowitz.

Jose Melendez-Perez, the heroic Orlando border inspector who turned away the likely would-be "twentieth hijacker," in part because "he gave me the chills."

Richard Clarke leaning forward in the witness chair. Clarke provided one of the most dramatic moments of the hearings when he opened his testimony by apologizing to the families of the victims of 9/11.

Director of Central Intelligence George Tenet testified before us twice, giving a vigorous defense of the CIA's pre-9/11 efforts while also acknowledging "we did not steal the secret."

Samuel Berger, former President Clinton's national security advisor, makes a point. Berger came under scrutiny for documents that were removed from the National Archives Reading Room during his preparation for this and other appearances before us.

Then National Security Advisor Condoleezza Rice is sworn in on April 8, 2004. The buildup to her testimony was enormous because of the White House's initial refusal to allow her to appear in public and under oath.

Condoleezza Rice faces the commission and a phalanx of cameras as she delivers her nationally televised testimony.

FBI Director Robert Mueller testifies before the commission. Mueller was very cooperative with the commission as we probed the FBI's many pre-9/11 short-comings and prepared to issue recommendations about its post-9/11 efforts at reform.

Former Mayor Rudy Giuliani tells the commission about his remarkable experience on September 11, 2001. The commission came under scrutiny for not being more probing in questioning the mayor.

Attorney General John Ashcroft is sworn in on April 13, 2004. In his testimony, he attacked Commissioner Jamie Gorelick for building a pre-9/11 "wall" between intelligence and law enforcement.

Chairman of the Joint Chiefs of Staff Richard Myers (FAR LEFT) is sworn in along with leading NORAD officials. The commission faced difficulties in getting to the bottom of NORAD's actions on September 11, 2001.

Tom Kean takes questions after our May 2004 New York hearing. Media interest in our work built as the commission's hearings went on.

U.S. Attorney Patrick Fitzgerald testifies at our hearing on al Qaeda and the 9/11 plot. Though Fitzgerald gained notoriety for his own high-profile investigation into the leak of a CIA officer's identity, he appeared before us because of his experience prosecuting al Qaeda–affiliated terrorists.

Patrick Fitzgerald

Lee Hamilton asks a question at our hearing on the national response and air defense on September 11, 2001.

The view from the back of the Mellon Auditorium in Washington, D.C., on July 22, 2004. This stately building was the perfect location for the rollout of our report.

8

A REMARKABLE DAY

CONDOLEEZZA RICE IN PUBLIC,
BILL CLINTON IN PRIVATE

I believe the title was "Bin Ladin Determined to Attack Inside the
United States."

— Condoleezza Rice, former assistant to the
president for national security, testifying
before the 9/11 Commission, April 8, 2004

I T SEEMED OUR COUNTERTERRORISM POLICY HEARING would not end.
For days afterward, the fallout from Richard Clarke's dramatic testimony resonated in a public and increasingly bitter debate.

Clarke's supporters pointed to sources that backed up the charge that
the Bush administration had not been focused on terrorism before 9/11:
for instance, a quotation from President Bush to Bob Woodward, in which
he said he did not feel "that sense of urgency" about al Qaeda before
9/11; Richard Armitage's acknowledgment at our hearing that "we
weren't going fast enough" to develop a counterterrorism strategy before
9/11; and a quotation by the former chairman of the Joint Chiefs of Staff,
Hugh Shelton, who said that before 9/11 the Bush administration pushed
terrorism "farther to the back burner" than it had been under President
Clinton.

White House officials, particularly Condoleezza Rice, were everywhere
countering Clarke's charges. On March 22, the day before our hearing,
Rice published an Op-Ed in *The Washington Post* entitled "9/11: For the
Record," in which she presented a vigorous defense of the Bush adminis-

tration and an implicit criticism of the Clinton administration. The core of her argument was: "Once in office, we quickly began crafting a comprehensive new strategy to 'eliminate' the al Qaeda network. The president wanted more than occasional, retaliatory cruise missile strikes. He told me he was 'tired of swatting flies.' "

Rice took to the airwaves to repeat her arguments on news shows. The Sunday after our hearing, she appeared in her own *60 Minutes* interview from the Old Executive Office Building, saying,

> I would like very much to know what more could have been done—given that it [terrorism] was an urgent problem. We were looking for a more comprehensive plan to eliminate al Qaeda. But we weren't sitting still while that plan was developing. We were continuing to pursue the policies that the Clinton administration had pursued.

Republicans in Congress also levied countercharges against Clarke. On the Friday after our hearing, Senate Majority Leader Bill Frist took to the Senate floor to demand the declassification of portions of Clarke's July 2002 testimony to the congressional Joint Inquiry into the 9/11 attacks, saying, "Mr. Clarke has told two entirely different stories under oath. . . . It is one thing for Mr. Clarke to dissemble in front of the media, in front of the press, but if he lied under oath to the United States Congress, it's a far, far more serious matter."

Clarke did not shrink from the spotlight. He appeared on NBC's *Meet the Press* the same Sunday that Rice appeared on *60 Minutes*. He demanded that all his testimony to the Joint Inquiry and the 9/11 Commission, in public and private, as well as Rice's private testimony before the commission and all of his pre-9/11 e-mails to Rice and her deputy, Stephen Hadley, be declassified. He expressed disgust with what he called "a general pattern of the White House and the Republican National Committee and the president's reelection committee distributing talking points like that to senators and to press and to media trying to make me the issue and trying to engage in character assassination." He also repeated his charge: "The president of the United States was active on these issues [terrorism] in the Clinton administration. The president of the United States was not active on these issues prior to 9/11 in the Bush administration."

The media defined the debate as about politics and personalities, not about getting the facts right about 9/11. Introducing his *Meet the Press* interview with Clarke, NBC's Tim Russert exemplified the way in which people were approaching what was characterized by many as "Clarke vs. Rice," saying, "Who is right? What are Clarke's motives? How will all this affect the race for the White House?" The "Who is right?" question was steering the public dialogue, with supporters of George W. Bush inclined to believe Rice's version of the story, and supporters of John F. Kerry inclined to believe Clarke's. Politics and personalities, after all, make more intriguing story lines than dispassionate fact-finding.

Because our questioning had split roughly along partisan lines, we were in danger of becoming a victim of the partisanship we had tried so hard to avoid. Polls showed that a majority of Republicans found our inquiry "too partisan," while a majority of Democrats differed. Many observers chastised the commission for degenerating into a partisan "blame game"—a view typified by a cartoon that appeared in the *Los Angeles Times* depicting all ten commissioners pointing fingers at one another while an al Qaeda terrorist stands off to the side thinking, "You've got to love this."

Underneath the partisan bickering, there was a desire in many quarters to get the facts right. The staff reports released at our hearing were widely praised. This interest was typified by *New York Times* columnist David Brooks, who went as far as to give them a plug:

> Warren Bass, Michael Hurley and Alexis Albion are not exactly household names. But they are a few of the authors of the outstanding interim reports released by the 9/11 Commission this week. In clear, substantive and credible prose, these staff reports describe the errors successive administrations made leading up to the terror attacks. More than that, they describe the ambiguities and constraints policy makers wrestled with. . . . If you want something serious, read the commission reports. You'll find them at www.9-11commission.gov.

Comments like this, reprints of the staff reports in newspapers, and an enormous number of online visitors downloading the reports from our Web site indicated that the commission could cut through the heat of the political battles if the output of our investigation shed light on the 9/11 story.

Still, we did have to reconcile Clarke's account with Rice's. To that end, our staff put together a memo that ran to eleven pages detailing their respective statements on thirty different issues. When viewed side by side, it was striking how much the disagreement was one of interpretation, and not of facts. Rice said terrorism was an "urgent priority" before 9/11; Clarke said it was "important" but "not urgent." Clarke said he had been "downgraded" as national coordinator for counterterrorism before 9/11; Rice said Clarke "wasn't demoted. We had a different organizational structure." Clarke said he gave the incoming Bush administration a "plan" to fight al Qaeda when President Bush took office; Rice said she received a "set of ideas" from Clarke. Important or urgent? Demoted or reorganized? A plan or a set of ideas? The list went on and on.

Yet even though Clarke's differences with Rice were largely semantic, he had offered those views in public, under oath—something the White House had refused to permit Rice to do. Time and again during her television appearances, she was asked the question posed by Ed Bradley, the *60 Minutes* interviewer: "The secretary of state, defense, the director of the CIA, have all testified in public under oath before the commission. If—if you can talk to us and other news programs, why can't you talk to the commission in public and under oath?" Clarke's views had an air of legitimacy because they had been made in the formal venue of our hearing. The majority of the general public was not inclined to accept that a legal issue like executive privilege should permit the White House to keep Rice from testifying for the public record, particularly since she was writing Op-Eds and appearing on television program after television program.

But the White House continued to refuse our request. The day after our hearing, we received a communication from Alberto Gonzales disputing several of the statements made at our hearing, particularly Richard Ben-Veniste's assertions that national security advisors had testified in public in the past. This was echoed in a "fact sheet" released publicly by the White House entitled "Correcting Misstatements from the 9/11 Commission Hearings: Factual Inaccuracies from the Commission's Hearings on March 23–24, 2004." Gonzales's communication—and the fact sheet—reiterated the White House's position: "Sitting National Security Advisors in fact regularly decline to testify publicly on policy matters before legislative bodies, such as the Commission."

The White House sought a middle ground between doing nothing and having Rice testify in public. Gonzales requested another private meeting between the commission and Rice at which she could answer Clarke's charges. The possibility of publicly releasing the proceedings of such a meeting was also raised. In this way, the public could be informed without setting a precedent for a national security advisor testifying publicly. The 9/11 Commission's position remained firm and unanimous. We told the White House that we were not the Congress, and there was precedent for national security advisors testifying in public; Philip Zelikow even faxed the White House a photograph of Admiral William D. Leahy—Presidents Roosevelt and Truman's equivalent of a national security advisor—appearing before the congressional Pearl Harbor inquiry.

Ultimately, the White House's position was unsustainable; they could not leave Clarke's account on the public record without a rebuttal by Rice. On March 30, less than one week after Clarke's testimony, we received a letter from Judge Gonzales agreeing to allow Rice to testify under oath. The letter stated that, in return, the commission had to accept two conditions. First, we had to agree in writing that Rice's testimony would not set a precedent for future testimony by national security advisors or White House officials—a condition we had long since agreed to; second, we had to agree that we would not seek further public testimony from White House officials—something that we had no plans to do.

The letter also contained a surprise. For months, we had sought meetings between President Bush and the full commission, and a meeting with Vice-President Cheney. The White House's position had been that the president would meet with only the two of us; however, Gonzales shifted this position, and proposed one joint meeting with President Bush, Vice-President Cheney, and the full commission. The reversal on these two issues was indicative of why it was important for us to have an open and transparent inquiry. Our interim reports, media appearances, and public hearings over the course of many months had exposed us to partisan mudslinging, and charges of grandstanding. But they had also enabled the commission to develop political clout.

It was an important moment for the commission. We now had an agreement with the White House on our two major pending access questions. We set the hearing date for the morning of Thursday, April 8—the same day we were scheduled to interview President Clinton in private at the commission offices in the afternoon. The drumbeat of public interest now shifted from the wake of our March 23–24 hearing to the build-up to Rice's testimony. Meanwhile, the commission had to prepare for a truly remarkable day.

CONDOLEEZZA RICE TAKES THE STAND

THERE WAS TREMENDOUS PRESSURE in the days leading up to the hearing. Our staff had extensive briefing materials at our offices, including nearly verbatim notes of our private interview with Rice; side-by-side comparisons of the comments of Rice, Richard Clarke, and others; and the timeline of precisely what had been happening on terrorism on nearly every day of Rice's tenure as national security advisor leading up to September 11, 2001. But additional questions to ask Rice were coming at us from all directions.

It is not unusual to get advice—much of it unsolicited—before a high-profile hearing. But this was quantitatively different. The 9/11 families were adamant that we ask a huge number of questions arising from their beliefs about what happened on September 11, 2001. Many of them had become convinced that there was some degree of foreknowledge of the 9/11 plot—a briefing to the president or to Condoleezza Rice about an imminent al Qaeda attack involving planes flying into buildings. They were convinced that Rice had avoided testifying in front of the congressional Joint Inquiry—and then the commission—because she wanted to avoid having to reveal this fact.

The advice did not end with the families. Entire Op-Ed pieces were devoted to listing "questions for Dr. Rice." Conspiracy theorists coordinated e-mails to commissioners, so each of us received hundreds of copies of the same set of questions to ask in support of various fringe theories. Calls and e-mails came to us from friends and former staff not heard from in years; we even had people trying to get our children to influence us to follow certain lines of questioning. Given the political stakes, members of Congress from both parties were reaching out to commissioners with suggestions.

One message came to commissioners on April 1 from Richard Ben-Veniste, the Democratic commissioner who had argued most passionately that Condoleezza Rice had to testify before us in public: "I will not be able to attend the Rice hearing, as I am scheduled to be in a trial and the judge will not permit me to be absent." It was a startling development. An hour later there was a follow-up message: "April Fool."

For each of our other hearings, two commissioners were designated as "lead questioners" for a witness or panel of witnesses; those two commissioners would each get fifteen minutes for questioning, and other commissioners followed, with five minutes each. However, because of the intense interest in Rice's testimony, we decided to have no lead questioners; commissioners would get ten minutes apiece. In presenting this plan the evening before the hearing, Lee looked at Ben-Veniste and said, "Richard, we have good news and bad news. The good news is we're going to go in alphabetical order. The bad news is we've decided that 'Ben' is your middle name."

This was characteristic of a dynamic that had built up within the commission over months of close cooperation. We had disagreements and came from different professional and ideological backgrounds. But we made an attempt to get to know one another as people, and found that we could laugh together as friends in addition to negotiating with one another as commissioners. But the two of us knew we were in a delicate and potentially dangerous state. People were watching the commission closely, and many on both sides of the political spectrum had expectations for the hearing that could not be fulfilled.

The buildup was overblown. This would not be the Watergate testimony of John Dean. There was going to be no revelation of gross negligence or criminal conspiracy. Since we'd seen all the documents—including the infamous August 6 PDB—we knew that no report of planes crashing into buildings had gone to Rice or President Bush. Since we had already interviewed Rice, we knew her side of the story. Yet what the hearing lacked in unpredictability, it made up for in historical value and political consequences.

Clarke's charges were devastating to an administration that had put fighting terrorism at the forefront of its argument for reelection. The week of the Rice testimony was also a particularly bloody one in Iraq, with more than thirty American soldiers killed by the Thursday of our hearing, and the prospect of a Shiite uprising in southern Iraq and Baghdad. Polls showed that Americans were increasingly uncertain about the Iraq war. With Rice appearing before us in public, it was as if the Bush administration's two signature policies—the war on terrorism and the invasion of Iraq—were being put on the stand.

All of the major television networks preempted their morning programming in order to broadcast the hearing live. People had to line up hours in advance to get a seat in the hearing room, which was as tightly packed as any you will ever see. One longtime Capitol worker told our staff that it was the most cameras that had ever been assembled in a single hearing room. When Rice finally opened the door from behind the dais and walked, alone, to her seat at the witness table, a surge of flashbulbs went off; in addition to the news photographers, many members of the audience were standing and snapping pictures with their own personal cameras.

The two of us were concerned by the prospect of commissioners dividing along partisan lines. The stakes were so high politically, and the spotlight so bright: questions had to be tough, but they also had to be fair. Before Rice gave her testimony, Lee took the unusual step of reading a brief opening statement: a message to the audience about our purpose, and a reminder to commissioners to use a respectful tone:

> If we are going to fulfill our mandate, a comprehensive and sweeping mandate, then we will have to provide a full and complete accounting of the events of 9/11, and that means that we are going to ask some searching and difficult questions. Our purpose is not to embarrass, it is not to put any witness on the spot. Our purpose is to understand and to inform.

When Rice stood, raised her right hand, and swore to tell the truth, the room exploded with sound: the noise of the cameras almost drowned out the words of the oath. Like our other witnesses, Rice had prepared a written statement; unlike our other witnesses, she read her entire statement aloud instead of briefly summarizing it or skipping certain parts. It was a stark contrast in style: whereas Clarke had dispensed with his statement and briefly apologized, Rice read every word.

The statement gave a careful and detailed depiction of the story Rice had told to us in private and provided to us in bits and pieces in her previous public appearances. The statement touched upon many themes that had emerged in our previous hearings. Rice acknowledged the continuity between Clinton and Bush, saying, "On an operational level, we decided immediately to continue pursuing the Clinton Administration's covert action authorities and other efforts to fight the [al Qaeda] network." She vigorously defended her boss, saying, "President Bush understood the threat, and he understood its importance." Her core argument was that the Bush administration was developing a more "comprehensive strategy" to fight al Qaeda throughout 2001. She acknowledged the spike in threat reporting in 2001, but said that the intelligence was not specific:

> The threat reporting that we received in the spring and summer of 2001 was not specific as to time, nor place, nor manner of attack. . . . In hindsight, if anything might have helped stop 9/11, it would have been better information about threats inside the United States, something made difficult by structural and legal impediments that prevented the collection and sharing of information by our law enforcement and intelligence agencies.

She portrayed the administration as active and engaged on the issue of terrorism before 9/11, while supporting many of the policies that it had taken since 9/11—for instance, the PATRIOT Act, the passing of which had removed some of those structural and legal impediments.

In nearly all of our previous public hearings, the two of us asked almost no questions. But for the Rice hearing, we wanted to set a tone for the questioning that was probing yet non-confrontational, so Tom opened. Because he knew the closeness with which the 9/11 families were watching the hearing, he asked a series of questions that had been passed to him beforehand by family members. Among the first questions he asked concerned the charge that the administration had focused too hastily on Iraq in the days after 9/11. Rice acknowledged that the president had speculated about the possibility of Iraq's involvement, saying, "It was a reasonable question to ask, whether indeed Iraq might have been behind this." In talking about meetings at Camp David the week after 9/11, she said, "There was a discussion of Iraq. I think it was raised by Don Rumsfeld. It was pressed a bit by Paul Wolfowitz." But she was adamant that all of the administration's attention became focused on Afghanistan.

Whereas Republicans had questioned Clarke harshly, Democrats challenged Rice aggressively. This trend was immediately apparent when Richard Ben-Veniste began his questioning. Ben-Veniste's prosecutorial style had been honed in courtrooms, and he challenged Rice repeatedly in the style of a cross-examination. He moved directly to the issue of the August 6 intelligence briefing to President Bush, asking: "Isn't it a fact, Dr. Rice, that the August 6th PDB warned against possible attacks in this country? And I ask you whether you recall the title of that PDB." She responded, "I believe the title was, 'Bin Ladin Determined to Attack Inside the United States.' "

It was a charged moment. So much attention had focused on our struggle to gain access to the PDBs, and so many rumors had swirled about the August 6 PDB. We had not previously been permitted to disclose its title; hearing it from the national security advisor under oath indicated an unprecedented and unexpected level of openness. The exchange between Ben-Veniste and Rice, however, quickly became a confrontation, as she tried to explain the context of the PDB:

> RICE: Now the PDB—
> BEN-VENISTE: Thank you.
> RICE: No, Mr. Ben-Veniste, you—
> BEN-VENISTE: I will get into the—
> RICE: I would like to finish my point here.
> BEN-VENISTE: I didn't know there was a point.

They continued to go back and forth in a somewhat acrimonious manner, with Rice asserting that the PDB possessed "historical" information rather than current reports of threats. The families' habit of applauding reemerged when Ben-Veniste called for the declassification of the PDB.

Jamie Gorelick pressed the issue of why the Bush administration had not held senior-level meetings on counterterrorism before September 2001, and why more had not been done to take defensive measures in response to the threat reporting over the spring and summer. Rice asserted: "We were in office 233 days. It's absolutely the case that we did not begin structural reform of the FBI." Like some of the Clinton administration officials who testified before us, though, Rice pointed out that the nation simply wasn't prepared to take dramatic action against al Qaeda before 9/11—either abroad or in reforming government at home—and said, "Until there is a catastrophic event that forces people to think differently, that forces people to overcome all customs and old culture and old fears about domestic intelligence and the relationship [between foreign and domestic intelligence], that you don't get that kind of change."

Bob Kerrey was often aggressive and unpredictable, and his questioning of Rice was no different. He began: "I'm not going to get the national security advisor 30 feet away from me very often." He then critiqued the tactics used by the U.S. armed forces in Iraq, saying, "I'm terribly worried that the military tactics in Iraq are going to do a number of things, and they're all bad." Sections of the audience broke into applause, but Kerrey, who can lose his temper, pleaded, "No, please don't. Please do not do that. Do not applaud." Kerrey turned his attention to Rice's characterization of President Bush's pre-9/11 efforts against al Qaeda, saying, "You said the President was tired of swatting flies. Can you tell me one example where the President swatted a fly when it came to al Qaeda prior to 9/11?" They went back and forth, with Kerrey cutting Rice off and saying, "We only swatted a fly once, on the 20th of August, 1998. We didn't swat any flies afterwards. How the hell could he be tired?"

Rice's answer echoed her testimony that the president wanted a comprehensive approach to fighting al Qaeda. Using technical language, she described the difference between approaching the threat "tactically" and "strategically." Kerrey took issue with her extended answers, accusing her of trying to "filibuster" him, saying, "It is not fair. I have been polite. I have been courteous. It is not fair to me." Parts of the audience applauded, while others booed, giving the room the atmosphere of a wrestling match. Kerrey also mistakenly called her "Dr. Clarke" on numerous occasions, prompting her to interject, "I don't think I look like Dick Clarke." The exchange was heated, and circled back to the August 6 PDB. Kerrey ended his questioning by announcing, "In the spirit of further declassification, this is what the August 6th memo said to the President, that 'the FBI indicates patterns of suspicious activity in the United States consistent with preparations for hijacking.' "

Having seen the August 6 PDB, we knew there was no reason why it could not be declassified and made available to the public—nothing within it betrayed sensitive sources and methods of intelligence collection by the United States, and the information was dated. At the conclusion of the hearing, Tom announced that we were requesting the full declassification of the item from the August 6, 2001, PDB entitled "Bin Ladin Determined to Strike in US."

The White House initially said no, but once again they had far more to lose by keeping the PDB secret than by making it public. Two days later, on April 10, it was declassified. Much of it was historical information. For instance, it begins, "Clandestine, foreign government, and media reports indicate Bin Ladin since 1997 has wanted to conduct terrorist attacks in the U.S. . . . Al-Qa'ida members—including some who are US citizens—have resided in or traveled to the US for years, and the group apparently maintains a support structure that could aid attacks." The conclusion of the PDB came the closest to detailing current threats:

> We have not been able to corroborate some of the more sensational threat reporting, such as that from a _____ service in 1998 saying that Bin Ladin wanted to hijack a US aircraft to gain the release of "Blind Shaykh" 'Umar 'Abd al-Rahman and other US-held extremists.
>
> Nevertheless, FBI information since that time indicates patterns of suspicious activity in this country consistent with preparations for hijackings or other types of attacks, including recent surveillance of federal buildings in New York.
>
> The FBI is conducting approximately 70 full field investigations throughout the US that it considers Bin Ladin–related. CIA and the FBI are investigating a call to our Embassy in the UAE in May saying that a group of Bin Ladin supporters was in the US planning attacks with explosives.

Declassifying the PDB was particularly important for the families, as it dispelled any notion that President Bush had received a warning about the date September 11, 2001, or planes flying into buildings, while also making public the kinds of warnings that were moving up the government hierarchy during the 2001 "summer of threat."

Yet the meaning of the PDB remained a matter of interpretation. Some argued that it contained no specific information that the president could have acted upon; others stressed that he should have been galvanized to take more aggressive action. That, too, was the case for the entire Clarke and Rice disagreement; the facts of the story were not in dispute, the interpretation of the story was. Rice's testimony was not going to settle that disagreement, but it did succeed in getting all of the facts and differing interpretations on the public record.

Reflecting on the hearing, we feel that the very fact that Condoleezza Rice testified was far more important than the information we obtained from her—much of which we already knew from her or other sources. For the media, it was the denouement to a compelling story of an embittered bureaucrat emerging from obscurity to challenge the president and his top advisors. For the families, it was a moment of accountability: the national security advisor was forced to endure close scrutiny and tough questioning. For Condoleezza Rice, it was a pivotal moment, as she assumed the burden of defending her own actions and those of her boss.

For the general public, it was educational: people could hear for themselves the story as told by the president's most senior advisor, comparing her account to Clarke's. Indeed, it was satisfying to hear that many teachers around the country had their classes watch the hearing live; for so many Americans, it was an unusual glimpse into the way our country makes national security policy. When the commission began in December 2002, a select few Americans knew the intricacies of how the government fights terrorism—the bureaucracies involved, the process of making policy, how the president is advised, or how the threat from al Qaeda had been confronted over several years. By the time our counterterrorism policy hearings ended with Condoleezza Rice's testimony, many aspects of the 9/11 story were in the public record. Any student of the commission's reports and hearings could now have a new and detailed understanding of the workings of the U.S. government.

But we had no time to reflect on this on April 8. When we finished the hearing, shortly before noon, we had several cars waiting for us outside of the Hart Senate Office Building, which were going to take us to interview the forty-second president of the United States.

INTERVIEWING PRESIDENT CLINTON

THE BULK OF THE ATTENTION on our inquiry focused on the Bush administration, but the time frame of our investigation—1998 to September 20, 2001—focused on the Clinton administration. As our hearing with Condoleezza Rice ended and the audience of press, 9/11 families, and interested observers filed out, we were on our way to an interview that was equally unprecedented, and substantively more important. But our climb to the very top of the Clinton administration was not without its stumbles.

Since Bill Clinton is out of office, Clinton White House records are under the authority of the National Archives. Under a law called the Presidential Records Act, the Archives accepts requests only from the White House and Congress, or in response to a court order when it concerns documents of former presidents within five years of the conclusion of a president's term. Thus we had to request Clinton White House documents through the Bush White House, which then coordinated our request with the Archives. The Archives then had to obtain the Clinton records from Little Rock, Arkansas, where they were being held while the William Jefferson Clinton Presidential Library was under construction.

The process did not end there. After the Archives assembled the Clinton records in Washington, D.C., they had to be reviewed by the White House, which had the authority to determine what Clinton documents were responsive to our requests. President Clinton also had the right to designate representatives to review the documents, in part to see if there were any executive privilege concerns. President Clinton's designees for this were his former national security advisor, Samuel Berger, and his former deputy White House counsel, Bruce Lindsey.

This led to a bizarre incident. In early 2004, Judge Gonzales called both of us with strange news: Sandy Berger was under investigation by the Justice Department for taking highly classified documents out of the National Archives Reading Room, where the information was being stored. Berger had been reviewing documents to prepare for his interview with 9/11 Commission staff, and for subsequent public testimony. Gonzales told us that the investigation was pending, and that we should not share the news that Berger was being investigated with anyone. The documents in question included an after-action report prepared by Richard Clarke that assessed the Clinton administration's response to the terrorist threats accompanying the millennium celebrations.

From our standpoint, the primary matter of concern was: Had we seen all of the documents we needed to see? The answer to that question was yes. The Justice Department assured us that copies of the documents in question had been sent by the Archives to the White House, and then made available to the commission: Berger was reviewing copies of documents that the commission had already acquired. When the matter became public several months later, the same week that we released our final report, it ignited a fierce controversy that led to Berger's resignation as a senior advisor to John Kerry's presidential campaign.

The Berger incident was not the last problem we had with Clinton documents. After his interview with commission staff, Berger went to the Archives and found documents that the commission had not yet seen that he wanted us to see. In February, Bruce Lindsey complained that the White House had failed to give the commission the full 10,800 pages of Clinton documents that the Archives had assembled in response to our document requests. Apparently, the White House had taken a narrower view than the Archives of what was responsive to our requests.

The story surfaced between the Clarke and Rice public testimony. *The New York Times* ran a front-page story headlined "Bush Aides Kept Clinton's Papers from 9/11 Panel." The implication was that the Bush administration deliberately withheld Clinton documents, perhaps because those documents cast a more favorable light on Clinton's counterterrorism efforts. But the reality was more legalistic: the Bush White House simply did not think the documents were responsive to our requests, or they felt they were duplicative and had been given to the commission in other ways.

Why was this important? One of the central issues of dispute about the Clinton counterterrorism policy was whether the CIA had been authorized to capture or kill Usama Bin Ladin through covert actions in Afghanistan. President Clinton's top advisors—particularly Berger—stressed that the president had authorized the CIA to kill Bin Ladin through what is called a Memorandum of Notification. But CIA agents in Afghanistan were unclear on this point, thinking that they were supposed to try to capture Bin Ladin before using deadly force, which is a far more difficult mission. Because of the ambiguity on this point, the commission had to see all of the relevant documentation.

To ensure that we saw everything, the Bush administration allowed the commission to dispatch an "Archives Review Team" from our staff. Philip Zelikow, General Counsel Dan Marcus, and Deputy General Counsel Steve Dunne went to the Archives at the beginning of April and reviewed all 10,800 pages of Clinton documents. The vast majority were, indeed, duplicative or unresponsive. However, the team did locate about fifty documents that were of interest to the commission. The majority of those fifty were documents that the commission had failed to request. The National Security Council is divided up into "directorates" by subject matter, and we had asked for documents that had passed through the NSC directorate on terrorism, headed by Clarke. Yet a small number of documents pertaining to terrorism come from a separate NSC directorate, one focused on intelligence; so at the late date of April 2004, we submitted an additional document request to get Clinton and Bush administration documents from this directorate.

This sounds highly technical, but it indicates the level of detail required to ensure that an investigation is comprehensive. The efforts of our Archives Review Team enabled us to go into our interview with President Clinton assured that our staff had seen every document necessary to comprehend his administration's efforts against terrorism, just as we had when meeting in private with all of Clinton's top advisors.

Interviewing Presidents Clinton and Bush was essential to fulfilling our mandate. Documents provide you with a record of orders and actions; interviews with advisors provide you with a view of how policies are developed, and how the chain of command operates within an administration. But if you do not talk to the person at the top, you cannot understand how an administration works. We wanted to know how the presidents understood the threat from al Qaeda before 9/11; what options they considered to combat al Qaeda; what actions they took and why; and what suggestions they had for our policy recommendations.

In February 2004, we sent letters asking to meet with President Clinton, Vice-President Gore, President Bush, and Vice-President Cheney. We knew the interviews with the sitting president and vice-president would be harder to get, as their appearances before an independent commission would be without precedent, and the White House had expressed resistance to this in our early conversations on the matter. Clinton and Gore accepted immediately; indeed, the former president seemed eager to speak to the commission.

The Clinton interview had been scheduled several weeks prior to April 8, and it was a matter of happenstance that Condoleezza Rice's calendar and our own coincided for the morning of April 8. We were determined to keep the meeting with President Clinton secret; the last thing we wanted was a horde of reporters camped outside various locations, waiting for Bill Clinton or commissioners to arrive. Surprisingly, the press did not find out about the interview until it was in progress.

After the Rice hearing ended, we literally ran to waiting cars, which took us to commission offices in the General Services Administration (GSA) Building at Seventh and D Street Southwest, near the Capitol. As it turned out, Clinton arrived late. He was flying to Washington from New York in a small plane. Because of post-9/11 security rules, his office had made arrangements with the FAA at Washington's Reagan National Airport to clear the plane's arrival, but the FAA supervisor who had cleared Clinton's plane was not on duty the day of our interview. The supervisor in charge knew nothing about the previous day's approval, so Clinton's plane was delayed on the tarmac in New York while his office struggled to obtain clearance for the former president to fly into Washington.

President Clinton was annoyed, as he was sensitive to his reputation for being late for meetings. After several phone calls, Clinton finally had to call the head of the FAA to get approval, but the plane still ended up being late. When Clinton arrived and told us about his problems with the FAA—an agency that we had had to subpoena for documents—Tom sympathized: "Welcome to our world."

President Clinton was taken into the building through an underground garage. The first thing he said to us was, "I went to bed early last night—at three in the morning." He had been up late nights trying to finish his book, *My Life;* he joked that his associates did not want him to be doing the interview at all, as he was under extraordinary time pressure to finish in time for June publication. He had taken a break from writing and editing to fly down, and he was well prepared: the work he'd done on his book had covered some of the same issues that we wanted to discuss.

The interview took place around a conference room table. Sandy Berger and Bruce Lindsey accompanied President Clinton, and several of our staff were present to take notes and ask some questions. We had agreed that commissioners would take turns questioning in reverse alphabetical order, so Jim Thompson went first and Richard Ben-Veniste last. The interview lasted four hours, and Clinton answered all our questions. He was expansive and candid. He clearly reflects on his own decisions and has a remarkable ability to recall specific events. He said he had gone back in his mind over and over again to think about what more he might have done to combat al Qaeda.

Bin Ladin's entrepreneurial approach to terrorism fascinated Clinton, as did the innovation of stateless terrorist attacks on states. He stressed that countering Bin Ladin's methods, which were essentially unprecedented in history, required entrepreneurial defenses. Clinton lamented the fact that, in war, defenses are often years behind offenses: when a cannon ball was invented to puncture castle walls, it took years to build new kinds of walls to repel new kinds of cannon balls.

There were tough and probing questions asked on the matter of whether President Clinton had ordered the CIA to capture or kill Bin Ladin. Clinton echoed Berger's comment, that after he launched cruise missiles at Bin Ladin in August 1998, there should have been no doubt what his intentions were with regard to the al Qaeda leader. The CIA, though, had come under fire in the 1980s for some of its actions in Central America, and the targeting of individuals—no matter how odious those leaders were—was approached with great caution. The directives that had gone down from the president and Berger authorized the use of lethal force during an operation, particularly by America's allies within Afghanistan, and Clinton told us that this had been his clear intent. But moving down the chain of command, it was customary for a more cautious interpretation to be made of his directives—for only an attempted capture of Bin Ladin. It showed the complexity of how a president's orders and intentions move through the government, particularly in the secret world of national security.

We also asked why there had been no response during the Clinton administration to the bombing of the USS *Cole* in October 2000. President Clinton said that if he had had a finding from the CIA and FBI saying that al Qaeda was responsible, he would have taken the issue to the UN Security Council for action, even if the finding came in January 2001, days before he was scheduled to leave office. That finding never came.

Through our questioning, we got a unique sense of the inner workings of the Clinton presidency. He discussed his dealings with foreign governments, his view of the various national security agencies, and his approach to intelligence. We discussed the presidential daily briefings, which were only a small part of the reading that Clinton did each morning, which included a variety of classified and unclassified memos and intelligence reports put together by Sandy Berger and his staff. Clinton said the secretary's morning summary, prepared by the State Department Bureau of Intelligence and Research, was more helpful to him than the PDB in providing context for understanding international developments.

Clinton also spoke extensively on foreign policy. At one point, the issue of Saudi Arabia came up. Clinton said, "Here's what I would do if I were the Saudi royal family." He then described at length what kind of reforms the kingdom should undertake, and spoke in surprising and impressive detail about the domestic political factors within the kingdom and how to deal with those factors while reforming.

Clinton had made a point of remembering details about each of the commissioners and asking them questions. Fred Fielding, who was the only Republican commissioner who had not met Clinton, came up to Lee afterward and said, "You know, he really is a nice man." News of the meeting leaked out about an hour before we had finished. When Clinton finally left after five o'clock, much of the staff at the GSA Building—from janitors, to food service employees, to office workers—had lined the hallway outside of our offices. Clinton moved down the line, shaking hands and chatting.

When we left our offices, a mass of reporters outside shouted questions at commissioners. President Clinton left through a separate exit, but at one point the reporters swarmed another passerby, whom they mistook for the former president. The two of us took a car to tape an interview for *The NewsHour with Jim Lehrer,* where we reflected on the remarkable day. We then taped an interview with Bill O'Reilly for *The O'Reilly Factor.* We were sensitive that conservative opinion was coalescing around a view that the 9/11 Commission was being used to damage President Bush, and O'Reilly's show was a good way to reach conservative viewers.

We had spent more than seven hours in detailed questioning. We had witnessed the historic occurrence of a sitting national security advisor raising her right hand to be sworn in before a panel of private citizens assembled as an independent commission, and had sat around a conference room table asking questions of a former president of the United States.

Through it all, we had endured the ordeal of the public spotlight through the Clarke-versus-Rice controversy. We had, in a few short weeks, reached an unusual and unplanned high level of notoriety for a Washington commission. At one point, Jamie Gorelick sent each of us the lead story from the satirical newspaper *The Onion.* Over a picture of the ten of us sitting on a dais during a hearing, the headline read "9/11 Commission Finds 9/11 Commission Was Preventable." Lee was not familiar with *The Onion;* for a moment, he thought the commission had a whole new controversy to confront.

9

BECOMING A TARGET

> Although you understand the debilitating impact of the wall, I can-
> not imagine that the commission knew about this memorandum.
> So I have declassified it for you and the public to review. Full disclo-
> sure compels me to inform you that the author of this memoran-
> dum is a member of the commission.
>
> — Attorney General John Ashcroft, testifying
> before the 9/11 Commission, April 13, 2004

THERE WAS NO RESPITE for the 9/11 Commission in April 2004. We interviewed former Vice-President Al Gore on April 9, Good Friday, the day after our hearing with Condoleezza Rice and interview with President Clinton. As with Clinton, we were discreet about the date and time, announcing the meeting only after it had taken place.

Vice-President Gore was forthcoming in a session that lasted nearly three hours. We asked about the development of counterterrorism policy through the Clinton administration, and Gore's growing awareness of Usama Bin Ladin and al Qaeda. We also asked about his leadership of a presidential commission on aviation security that released its findings in 1996, recommending that aviation security be treated as a "national security issue," though focusing on the threat of sabotage, not hijackings. Gore was particularly candid and critical in discussing his view of the problems within the FBI, and repeated President Clinton's assertion that the Clinton administration had been ready to respond aggressively to the attack on the USS *Cole* if it received a finding from the CIA and FBI assigning responsibility to al Qaeda, even if that finding came in December, as Gore was immersed in the recount of the 2000 presidential election.

The commission remained in the spotlight over Easter weekend. On Saturday, April 10, the August 6 PDB was declassified and reprinted in newspapers around the country. Accompanying the PDB were stories about our upcoming hearing on "law enforcement and the intelligence community," which was scheduled for the following Tuesday and Wednesday, April 13–14. Over two days, we would hear from the current and former attorneys general, the director of central intelligence, and the current and former directors of the FBI.

Telling the intelligence and law enforcement story of 9/11 was a top priority for the commission. There was broad consensus in the country that 9/11 had revealed fundamental problems with U.S. intelligence agencies. We wanted to explore possible policy recommendations. We also hoped to move from the more politicized terrain of White House decision-making to more technical questions, such as how to enhance intelligence collection and analysis and information sharing within the U.S. government. But this hope was misplaced.

Some Republicans in the Congress and the media had always been skeptical of the commission, particularly during our high-profile disputes with the White House over access to documents and people. This skepticism moved to alarm when Richard Clarke blasted President Bush at our hearing, and some Democratic commissioners praised Clarke and asked tough and pointed questions of Condoleezza Rice. On the Senate floor, Senator Mitch McConnell (R-Ky.) spoke for many when he said, "Sadly, the commission's public hearings have allowed those with political axes to grind, like Richard Clarke, to play shamelessly to the partisan gallery of liberal special interests seeking to bring down the President."

When the publication of the August 6 PDB was followed by news stories that contained leaks from an upcoming commission staff statement with criticism of Attorney General John Ashcroft, the discontent became focused more directly on the commission. Ashcroft's spokesman, Mark Corallo, cited Democratic commissioners Jamie Gorelick, Richard Ben-Veniste, and Tim Roemer, saying, "Some have political axes to grind." It set the stage for a contentious hearing, at which we would be confronted by the most aggressive challenge to the commission's credibility waged to date.

The congressional Joint Inquiry into the 9/11 attacks shed light on many pre-9/11 intelligence failures. The phrase that came up again and again was a "failure to connect the dots." Bits and pieces of the 9/11 plot were scattered throughout America's intelligence and law enforcement agencies, but before September 11, nobody had put all of this information together: agencies did not share information; leads were not followed aggressively enough; warning signs detected over the summer of 2001 did not help us stop the attacks.

The Joint Inquiry recommended sweeping reforms (as had congressional committees and commissions for decades before 9/11). But few of these reforms were implemented. The law creating the commission specifically charged us to look at the Joint Inquiry's recommendations. This, joined with a broad consensus that the status quo was unacceptable, generated considerable anticipation about our intelligence recommendations. Would we call for the creation of a new domestic intelligence agency to replace the FBI? Would we call for a broad reorganization of America's intelligence community?

Many commissioners had worked extensively on intelligence issues, in the executive branch or on the congressional Intelligence Committees. We were familiar with various theories for how to fix intelligence, and heard many proposals throughout our inquiry. But we did not want to simply pick a model. As a starting point for our recommendations, we wanted to look back at 9/11 to understand why our intelligence agencies had failed to get the job done. Why hadn't we collected the pieces of data, shared the information, analyzed the big picture, or put together an operation that could stop this catastrophic attack? From those answers, we would determine what changes needed to be made to help prevent the next 9/11, taking into account the reforms already undertaken at the CIA, FBI, and our other intelligence agencies. In short, our recommendations would emerge from the facts uncovered in our investigation.

Our morning panel of witnesses on April 13 included Louis Freeh, the FBI director from 1993 to the spring of 2001, and Janet Reno, the attorney general under President Clinton. The staff statement opening the hearing ran through the FBI's pre-9/11 efforts, cataloguing the attacks or foiled terrorist plots of the previous decade: the 1993 World Trade Center bombing; the 1993 plot to blow up several New York City landmarks; the "Manila plot" to blow up several airplanes over the Pacific Ocean in 1994; the bombing of the Khobar Towers in Saudi Arabia that killed nineteen U.S. military personnel in 1996; the bombings of two American embassies in 1998; the foiled plots for attacks to coincide with the millennium; and the bombing of the USS *Cole* in 2000.

The FBI, which was the lead agency for domestic counterterrorism before September 11, 2001, approached these terrorist incidents as a matter of law enforcement. Information was gathered to prosecute individual cases, not to be widely disseminated, analyzed, and acted upon. A piece of evidence was a clue to a particular case, not a dot to be connected to other information scattered throughout the government that might help us understand an organization such as al Qaeda. Intelligence was not widely available within the FBI, or made available to other intelligence agencies. Our staff concluded: "As a result, it was almost impossible to develop an understanding of the threat from a particular international terrorist group."

The FBI tried different reforms to focus on terrorism before 9/11, but these efforts came up short. First, despite a stated goal to focus on counterterrorism, the Bureau had trouble making it a priority: for instance, on September 11, 2001, just 6 percent of the FBI's personnel were working on terrorism. Second, the FBI's efforts to pursue terrorists within the United States were impaired, in large part because of a "wall" between law enforcement and intelligence: for instance, there were burdensome restrictions on the circumstances under which the CIA and FBI could share information, particularly about a suspected terrorist who had not yet committed a crime. Third, the FBI did not sufficiently develop counterterrorism capabilities before 9/11: for instance, by hiring, training, or promoting people with necessary skills and expertise, such as Arabic linguists or terrorism analysts. These factors and others painted a picture of an institution ill suited to taking the lead in preventing terrorist attacks before September 11, 2001.

Director Freeh was questioned sharply. Tom said to him, "I read our staff statements as an indictment of the FBI over a long period of time. You tried reforms. You tried very hard to reform the agency. According to our staff report, those reforms failed." Freeh pointed again and again to the pre-9/11 context. Because terrorism was not a national priority before September 11, he said, the FBI did not get adequate resources or legal authorities to go after al Qaeda: "I would ask that you balance what you call an indictment, which I don't agree with at all, with the two primary findings of your staff—one is that there was a lack of resources and, two, there were legal impediments." After 9/11, Freeh argued, the FBI got these resources and legal authorities because Americans had made combating terrorism a top priority.

Attorney General Reno acknowledged that the FBI had significant problems sharing information, saying, "One of the frustrations is that the bureau, even when it finds that it has something, doesn't share." Like

Freeh, she pointed to the pre-9/11 context, recalling that even within the task of counterterrorism, her focus went well beyond al Qaeda, particularly in the aftermath of the Oklahoma City bombing, in 1995. She also disputed the proposal for a new domestic intelligence agency, saying: "The worst thing you can do is create another agency, and then we'll be back talking about whether they can share here or there or what. Let's try to work through it." In her view, the reforms taken by the FBI after 9/11 had put the Bureau on the right track.

Our second staff statement reviewed the threats coming into the intelligence community in 2001, including intelligence reports with headlines such as "Bin Ladin Planning Multiple Operations," "Bin Ladin Network's Plans Advancing," "Bin Ladin Planning High-Profile Attacks," and "Bin Ladin Threats Are Real." The statement reported: "A Terrorist Threat Advisory in late June indicated that there was a high-probability of near-term 'spectacular' terrorist attacks resulting in numerous casualties," and that George Tenet, the director of central intelligence, had told our staff in a private interview that "in his world 'the system was blinking red' " over the summer of 2001. However, the staff also reported, "Despite the large number of threats received, there were no specifics regarding time, place, method, or target."

The statement went through the missed opportunities to uncover the plot. The CIA knew two of the 9/11 hijackers to be terrorists—Khalid al Midhar and Nawaf al Hazmi—but the FBI was not informed until August 2001 that those men might be in the United States, at which point the Bureau did not aggressively pursue the lead. A memo drafted in July 2001 in the FBI's Phoenix field office warned of the "possibility of a coordinated effort by Usama Bin Ladin to send students to the United States to attend civil aviation schools." But the memo did not reach FBI headquarters and was not shared with other intelligence agencies until after 9/11. In August 2001, Zacarias Moussaoui was detained in Minneapolis, and an FBI agent expressed his concern to FBI headquarters that Moussaoui was a terrorist potentially interested in hijacking. But the information was not acted upon or publicized before 9/11. Information within the CIA and FBI that could have identified or obstructed the hijackers was not connected to the surge in threat reports; it was not shared vertically within the agencies, and it was not shared horizontally across agencies.

Thomas Pickard, the acting director of the FBI until September 4, 2001, testified that he did not learn about the Phoenix memo or the arrest of Zacarias Moussaoui until hours after the 9/11 attacks, saying, "It keeps me up at night, thinking: If I had that information, would I have had the intuitiveness to recognize, to go to the president, to do something different?" Pickard also said that Attorney General Ashcroft was not focused on the issue of terrorism before 9/11. According to Pickard, Ashcroft had asked him not to include terrorism during his FBI briefings, and did not give the FBI the counterterrorism funding it requested in spring 2001. In response to this cut in funds, Pickard said, "I spoke to the Attorney General briefly and asked him if I could appeal it, and he told me yes, I could; put it in writing. I had our finance and counter-terrorism people put together an appeal on that decision. And then on September 12th, I read the denial of that appeal from the Attorney General."

Pickard's account of his relationship with Ashcroft had already been made public over the weekend, when some of the contents of our staff report had been leaked to the press, drawing the ire of the attorney general's office; we do not know where the leaks came from. The morning of the hearing, *The New York Times* printed a story with the headline "9/11 Panel Is Said to Offer Harsh Review of Ashcroft." The opening paragraph of the story read:

> Draft reports by the independent commission investigating the Sept. 11 attacks portray Attorney General John Ashcroft as largely uninterested in counter-terrorism issues before Sept. 11 despite intelligence warnings that summer that al Qaeda was planning a large, perhaps catastrophic, terrorist attack, panel officials and others with access to the reports have said.

Unlike our other witnesses, Ashcroft refused to give us his testimony in advance of his appearance, despite our repeated requests. In the hearing room, one of his aides was literally sitting on a pile of copies of the testimony to prevent anyone from reading it. So when Ashcroft took his seat at the witness table, we were in the unusual position of having no idea what he was about to say. As he stood and raised his hand to be sworn in, a pack of his aides fanned out in the crowd, distributing the testimony to the audience and assembled media.

All of our witnesses, to some extent, defended the record of the administration they worked for, and several offered implicit criticisms of the other party's administration—none more so than Attorney General Ashcroft. He testified: "The single greatest structural cause for September 11 was the wall that segregated criminal investigators and intelligence agents. Government erected this wall. Government buttressed this wall. And before September 11, government was blinded by this wall." He described how information was not shared within the FBI or between the FBI and other agencies because of these legal restrictions. He stressed that "somebody did make these rules. Someone built this wall." He went on to describe at length a particular Justice Department memo from 1995 that dealt with this "wall," concluding, "I cannot imagine that the commission knew about this memorandum. So I have declassified it for you and the public to review. Full disclosure compels me to inform you that the author . . . is a member of the commission."

The declassified memo, which was included in the press packet distributed along with Ashcroft's testimony, had been authored by Jamie Gorelick in 1995, and been sent to, among others, FBI Director Freeh, and Mary Jo White, the U.S. Attorney for the Southern District of New York. The memo addressed the investigation into the 1993 World Trade Center bombing, which was being prosecuted by White's office, detailing how the "counterintelligence investigation" was to be separated from the "criminal investigation" of the attack. The implication was that the memo erected a wall between intelligence and law enforcement in the government, so that those prosecuting terrorism cases could not exchange information with those working on intelligence matters; this was what Ashcroft had called the "greatest structural cause for September 11." Thus the blame for 9/11, in Ashcroft's view, rested not only on the Clinton administration's Justice Department, but also on a member of the 9/11 Commission: Jamie Gorelick.

The attorney general's claim was overstated. The "wall" was a set of rules for the exchange of information between intelligence investigations and criminal investigations that evolved at the Justice Department in the 1980s in response to a series of court decisions. The 1995 guidelines reinforced those rules. In August 2001, Ashcroft's own deputy, Larry Thompson, ratified those same guidelines in writing. The wall was not dismantled until 2002, after the passage of the PATRIOT Act. The wall, which reflected Americans' reticence about spying within our borders or linking foreign and domestic intelligence, was certainly a crucial part of pre-9/11 information-sharing problems. But it was not the creation of Jamie Gorelick or any one individual.

Our staff was well aware of the wall's history, and they gave Jamie Gorelick some materials to use for questioning Ashcroft. Slade Gorton leaned over to Gorelick on the dais and said, "Don't you ask those questions. That's for me." So Gorton, a former Republican Senate colleague of Ashcroft's, asked:

> Your second issue is a severe criticism of the 1995 guidelines that, as you say, imposed draconian barriers to communications between law enforcement and the intelligence community—the so-called

wall. I don't find that in the eight months before September 11th, 2001 that you changed those guidelines. In fact, I have here a memorandum dated August 6th, from Larry Thompson, the fifth line of which reads, "The 1995 procedures remain in effect today." If that wall was so disabling, why was it not destroyed during the course of those eight months?

Ashcroft countered that the memorandum issued on August 6 was "a step in the direction of lowering the wall, providing for greater communication." Gorton responded: "But it was after August 6, 2001, that Moussaoui was picked up and the decision was made in the FBI that you couldn't get a warrant to search his computer. So those changes must not have been very significant." Ashcroft responded, "I missed your question, Commissioner."

Other Republican commissioners had tough questions for Ashcroft, while Gorelick did not ask any questions pertaining to the wall. This was in accordance with our policy on conflicts of interest: as a commissioner, she was recused from working on parts of our investigation related to her work as deputy attorney general. But it was also an important shift from the previous hearings, where Democrats asked tougher questions of Condoleezza Rice, and Republicans asked tougher questions of Richard Clarke. This time we had a witness stretching the facts to make an interpretation; it sent a powerful message that members of that witness's own party were challenging that interpretation.

The next morning, coverage of our hearing split between the accusations regarding Gorelick and the wall, and the information released in our staff reports about the FBI. Our opening staff statement of the second day highlighted a fundamental problem facing the intelligence community: "Today's Intelligence Community is a collection of agencies which were largely created to help wage the Cold War." The statement summarized the divisions present in how government approaches intelligence: the CIA collects and analyzes intelligence from abroad, performing "human intelligence," or spying; the Department of Defense operates the vast majority of the satellites that take photographs, prepare maps, and intercept communications and conversations, known as "signals intelligence"; the FBI is in charge of security within the United States, known as "domestic intelligence." Other Cabinet departments have their own intelligence units that collect and analyze information: for instance, the State Department has a "Bureau of Intelligence and Research" that provides assessments for the secretary of state.

As director of central intelligence (DCI), George Tenet's two responsibilities were running the CIA and coordinating the efforts of the fifteen intelligence agencies spread across the government. The statement pointed out: "The DCI controls the CIA, but other cabinet secretaries and the FBI Director direct their parts of the Intelligence Community." This organizational structure contributed to some of the pre-9/11 problems. A directive issued by Tenet on December 4, 1998, illustrated the problem. The directive read: "We are at war [with al Qaeda]. I want no resources or people spared in this effort, either inside the CIA or the Community." The directive is dramatic. But the staff statement continues, "Unfortunately, we found the memorandum had little overall effect on mobilizing the CIA or the Intelligence Community. . . . Almost all of our interviewees had never seen the memo or only learned of it after 9/11."

As DCI, Tenet lacked authority over the budgets and personnel of the various intelligence agencies beyond the CIA; for instance, he controlled less than 20 percent of the overall spending on intelligence. This led, in part, to an inability to coordinate a response to al Qaeda that could have drawn on all of the government's intelligence resources and made his words "We are at war" a reality. The statement concludes by bringing the pre-9/11 example up to date: "The DCI labored within—and was accountable for—a Community of loosely associated agencies and departmental offices that lacked the incentives to cooperate, collaborate, and share information. . . . As a result, a question remains: Who is in charge of intelligence?"

Our first witness was Tenet, who was making his second public appearance before us. In his testimony, he attributed some of the pre-9/11 failings to the "significant erosion in resources and people" dedicated to intelligence in the aftermath of the cold war, including the loss of 25 percent of personnel and billions of dollars in budget cuts. He was also blunt in saying, "We made mistakes" before 9/11. Specifically, he cited the failure to put future hijackers Hazmi and Midhar on terrorism watch lists, even though they were known to the CIA; the fact that terrorism watch lists in the government were "haphazardly maintained"; and the lack of "government-wide capability to integrate foreign and domestic knowledge." Because of these and other failings, he said, "we all understood Bin Ladin's attempt to strike the homeland, but we never translated this knowledge into an effective defense of the country."

Tenet outlined some of the steps he was taking to bolster the U.S. intelligence capability. Speaking of the need to get better human intelligence, he offered the opinion, "It will take us another five years to have the kind of clandestine service our country needs." In the questioning period, Tom expressed surprise at this: "I wonder whether we have five years." John Lehman also suggested the need for more robust reform, saying to Tenet, "You've done a terrific job in the evolutionary change, but it's clearly not been enough. Revolution is coming." In response to a question from Lehman about how to institute revolutionary change, Tenet said, "My personal view is that you really do need an outside group engagement, recommendations to come forward."

The final witness was Robert Mueller, the director of the FBI. Mueller had become director on September 4, just a week before the 9/11 attacks. Since then, he had implemented sweeping reforms to make counterterrorism the FBI's top priority. For months, we had considered whether those reforms settled the core question of whether an institution devoted to law enforcement (gathering information to prosecute cases after crimes had taken place) could reorient itself to focus on prevention (gathering information that enabled you to stop crimes from happening). To answer that question, we conducted a far-reaching investigation of the FBI's pre-9/11 performance and post-9/11 reforms. Our staff traveled to FBI field offices around the country, interviewed well over 300 FBI witnesses, and reviewed more than 1.7 million pages of FBI documents, just as Director Mueller reached out to us repeatedly to explain his reforms.

The final staff statement of the hearing assessed these post-9/11 FBI reforms, saying, "We believe the FBI is a stronger counterterrorism agency than it was before 9/11." Among the reforms were significantly increased funding; enhanced legal authorities, including the elimination of the wall between intelligence and law enforcement; recruitment of more anti-terrorism personnel; the development of new capabilities and technologies; and a widespread understanding that terrorism is the FBI's top priority. However, the statement pointed to remaining needs: hiring more analysts and linguists; establishing better communication between the FBI's field offices and its headquarters; improving coordination between the FBI and state and local law enforcement; and assessing the role of the FBI within the intelligence community. Despite improvements, a core problem was still the sharing of information; our staff concluded: "We found there is no national strategy for sharing information to counter terrorism."

In his testimony, Mueller strongly opposed the creation of a new domestic intelligence agency, arguing that "splitting the law enforcement and the intelligence functions would leave both agencies fighting the war on terrorism with one hand tied behind their backs." He was, however, candid in acknowledging: "The FBI's strength has always been, is and will be in the collection of information. Our weakness has been in the integration, analysis and dissemination of that information. . . . We want to make the FBI better." In questioning, commissioners offered praise of Mueller's efforts, and of Mueller personally. Tom spoke for many commissioners when he said, "Everybody I talk to in this town, a town which seems to have a sport in basically not liking each other very much—everybody likes you, everybody respects you, everybody has great hopes that you're actually going to fix this problem." But the good feeling toward Mueller alone was not going to guarantee a good future for the FBI. Our general impression was that the reforms under Mueller had put the FBI on the right track, but they had to be institutionalized, and they had to be supplemented by better information sharing across the government.

It was a productive hearing. We focused on the key problems in the years and months leading up to 9/11: problems sharing information, coordinating analyses and effort within and across different agencies, and connecting warnings about attacks to effective action. We also heard about increases in funding, personnel, and granting of legal authority to fight terrorism that had been made since 9/11, such as the authority to put suspects under surveillance before they have committed a crime. The question to consider was whether the huge problems revealed by 9/11 had been adequately corrected, or whether more reform was needed.

But if the hearings were a substantive success, they left us with a huge political problem. During the second day of our hearing, the chairman of the House Judiciary Committee, James Sensenbrenner (R-Wisc.), called on Jamie Gorelick to resign from the 9/11 Commission, describing her work from 1994 to 1997 in the Clinton Justice Department "a crippling conflict of interest," and saying, "Commissioner Gorelick is in the unfair position of trying to address the key issue before the Commission when her own actions are central to the events at issue. . . . The public cannot help but ask legitimate questions about her motives." Sensenbrenner widened his target from Gorelick to the entire commission, saying, "I believe the Commission's work and independence will be fatally damaged by the continued participation of Ms. Gorelick as a Commissioner."

We received Sensenbrenner's statement in the middle of our hearing, and other Republican members of Congress soon began to put out statements echoing Sensenbrenner's demand for Jamie Gorelick's resignation. Gorelick was upset, and went outside the hearing room to call Senator Tom Daschle, who had appointed her to the commission. Tom Kean followed her, saw her on the phone, and asked her what she was doing. "I'm calling Daschle and Leahy," she said, referring to Patrick Leahy, the ranking Democratic member on the Senate Judiciary Committee. Tom replied, "You don't need them to help you. You need us to help you. We'll take care of it."

FACING AN ONSLAUGHT

SLADE GORTON SUGGESTED THAT ALL the Republican commissioners hold a press conference after the hearing to defend Jamie Gorelick, but the two of us said that this was unnecessary—we would do it. Still, Republican commissioners made immediate statements defending Gorelick. John Lehman said, "Jamie Gorelick has made a very good contribution, and she's one of the really savvy, nonpartisan of the bipartisan members." In a press conference, Tom went further, saying, "She's in my mind one of the finest members of the commission, one of the hardest-working members of the commission, and, by the way, one of the most nonpartisan and bipartisan members of the commission. So people ought to stay out of our business." Telling the chairman of the Judiciary Committee to "stay out of our business" may not have been the most diplomatic phrasing, but it came at the end of a long two days of hearings.

The commission had never enjoyed smooth relations with Republicans in the House of Representatives. Many representatives had opposed the creation of the commission in the first place, and had opposed increasing our funding and extending our deadline. Structurally, we had a problem because there was no former Republican congressman on the commission. Slade Gorton, a former Republican senator, met often with the Senate Republican caucus and Bill Frist, the Republican majority leader. Former Congressman Tim Roemer kept in contact with Democratic members of the House, and former Senator Bob Kerrey did the same with Senate Democrats. But we had no commissioner who could maintain a level of trust and regular consultation between the commission and the House Republican caucus. Jim Thompson could reach out to Speaker Dennis Hastert; Lee spent significant time on Capitol Hill and spoke with members of both parties; and other commissioners knew individual House Republicans. But too often we found ourselves performing damage control.

The Friday after our hearing, Tom received an angry letter from the House majority leader, Tom DeLay, who unleashed a series of complaints. DeLay expressed outrage over "the camera-driven tone of the hearings," "commissioners fanning out across media programs," and commissioners expressing "startling disrespect for Congress." He then accused the commission of endangering the lives of Americans serving abroad, saying:

> Partisan mudslinging, circus-atmosphere pyrotechnics, and gotcha-style questioning do not get us closer to the truth. They serve as dangerous distractions from the global war on terror. They undermine our national unity and insult the troops now in harm's way, to say nothing of those who have already given their lives in this conflict. And make no mistake, enemies of freedom will try to conclude from such antics that the United States is unserious about the threat to civilization posed by international terror. Put simply, Mr. Chairman, politicization of the commission not only undermines its credibility; it undermines the war effort and endangers our troops.

DeLay concluded his letter by expressing his "growing concern about the recent revelations regarding Commissioner Gorelick," suggesting that her conflict of interest further compromised the commission's credibility.

It was a direct attack on the 9/11 Commission's credibility and a politically devastating letter to receive with just three months left in our inquiry. As majority leader, DeLay was highly influential, and his views presaged a broad discontent in his caucus. Whereas previous outrage had been expressed about a particular witness such as Richard Clarke, or even a particular line of questioning by Democratic commissioners, DeLay's letter indicted the nature of our entire inquiry. If the leadership of the House of Representatives rejected our report, we would have little chance of getting our recommendations passed into law.

We received the letter on a Friday afternoon, after it was released to the media. Tom drafted a response, answering each of the criticisms brought up by Congressman DeLay. On the issue of public hearings, Tom wrote, "The Commission has held public hearings because of our belief that the American people need to be brought into the discovery of the facts." On the issue of the troops, Tom wrote, "There is no other country in the world that would allow an open investigation of this kind. . . . It is this tradition of freedom that our troops around the world defend, and we salute them." On the issue of partisanship, Tom pointed out that the commission had held no votes that broke down along partisan lines, and that commissioners had deep respect for one another. On the question of integrity, Tom stated the commission's recusal policy, specifying, "Commissioner Gorelick has recused herself from the Commission's work on any of her decisions or actions as Deputy Attorney General." The letter concluded by addressing the issue of the Congress:

> We have profound respect for the Congress of the United States. My father served for twenty years in Congress; the Vice-Chair served in Congress for thirty-four years. Nine Commissioners were appointed by Congress; four served in Congress. The authority for the Commission, its funds, and the extension of its existence for sixty days, came from the Congress. Our recommendations will require the support of the Congress. We have always welcomed the input we have received from Members of Congress of both parties. . . . As you state, "We are all in this together." When you or one of your colleagues have further thoughts, please pick up the phone, and let's talk about it.

Lee offered to co-sign, but because DeLay's letter had been addressed specifically to Tom, the response letter went out over only Tom's signature.

We also faced criticism that went beyond the issue of Jamie Gorelick and came from beyond the Congress. We have recounted the many benefits of being open and transparent, but when you're in the public eye, you also become a target. The second day of our hearing, the *New York Post* ran a front-page editorial with the headline "National Disgrace," lambasting the commission for publicly raising questions about warnings that preceded 9/11.

The next day, a story ran on the front page of *The New York Times* with the headline "Panel Members Talking Freely (Some Critics Say Too Freely)." The article quoted people ranging from Senator Arlen Specter to former President Gerald Ford expressing concern that commissioners were talking too much in the media. The *Times* also ran an Op-Ed with the headline "From One Commission to Another: Shut Up." Juliette Kayyem and Wayne Downing, who served on a National Commission on Terrorism in 1999, argued that their commission, which did not speak to the media until it released its report, was a model for us to follow, writing, "While open testimony is important for the American public, open pontificating by the commissioners is not." They advised us to impose a "gag order" on commissioners until the release of our report.

We did not impose such a "gag order" during our work for several reasons. First, because we were dealing with 9/11, we did not think it would be possible; there was going to be public interest, and we saw little reason to encourage commissioners to hide from that interest. In a world of twenty-four-hour news cycles, someone was going to be talking about the 9/11 Commission, so it might as well be us, and not exclusively our critics. Second, we felt that an open discussion about 9/11, no matter how painful, was healthy. Third, we had a commitment to the 9/11 families to be open and transparent throughout our work. Finally, we were not inclined to order our fellow commissioners around; they probably would not have listened to us anyway.

However, in the spring of a bitter presidential election year, being public meant being caught in the partisan cross fire. In the wake of the Ashcroft testimony, we needed to keep our heads down, so we did suggest to commissioners that we take a lower profile in the coming weeks, and refrain from issuing preliminary judgments about what was going to be in our report. But that did not stop the deluge of complaints focused on Jamie Gorelick.

The second half of April brought a steady drumbeat of criticism of Gorelick in the conservative media. *The Washington Times* ran a story on her nearly every day for two weeks, and Op-Eds with headlines such as "Investigator or Obstructionist?" and "Gorelick Must Go." *The Wall Street Journal* ran editorials on the subject. The first, headlined "Gorelick's Wall," declared, "Where is the outrage? . . . From any reasonably objective point of view, the Gorelick memo has to count as by far the biggest news so far out of the 9/11 hearings." The editorial concluded, "It's such a big conflict of interest that the White House could hardly be blamed if it decided to cease cooperation with the 9/11 Commission pending Ms. Gorelick's resignation and her testimony under oath as a witness." The conservative talk radio and cable television airwaves generated further outrage over "the wall" and Gorelick's participation on the commission.

It was a difficult time for Jamie Gorelick. She had been a public figure, but not an elected official or a Cabinet member, and had never before been subjected to such intense and sustained public criticism. It also brought out some lunacy. Hate mail came in, and at one point a bomb threat was phoned in to her home. She became worried about her children, the FBI had to be notified, and the Montgomery County bomb squad searched her home.

Gorelick decided to take on her critics, publishing an Op-Ed in *The Washington Post* entitled "The Truth About the Wall." She argued that she did not invent the wall, and that its existence had been perpetuated by John Ashcroft's own Justice Department. But taking on the matter in a public format did not serve to diminish the controversy. Indeed, it only escalated. On April 22, the two of us received a letter drafted by

Senator Christopher Bond—John Ashcroft's former fellow senator from Missouri—and signed by ten other Republican senators, calling on Gorelick to testify in public before the commission. On April 26, a letter from Congressman Lamar Smith (R-Tex.), signed by seventy-four Republican congressmen, was sent directly to Gorelick, demanding answers to five detailed questions about her tenure as deputy attorney general. Meanwhile, the rhetoric continued to flow from Capitol Hill. Perhaps the best line came from Congressman Jack Kingston (R-Ga.), who put out a statement saying, "The commission is a reunion of political has-beens who haven't had face time since *Seinfeld* was a weekly show."

Our response was dispassionate. The two of us answered each congressional letter, including the one addressed directly to Gorelick, focusing on the facts and not on the rhetoric. We explained that Gorelick had, in fact, been interviewed by our staff in private about her time as deputy attorney general, and had been recused from participating in our inquiry into that period, as well as into any pre-9/11 issue regarding "the wall"; yet we declined to call her as a public witness, as no other deputy-level officials were called as witnesses during our 2004 public hearings. We assured people that our investigation of the wall was ongoing, and would be addressed in our final report.

It was a difficult two weeks. Unfortunately, a legitimate question—the restrictions on information sharing between intelligence and law enforcement—was being used as a tool to bludgeon Jamie Gorelick, implicate the Clinton administration, and undermine the credibility of the commission before we had even issued our report. It did, however, bring the commission together. People who had just tuned in to the Clarke and Rice hearings may have seen ten commissioners acting as partisans, but as each of us defended Gorelick, people could see ten individuals with great respect, even affection, for one another. As Jamie said at one point, she found she had nine brothers.

In addition to writing letters, we made a concerted effort to consult more actively with members of Congress. The two of us met with Speaker Hastert, Majority Leader DeLay, and the full Republican leadership team for the first time, and tried to resolve our differences. We did not win over everyone, but we did make progress in assuring Speaker Hastert and Congressman DeLay that we were not a runaway commission intent on tarring and feathering the president. DeLay emerged from the meeting declaring that he "felt better" about the direction of the commission. Jim Thompson was also important through this period because of his personal relationship with Hastert.

But on April 28, we received another surprise from the attorney general. The commission had flown to Tampa, Florida, to tour the headquarters of the United States Central Command, which was coordinating the war effort in Afghanistan. We flew back to Washington on a military aircraft. When we landed at Andrews Air Force Base outside of Washington, Jamie Gorelick received an e-mail on her BlackBerry notifying her that several more memos from her time as deputy attorney general had been declassified and posted on the Justice Department's Web site, complete with her own handwritten notes in the margins—documents that the commission had not yet received.

Gorelick became upset. The memos were likely to spark more outrage and another round of calls for her resignation. She said people were trying to destroy her reputation and bring down the commission. She even offered to resign. Heightening the tension was the fact that the next day the commission was scheduled to interview President Bush and Vice-President Cheney in the Oval Office.

INTO THE OVAL OFFICE

We could not fulfill our mandate without talking to George W. Bush. There were questions that only he could answer: about what intelligence he received on al Qaeda leading up to the attacks; how he had acted to combat terrorism before 9/11; what happened on the day of September 11, 2001; and what steps he took in the days after 9/11 to launch a war on terrorism.

In 1964, Lyndon Johnson sent a three-page letter to the Warren Commission, which was investigating the assassination of President Kennedy, even though Johnson had been a witness to the assassination; Gerald Ford testified before a congressional subcommittee as president to explain his pardon of Richard Nixon; and Ronald Reagan met twice in private with the commission investigating Iran-Contra. But there was no direct precedent for the access we were seeking. Considering the Bush administration's devotion to the principle of executive privilege, we knew they would be reluctant to set any precedent for future commissions to interview a sitting president of the United States.

On February 13, 2004, we sent separate letters to President Bush and Vice-President Dick Cheney requesting interviews. Within two days, the White House responded that the president was agreeable to meeting with the two of us—not with the full commission—and that the meeting would last only one hour.

These limitations were unacceptable. We were respectful of the president's time, but an hour would not be long enough for us to get the information we needed. We also felt strongly that all ten commissioners had to be present. Each commissioner had been appointed because he or she brought particular expertise, and represented a different point of view on a broad ideological spectrum. Our report would be enriched, and the public would have more confidence in our findings, if those perspectives and viewpoints were represented in the questioning of the president. Furthermore, the limitations could create a strain within the commission, as other commissioners might perceive it as a slight—particularly to the Democrats. Not that they could not make light of the situation—in one of our meetings on the subject, Richard Ben-Veniste said he could not understand why all ten commissioners could not attend the meeting with the president. Jamie Gorelick turned to him and said, "It's because of you, Richard."

Pressure grew on the White House to loosen its restrictions. The 9/11 families were adamant that all ten commissioners be present; indeed, they wanted the president and vice-president to testify in public, under oath—a request that we felt was excessive and out of place in the American constitutional system. Senator Kerry cited the one-hour restriction to accuse the president of "stonewalling." (President Clinton had agreed to an interview with the full commission without a time limit.) Above all, there simply was not a clear reason for the White House's restrictions on time and attendance. As was the case with the PDBs and the public testimony of Condoleezza Rice, the White House had more to lose in the public eye by restricting access than by granting it.

On March 10, the White House announced that the meeting with the president could go longer than one hour, but would still be limited to the two of us. As the commission received more and more attention through the month of March, we continued to say that we appreciated the president's willingness to meet with us, but favored a meeting attended by all ten commissioners. Then, on March 30, the White House surprised us by offering to have both President Bush and Vice-President Cheney meet with the full commission.

Much attention focused on the fact that President Bush and Vice-President Cheney had decided to meet with us together. This was not our decision, and we originally requested separate meetings. However, we did not think it necessary to push the White House. Together or apart, we could ask the president and vice-president the questions that we needed answered to write our report. It was not a perfect solution, but it was sufficient.

Another condition was that there could not be a recording or transcript of the meeting. For the purpose of accuracy, a recording and transcription was our preference, and some journalists argued that it was necessary to make a transcription or recording for a historical record; but the White House position was firm. Again, this was tied to their view of presidential privilege. We were permitted one staff member—Philip Zelikow, our staff director—to attend as a note taker, and commissioners also took notes.

There was intense media interest in the meeting. Coming, as it did, after a month of high-profile hearings and political controversy, it was both a historical event and, in the eyes of many, a meeting that would have political consequences. But our interest was in getting information for our report. If anything, we were eager to avoid the partisan flashes that had increasingly inflamed our work. Even the slightest hint or perception of public criticism of President Bush would unleash partisan warfare; so—as we had done for our interview with President Clinton—we advised commissioners to avoid making any comment on the contents of our meeting, despite the many interview requests that were coming to each commissioner. Our findings and judgments would be reserved for our report.

The other pending issue was the Jamie Gorelick controversy. The Justice Department had, in our view, acted unfairly and in bad faith in declassifying and posting more of her memos on their Web site. If the information was vital to our investigation, it should have been provided to us, not used in such a political fashion. The whole issue was dragging on too long, and distracting us from our work. The night before the meeting with the president, Tom came from Andrews Air Force Base to a hotel in downtown Washington. He called Andrew Card and got right to the point, saying: "Andy, I'm mad. And this is going to be the first thing I ask the president about tomorrow." Card did not know about the memos having been posted on the Web site, and said that the president didn't know about it either. He told Tom he would look into it.

The next morning was warm and cloudless, and commissioners met at the southwest gate to the White House a little before nine o'clock. Like any visitors to the White House, we had to pass through security checkpoints and weapons screening. We were met by lawyers from the counsel's office and led to the Roosevelt Room, adjacent to the Oval Office. The commission's meeting with the president and vice-president was scheduled for nine-thirty, and before the full meeting the two of us were scheduled to have a session alone with the president. While the rest of the commission waited in the Roosevelt Room, we were ushered into the president's private office.

The first thing President Bush told us was that he disapproved of what the attorney general had done. He agreed that it was unfair to put the Gorelick memos on the Internet when they had not been delivered to us, and said that this kind of behavior would stop. We then spoke a little bit about the progress of our investigation. The president said he was energetic and had been looking forward to the meeting. After a short conversation, the rest of the commission was brought into the Oval Office. The president began by repeating to the full commission what he had told us: he did not agree with the memos having been posted on the Justice Department's Web site, and they would be removed. At that point, we knew that the controversy over Jamie Gorelick's service on the commission was largely behind us.

The president and vice-president sat in high-backed chairs with their backs to the large Oval Office fireplace. Accompanying them were Judge Gonzales and two of his aides, who said little through the course of the meeting. The commissioners were seated on couches and chairs arranged in a semi-circle facing Bush and Cheney. The entire room was bathed in light from the brilliant spring sunshine coming in through the large windows that face south, toward the National Mall and the Jefferson Memorial.

The two of us opened the questioning, as we had a number of issues that the staff had given us that were essential for the drafting of the report. We asked about the surge in threat reporting over the spring and summer of 2001: What information was making its way up to the president? The president's answers echoed what we had heard from others: the vast majority of the threats pointed overseas, and there was a lack of specificity regarding what kinds of attacks to expect.

We also asked about the events of the day of September 11, 2001. With the president reading to schoolchildren in Sarasota, Florida, and the vice-president in Washington, it was a chaotic morning. In the space of two hours, three hijacked planes hit their intended targets, one was crashed by the heroic actions of its passengers, an order to shoot down civilian aircraft was given, the nation and the military were put on high alert, and the president addressed the nation and was evacuated onto Air Force One. We wanted a precise understanding of the sequence of events and the decision to shoot down civilian aircraft, while getting the president's and vice-president's views on whether they had been well served by the national crisis-management capability in place on September 11, 2001.

We also asked about recommendations. As the only commander-in-chief to serve during the war on terrorism, President Bush had a singular view of what intelligence was most useful to him, what it was like to make decisions to fight against a stateless enemy, and how his administration was organized to fight terrorism. We sought his opinion on what problems had been revealed by 9/11, what was working better in the months and years since, and what could be improved.

When the questioning moved to other commissioners, time became a concern. The two of us had taken about an hour to ask our questions, and we intended to hold each commissioner to ten minutes. As Richard Ben-Veniste approached ten minutes, Tom eyed his watch and cut in to suggest that Ben-Veniste wrap up so that we could move on to other commissioners. President Bush turned to Tom and said, "This is the Oval Office. I make the rules." He then turned back to Ben-Veniste and said, "Richard, go on to your next question."

Any strain was lifted. Commissioners asked every question they had, covering all the parts of the 9/11 story involving the Bush administration that had emerged throughout our work: the transition from Clinton to Bush; the decision not to retaliate for the bombing of the *Cole;* the development of a new strategy to fight al Qaeda; the immediate response to 9/11; and the invasion of Afghanistan and the onset of the war on terrorism. Bush spoke expansively on these topics, answering the vast majority of questions; Cheney spoke only when asked a question, or when the president turned to him and asked if his recollection of a particular matter was different.

The journey from our appointment as chair and vice-chair to our presence in the Oval Office had been so full of activity that we occasionally lost sight of the enormity of what was taking place. We had been given access to the most secret information in the government, and every official whom we had sought to interview we had interviewed—many in public. The journey was not without its difficulties—logistically, legally, and politically. But in few other countries in the history of the world could you find ten independent citizens sitting in the seat of power, asking the elected leader of the country questions about a national catastrophe.

The meeting went on so long that it put Lee in an impossible situation. As president of the Woodrow Wilson International Center for Scholars, he often hosted visiting dignitaries. That day, the recently elected prime minister of Canada, Paul Martin, was scheduled to make a major foreign policy address at the Wilson Center—the only such address he would be making in his first official visit to Washington. Lee had personally offered the invitation to the prime minister a year in advance, and was scheduled to introduce him in front of a crowd of one thousand people shortly after noon.

The meeting with President Bush had originally been scheduled for April 28. When it was moved to the twenty-ninth, Lee explained that he had to leave by noon. To accommodate him, the White House rescheduled the meeting from 10:00 to 9:30, thinking it would last only two hours. But since the president imposed no time limit, the meeting extended well past noon, and Lee had to excuse himself to go meet and introduce the prime minister. He had told President Bush and Vice-President Cheney of his commitment in advance, and had asked all of his questions by the time he left. Both Bush and Cheney were gracious when he got up to leave along with Bob Kerrey, who was attending a meeting on Capitol Hill. But Lee's departure became yet another source of controversy.

The meeting concluded at 12:40. President Bush walked out into the Rose Garden to make a statement and take a few questions. He said, "I'm glad I took the time. This is an important commission, and it's important that they asked the questions they asked so that they can help make recommendations necessary to protect our homeland." The commission put out a statement saying that we "found the President and the Vice President forthcoming and candid. The information they provided will be of great assistance to the Commission as it completes its final report."

That afternoon, the White House press secretary, Scott McClellan, was asked about the demands for Jamie Gorelick to testify in public before the commission, and about the documents posted on the Justice Department Web site. He responded, "We were not involved in it. I think the president was disappointed about that." He went on to say that this disappointment had been "communicated to the Justice Department." With that statement, the bull's-eye on Jamie Gorelick and the commission faded significantly. A diminishing chorus of outrage continued in some conservative media, but the effort to discredit Gorelick and the commission lost momentum. "The wall" could now be discussed and evaluated as a question of policy, not as a point of personal integrity or political expediency.

The commission had been exposed to the clamor and convulsions of partisan Washington. But instead of being pulled apart, we had come together: in defense of a colleague under fire, and through extraordinary meetings with presidents of two parties. For a few days after our interview with President Bush and Vice-President Cheney, we took some shots, as some expressed outrage over Lee and Kerrey's early departure; but even some of these voices raised in protest began to tire. The ten commissioners, despite our partisan and ideological differences, had stuck together.

Meanwhile, we had assembled a vast amount of information about 9/11, and presented much of it in public. We had learned about short-comings and structural flaws in our intelligence community, and the decisions made—and not made—by the most senior officials in two administrations. Yet while we had seen passions inflamed by the subject of 9/11, we were now going to turn to the place where the emotions were more intense, and the wounds fresher.

10

THE TRAUMA OF NEW YORK

That day we lost 2,752 people at the World Trade Center; 343 were firefighters. But we also saved 25,000 people. And that's what people should remember because firefighters and rescuers went in and they knew it was dangerous, but they went in to save people. And they saved many.

— Joseph Pfeiffer, deputy assistant chief, Fire Department of New York, as quoted in 9/11 Commission staff statement on emergency preparedness and response

THERE WERE TWO RESPONSES to 9/11 in the United States: the horror experienced by the nation, and the acute trauma experienced by greater New York. If people around the country will never forget televised images of the day, people in and around New York will never forget their direct experience of billowing black clouds drifting over Lower Manhattan and across the river to Brooklyn, the acrid residue in the air, the posted pictures and descriptions of those missing in the World Trade Center, the months of funerals, and the unfathomable absence of the most prominent presence from Manhattan's skyline.

Our task in New York City went beyond merely connecting to the emotions of the day. The statute creating the 9/11 Commission mandated that we provide "a full and complete accounting" of the "preparedness for, and immediate response to, the attacks." Any account of the "immediate response" had to start in northern Virginia and Lower Manhattan, where firefighters, police, and rescue workers—not presidents, spies, or soldiers—were on the front lines. Thus we faced the complex and emotionally fraught task of telling the story of what had happened over the course of one hundred terrible minutes in New York on the morning of September 11, 2001, from the moment, at 8:46 a.m., when American Airlines Flight 11 crashed into World Trade Center 1, to the moment, at 10:26 a.m., when World Trade Center 1 became the second of the towers to collapse.

Enveloping this already challenging political and legal picture was emotional protectiveness: the events of the day and the countless acts of individual heroism had become mythologized in the New York City area and within response agencies such as the New York Police Department (NYPD) and Fire Department (FDNY). Many people were extremely sensitive to any hint of criticism that might accompany a comprehensive assessment of the emergency response on the morning of September 11. Conversely, the families of many victims who perished in the towers were demanding answers to a litany of questions.

The response at the Pentagon was simpler for us to understand and evaluate. The attack took place at a federal location and was contained to a specific portion of the Pentagon. While the circumstances were extraordinary, and the fire was exceptionally difficult to fight because of the jet fuel feeding the flames, it was possible to fight the fire and complete a rescue operation. Our staff was aided by a thorough after-action report prepared by Arlington County, which covered all aspects of the response: from the military response efforts to the performance of local firefighters. Indeed, most of the work done by our staff conformed to what was in the original after-action report.

The New York response was more complicated by multiple orders of magnitude. It involved a fire, police, and rescue operation in two buildings that soared more than one hundred stories tall, with thousands of victims and thousands more who were rescued. The heart of the two fires occurred well above the seventieth floor of both towers, and the fires were impossible to put out. The event had the added horror of the unforeseen collapse of the two towers within less than two hours of the first plane's impact, destruction that enveloped all of Lower Manhattan in the emergency response and evacuation, and led to the collapse of several more buildings. It was the most challenging municipal emergency response in the history of the United States.

Our New York investigation was run out of the commission office at

26 Federal Plaza in Lower Manhattan, where we had ten employees working under John Farmer, the former attorney general of New Jersey. Farmer's work was complicated when he also took on leadership of our investigation into the response of the FAA, NORAD, and the nation's leadership. But we had excellent staff members in New York, who knew the terrain. Their work was spearheaded by Sam Caspersen, our New York counsel, and George Delgrosso, a former homicide detective with the NYPD.

Our staff team in New York had several areas of inquiry. First, they looked at the safety and security features of the World Trade Center. Second, they examined whether the evacuation of the buildings on September 11 matched existing plans, and how those evacuations had proceeded. Third, they looked at how the response was managed: who was in charge at the site, how the different response agencies worked individually and together, and how communications were maintained in such a chaotic environment.

As with the federal government, in New York City we dealt with multiple agencies, including some that did not always get along. Our requests encompassed the FDNY and NYPD, which were notoriously competitive; the Office of Emergency Management (OEM), which was set up in the years preceding 9/11 to respond to crisis situations; the office of then Mayor Giuliani, which saw the 9/11 response as the cornerstone of the mayor's legacy; the office of current Mayor Michael Bloomberg, which was in the process of preparing guidelines for responding to future attacks; and the Port Authority of New York and New Jersey, the bistate agency that administered the World Trade Center and maintained its own police force on-site.

The commission made extensive document requests. We asked for FDNY, NYPD, and Port Authority pre-9/11 emergency plans; FDNY, NYPD, and Port Authority dispatch records and operational logs from September 11, 2001; tapes and transcripts of 911 calls; and radio communication tapes and transcripts for all FDNY, NYPD, and Port Authority communications on 9/11. Both the FDNY and NYPD had done their own internal after-action reports on 9/11, and had commissioned McKinsey & Company—a private management consulting firm—to prepare those reports. So we requested transcripts of all interviews with police and firefighters conducted during those studies.

With our document requests, the commission entered into New York City's already strained legal situation. In the aftermath of 9/11, the city's legal department confronted lawsuits from multiple family groups seeking compensation, and from other parties seeking information about 9/11. For instance, *The New York Times* had filed a request under the Freedom of Information Act asking for the same 911 tapes and police and firefighter interview transcripts as the commission. The city had declined those requests, citing privacy assurances it had given to the families of people recorded on the 911 tapes, and to interviewees from the NYPD and FDNY. They did not want to turn the materials over to us because they feared it would set a precedent for their pending litigation.

We sought a compromise with the city's lawyers. In late September, our general counsel, Dan Marcus, sent a letter to the city pledging to give the same assurances to the victims' families and the FDNY and NYPD interviewees as the city, saying, "We acknowledge the privacy interests of individual victims, their families, and first responders, and will not disclose their names or personal information . . . in our public report without further consultation and agreement with the city or the individual in question." Marcus also agreed that all commission documents obtained from New York City would be turned over to the National Archives with the understanding that "personal, deliberative and other sensitive documents" would not be disclosed for an extended period of time, up to fifty years. Marcus also pointed out that Freedom of Information requests were not applicable to the commission; thus the city would not be setting a precedent for *The New York Times* lawsuit by turning over documents to us.

Still, the city resisted. By November 2003, four months had elapsed since we issued our document requests. John Farmer made a presentation on the issue at a November 19 commission meeting at Drew University, and commissioners unanimously decided to issue a subpoena. That evening we took vans back to the commission's hotel, and our staff drafted a statement announcing the subpoena during the drive back to New York.

The FAA and the Department of Defense responded to our subpoenas by agreeing to turn over documents, but New York City responded with defiance. Edward Skyler, Mayor Bloomberg's press secretary, put out a statement saying, "It will take a court order to make the city violate the privacy of those we lost. It is also puzzling why the commission is trying to distract the public by focusing on the city's response as opposed to the question we all want answered—how this savage terrorist attack was planned and executed without any warning." The claim that we were going to violate anyone's privacy was either ill informed or disingenuous, as we had offered in writing to give the same privacy assurances as the city had; the notion that we were issuing a subpoena to distract people was absurd, as we were specifically mandated to give a full account of the emergency response in New York.

A court battle over whether or not the subpoena could be enforced was in nobody's interest. We did not want extended court proceedings to keep us from getting the materials in time to prepare our report. The city had little incentive to take on the Justice Department (which agreed to represent the commission) in a fight it was likely to lose. John Farmer sat down with the city's legal department to reach a settlement. While Farmer and the city's lawyers were negotiating, the Justice Department was ready to take the matter to court. The difficult issue for the city would be backtracking from the tough statements made in the wake of the subpoena, but on the eve of a December 4 court date, a settlement was reached.

Under the agreement, the commission received copies of all the tapes and transcripts we requested, with personal information (such as names) redacted. The commission was granted access to all of the unredacted materials seven days a week at city offices, which were only a few blocks from the commission's New York office. Furthermore, we could take notes on the unredacted materials, and agreed to use personal statements or information from the tapes and transcripts only after getting consent from the individuals in question. That way, we would see everything we needed to see, and the city could claim that it was still protecting the information and the privacy of those named in the tapes and transcripts. The city also agreed to respond to all other outstanding commission document requests by December 31, 2003.

With the legal issues behind us, we could get on with our investigation. Our staff conducted hundreds of interviews with police, firefighters, and emergency personnel who responded on September 11, 2001. Unlike the majority of our interviews in Washington, nearly all of our New York interviewees had lost friends and loved ones on 9/11, and were being asked to recall painful and horrifying personal experiences. Many of these interviews included officials from the National Institute of Standards and Technology (NIST), which was conducting its own inquiry into why the towers had collapsed—an inquiry that included the emergency response. NIST, which had a budget for its inquiry that was twice the size of the entire commission budget, at first resisted cooperation. But over time we developed an effective and efficient working relationship that aided both of our inquiries.

In addition to emergency response personnel, our staff interviewed representatives of several of the private-sector tenants of the World Trade Center; civilians who had survived the attacks; the leadership of the FDNY, NYPD, and Port Authority; the top aides to Mayor Giuliani and

Mayor Bloomberg; and the two mayors themselves. Ultimately, our New York staff conducted more than two hundred interviews, in addition to reviewing hundreds of hours of audiotape and reading tens of thousands of pages of documents.

Divergent views emerged. Most people were proud and certain that the city's response had been coordinated, courageous, and effective in saving the lives of the vast majority of people inside the World Trade Center on the morning of September 11. But some firefighters and families of firefighters who died on September 11 expressed anger and frustration that poor coordination and communication among emergency response agencies had led to an unnecessarily high loss of life, particularly among firefighters.

There was some wariness with regard to the commission. As with federal agencies, individuals may have been asking themselves what could be gained by cooperating with a commission that could challenge the laudatory view of New York's 9/11 response. But our New York staff reached out to third parties and established connections. For instance, Dennis Smith, a former firefighter who has written extensively about the FDNY and the 9/11 response, was helpful in providing information from interviews that he had done, and pointing our staff toward people who he thought were important to interview.

In preparation for our hearing in New York City, our staff pulled the huge amount of information it had collected about the morning of September 11 into a coherent timeline. Each staff member was assigned to a different story—police, fire, Port Authority, and civilian. But it was difficult to convey in words alone what happened on the day of the attack. Thus Farmer and his team brought on a video producer, Allison Prince, to help them prepare the staff statement on "emergency preparedness and response."

Working with Prince, our staff videotaped several interviews with civilians and emergency responders who were in the World Trade Center on 9/11. They also obtained access to footage filmed by Jules and Gédéon Naudet, French brothers who were filming a documentary about a rookie firefighter when they found themselves in the middle of the 9/11 rescue operation. The resulting Naudet brothers' documentary, entitled *9/11,* originally aired on CBS in March 2002, but our staff received the raw, uncut footage filmed on September 11. It is remarkable material: it begins with the only existing image of the first plane crashing into World Trade Center 1, and continues as the Naudet brothers accompany firefighters to a command post in the lobby of World Trade Center 2.

The result was an extraordinary multimedia presentation. Moving minute by minute from 8:46 a.m., when American Airlines Flight 11 hit the North Tower, to 10:26 a.m., when the North Tower collapsed, the staff statement intersperses footage of the day and videotapes of interviews with civilian and emergency-response survivors. The most fascinating segments take place when two fire chiefs who were in the Naudet brothers' footage are filmed watching the tape of themselves on 9/11, and commenting on what was taking place. The staff statement thus provides a narrated description of what took place; conveys in images the stunning and horrifying velocity of the events of September 11; and underscores the powerful emotions of the day by featuring those who survived.

Originally, our staff wanted a full two hours to present the statement, but we were pressed for time, and thus trimmed the presentation down to one hour and fifteen minutes. We had other last-minute complaints about the hearing agenda. Mayor Bloomberg, who was not invited to testify because he had appeared at our first hearing, asked to testify; to accommodate him, we added a fifteen-minute slot toward the end of our second day. Then, leaders from the city's powerful police and firefighter unions publicly complained that they had not been invited. In a further complication, Bloomberg announced his new citywide plan to deal with future large-scale disasters the Friday before our hearing.

The increasing number of voices demanding to be heard was indicative of the varying political and bureaucratic agendas awaiting us in New York City. More than that, though, we were providing the most prominent forum to date at which New Yorkers would directly revisit September 11, 2001. Our goal was to present facts dispassionately, but we discovered that it was impossible to address 9/11 in New York without rousing passions.

HEROISM AND HARD QUESTIONS

THE MONDAY NIGHT BEFORE THE HEARING, we had a working dinner at the New School University. Bob Kerrey was generous enough to offer as a hearing venue the university's Tishman Auditorium, located on West Twelfth Street in Lower Manhattan. In addition to the large space, Kerrey's staff provided us with invaluable logistical help in preparing for a packed crowd of hundreds, and procuring the audiovisual equipment our staff needed to make its opening presentation.

During dinner, John Farmer briefed commissioners on what to expect at the hearing. Emotions would be very raw. For Mayor Giuliani, his leadership team, and many of the police and firefighters who would be in attendance, the 9/11 emergency response was defined by the heroism of the individuals involved, and shadowed by the loss of many close friends and associates: any criticism, even of technical capabilities such as radio communications, could be perceived as an assignment of blame and an attempt to tarnish the 9/11 legacy. On the other hand, many of the 9/11 families and some of the firefighters who would be at the hearing believed that the true story of 9/11 had not been told: they were arguing that radios had not worked, command and control issues had hindered the response, and evacuation orders had never reached firefighters in the North Tower.

Both sides would be looking to the commission to support their point of view. The reality, of course, lay somewhere in between: a response could be both heroic and effective, while also revealing problems that needed correcting. Our goal was to point out those deficiencies so that they could be corrected, while also recounting the awesome achievement of the rescuers. But we anticipated tension. This was the first, and probably the only, gathering at which city officials would testify in front of an audience split between fervent supporters and emotional critics.

Tuesday morning was overcast. A local graphic designer had unfurled a huge banner on a building near the New School with the words NEVER FORGET and a list of all who had died on 9/11. Dennis Smith had an Op-Ed in *The New York Times* that presaged some of the points we would make, saying, "I have reluctantly come to the belief that the crisis at the World Trade Center was worsened by a lack of cooperation between the Fire and Police Departments." Many of the local network affiliates in New York were preparing to carry our two days of hearings live. Outside and inside the auditorium, there was the sense of a family preparing to undergo a long-festering painful discussion.

The opening staff statement began with the warning "We wish to advise the public that the details we will be presenting may be painful for you to see and hear. Please consider whether you wish to continue viewing." The first section gave an overview of the World Trade Center complex: how the 1993 bombing revealed serious shortcomings in preparedness, as it took nearly ten hours to completely evacuate the buildings, and how the Port Authority provided $100 million in upgrades after 1993, including better lighting and glow-in-the-dark signs in stairwells, a redesigned command board to monitor all elevators, and a new "repeater system" that used an antenna on top of World Trade Center 5 to enable firefighters' radios to work better in the high-rise towers.

One emotional issue was the towers' rooftops. Some families and 911 operators received terrifying phone calls from people trapped in the buildings who were trying to go up to the roof. The Port Authority kept these doors locked for a variety of reasons, and the NYPD would not have been able to make helicopter evacuations at that height. But in advance of 9/11, "civilians were not informed that rooftop evacuations were not part of the Port Authority's evacuation plan. They were not informed that access to the roof required a key. The Port Authority acknowledges that it had no protocol for rescuing people trapped above a fire in the towers."

The statement provided an overview of the four emergency response agencies on 9/11: the FDNY, NYPD, Port Authority Police Department (PAPD), and Office of Emergency Management. The OEM had been created in part to address the rivalry between the FDNY and NYPD, a rivalry that impeded the agencies' ability to work under a unified command. The statement read "This rivalry has been acknowledged by every witness we have asked about it. . . . By September 11 neither had demonstrated the readiness to respond to an 'Incident Commander' if that commander was an official outside of their Department. The Mayor's Office of Emergency Management had not overcome this problem."

The statement divided the one hundred minutes of the emergency response of the morning of 9/11 into four phases. The first phase started at 8:46 a.m. Video screens in the auditorium went on and the audience let out a gasp as the Naudet brothers' footage showed American Airlines Flight 11 slamming into the North Tower. The excerpt that followed spoke to the detailed nature of the staff's work:

> A jet fuel fireball erupted upon impact, and shot down at least one bank of elevators. The fireball exploded onto numerous lower floors, including the 77th, 50th, 22nd, West Street lobby level, and the B4 level, four stories below ground. The burning jet fuel immediately created thick, black smoke which enveloped the upper floors and roof of the North Tower. The roof of the South Tower was also engulfed in smoke because of prevailing light winds from the north.

Tears were in the eyes of many in the audience, some of whom had lost a loved one at the moment of the plane's impact.

The evacuation that followed the plane's impact was recalled in video clips of civilian survivors telling their stories. A point of controversy was the repeated notice to occupants of the South Tower to stay at their desks. The staff statement read "The protocol against evacuation, of telling people to stay where they were, was one of the lessons learned from the 1993 bombing. . . . Many of the injuries after the 1993 bombing occurred during the evacuation." Thus many people in the South Tower, which had not yet been hit, were advised by the Port Authority and 911 operators to stay at their desks. This decision was revised shortly before 9:00 a.m. by firefighters on the scene, but the instruction to evacuate did not reach many people in the South Tower because of poor communications, and the public address system continued to advise people to stay put: "As a result of the announcement, many civilians in the South Tower remained on their floors. Others reversed their evacuation and went back up."

The review of the FDNY response drew heavily on interviews with two FDNY fire chiefs, Joseph Pfeiffer and Peter Hayden, who were filmed on the morning of September 11 by the Naudet brothers, and filmed by our staff watching and commenting on the footage of their actions on the morning of 9/11. The opening footage shows Pfeiffer in the lobby of the North Tower setting up an FDNY command. Watching footage of himself, Pfeiffer explains, "What you see is the beginning of an Incident Command System, where things are placed in order, and command is taken immediately." The presentation then plays the footage of Pfeiffer on 9/11, giving orders to his men: "We have a number of floors on fire; it looks like a plane was aiming towards the building. Transmit a third alarm. We will have a staging area."

The first two key decisions made by the fire chiefs shortly before 9:00 a.m. were to evacuate the full World Trade Center complex— including the South Tower, which had not yet been hit; and that the fire in the North Tower would not be fought, so that the FDNY would perform "strictly a rescue mission." Chief Pfeiffer also determined that the elevators were not working; he explained, "Without elevators, it meant that the firefighters carrying a hundred pounds of equipment would have to climb some ninety floors just to get to where we could start a rescue operation for people trapped above the damaged area." The footage shows badly burned civilians walking into the lobby as Pfeiffer sets up his command post; and the two chiefs talking to each other and on radios as firefighters start the long climb up the stairwells. As one group of firefighters moves upstairs, Chief Pfeiffer comments, "What you see here is—this footage—is actually my brother going upstairs. As so many other firefighters, this was the last time we saw them."

The statement reviewed the initial activities of the other emergency response agencies. The NYPD cleared New York City's major thoroughfares so that emergency vehicles could get to the World Trade Center, and closed "bridges, subways, PATH trains, and tunnels into Manhattan." The PAPD commanding officer ordered an evacuation of civilians from the World Trade Center, but this order was not widely received: "The order was issued, however, over a radio channel which could be heard only by officers on the Port Authority WTC command channel. There is no evidence that this order was communicated to officers in other Port Authority Police commands or to members of other responding agencies." Meanwhile, the OEM was setting up an emergency operation center at its headquarters in building 7 of the World Trade Center complex.

"Phase one," the first seventeen minutes of the hundred minutes, is summarized: "Well over one thousand first responders had been deployed, evacuations had begun, and the critical decision that the fire could not be fought had been made." The description of phase two begins with the all-too-familiar footage of United Airlines Flight 175 banking in the air and plowing into the South Tower at 9:03 a.m. An excerpt of an interview with a civilian survivor who was on the eighty-first floor in the South Tower, Stanley Praimnath, provides a harrowing vantage point:

> I am looking to the direction of the Statue of Liberty, and I am looking at an airplane coming, eye level, eye contact, toward me—giant gray airplane. I am still seeing the letter *U* on its tail, and the plane is bearing down on me. I dropped the phone and I screamed and dove under my desk. It was the most ear-shattering sound ever. The plane just crashed into the building. The bottom wing sliced right through the office and it stuck in my office door twenty feet from where I am huddled under my desk.

Interviews with survivors go on to detail the evacuation that ensued and how, in the words of the staff statement, "civilians became first responders" as they helped their disabled colleagues down darkened and smoke-filled stairwells. Nine-one-one operators were often not helpful. One survivor told a story of being put on hold twice when he called from the forty-fourth floor to report that someone was injured and needed a stretcher. The operators continued to advise callers to remain where they were even after an evacuation order had been given for both towers.

The statement described further radio communications problems. The "repeater system" installed after the 1993 bombings to facilitate radio communication had not been activated because a chief thought that it was broken. The statement read "The system was working, however, and was used subsequently by firefighters in the South Tower." This led in part to a situation where

> the Chiefs in the North Tower were forced to make decisions based on little or no information. . . . Unfortunately, no FDNY chiefs outside the South Tower realized that the repeater channel was functioning and being used by units in the South Tower. Chiefs in the

North Tower lobby and outside were unable to reach the South
Tower lobby command post initially.

The confusion was described by Chief Hayden: "People watching on TV
certainly had more knowledge of what was happening a hundred floors
above us than we did in the lobby." The statement summarized phase two:
"First responders assisted thousands of civilians in evacuating the towers,
even as incident commanders from responding agencies lacked knowledge of what other agencies and, in some cases, their own responders
were doing."

The video then showed the South Tower collapsing at 9:59 a.m., starting "phase three." Chiefs Pfeiffer and Hayden, who were in the lobby of
the North Tower, were not aware of the South Tower's collapse. They
knew something had happened, as the air had gone black with smoke and
debris, but they did not know what. As Chief Hayden says, "We were completely unaware that the South Tower had collapsed. I don't ever think it
was in our realm of thought." Still, they issued an order for all firefighters
to leave the North Tower. Pfeiffer recalled: "I got on the radio and I said,
'Command to all units in Tower One. Evacuate the building.' "

This was a sensitive issue. Many family members of deceased firefighters were angry that the evacuation order did not reach all the firefighters
in the North Tower. The commission statement explained the various reasons for this: the high-rise environment blocked some radio transmissions; one of the radio channels became overwhelmed after the South
Tower collapsed; some firefighters in the North Tower were using a radio
channel meant for use in the South Tower; some firefighters did not have
radios with them because they had reported at the World Trade Center to
help out even though they were off duty; others did hear the evacuation
order but stayed where they were to assist civilians. Meanwhile, "the Police
Department had a better understanding of the situation." NYPD heli-
copters were able to radio units on the ground that the South Tower had
collapsed, and at 10:08 they reported that the North Tower was likely to
collapse. Yet without a unified incident command and effective radio
communications, "there was no ready way to relay this information to the
fire chiefs in the North Tower."

The statement concluded with the collapse of the North Tower, and a
summary of the human cost of the day:

> The FDNY Chief of Department and the Port Authority Police
> Department Superintendent and many of their senior staff were
> killed. The Fire Department of New York suffered the largest loss of
> life of any emergency response agency in U.S. history. The Port

Authority Police Department suffered the largest loss of life of any American police force in history. The New York Police Department suffered the second largest loss of life of any police force in U.S. history, exceeded only by the loss of Port Authority police on the same day. The nation suffered the largest loss of civilian life on its soil as a result of a domestic terrorist attack in its history.

The last word went to Chief Pfeiffer, who had witnessed footage of his brother ascending the stairs of the North Tower to save lives—only to lose his own:

> What happened inside [the North Tower] now happened outside. This beautiful sunny day now turned completely black. We were unable to see the hand in front of our face. And there was an eerie sound of silence. That day we lost 2,752 people at the World Trade Center; 343 were firefighters. But we also saved 25,000 people. And that's what people should remember because firefighters and rescuers went in and they knew it was dangerous, but they went in to save people. And they saved many.

As our staff got up to leave the witness table, the screen went black. Many in the audience were in tears; others sat in somber silence.

Our first panel of witnesses, the former director of the Port Authority, and former chief of the Port Authority Police, were questioned about the command and control, communications, and 911 problems. But the sharpest exchanges came during our second panel, with former Police Commissioner Bernard Kerik, former Fire Commissioner Thomas Von Essen, and former OEM Director Richard Sheirer. Each man gave an impassioned defense of his agency, and the preparedness of New York City under the leadership of Mayor Giuliani, whom they each continued to work for as partners in the private consulting firm Giuliani & Associates.

Slade Gorton asked about the problems with the 911 system, pointing out that it was the only number most civilians in the towers could call, "yet 911 didn't know what to tell them to do." Gorton then asked who had been in charge of "what was going on and communicating that with 911 people so that 911 people could provide up-to-date and valuable information to people who called in." Both Kerik and Von Essen could not identify anyone performing that function, beyond the supervisors from their respective agencies—the NYPD 911 supervisor and the FDNY dispatcher. Sheirer pointed out that the volume of calls overwhelmed the system.

Gorton responded, "I am even more troubled now than when I began this series of questions." At that point, as often happened over the course of the two days, the audience broke into loud applause.

Several other commissioners asked questions about the problems in communications and the lack of coordination between the FDNY and the NYPD, but Kerik and Von Essen downplayed the communications failures, and largely denied that the rivalry between the agencies had had an effect on 9/11. The most pointed questioning came from John Lehman. Lehman was particularly interested in the issue of radio communications because he had dealt with similar challenges as secretary of the navy, when he had to help integrate the command and control operations of the U.S. Marine Corps and the U.S. Navy, coordinate communications with the other military services, and manage competitive rivalries among the military services. Lehman began his questioning:

> Gentlemen, I'm aware of the history and of the traditions and of the politics that have shaped the public service agencies in this city over many, many years, and I agree with you all that we certainly have the finest police and fire departments, Port Authority Police, anywhere in the world. And as you said, Mr. Sheirer, they're the proudest. But pride runeth [*sic*] before the fall. And I think the command and control communications of this city's public service is a scandal.

Loud applause broke out, and Tom had to call for order. Lehman continued: "It's not worthy of the Boy Scouts, let alone this great city. . . . It's a scandal that there's nobody that has clear line authority and accountability for a crisis of the magnitude that we're going to have to deal with in the years ahead." He then asked a series of questions about potential fixes in the management of the emergency response services and the procurement of equipment.

Lehman was addressing two core problems illustrated in the staff statement: the failure to establish an interagency unified command at the World Trade Center, and the lack of cross-communications among the FDNY, NYPD, and Port Authority radios. The witnesses, however, responded as if they and their agencies were being personally attacked. Kerik declared that the police commissioner had clear authority over his department, prompting Lehman to cut in and say, "You missed my point. I'm not criticizing any of the agencies. I think they do have very fine line authority and accountability. I'm talking about amongst the agencies." But it was Von Essen who bristled the most. He said, "I couldn't disagree with you more," and gave a strong defense of the FDNY and his authority as commissioner. Then he said, his voice filled with emotion, "You make it sound like everything was wrong about September 11th or the way we function. I think it's outrageous that you make a statement like that." Applause broke out again, this time from supporters of Von Essen and Kerik, prompting boos from some of the families of victims.

The hearing continued like this, with any critique of the city's emergency response planning treated as an attack on the city's entire response on 9/11, and the audience erupting in applause in support either of tough questioning or of tough answers. After the hearing, Kerik and Von Esssen stoked the controversy. Kerik said of Lehman, "It's almost pitiful that this is what he had to stoop to in order to get his name in lights." Von Essen called the comments "outrageous," and added, "If I had the opportunity, I probably would have choked him, because that's what he deserved."

That evening, the commission had dinner at John Lehman's apartment on the Upper East Side of Manhattan. We reviewed the events of the day, and enjoyed a view over Central Park, with little idea of how much controversy we had generated. The purpose of the hearing was to get people in New York and around the country to focus on the facts of 9/11 and the issues that needed correcting; instead, the media coverage, particularly on television and in tabloid newspapers, was dominated by precisely the kind of emotional response that we were seeking to move past.

The next morning, we awoke to a huge one-word headline on the front page of the *New York Post:* "INSULT!" Over a picture of a firefighter kneeling at Ground Zero on 9/11, the *Post* editorialized: "Memo to 9/11 Commission: This Man Is a New York Hero. Not a Boy Scout." The front-page editorial continued: "The bravery and selflessness of [firefighters] have been lost on the mean-spirited commission of outsiders." The *Daily News* piled on with a column that read, "[Lehman] should get down on his hands and knees and beg forgiveness of the public servants he insulted if he wants to preserve a scrap of his reputation. If he wants to be able to walk the streets of New York. If he wants the 9/11 Commission ever to be taken seriously."

There was a soft rain falling as the audience filed into the Tishman Auditorium. Given the omnipresence of New York's tabloid newspapers at newsstands and vending machines, everyone had seen the negative coverage, even if they hadn't read it. Our first witness was Mayor Giuliani, the man who had become the symbol of the city's lionization after 9/11, and also the foremost target of some of the 9/11 families' ire. Looking out at the audience, we saw families holding signs that read FICTION and LIES, just as we saw many others who were there to support the mayor. Both sides knew many who had perished on 9/11: some were overwhelmed with anger at the loss of their loved ones; others were overwhelmed with anger at the notion that any fault could be found with the 9/11 response.

We began with a staff statement that assessed the private- and public-sector crisis management on 9/11. For the private-sector tenants in the World Trade Center, the statement found that the evacuation efforts below the points of impact had been largely successful, particularly for a company such as Morgan Stanley, which practiced its evacuation plans repeatedly. For communications to employees during the crisis, and continuity of operations for companies in the days following 9/11, performance was mixed: few companies in the World Trade Center had anticipated or prepared for such a large-scale calamity. The statement suggested that the commission consider recommending national standards for private-sector preparedness for terrorist attacks and large-scale disasters.

The statement also provided an overview of the Pentagon emergency response, concluding, "The response to the 9/11 terrorist attack on the Pentagon was mainly a success for three reasons: first, strong professional relationships and trust established among emergency responders; second, the adoption of an Incident Command System; and third, the pursuit of a regional approach to response." The fire, police, and federal response agencies had performed multiple drills together, and operated efficiently under the unified command of the Arlington County Fire Department. However, while there were broad lessons to draw from the effective Pentagon response, the statement pointed out "Several factors facilitated the response to this incident, and distinguish it from the far more difficult task in New York."

Regarding the New York response, the statement praised the judgment of the FDNY commanders at the scene and the actions of the emergency response personnel. Drawing on the information presented the previous day, it pointed out that "effective decision-making in New York was hampered by limited command and control and internal communications." This was due in part not only to the enormity and unforeseen nature of the incident, but also to problems in communications equipment, to the fact that 911 operators and the FDNY's dispatchers were not integrated into the response, and to the fact that so many firefighters from all parts of the city had rushed to the scene. The statement ended by looking toward recommendations: "The task looking forward is to enable first responders to respond in a coordinated manner with the best situational awareness possible."

Mayor Giuliani sat at the witness table by himself, with his wife seated behind him. He opened by addressing the question of blame, saying, "Our enemy is not each other. Catastrophic emergencies and attacks have acts of great heroism attached to them. They have acts of ingenious creativity attached to them, and they have mistakes that happen." He continued: "So our anger should clearly be directed, and the blame should clearly be directed, at one source and one source alone, the terrorists who killed our loved ones." Many in the audience applauded.

Giuliani then gave a meticulous account of what he had done on September 11. He described hearing of the attack during a breakfast meeting, traveling downtown past a hospital amassing doctors and stretchers, hearing rumors of other attacks throughout the country, seeing people jumping from the top floors of the towers, setting up a command post, being covered by debris while on the phone with Vice-President Cheney when the South Tower collapsed, traveling up to the police academy to set up a new command center, and holding press conferences to reassure the public. He stressed that the evacuation of the towers had been generally orderly because firefighters and police calmed people, and he highlighted the importance of that achievement: "Rather than giving us a story of men—uniformed men fleeing while civilians were left behind, which would have been devastating to the morale of this country—they gave us an example of very, very brave men and women in uniform, who stand their ground to protect civilians."

Giuliani spoke calmly and articulately, and with emotion. He offered a vivid picture of the morning of September 11, and an impassioned yet reasoned defense of the heroism and quality of the response. Coming, as it did, in the wake of such an emotional first day—and such an outbreak of controversy—his testimony had a mesmerizing effect.

Each commissioner opened his or her questioning with lavish praise. The normally hard-hitting Richard Ben-Veniste started by saying, "Your leadership on that day and in the days following gave the rest of the nation, and indeed the world, an unvarnished view of the indomitable spirit and the humanity of this great city, and for that I salute you." Jim Thompson thanked Giuliani for "setting an example for us all"; Tim Roemer acknowledged his "brave and courageous leadership"; John Lehman said, "There was no question to the world that the captain was on the bridge"; and Tom said, "New York City on that terrible day in a sense was blessed because it had you as a leader."

There was a reluctance to ask Giuliani the kinds of probing questions that had been asked of Kerik and Von Essen the day before. Giuliani did acknowledge that the police and firefighters "should have radios that are interoperable," and that the 911 system had been insufficient, saying, "Should it have been larger, should it have been anticipated? Yes, but it wasn't." But there were no questions posed to him about communications problems between police and firefighters in the towers, or why New York City had built its emergency response command center in World Trade Center 7 after the complex had been the target of the 1993 terrorist attack.

As the questioning period went on, some families in the audience became audibly upset. Near the end of the session, Slade Gorton detailed the successes of the rescue operation, asking, "Would it be accurate to say that your people saved, at this cost of 403 of their own lives, 99.5 percent or more of the people they could conceivably have saved?" In his answer, Giuliani said that firefighters who had received an evacuation order chose to stay and save lives. At this point, the audience erupted into shouting. Some yelled, "Talk about the radios!" or "Put one of us on the panel!" or "My son was murdered because of your incompetence!" Others started trying to shout them down; many people were standing.

Emotions boiled over. Tom tried to restore order. Giuliani said, calmly, "It's understandable." Gorton said to Giuliani, "That record is absolutely extraordinary," which fed the commotion further. The hearing was able to proceed, but there was an uneasy feeling. When Lee concluded the questioning by saying, "It's important that I simply express to you my appreciation," there was another outburst. Both Giuliani supporters and detractors were shouting at each other. The police had to remove two protesters. Some demanded that we ask "real questions." Another raised voice said, "My brother was one of the firemen that was killed and I think the mayor did a great job, so sit down and shut up!"

Our next panel included Dennis Smith; Edward Plaugher, the chief of the Arlington County Fire Department; and Jerome Hauer, a former head of New York's OEM. Chief Plaugher argued in favor of a unified incident command, and reaffirmed his statement to our staff that "the lack of a unified command dramatically impacted the loss of first responder lives on 9/11 in New York City." Dennis Smith echoed that point, saying of the police and firefighters, "These men did not get together that day and they should have been together. And I think, had they been together, that the communications system would have been a little different. And God knows, you know, maybe not as many people would have died."

Mayor Bloomberg followed, deriding a homeland security funding system in which Wyoming gets $38.31 per person in federal funds, while New York gets only $5.47, and calling this "pork-barrel politics at its worst." He also defended his new incident command plan, while criticizing "armchair quarterbacks" who criticize the FDNY and NYPD. Secretary of Homeland Security Tom Ridge followed Bloomberg and echoed the mayor's view that homeland security funding should go to the most likely and vulnerable targets for terrorism, saying, "Population density, critical infrastructure and threat should drive most of the money." Ridge also endorsed a voluntary standard for private-sector preparedness and emergency preparedness, two welcome developments.

When the hearing concluded, amid some final yelling from the audience, we were exhausted. It had been a trying and emotional two days. We issued a statement summarizing what we had learned and expressing our "profound admiration for the first responders of 9/11. . . . Their acts of heroism exceed our ability to praise." We also outlined the problems caused by a lack of evacuation preparedness, by 911 operators and FDNY dispatchers who "were not adequately integrated into emergency response," and by the "limited command and control and internal communications" of the response agencies. Meanwhile, Mayor Giuliani answered press questions in the light rain outside the hearing, saying that he was upset by John Lehman's comment and thought he should apologize.

We had succeeded and we had failed. We had wanted to examine the facts of the 9/11 emergency response in New York City. Of course, given the size and unpredictability of the attack, there were going to be shortcomings in New York's preparedness and capabilities: nobody could have responded flawlessly. We had wanted to identify those shortcomings so that they could be corrected, while also honoring the amazing heroism and achievement of the emergency responders. If anything, their success in safely evacuating so many people was achieved in spite of some of the flaws in communications and command and control.

Yet it proved difficult, if not impossible, to raise hard questions about 9/11 in New York without it being perceived as criticism of the individual police and firefighters or of Mayor Giuliani. If our witnesses in Washington had been disinclined to acknowledge pre-9/11 failings because of the potential political fallout, our New York witnesses had seemed to regard it as acknowledgment of culpability for people dying—many of whom they were acquainted with—or as a threat to the phenomenal legacy that had emerged out of the ashes of the World Trade Center. To those assembled in our hearing audience, it seemed that there was no middle ground: either the response to 9/11 was heroic and as good as it could have been, or it was a terrible failure, and individuals had to be blamed.

The questioning of Mayor Giuliani was a low point in terms of the commission's questioning of witnesses at our public hearings. We did not ask tough questions, nor did we get all of the information we needed to put on the public record. We were affected by the controversy over John Lehman's comments, and by the excellent quality of the mayor's presentation. That is not to say we should have attacked him to satisfy his critics in the audience; but we did not question him in the same manner that we questioned other witnesses in getting information on the public record.

Still, the New York hearings were good for the commission and good for New York. We learned not only a great deal about the challenges of responding to large-scale attacks, but also a lesson about the emotions of 9/11 that could not be learned elsewhere. We revisited the day of 9/11, and saw the continued emotional fallout of that day on the lives of individuals and the psyche of the city. For New York it was, perhaps, a first step: a confrontation with the trauma of September 11, and a much-needed dialogue on how to prepare for the next attack. Even the bitter recriminations that erupted in our hearing room may have been a necessary catharsis.

Our goal was now to get the story right in our report, and determine what recommendations might help New York City and others in preparing for and responding to future catastrophes. Our remaining two days of hearings would confront 9/11 from two very different perspectives: that of the terrorist plotters, and that of our nation's leaders.

11

THE ENEMY

What our staff statement found is there is no credible evidence that
we can discover, after a long investigation, that Iraq and Saddam
Hussein in any way were part of the attack on the United States.

— Tom Kean, speaking at a press conference,
June 18, 2004

WHO IS THE ENEMY? Many Americans asked this question after September 11, 2001, and it was one of the most frequently asked questions within the commission. There was a wide range of answers.

There were nineteen hijackers working under the leadership of Usama Bin Ladin. More broadly, there was al Qaeda, a terrorist network headed by Bin Ladin and based in Afghanistan, with operatives and affiliates around the globe. Beyond that, there were more terrorist groups and extremists with the will and capability to do the United States harm— "terrorist groups with global reach," as President Bush put it in his address to a joint session of Congress on September 20, 2001.

Our goal was to understand this enemy. We split our staff team working on al Qaeda into two separate investigations to deal with two separate questions: staff team 1 focused on the history and organization of al Qaeda; staff team 1A focused on unraveling the 9/11 plot. Our al Qaeda inquiry was unique. Whereas our other staff teams were looking at the actions of individuals and agencies within the United States government, our al Qaeda investigation had to gather bits and pieces of information about a foreign terrorist organization. The subject was diffuse and clandestine, having operated in some of the most shadowy and least understood corners of the globe.

The leader of our staff team looking at the history and organization of al Qaeda was Doug MacEachin, whom Philip Zelikow recruited from his retirement home in France. MacEachin was assisted by an able and experienced group of analysts and investigators. An amiable and garrulous man, by the time of his retirement in 1994, MacEachin had risen to become the CIA's deputy director for intelligence. In the ensuing years, he focused on intelligence and history, writing studies on Japan at the end of World War II, the Soviet invasion of Afghanistan, and the crisis in Poland in 1980–1981. His analytical ability, historian's eye, and widespread contacts in the intelligence community served us well.

MacEachin's team had to deal with an organization that had developed in stages. Al Qaeda's history reached back to the jihad against the Soviet Union in Afghanistan in the 1980s; extended over a several-year period from 1991 to 1996, when Usama Bin Ladin lived and built up his organization in Sudan; spanned 1996–2000, when Bin Ladin and his lieutenants returned to Afghanistan, constructed their base of operations, issued fatwas against the United States, and carried out attacks; and continued through the post-2000 ascendancy of al Qaeda as a global actor and target of the United States.

Different members of the staff took on these different time periods, and probed information from across the intelligence community. One challenge was distinguishing what we knew and thought at a particular time from what we knew now. For instance, when Bin Ladin was in Sudan, much of our thinking at the time was that he was mainly a financier of extremism setting up a business empire. We now knew that he was establishing a foundation for international jihad during his years in Sudan, and had participated in attacks against U.S. forces in Yemen in 1992, and in Mogadishu, Somalia, in 1993.

There were many key questions to answer. What were al Qaeda's roots? What attacks had it participated in against the United States? Was al Qaeda motivated by religious ideology, or by opposition to American policies in the Islamic world? Had al Qaeda received support from states such as Saudi Arabia, Pakistan, Iran, or Iraq? How was al Qaeda funded? How did al Qaeda recruit operatives? Did al Qaeda seek or have weapons of mass destruction? What was Usama Bin Ladin's role? Some of these questions, we knew, would be of acute public interest: for instance, those regarding the allegations of Saudi support for 9/11, or the question of Iraq's relationship with al Qaeda.

In assembling materials and drafting a history of al Qaeda, our staff found themselves asking why nobody within the government had done so before. Given the day-to-day demands of government, nobody had stepped back, read everything there was to read, and tried to figure out precisely what the United States was facing with this new kind of enemy. For instance, given the fact that we knew al Qaeda had performed suicide operations by driving trucks into targets, given our knowledge that al Qaeda had considered hijacking airplanes, and given Usama Bin Ladin's growing ambition to attack the United States in a spectacular fashion, it was a logical step to consider planes flying into targets. But government sometimes lacks incentive for people to put their feet up on the desk, draw on diverse sources, and imagine what might come.

There was substantial overlap between MacEachin's team and the staff team headed by Dietrich Snell, which was focusing on the 9/11 plot. In studying al Qaeda generally, you learn a lot about the context for and participants in the 9/11 plot. In studying the 9/11 plot, you learn a lot about al Qaeda and how it recruits, plans, finances, and carries out operations. Thus the two teams often found themselves cooperating in interviews with different intelligence officers, and reviewing similar documents.

There was also a wealth of expertise spread throughout the rest of our staff. For instance, as Snell and his investigators pieced together the story of 9/11, they could turn to our border security team to learn about how the nineteen hijackers permeated American borders; to the aviation security team to learn about how they got on the airplanes; and to the terrorist financing team to learn how al Qaeda finances its operations, and paid for the 9/11 attacks. The same was also true in reverse—as Snell's team put together a detailed record of the conspiracy, other teams often turned to them for information.

There were various other sources of information to help unravel the plot. The FBI's PENTTBOM investigation was a crucial source, as was the government's investigation into Zacarias Moussaoui. After our extended negotiations over access to detainees, information began flowing to the commission from interrogations with top 9/11 plotters such as Khalid Sheikh Mohammed and Ramzi Binalshibh, and our staff was able to submit hundreds of questions for these detainees through the CIA.

As with al Qaeda's history, there were many key questions about the 9/11 conspiracy. How had the 9/11 plot been conceived? What had motivated the nineteen hijackers to join al Qaeda and sacrifice their lives to kill innocent civilians? Had the hijackers received any support from foreign governments? What was Zacarias Moussaoui doing in flight school? Had Mohammed Atta met with an Iraqi intelligence officer in Prague in

April 2001, as had often been alleged? Had the hijackers received help from sleeper cells within the United States?

The answers to each of these questions had far-reaching ramifications. For instance, a finding of foreign support for the 9/11 plot, or of a support structure within the United States, would have raised pressing concerns. The investigation into the latter question focused on two of the hijackers, Nawaf al Hazmi and Khalid al Midhar, who lived openly under their own names in Southern California. Unlike the other hijackers, Hazmi and Midhar had spent little time in the West before coming to Los Angeles on January 15, 2000. They spoke little if any English, and were not met by another plotter upon their arrival in the United States. Yet, after a two-week stay in Los Angeles, they managed to get settled in an apartment in San Diego.

There has been much public speculation about how these two newcomers got a foothold in a totally alien environment. Press accounts after 9/11 detailed how they attended the King Fahd Mosque in Los Angeles, whose imam, Fahad al Thumairy—a diplomat at the local Saudi Arabian consulate—was known for his extremist views. Further accounts detailed how Omar al Bayoumi, a Saudi citizen who was living in San Diego, helped the two hijackers find an apartment in San Diego after meeting them on February 1, 2000, at a restaurant in Los Angeles; and how the hijackers lived with an FBI informant while in San Diego.

Different theories have been advanced. Did Fahad al Thumairy aid the future hijackers at the behest of Saudi intelligence? Did Omar al Bayoumi belong to some kind of al Qaeda sleeper cell in Southern California that provided a support network for Hazmi and Midhar upon their arrival? Does the example of Hazmi and Midhar's arrival in Southern California illustrate how al Qaeda has sleeper cells within the United States, or how it receives support from elements inside the Saudi government?

This was an area where the FBI had done a lot of work—gathering evidence and interviewing scores of people—so for our staff it was a matter of sorting through the FBI materials, talking to the FBI agents involved, and identifying witnesses of particular interest. The starting point was telling the story as completely as possible: What, precisely, did Hazmi and Midhar do after arriving in the United States?

In the process of telling that story, our staff pursued the question of who provided the two men with support. In California, the staff interviewed a number of people who had encountered Hazmi and Midhar. In October, Snell and Zelikow interviewed Omar al Bayoumi in Riyadh, Saudi Arabia, with an FBI agent and Saudi official present. Bayoumi recalled having met the two future hijackers in a restaurant after over-hearing them speaking in a Gulf Arab accent. He said he encouraged them to move to San Diego, and helped them in various ways—by locating an apartment for them, co-signing their lease, and lending them his cell phone. But he denied knowing of their affiliation with al Qaeda or their nefarious plans. He told our staff that he condemned the 9/11 attacks, and was distressed by the speculation about his involvement.

In February, our staff returned to Riyadh to interview a number of people, including Fahad al Thumairy, the former Saudi diplomat and imam in Los Angeles. Thumairy said he did not recognize photographs of Hazmi or Midhar—a denial we found suspect because of Hazmi and Midhar's confirmed associations with people at the King Fahd Mosque, but that was not implausible, as many young men passed through the mosque. Our staff also tracked many leads regarding Thumairy's actions in Los Angeles, and the possible actions of Hazmi and Midhar in their two weeks in Los Angeles, but did not find anything to conclusively suggest a firm connection between Thumairy and the two hijackers.

These cases—which were not the only suspicious examples of help provided to Hazmi and Midhar—indicate how our staff faced the same problems confronting law enforcement and intelligence. There were plenty of dots to connect about Hazmi and Midhar's actions in Southern California, but connecting them with certitude was not easy—even with the benefit of hindsight. To some, the fact that Thumairy had been in contact with two hijackers and that Bayoumi had aided them was enough to infer that they must have been aware of the plot, or even part of the conspiracy. But, lacking corroborating evidence, one cannot be certain. Particularly in a culture that places such a value on hospitality, where does one distinguish between hospitable acts on behalf of two recent émigrés, and participation in the 9/11 conspiracy?

California was just one aspect of the story, and one instance where our staff traveled to pursue leads. In Saudi Arabia, they also talked to Saudi law enforcement, the families of several of the so-called muscle hijackers who were recruited for the 9/11 operation in 2001, and even Saudis who had been identified by Khalid Sheikh Mohammed as runners-up to be included in the 9/11 operation.

In February 2004, several staff members traveled to Berlin, where they met with German prosecutors. Three of the 9/11 pilots, including ring-leader Mohammed Atta and co-conspirator Ramzi Binalshibh, had emerged from an al Qaeda cell in Hamburg. On September 12, 2001, the German government had launched the largest criminal investigation in its history of the Hamburg cell—an investigation that led to the prosecution of several alleged accomplices of Atta and the other pilots, Marwan al Shehhi and Ziad al Jarrah. The German government had gathered the most extensive evidence available on how the Hamburg cell was recruited and integrated into the 9/11 plot.

The Germans provided detailed profiles of the conspirators—their activities in Germany and their backgrounds. Each was well educated and came from a relatively well-off family. Each became increasingly anti-American and anti-Semitic during his time in Hamburg, and fell in with extremist elements that led him to al Qaeda in 1998 or 1999. By 2000, all were pursuing the 9/11 plot. The issue of motivation was one that the 9/11 Commission grappled with: What motivated these men to commit such a heinous act? For instance, Jarrah posed a vexing example. He came from a successful family. There was a period when he enjoyed living in Germany—drinking alcohol, going out to nightclubs, and wearing Western clothes. Even through his growing extremism and his association with al Qaeda, he remained close to a girlfriend, visiting her on a one-way plane ticket to Germany just a month before the attacks took place. By all accounts, he was a man who appeared to have a lot to live for.

So what was it about Jarrah, or about al Qaeda, that had enabled him to take his own life while killing so many whom he did not know? We had many debates within the commission about whether the hijackers were motivated more by extreme religious beliefs or by a hatred of American policies, such as our support for Israel or governments like Saudi Arabia. The motivations of these individual men—who are no longer alive—are perhaps unknowable.

Working with the FBI, our staff also pieced together the final months, weeks, and days before 9/11: the hijackers' movement in places such as Las Vegas; Boston; Coral Springs, Florida; and Paterson, New Jersey. The evidence included cell phone records, flight itineraries, hotel and apartment receipts, and even footage of the hijackers, all of which allowed us to reconstruct in some detail the hijackers' paths leading up to the moment when they boarded planes on the morning of September 11, 2001.

One lighthearted moment occurred during the intensity of hearing preparation when Snell was briefing the commission. He displayed two sets of still photos from video of Atta cashing a check at a teller's window in Virginia Beach. Before showing the images, Snell addressed the fact that there had been a lot of questions raised about the support network for the hijackers in the United States. He said that the staff might have found a shocking development that provided the answer. Then he showed one of the photos, which depicted Atta in line at the bank. Directly behind him was a man with a crew cut, a man who looked just like Lee. Needless to say, Lee took a good deal of ribbing for this from his fellow commissioners.

PRESENTING THE PLOT

OUR JUNE 16 HEARING WAS a unique opportunity to educate the commission and the American public about al Qaeda. We planned a morning panel to present an overview of al Qaeda, and an afternoon panel to focus on the 9/11 plot. The following day, June 17, we would close the circle on our public hearings by holding a hearing on the realization of the plot: the deadly voyages of the hijacked planes, the confused responses of the FAA and NORAD, and the actions of the nation's leadership.

For our witnesses on al Qaeda, we invited working-level officials: FBI special agents who had investigated al Qaeda, CIA analysts, and a federal prosecutor who had tried several terrorism cases. Instead of hearing from senior officials who were the recipients of analytical assessments, we wanted to hear directly from the people who prepared those assessments. By having experts, rather than the leadership of the FBI and CIA, we also might keep the focus where we wanted it: on the history of al Qaeda and 9/11, rather than on bureaucratic or political concerns.

The FBI and CIA resisted. As a general rule, both are reluctant to let mid-level officials testify in public—in part because senior officials are supposed to serve as the public face of the agencies, and also because they have concerns about spotlighting people who do their work in the shadows. Both the FBI and CIA insisted that they be able to send senior officials to testify alongside the witnesses we had invited. This was not our choice—as in the case of interview "minders," we were concerned that a witness might be less forthright with a superior sitting next to him or her at the witness table. But in order to get the witnesses we wanted, we had to accede.

The CIA also insisted that their witnesses testify under pseudonyms. Although the witnesses were analysts and not clandestine operatives, the CIA was worried that they and their families would be put in danger if their names were revealed in a hearing that would be widely viewed around the world. Thus on the hearing agenda we had to list CIA witnesses simply as "CIA official." In questioning the witnesses, we had to refer to one witness under the assumed name "Ted Davis"; another, more ambiguously, we had to call "Dr. K."

We had one witness fall through at the last minute. To get the best possible view of the Hamburg cell, we had invited an official in the German Public Prosecutor's Office whom we had interviewed in Berlin. It is unusual to have a foreign official testify at U.S. hearings, and we tried to negotiate a number of conditions—for instance, that he would not be sworn under oath, and that his testimony would be used only by the commission (not in other criminal proceedings). But shortly before our hearing, the German government decided against allowing his testimony.

Our hearing venue was the auditorium of the National Transportation Safety Board (NTSB) on L'Enfant Plaza, just east of the National Mall in Washington, D.C. The NTSB has a state-of-the-art facility with sophisticated audiovisual capability, useful in enabling our staff statements to be accompanied by multimedia presentations. Outside, the weather had already turned hot and humid—a sign that we were moving closer to our summer deadline—and the cool interior of the NTSB was a welcome escape from the Washington weather. The auditorium, which held several hundred people in sloped, theater-style seating, was nearly filled when we began our hearing with a staff statement entitled "Overview of the Enemy."

The statement gave a history of al Qaeda. It began by describing how Bin Ladin was a "significant player" among the Arabs who traveled to Afghanistan to resist Soviet occupation in the 1980s, and how, "following the defeat of the Soviets in the late 1980s, Bin Ladin formed an organization called 'The Foundation' or al Qaeda. Al Qaeda was intended to serve as a foundation upon which to build a global Islamic army." The distinction between *foundation* and *base*—which *al Qaeda* is often translated to—is important. Whereas *base* implies some geographic focus, *foundation* more accurately reflects al Qaeda's role as a source of ideas, inspiration, funding, and operatives for a more diffuse global jihad.

The staff statement detailed Bin Ladin's years in Sudan from mid-1991 to 1996, where he decided to focus his efforts against the United States rather than Israel or Arab regimes because he thought the United States was "the head of the snake." He formed an organization that included several "committees": a foreign purchases committee buying weaponry and equipment; a political committee issuing fatwas; a finance committee raising funds and allocating resources; a security committee in charge of intelligence; an information committee responsible for media

and propaganda; and a military committee with subcommittees for training and the administration of training camps. An advisory council of Bin
Ladin and his top associates ran the organization.

While Bin Ladin built his organization, he also aided attacks on U.S.
troops in Yemen in December 1992, and Somalia in October 1993. In
addition to sponsorship from Sudan and contacts with Iran, the staff statement also addressed Bin Ladin's connections with Iraq:

> Bin Ladin also explored possible cooperation with Iraq during his
> time in Sudan, despite his opposition to Hussein's secular regime.
> Bin Ladin had in fact at one time sponsored anti-Saddam Islamists
> in Iraqi Kurdistan. The Sudanese, to protect their own ties with
> Iraq, reportedly persuaded Bin Ladin to cease this support and
> arranged for contacts between Iraq and al Qaeda. A senior Iraqi
> intelligence officer reportedly made three visits to Sudan, finally
> meeting Bin Ladin in 1994. Bin Ladin is said to have requested
> space to establish training camps, as well as assistance in procuring
> weapons, but Iraq apparently never responded. There have been
> reports that contacts between Iraq and al Qaeda also occurred after
> Bin Ladin had returned to Afghanistan, but they do not appear to
> have resulted in a collaborative relationship. Two senior Bin Ladin
> associates have adamantly denied that any ties existed between
> al Qaeda and Iraq. We have no credible evidence that Iraq and
> al Qaeda cooperated on attacks against the United States.

This was the only paragraph of the statement that dealt with Iraq, but it
would receive by far the most attention of anything said at the hearing. At
the time, the United States was less than two weeks away from handing
over sovereignty to an interim Iraqi government amid an increasingly
bloody insurgency. Criticism of President Bush's Iraq policy—and his
decision to go to war—were a daily occurrence in the presidential campaign.

The statement detailed Bin Ladin's return to Afghanistan in 1996 and
merger with the terrorist group Egyptian Islamic Jihad, estimating that "as
many as 20,000" people trained in al Qaeda camps in Afghanistan
between May 1996 and 9/11. On the issue of financing, the statement
addressed Saudi Arabian support, finding that "there is no convincing evidence that any government financially supported al Qaeda before 9/11."
However, "al Qaeda found fertile fundraising ground in the Kingdom,
where extreme religious views are common and charitable giving is essential to the culture and, until recently, subject to very limited oversight."

Al Qaeda's annual budget was estimated at $30 million, with the money going to "terrorist operations, maintaining terrorist training camps, paying salaries to jihadists, contributing to the Taliban, funding fighters in Afghanistan, and sporadically contributing to related terrorist organizations. The largest expense was payments to the Taliban, which totaled an estimated $10–$20 million per year."

The statement concluded with an overview of al Qaeda today. It found that "the organization is far more decentralized," as its leadership has dispersed from Afghanistan, and individual cells have taken on far more authority. The gravest threat comes from potentially catastrophic attacks: "Al Qaeda remains extremely interested in conducting chemical, biological, radiological, or nuclear attacks." Through the 1990s, al Qaeda attempted to buy uranium for a nuclear weapon, and had an "ambitious biological weapons program." The statement ended: "Regardless of the tactic, al Qaeda is actively striving to attack the United States and inflict mass casualties."

In testimony, we heard from Deborah Doran, an FBI special agent who had pursued al Qaeda worldwide. John Pistole, the FBI's executive assistant director for counterintelligence and counterterrorism, accompanied her. From the CIA, we heard from "Dr. K," who was accompanied by "Ted Davis," a senior CIA official. Our third witness was Patrick Fitzgerald, a U.S. Attorney from the Northern District of Illinois who had prosecuted al Qaeda cases, and who was in the news for his investigation into the leak of the name of covert CIA officer Valerie Plame, whose husband, Ambassador Joseph Wilson, had disputed the Bush administration's claim that Iraq sought to purchase uranium in Niger.

Fitzgerald's leak investigation would last more than another year and result in the indictment of Vice-President Cheney's chief of staff, I. Lewis "Scooter" Libby, for perjury and obstruction of justice. For our purposes, though, Fitzgerald was a unique and trusted source of expertise on al Qaeda.

The starkest warning in testimony came from Dr. K, who spoke about the current and future threat from al Qaeda. He cautioned against complacency, pointing out that al Qaeda waits patiently for years before an attack, and that the extremist ideology that led to violent attacks against the United States went well beyond Bin Ladin and al Qaeda: "Even after Bin Ladin and al Qaeda are defeated, the global jihadist movement will continue to exist. That movement may again produce another Bin Ladin or al Qaeda as long as there are individuals who are willing to use violence to redress perceived wrongs."

With the United States faced with an enemy that is, in President Clinton's words, "entrepreneurial," with a global network, ideological adherents that may number in the millions, and a willingness to die for their beliefs, Jim Thompson asked the question that went to the heart of several of our prospective foreign policy recommendations: "How in the world do we ever expect to win this war?" Dr. K answered by dividing the challenge into two categories: first, the segment of the Islamic world who "believe they have an individual duty to the Muslim community to pursue violent jihad," which must be opposed with force; and second, "those folks who have not made that transformation"—that is, the broader Islamic world that can be reached and hopefully persuaded "to find alternative means of channeling their sentiments through constructive, nonviolent means."

It was an important distinction: the core enemy of al Qaeda and its supporters, and the broader ideological challenge from jihadist extremism that could be opposed nonviolently. Patrick Fitzgerald echoed that answer, saying that "there's no silver bullet" for winning the war. Fitzgerald divided his approach into the "short term and the long term"—with a short-term period of several years in which we pursue the immediate enemy. Addressing the broader challenge, Fitzgerald said, "The long-term solution is to win their hearts and minds. But we're not going to win the hearts and minds of the people who are already sworn to kill us. . . . What we have to do is win the hearts and minds of people who could be allies and work with us. We want to win the hearts and minds of people before they go over to al Qaeda." This analysis would prove important to us when we considered recommendations about how to reach out to the Islamic world.

Addressing a question regarding the immediate enemy—those sworn to kill us—Tom asked the panel about whether or not there were al Qaeda cells within the United States. John Pistole answered, "Absolutely," saying that such cells needed to be understood as a combination of possible operatives and "facilitators . . . fund-raisers, recruiters." Deborah Doran concurred, and said that since 9/11, further attacks against the United States had been averted, citing specifically "a few aviation attacks against both the East and West Coasts." Lee pursued the question of al Qaeda within the United States, asking about "not the intent [but] the capabilities of al Qaeda today to attack." Everybody we talked to, in public and in private, agreed that al Qaeda wanted to attack the United States. Few had given us a clear sense of al Qaeda's capability to do so. John Pistole replied, "The short answer is we know very little about their capability to attack. We know much more about their intent and know very little about their capability."

The panel was followed by our second staff statement of the day, this one titled "Outline of the 9/11 Plot." The statement began with the plot's origins: Khalid Sheikh Mohammed (KSM) conceptualized the plan and decided that al Qaeda had a willingness to carry it out after the 1998 embassy bombings. The statement read: "In early 1999, Bin Ladin summoned KSM to Kandahar to tell him that his proposal to use aircraft as weapons now had al Qaeda's full support." The statement painted a picture of KSM as the mastermind and chief operative, and Bin Ladin as providing leadership and institutional support. The statement then profiled the "Hamburg cell" and how its members came to join al Qaeda: Atta and the others meeting extremists in Hamburg, traveling to Afghanistan and meeting with Bin Ladin's deputy, Mohammed Atef, "who directed them to return to Germany and enroll in flight training." Bin Ladin met with Atef to discuss the targets for the attack: "the World Trade Center, which represented the U.S. economy; the Pentagon, a symbol of the U.S. military; and the U.S. Capitol, the perceived source of U.S. policy in support of Israel."

The story of Hazmi and Midhar's time in Southern California was told at some length. The statement refers to an interrogation with KSM in which, "recognizing that neither Hazmi nor Midhar spoke English or was familiar with Western culture, KSM instructed these operatives to seek help from the local Muslim community." The statement details how this occurred: Hazmi and Midhar's meeting with Bayoumi, and their move to a unit in Bayoumi's apartment complex in San Diego. Regarding Bayoumi's intentions, the statement concluded, "While it is clear that Bayoumi helped them settle in San Diego, we have not uncovered evidence that he did so knowing that they were terrorists, or that he believed in violent extremism."

On the controversial issue of the alleged meeting in Prague between Mohammed Atta and an Iraqi intelligence officer on April 9, 2001 (an allegation made by a single Czech source), the statement concluded, "Based on the evidence available—including investigation by Czech and U.S. authorities plus detainee reporting—we do not believe that such a meeting occurred." The staff then showed the photo of Atta at a bank in Virginia on April 4, 2001 (though not the photo in which the man behind Atta looks like Lee), and reviewed the records of phone calls made from Atta's cell phone on April 6, 9, 10, and 11, and evidence that he was in Coral Springs, Florida, on April 11. They found no evidence that Atta left the United States or entered the Czech Republic in that period, and Czech officials did not have evidence that anyone who looked like Atta crossed their border in that time frame, or was by the Iraqi embassy on April 8.

The hijackers who helped commandeer the planes but did not fly them were then profiled: "The muscle hijackers were between 20 and 28 years of age and had differing backgrounds. Many were unemployed and lacked higher education, while a few had begun university studies. Although some were known to attend prayer services regularly, others reportedly even consumed alcohol and abused drugs" despite Islamic proscription of such behavior. The statement described how they were recruited out of Saudi Arabia and traveled to Afghanistan in 1999 and 2000, where they were "picked by Bin Ladin himself for what would become the 9/11 operation." Beginning in late April 2001 they began arriving in the United States.

After describing last-minute preparations such as casing airplanes and airports and buying tickets for September 11, the statement provided an overview of the financing: "We estimate that the 9/11 attacks cost somewhere between $400,000 and $500,000 to execute. The operatives spent over $270,000 in the United States, and the costs associated with Zacarias Moussaoui . . . were at least $50,000." Expenses included money for flight school, living accommodations, incidentals, and travel and came to the hijackers via wire transfers or overseas bank accounts, or in the form of cash and traveler's checks that the hijackers brought with them. The hijackers used bank accounts opened under their own names. The origin of the money could not be specified, but there was no evidence that it came from people within the United States. The statement pointed out that $400,000 to $500,000 would not be hard to find within al Qaeda's $30 million annual budget.

The statement revealed that detainees were reporting that the attacks were planned to be even bigger, including "CIA and FBI headquarters, unidentified nuclear power plants, and the tallest buildings in California and Washington State." KSM was going to fly the final plane, land it, and make "a speech denouncing U.S. policies in the Middle East." There were also plans to hijack planes in Southeast Asia—either to blow them up in midair or to crash them into targets in South Korea, Singapore, or Japan—but it was decided that this would be too complex. Several other aspects of the plot changed. Hazmi and Midhar were originally meant to be pilots, but were unable to understand flight school. Additional Saudi "muscle hijackers" either backed out, could not acquire travel documents, or were "removed from the operation by al Qaeda leadership," thus denying al Qaeda the twenty-five or twenty-six hijackers originally planned for the four planes.

Among the four pilots, "friction developed between Atta and Jarrah," and Jarrah even considered dropping out of the plot, at one point flying to visit his girlfriend in Germany on a one-way ticket. In July 2001, the staff concluded, "KSM wanted money sent to Moussaoui to prepare him as a potential substitute pilot in the event Jarrah dropped out." Drawing on interrogation reports, the staff reported that Binalshibh described Moussaoui as part of the 9/11 operation, while KSM described him as part of a "second wave of attacks on the West Coast after September 11." The arrest of Moussaoui on August 16 did not cause the plot any difficulty. Jarrah returned to the United States on August 5 and, as he subsequently demonstrated, resolved any doubts that he may have had about participating in the operation.

The staff reported that "the date of the attacks apparently was not chosen much more than three weeks before September 11." In the final days, Taliban leader Mullah Omar and other al Qaeda leaders opposed going forward with the attacks. The statement concluded with a portrayal of Bin Ladin's strong leadership role within the organization:

> Bin Ladin also thought that an attack against the United States would reap al Qaeda a recruiting and fundraising bonanza. In his thinking, the more al Qaeda did, the more support it would gain. Although he faced opposition from many of his most senior advisers . . . Bin Ladin effectively overruled their objections, and the attacks went forward.

In the panel that followed, we heard from three more FBI special agents who had worked on the 9/11 investigation, and two CIA officials. Much of the questioning focused on unsettled questions. Fred Fielding asked why Mohammed Atta began September 11 by flying from Portland, Maine, to Boston to connect to American Airlines Flight 11. Supervisory Special Agent James Fitzgerald said that the FBI had looked closely at that question and concluded: "[T]he best indication we have of why he did what he did is from that detainee reporting indicating that he probably did so to minimize the amount of people who would be arriving at Flight 11 at one time." Apparently, he did not want five Arab men all arriving at Boston's Logan Airport at once for Flight 11.

Tim Roemer focused on Hazmi and Midhar's connections in California. He asked about a man named Mohdar Abdullah; on September 12, a car registered to Hazmi was recovered at Washington's Dulles Airport with Abdullah's address in it. Special Agent Jacqueline Maguire explained that Abdullah was interviewed repeatedly and investigated by the FBI. As with other individuals pursued by the FBI and by our staff in Southern California, Hazmi and Midhar's connection to the hijackers could be proven, but the intent to aid in attacks on the United States could not be demonstrated. Roemer then brought up a more damning report that had recently come to light: Mohdar Abdullah had been jailed in an immigration facility, and a fellow inmate had written the Department of Homeland Security to report that he had bragged to other inmates that he had had foreknowledge of 9/11. Maguire said that the FBI had been unable to corroborate those accounts with other inmates, adding that the agent assigned to the case had "had to take it from where it was coming, from an individual who's awaiting deportation, who's been incarcerated."

Looking forward, Jamie Gorelick asked what the FBI was doing to prevent further occurrences of local mosques unwittingly providing assistance to people who meant to do the United States harm—or, as she put it, "Don't be unwitting helpers to bad actors." John Pistole answered that the FBI's fifty-six field offices had all been directed to engage their local Arab American and Muslim American leaders for that purpose, "to help us identify people who may be in their community who are out of place, who are recent émigrés who may be here—anything that would be suspicious to them to help us do our job."

Lee returned to the question of motivation. He asked the agents, "You've looked [at] and examined the lives of these people as closely as anybody. It's an extraordinary thing to be able to motivate someone to kill themselves. . . . [W]hat have you found out about why these men did what they did? What motivated them to do it?" Within the commission, the debate had focused on whether the hijackers were motivated by their view of religion or by their hatred of American policies.

The panelists' answers pointed to a mixture of both. Fitzgerald said, "I believe they feel a sense of outrage against the United States. They identify with the Palestinian problem, they identify with people who oppose repressive regimes, and I believe they tend to focus their anger on the United States." Maguire pointed out differences among the nineteen— some had higher education; some had been involved with drugs and alcohol. Supervisory Special Agent Adam Drucker said many of them did not know they would be used in suicide operations when they first went to Afghanistan; they could have been drawn there for different ideological reasons, and then gone through indoctrination: "I think the backgrounds differ. Some were deeply religious, some were drug users, and just seemed to be lost in life a little bit. I think when you get to Afghanistan, however, you know, there is a strong religious-type background in those camps."

The issue of the hijackers' motivations is baffling to most Americans, who could not imagine taking their own lives for such a cause. Lee remained uncertain, saying, "We hang onto life with everything we have, but these men give it up. They give it up at the most promising age—19 to 28. Why did they do it?" John Pistole answered in a way that suggested the ongoing challenge:

> [I]t's for the reasons suggested and also for the idea of reward and for the idea of doing something beyond what you may achieve in your normal, everyday life—you achieve some type of status that you would not have. Now, we have some information to that effect but, obviously, given what's going on in Iraq every day, where we have—virtually every day—additional suicide bombers. There are people with that similar background and perspective.

We had learned much about an amorphous enemy—a core of operatives, and a broader ideological movement. We had learned about their most successful operation, and talked about the challenges that lay ahead in combating this enemy. Chief among those challenges was forging a strategy that could stop people from doing what nineteen men had done on 9/11, and what people were doing nearly every day in Iraq—killing themselves to kill others. But in the days ahead, the focus with regard to the commission would not be on that question of motivation; it would be on the question of Iraq.

WHAT KIND OF RELATIONSHIP?

WE DID NOT EXPECT, NOR were we prepared for, the controversy that erupted over our staff's characterization of the relationship between Iraq and al Qaeda. Certainly we knew it was an issue that would be closely watched—as Lee said to the staff, this was one of those situations where "we really need to nail this one." But it was merely a topic of two paragraphs in a staff statement presented at a hearing that provided significant new details about al Qaeda and the 9/11 plot—including public revelations of what was being said in detainee interrogations, and a new portrayal of Zacarias Moussaoui's role in the conspiracy. In fact, we were more focused on the attention that might be paid to our account of the relationship between Saudi Arabia and its citizens and al Qaeda than we were on a possible Iraq-9/11 connection.

Nonetheless, most of the immediate news coverage of our hearing focused on the fact that we had found no connection between Saddam Hussein and the 9/11 attacks. This was understandable, in large part, because the Bush administration had repeatedly tied the Iraq war to September 11—insinuating in some people's minds a link between Iraq and the attacks themselves, as at different junctures a majority of Americans believed that Saddam Hussein was involved in 9/11.

The following morning, June 17, *The New York Times* had a four-column headline declaring "Panel Finds No Qaeda-Iraq Tie." As we were holding a hearing on the response to 9/11 by the FAA, NORAD, and the nation's leaders, President Bush was asked about the Iraq–al Qaeda issue after a meeting of his Cabinet. He said, "The reason I keep insisting that there was a relationship between Iraq and Saddam and al Qaeda is because there was a relationship between Iraq and al Qaeda." Citing some of the information from our staff statement about meetings between Bin Ladin and Iraqi intelligence in Sudan in the mid-1990s, Bush elaborated, "This administration never said that the 9/11 attacks were orchestrated between Saddam and al Qaeda. We did say there were numerous contacts between Saddam Hussein and al Qaeda. For example, Iraqi intelligence officers met with Bin Ladin, the head of al Qaeda, in the Sudan. There's numerous contacts between the two."

While the administration was unhappy with the coverage of the "Iraq–al Qaeda" story, their ire was directed at the media, not the commission. In an interview the same day, Vice-President Cheney focused on *The New York Times* headline: "What *The New York Times* did today was outrageous." He added, "The press wants to run out and say there's a fundamental split here now between what the president said and what the commission said. . . . The press is, with all due respect—and there are exceptions—oftentimes lazy, oftentimes simply reports what somebody else in the press said without doing their homework."

The issue was quickly swept up into the presidential campaign. The decision to go to war in Iraq was the most important of President Bush's first term; Democrats were beginning to make the credibility of that decision a key issue in their campaign. Speaking to reporters, John Kerry said, "The president owes the American people a fundamental explanation about why he rushed to war for a purpose that it now turns out is not supported by the facts. . . . That is the finding of this commission."

That afternoon, we held a press conference after our hearing, and were asked by a reporter from Talk Radio News Service how we felt now that "President Bush has disputed your finding that there was no collaborative relationship between Saddam Hussein and al Qaeda."

Tom answered:

> Well, what we're going on is the evidence we have found. What we have found is that, were there contacts between al Qaeda and Iraq? Yes. Some of it is shadowy, but there's no question they were there. That is correct. What our staff statement found is there is no credible evidence that we can discover, after a long investigation, that Iraq and Saddam Hussein in any way were part of the attack on the United States.

Lee added, "I must say I have trouble understanding the flack over this." He repeated that the commission's finding was that al Qaeda and Iraq did have "connections," but that there was no evidence of cooperation "with regard to attacks on the United States."

The issue did not go away. Iraq was a prominent issue in American politics, so anything the commission said about Iraq was certain to be politicized. We had spent a great deal of time trying to be as precise and fact-based as we could. Yet the controversy went beyond what was contained in our mandate. We were focused on 9/11 specifically, and, more broadly, on the history of al Qaeda before 9/11. Thus we were investigating any possible collaboration between Iraq and al Qaeda on the 9/11 attacks, and any history of collaboration predating 9/11. In that respect, we said that there was no collaboration between Iraq and al Qaeda on the 9/11 attacks. There were "contacts" before 9/11; we had not found that those contacts had led to a collaborative or operational relationship against the United States; on the issue of the alleged Prague meeting between Mohammed Atta and an Iraqi intelligence officer, we found no evidence that could have led us to conclude that it ever happened.

The issue of state sponsorship of terrorism was one that we confronted with several countries—Saudi Arabia, Pakistan, Iran, Iraq, and Sudan—and with the Taliban. On Saudi Arabia, for instance, we found substantial support for al Qaeda—in money and manpower—from within the kingdom; we did not find official Saudi government support. On Pakistan, it was widely known that elements within Pakistani intelligence had ties to the Taliban and al Qaeda in the years leading up to 9/11. Later in our inquiry, we received a report that Iran may have facilitated the passage of some of the 9/11 hijackers, for instance by not stamping their passports;

we did not find that Iran had foreknowledge of or participated in the 9/11 conspiracy.

The point is terrorists exist in a shadowy world; contacts are made under ambiguous circumstances, for ambiguous reasons. We presented the facts about those contacts as clearly as we could. Those who opposed the war cried out, "See! The commission found no cooperation between Iraq and al Qaeda." Those who supported the war countered, "See! The commission found numerous contacts between Iraq and al Qaeda."

The controversy continued in this manner for several days, with arguments and articles spinning our findings in either direction. We continued to relate the facts, as they were summarized in our staff statement. Speaking that Sunday, June 21, on the ABC Sunday talk show *This Week*, Tom spoke to the complexity of the situation: "All of us understand that when you begin to use words like *relationship* and *ties* and *connections* and *contacts*, everybody has a little different definition with regard to those statements." It was emblematic of how carefully our words were weighed. With Richard Clarke and Condoleezza Rice, it had been a question of whether terrorism was an "important" or "urgent" priority. Now it was a question of whether there were "ties" or "connections" or "contacts" between Iraq and al Qaeda.

One additional controversy was sparked when Vice-President Cheney said he "probably" had evidence about the Iraq–al Qaeda relationship that the commission did not have. We responded by asking the vice-president for any information his office might have that we would need to fulfill our mandate. Over the course of the next two weeks, our staff reviewed the evidence we had collected on the Iraq–al Qaeda question, and determined that we did have all of the information available. On July 6, the two of us drafted a statement that read, "After examining available transcripts of the Vice President's public remarks, the 9/11 Commission believes it has access to the same information the Vice President has seen regarding contacts between al Qaeda and Iraq prior to the 9/11 attacks." The vice-president's office was shown the statement and raised no objection to it.

In some ways, the Iraq–al Qaeda issue was frustrating. As with previous hearings, much substantive work had been overshadowed by a single question or controversy. Yet the nature of the controversy spoke to the standing of the 9/11 Commission. Nobody attacked our findings. On the contrary, a kind of fervent competition broke out between the two sides to interpret our findings in a way that would cast each group in the better light.

We also learned yet another lesson about the importance of language. People reviewed what we said down to a single word or phrasing. In drafting our report, we had to be cognizant of this. Indeed, the day after our hearing on al Qaeda and the 9/11 plot, we looked at a response that had been mischaracterized precisely because care had not been taken to lay out the facts in a judicious manner.

12

THE STORY IN THE SKY

CONSPIRACY THEORIES AND
CORRECTING A RECORD

We fought many phantoms that day.

— General Richard B. Myers, former chairman of
the Joint Chiefs of Staff, testifying before the
9/11 Commission, June 18, 2004

CONSPIRACY THEORIES PLAY A PECULIAR ROLE in American discourse. Whenever there is a particularly surprising, traumatic, and influential moment in our history, people are left with unsettling questions. Who did this? How could it happen?

It is impossible to answer those questions to the satisfaction of all. There are still debates about who was involved in the assassination of Abraham Lincoln; and theories that the United States or United Kingdom had foreknowledge of the Pearl Harbor attack; and there is of course a veritable industry around the question of who killed John F. Kennedy.

Within the world of conspiracy theory, there is a range of opinion and rationality. Many people have reasonable questions about how Lee Harvey Oswald could have acted alone in assassinating President Kennedy; a smaller subset of conspiracy theorists propagate outrageous notions: Kennedy was assassinated by the CIA or by some shadowy secret society of the rich and powerful. For whatever reason, people feel the need to create these stories—to fill in their doubts about an event; to substantiate their ideological viewpoint; to have something to believe in; or, perhaps, simply because the conspiracy theory is more compelling than the reality.

September 11 has generated its own share of conspiracy theorists, and in the twenty-first century the Internet provides an ideal forum for people to exchange theories and mobilize their efforts. Throughout our inquiry, our offices received a steady flow of e-mails, letters, pamphlets, articles, books, videotapes, and Web site addresses from conspiracy theorists. In public forums or on call-in television and radio shows, we often confronted questions about one conspiracy theory or another. Before and after our public hearings, it was common for somebody to approach us and demand to know why we weren't asking questions about one theory or another.

These questions ranged from small to large, rational to irrational. For instance, some people raised important questions about specific topics that might have shed light on the 9/11 plot. Did al Qaeda have sleeper cells in the United States? Did stock trading in the days leading up to 9/11 indicate that some people had foreknowledge of the attacks?

Then there were the more irrational theories. Did the U.S. government have foreknowledge of the attacks? Did the military issue a "stand-down" order on 9/11 to allow the attacks to take place? Did a missile hit the Pentagon instead of a plane? The people who asked these questions often rejected the notion that the attacks were the work of al Qaeda, a foreign terrorist organization, despite overwhelming evidence of this; instead, they were determined to believe something else. Sometimes they would link 9/11 to other events from the past—Iran-Contra, Watergate, the Kennedy assassination—or, regrettably, to a perceived global Jewish conspiracy. We even heard from people who argued that 9/11 was the work of a particular movie star, a computer, or extraterrestrials.

We talked within the commission about how to deal with such theories. As we detailed in chapter 1, we established core principles for our inquiry in part to avoid the kinds of conspiracy theorizing that have followed in the wake of other inquiries. So we decided to be open and transparent so that people could see how we reached our conclusions about 9/11, and we demanded access to every document and witness in part to demonstrate that we had left no stone unturned in our investigation. We also adopted a policy of openness to the general public: people could send information to our offices, and somebody on our staff would review that information.

In addition to getting material at our offices, commissioners were often approached by the public: in airports, supermarkets, or simply on the street. In these situations, we listened politely to the theories that came our way. Sometimes, though, they were baffling. One woman approached

Tom and, in an extremely agitated voice, told him that before 9/11, Mohammed Atta had come to her house, knocked on her door, and spoke to her at some length about what he was going to do. "I told the FBI," she said, "but they wouldn't listen. And now I'm scared that he'll come again." Tom paused a moment before saying, "But he's dead."

For people with this level of belief in the unbelievable, we could not address things to their satisfaction. Instead, we dealt with conspiracy theories that fell within the realm of our factual investigation. If, in the course of our inquiry, we could address or knock down a particular conspiracy theory, we did so.

Some questions were dealt with indirectly. For instance, one of the most absurd theories was that a U.S. missile, not a plane, hit the Pentagon. Our staff told the story of American Airlines Flight 77 in such detail—with radar tracking, air traffic control conversations, calls from the plane, and a timeline of the flight's movements—that it simply was not credible to advance a theory that anything but American Flight 77 crashed into the Pentagon. It is also a great disrespect to the men and women who died on the airplane, as well as to the U.S. military, to suggest that a U.S. missile hit the Pentagon.

Other, more reasonable questions we dealt with directly. In the previous chapter we detailed the lengths our staff went to in assessing the question of whether there was an al Qaeda sleeper cell that helped two of the hijackers in Southern California. On the question of stock trading before 9/11, our staff team on terrorist financing, ably led by John Roth, supplemented exhaustive inquiries by the Securities and Exchange Commission (SEC) and the FBI undertaken in the aftermath of 9/11. Our staff had complete access to the reports and officials involved in the government investigations, and also spoke with nongovernmental groups such as the New York Stock Exchange and foreign officials, while also drawing on the commission staff's investigation of al Qaeda.

There was, indeed, unusual trading in the days before 9/11: an unusually high volume of trades on the parent companies of American and United Airlines. However, all of these trades left clear paper trails—as does all trading in U.S. markets—and were demonstrably part of a legitimate and innocuous trading strategy; the same held true for trading in foreign securities or U.S. securities overseas. Furthermore, no evidence turned up about al Qaeda or the 9/11 plot that pointed to profiteering from such stock trading. On the matter of pre-9/11 trading, we were thus able to determine that potentially suspicious behavior was, in fact, explainable and unrelated to the attacks.

Another issue that drew widespread attention was the report that Saudi citizens—including members of the Bin Ladin family—had been allowed to fly out of the United States in the days after 9/11, when the nation's airspace was still closed. Indeed, we received as many questions about this issue—particularly from members of Congress—as any other topic within our mandate. Some saw it as negligent on the part of the government or the FBI to let potential suspects out of the country. Others saw it as further proof that Saudi Arabia enjoys an undue and distasteful amount of influence in the United States. With the spring 2004 release of the movie *Fahrenheit 9/11,* director Michael Moore and others seized on the so-called Saudi flights as an example of the Bush family's close ties to the Saudi royal family.

Like the Iraq–al Qaeda issue, the question of the Saudi flights was one where we told our staff that we had to "nail this down." We spoke with the FBI; the Saudi embassy; Richard Clarke, who headed the crisis management for the National Security Council in the days after 9/11; and President Bush, Vice-President Cheney, and other senior officials.

What we found did not match up to the more nefarious charges. The Saudi embassy contacted the FBI about possibly evacuating some Saudi nationals, fearing reprisal attacks; the FBI prescreened the Saudi nationals, including the members of the Bin Ladin family, before permitting them to leave, and many were interviewed; Richard Clarke approved the departure of the planes only after he had been told that the FBI had reviewed the passengers to its satisfaction; and none of the planes departed the United States before September 14, 2001, when U.S. airspace was reopened.

A lesson from both the Saudi flights and the stock trading before 9/11 is that where there is smoke, there is not necessarily fire. The idea of many members of the Bin Ladin family (which numbers in the hundreds) flying out of the United States on chartered jets several days after 9/11 is suspicious, and may remain distasteful to some people. But that does not mean that those members of the family were involved in 9/11, or that the U.S. government was negligent in allowing them to leave. The fact that people traded an unusually high volume of stock in the airlines that ended up being used in the 9/11 plot certainly merits attention, but that suspicion does not confirm that those doing the trading had foreknowledge of the 9/11 attacks.

Still, even with evidence to the contrary, some people allow their beliefs to cloud their view. Those who disapprove of the U.S.-Saudi relationship may continue to believe that there was something reprehensible about those chartered flights, just as those who are convinced that Iraq was responsible for the 9/11 attacks continue to reject our finding that it wasn't. In the more extreme realm, those who loathe the United States or the Bush administration continue to harbor notions that the U.S. government was complicit in the 9/11 attacks.

All we could do was present, in an open and transparent manner, all of the facts that could possibly be gathered about 9/11. Because these facts did not always accord with people's views, the commission itself became a target of conspiracy theorists, who charged that commissioners and staff were engaged in a cover-up because of conflicts of interest. Here, too, is an odd disconnect: just because one member of the staff or commission had past ties to a certain individual, agency, or industry does not mean that all ten commissioners and eighty staff were thus engaged in a mass cover-up of 9/11. The absurdity of this kind of theorizing is evident when one considers that the ten commissioners came from a broad spectrum of expertise and ideology, as did our nearly eighty staffers.

The lengths that some people will go to in order to convince themselves of a conspiracy are astonishing. When presented with evidence to the contrary, they will simply reject that evidence. Yet when there are indeed inconsistencies in official versions of events, people with conspiracy theories are only emboldened to fill those gaps with their own alternative histories. Conspiracy theories are like mushrooms: they grow where there is no light. Throughout the course of our inquiry, the topic that invited the most skepticism—and thus the most conspiracy theorizing—was the performance of the FAA and NORAD on the day of September 11, 2001.

CONFUSION IN THE SKY, CONFUSION AFTER THE FACT

WHAT HAPPENED IN THE SKY above the United States on September 11, 2001? That question focused on a period of hours, rather than years; yet it was one of the most complicated and difficult aspects of our investigation.

The 9/11 story in the sky involved mainly three entities: the FAA, NORAD, and the civilian leadership at the top of the chain of command: President Bush, Vice-President Cheney, Secretary Rumsfeld, and other senior officials. There were many questions to answer about how these three entities operated on 9/11, among them: When did the FAA learn of the hijackings? When did the FAA notify the military, specifically NORAD, of the hijackings? What did NORAD do after it received these notifications? What did the nation's civilian leadership do? When was an order given to authorize the military to shoot down civilian aircraft? Why did NORAD fail to intercept any of the hijacked planes?

To appreciate the complexity of the task, put yourself back to the day of 9/11. American Airlines Flight 11 was the first of the four planes to take off, at 7:59 a.m.; United Airlines Flight 93 crashed into a field in Shanksville, Pennsylvania, at 10:03 a.m. During those two hours and four minutes, those responding to the events as they unfolded experienced the same chaos and confusion as many Americans watching the events on television.

They had not trained for the scenario they were facing. Before 9/11, NORAD's main focus had been repelling an air attack on America by foreign bombers or ballistic missiles, not by civilian aircraft. Because of that focus, the military's radar was generally pointed outward, so NORAD was dependent upon the FAA for readings within the continental United States. The FAA's protocol for hijackings was to track the planes and get them safely to the ground. Because we had not imagined hijacked civilian airliners being used as guided missiles, the FAA was not a major component of America's planning for an "air attack"—the National Military Command Center's protocol for a conference call with relevant agency representatives in the event of an air attack on America did not include a representative from the FAA. Meanwhile, the president and vice-president had not considered scenarios in which they would have to assert command and control during an attack on America by hijacked civilian airliners.

The task for our staff was determining how the FAA, NORAD, and national leadership were prepared, and creating a detailed timeline that could depict who was doing what at a specific time on 9/11, and how those actions were coordinated. Our document requests covered the FAA and NORAD's pre-9/11 protocols; the various logs, tape recordings, and radar transmissions from 9/11; after-action reviews prepared in the wake of 9/11; the president's daily schedule and diary from the day of 9/11; logs and notes from the White House Situation Room; and other documentary evidence from the day. Our staff also conducted a huge number of interviews around the country, with individuals ranging from airport security screeners, to FAA air traffic controllers, to NORAD operators, to the leadership of the FAA and NORAD. We also asked the president and vice-president to recall in detail their actions on that day.

As we discussed in chapter 4, we encountered problems with document access with both the FAA and NORAD that led to subpoenas in October and November 2003. While cooperation significantly increased after those subpoenas, the delays and gaps in document release significantly set back the work of our staff team assigned to the day of 9/11. Because of those delays, interviews had to be rescheduled after our staff reviewed new materials, and our hearing on the subject had to be delayed.

The delays in document production were further complicated by discrepancies we uncovered between the FAA's and NORAD's official accounts of 9/11 and the facts we were uncovering in documents and interviews. These discrepancies led us to increase the number of commission staff working on the FAA/NORAD story from one to seven. The problems stemmed from several accounts of 9/11 that dealt with when the FAA notified NORAD of the four hijackings, and what NORAD did with those notifications. The first of those accounts was a press release published by NORAD on September 18, 2001; another came in a book published within a year of 9/11 by the Department of Defense entitled *Air War over America*. In addition, FAA and NORAD officials testified in a series of congressional hearings in the fall of 2001, and in front of the commission in May 2003.

One example of the discrepancies between these accounts and reality involves United Flight 93. In its September 18, 2001, press release, NORAD said that the timing of the FAA's notification to NORAD of the United 93 hijacking was not available. In public testimony before the commission in May 2003—a year and a half after the attacks—NORAD officials said that the notification took place at 9:16 a.m., forty-seven minutes before the plane crashed in Pennsylvania. In reality, though, United 93 had not yet been hijacked at 9:16 a.m.—the last transmission from the pilot of United 93 did not occur until 9:28 a.m. In their investigation, our staff found that the notification took place at 10:06 a.m.—three minutes after the flight had already crashed.

Another example is the FAA notification to NORAD about the hijacking of American Airlines Flight 77. In its September 18, 2001, press release and in testimony before the commission in May 2003, NORAD said that the notification took place at 9:24 a.m., almost fourteen minutes before American 77 crashed into the Pentagon. Yet our staff determined that there was no notification to NORAD that American 77 was a hijacking before the crash time at 9:37; instead, at 9:34, there was notification that American 77 was lost and that its location could not be determined. At 9:36, NORAD received notice that a plane—not necessarily American 77—was six miles from the White House.

These inaccurate notification times explained in part the military's puzzling account of its own actions on 9/11. At 8:46, NORAD's Northeast Air Defense Sector (NEADS) scrambled fighter jets from Otis Air Force Base in Massachusetts in response to the report of American Flight 11's hitting the North Tower. At 9:24, NEADS scrambled air force jets from Langley Air Force Base in Virginia, directing them to fly east over the Atlantic Ocean. In its published accounts, and in testimony before the commission, NORAD claimed that the Langley jets were scrambled in pursuit of United 93 and American 77. Yet that was impossible. At 9:24, NORAD had not yet been notified that American 77 had been hijacked, and United 93 had not yet been hijacked.

So why were air force jets scrambled from Langley at 9:24? In working with the contemporaneous materials from the day of 9/11—notes, logs, tape recordings—our staff found that the people at NEADS had been told that American 11 had turned and was headed south toward Washington, when in fact American 11 had already crashed into the World Trade Center. The air force jets from Langley were thus pursuing a phantom aircraft—American 11, not United 93 or American 77.

These gaps were significant and apparent to people who dug deeply into the facts. In short, if the military had had the amount of time they said they had—forty-seven minutes to shoot down United 93, or even fourteen minutes to shoot down American 77—and had scrambled their jets, it was hard to figure how they had failed to shoot down at least one of the planes. A careful examination of the facts compared with the NORAD account also revealed other problems—it just didn't make sense why NORAD's scrambled aircraft were sent out over the Atlantic Ocean if they were pursuing United 93 and American 77.

These discrepancies provided fuel for the conspiracy theorists' fire. Many people did their own research of the FAA and NORAD timelines, and read *Air War over America*, and found that something did not add up. This uncertainty gave rise to various theories as to what happened on 9/11: for instance, the military did not shoot down the planes because it had a "stand-down" order to permit 9/11 to happen. In this way, the FAA's and NORAD's inaccurate reporting after 9/11 created the opportunity for people to construct a series of conspiracy theories that persist to this day.

Fringe conspiracy theorists were not the only people who noticed the discrepancies; many of the 9/11 families were far more concerned with the FAA/NORAD story than they were with issues of CIA activities or counterterrorism policy making in the years leading up to 9/11. They wanted to know why the government had not saved more lives on 9/11—perhaps by shooting down United Airlines Flight 175 before it crashed into the South Tower of the World Trade Center, or American 77 before it crashed into the Pentagon.

Indeed, many of the families' most detailed and frequently asked questions dealt with the FAA and NORAD. As it became apparent that FAA and NORAD officials had been inaccurate—if not untruthful—in making public statements, including in testimony before Congress and the 9/11 Commission, the families became more upset. The notion that they were not being told the truth fed their mistrust of the government, and nearly aligned some of them with the conspiracy theorists.

All of these factors made our task more difficult. But the good news was that a wealth of source material existed: once we received the materials we needed, there were ample logs, tapes, and other evidence to construct a timeline for the day of 9/11. For our staff, it became a methodical process of rebuilding the record from scratch. When they took their corrected record to NORAD, however, they found resistance. Even with the evidence, there was some pushback from NORAD officials, who insisted that their original timelines had been correct. Ultimately, though, the contemporaneous materials that our staff acquired after the subpoena proved incontrovertible, and the military acknowledged the accuracy of our corrected record in advance of our June 2004 public hearing.

On the origin of the order to shoot down civilian aircraft, however, there was less documentary evidence. Vice-President Cheney issued the shoot-down order from the bunker underneath the White House shortly after 10:00 a.m. He told us that he discussed the order beforehand in a phone conversation with President Bush—who was aboard Air Force One—shortly after he entered the bunker at around 9:58 a.m. There was no documentary evidence of this call—either in log entries from the day or from the notes of the people sitting next to the vice-president.

There was evidence about whether the shoot-down order reached military pilots in the sky. Based on transcripts of conference calls, logs of phone calls, and interviews, our staff found that the shoot-down order did not reach the NORAD pilots until after all of the hijacked planes had crashed—well after the vice-president thought that it had reached the pilots—and that the order was for the pilots to identify the types and tail numbers of the planes, not to shoot them down. Piecing together all of this information took time. The tape recordings and logs from the day were extremely important—they provided a real-time record of what was happening that enabled our staff to relive the day, instead of relying solely on people's memory or their hurried notes of what took place.

Another challenge was figuring out how to present the information to the public in an understandable format. As in New York, the staff team generated a statement for our June 18, 2004, hearing that featured a multimedia presentation. To illustrate what was going on, they played various audiotapes of the pilots from the hijacked planes talking to the FAA, FAA controllers talking to FAA headquarters, and FAA controllers talking to NORAD. They also constructed graphics to depict the movement of the hijacked flights, as well as the location of military aircraft in the air that morning. The National Transportation Safety Board, which conducts frequent investigations of airline crashes, was particularly helpful in lending its expertise and assistance in setting up the presentation.

In drafting the staff statement, we faced some difficulty in how to tell the story of the shoot-down order. In the statement, the staff pointed out that there was "no documentary evidence" of the call described to us by the vice-president and president, despite the fact that logs and notes were being taken of phone calls. On the other hand, the record-keeping that morning was incomplete, and both the vice-president and president had said that the call took place.

The White House, which reviewed all of our staff statements for pre-publication review, objected to the language used by our staff in a draft of the statement, and the vice-president's office wrote us a letter outlining their objections. In reviewing the language of the statement, we faced the same kind of ambiguity that had confronted us on other questions: there was no documentary evidence of the call, yet the documentary evidence from the day was not sufficient to declare that the call had not taken place. As was our practice in other matters—whether it was the conflicting accounts of Richard Clarke and Condoleezza Rice, or the suspicious contacts between Hazmi and Midhar and some individuals in Southern California—all we could do was present the evidence as we had gathered it. So we recounted in the staff statement both the recollections and assertions of the president and vice-president, while also noting that "there is no documentary evidence for this call, although the relevant sources are incomplete."

The other issue to resolve in advance of the hearing was how to handle the discrepancies in the earlier FAA and NORAD statements in testimony before the commission. Our staff was exceedingly frustrated by their problems with the FAA and NORAD. Fog of war could explain why some people were confused on the day of 9/11, but it could not explain why all of the after-action reports, accident investigations, and public testimony by FAA and NORAD officials advanced an account of 9/11 that was untrue.

There was discussion within our staff about whether or not to investigate how the inaccurate story became the official account presented by NORAD and the FAA. The issue was presented to the commission in May 2004, in an extended memo and presentation. At that point, we did not have time to launch a separate investigation into why the FAA and NORAD had presented inaccurate information in public, nor was that question clearly under the commission's mandate. We decided to refer the matter to the inspectors general at the Departments of Transportation and Defense. The results of those two investigations are still pending as of this writing.

A FINAL HEARING

THE LAST DAY OF OUR FINAL HEARING was June 17 at the National Transportation Safety Board. It was a significant day, as we were presenting information to correct a flawed record, and dealing with a topic that was uniquely important to the families. Coming as it did the day after our dialogue on the 9/11 plot, the hearing was somewhat overshadowed by the brewing political controversy over our findings about al Qaeda and Iraq. Controversy aside, though, ending our hearings by addressing the events of the day of 9/11 was fitting.

As with our hearing on the day of 9/11 held in New York, we opened this one with an extended multimedia staff statement. The statement began with an overview of the pre-9/11 missions of the FAA and NORAD. Within those missions, the protocols for dealing with hijackings assumed that the hijacked aircraft would not turn off its transponder signal in order to "disappear"; that "there would be time to address the problem through the appropriate FAA and NORAD chains of command; and the hijacking would take the traditional form, not a suicide hijacking designed to convert the aircraft into a guided missile." One issue that had been seized upon by conspiracy theorists was that the FAA and NORAD had not followed their protocols on 9/11. But the reason for this was that, as our staff stated, "the existing protocol was unsuited in every respect for what was about to happen. What ensued was the hurried attempt to create an improvised defense by officials who had never encountered or trained against the situation they faced."

The statement then tracked the story of each of the four flights, beginning with American Airlines Flight 11. Particularly haunting was the playing of the tape of an audio transmission from American 11: "We have some planes. Just stay quiet, and you'll be okay. We are returning to the airport." The voice likely belonged to Mohammed Atta. The staff statement then outlined the response of the FAA, playing communications of the FAA notifying NORAD's Northeast Air Defense Sector (NEADS):

> FAA: Hi. Boston Center TMU, we have a problem here. We have a hijacked aircraft headed toward New York, and we need you guys to, we need someone to scramble some F-16s or something up there, help us out.
>
> NEADS: Is this real-world or exercise?
>
> FAA: No, this is not an exercise, not a test.

The statement then detailed how NORAD scrambled F-15s but did not know precisely where to send them because the FAA was still trying to pick up American 11 on radar. The notification from the FAA, which took place nine minutes before Flight 11 crashed into the North Tower of the World Trade Center "was the most the military would receive that morning of any of the four flights."

The story for the other three flights was one of confusion. For United Airlines Flight 175, which crashed into the South Tower, NORAD had no advance notification. For American Airlines Flight 77, which crashed into the Pentagon, the FAA actually lost track of the plane for more than thirty minutes as it turned around and headed back east, toward Washington. For United Airlines Flight 93, which crashed in Pennsylvania, we again heard the voice of one of the hijackers—this time pilot Ziad al Jarrah—saying, "Uh, this is the captain. Would like you all to remain seated. There is a bomb on board and are going back to the airport, and to have our demands [*unintelligible*]. Please remain quiet."

Even though the FAA knew of the hijacking of United 93, "no one from either the Command Center or FAA headquarters requested military assistance regarding United 93. Nor did any manager at FAA headquarters pass any of the information it had about United 93 to the military." Thus the military would not have been able to intercept the flight anyway, even had its passengers not heroically forced it to crash, probably saving the Capitol or the White House. Meanwhile, NORAD did scramble jets; only those jets were pursuing an airliner that had already crashed—American 11—because the FAA had mistakenly notified the military that American 11 was heading south, toward Washington.

The staff statement detailed the conflicting accounts provided by NORAD to the 9/11 Commission in May 2003—of the notification time for the hijackings of United 93 and American 77, and of the scrambling of fighters to pursue United 93 and American 77. Another error cited by our staff was a failure by the military to acknowledge that it was pursuing American 11 after it had crashed into the World Trade Center: "[T]his response to a phantom aircraft [American 11] was not recounted in a single public timeline or statement issued by FAA or Department of Defense." The statement tied this failure to the suspicions that emerged after 9/11: "In fact, it was inaccurate accounts of what happened that created questions about supposed delays in the military's interception of hijacked aircraft."

On the matter of the nation's civilian leadership, the statement described how senior officials struggled to figure out what was going on while trying to take control of the situation. NORAD's top commanders did not coordinate with their FAA counterparts. President Bush was reading with schoolchildren in Sarasota, Florida, and after his visit there ended, he was rushed to Air Force One, which took off, climbing rapidly to avoid attack, without a destination. Vice-President Cheney entered a conference room underneath the White House "shortly before 10:00." The statement said, "The Vice President recalls being told, just after his arrival, that an Air Force combat air patrol (CAP) was up over Washington. At 9:59, a White House request for such a CAP was communicated to the military through the Air Threat Conference," a telephone conference call of senior officials.

On the origin of the shoot-down order, the statement presented the accumulated evidence: the vice-president recalled talking to the president shortly after entering the conference room; the president "said he remembered such a conversation, and that it reminded him of when he had been a fighter pilot"; the vice-president's military aide and Condoleezza Rice remembered a conversation taking place shortly after the vice-president entered the conference room. Yet "there is no documentary evidence for this call, although the relevant sources are incomplete." Among the documentary evidence for the day were notes taken by the vice-president's chief of staff and by Lynne Cheney, who "did not note a call between the President and Vice President immediately after the Vice President entered the conference room."

The rest of the story is also one of struggling to gain awareness and control of the situation. The shoot-down order did not get to NORAD until 10:31, well after all of the hijackings had concluded. Secretary of Defense Rumsfeld, who is in the chain of command, did not get on the Air Threat Conference until 10:39 because he had been assisting Pentagon rescue efforts. At one point, Vice-President Cheney, believing that the military had shot down hijacked civilian aircraft, told Rumsfeld that "it's my understanding they've already taken a couple of aircraft out."

Our first panel of witnesses comprised military leaders, including General Richard Myers, then chairman of the Joint Chiefs of Staff; General Ralph Eberhart, the commander of NORAD; and retired Major General Larry Arnold, who was a NORAD commander for the continental United States on 9/11 and who testified before the commission in May 2003. In his opening statement, General Myers reasserted the notion that a pre-9/11 mind-set hampered the country's 9/11 response: "[O]ur military posture on 9/11, by law, by policy and in practice, was focused on responding to external threats, threats originating outside of our borders."

During questioning, Richard Ben-Veniste asked General Arnold about his inaccurate testimony from May 2003, specifically why there was no mention that NORAD jets were pursuing American 11, and why there was no mention that NORAD had received no notification of the American 77 hijacking. Arnold responded by saying that the 9/11 Commission staff had "helped us reconstruct what was going on." Pointing out that the military after-action report on 9/11 was "skewed," Ben-Veniste said, "General Arnold, surely by May of last year when you testified before this commission, you knew those facts." Arnold replied, "I didn't recall those facts in May of last year." A tense exchange ensued in which Ben-Veniste repeatedly pointed out that those facts were widely available, and Arnold repeatedly said he had been unaware of the details of the story.

John Lehman inquired about the chain of command on 9/11, asking General Myers, "Who was in charge on 9/11? Was it NORAD commander? Was it you? Was it NMCC? Was it SecDef? Was it FAA?" General Myers asserted that the chain of command was in place, though there were gaps when Secretary Rumsfeld was in the Pentagon's parking lot, and since the president was sometimes out of reach. Indeed, one of the frustrations expressed to us by President Bush in our interview with him was that he could not remain in contact with people because the phones on Air Force One were cutting in and out. General Myers assured us that these communications problems had been corrected.

Slade Gorton asked about the shoot-down order. In our staff interviews, General Arnold had said that he would have authorized a shoot down of civilian aircraft even without an authorization from the secretary of defense or president. Gorton asked if that assertion was correct. Arnold responded that he would have authorized air force jets to surround the hijacked aircraft and "God help me if I ever had to do this, we would have given the order to shoot them down. . . . We fully anticipated that we would get presidential authority." Yet even within NORAD, there was some disagreement on this point, as General Eberhart reiterated that NORAD had ordered its jets only to "identify type and tail numbers" of the hijacked planes, and would not have done more without authorization from the chain of command.

Perhaps the most surprising statement of the morning came when General Eberhart stated his belief that if 9/11 happened today, NORAD could shoot down all four hijacked airliners if it received notification at the moment the planes were hijacked. Tom sought to clarify this, asking, "So you would have had the seven minutes, five minutes, 14 minutes, and 47 minutes" to shoot down the planes. Eberhart replied, "Yes sir." The basis for his assumption was a computer model.

Our second panel comprised senior FAA officials, including Monte Belger, who was acting deputy administrator on 9/11. Like General Myers, Belger stressed the inadequacy of pre-9/11 protocols in his opening statement: "On the morning of 9/11, it became clear that the historical procedures, the protocols, and the communication links were not adequate." He stressed, however, the FAA's success in grounding more than 4,500 aircraft that were in the skies over the United States on the morning of September 11, 2001, by 12:16 p.m.

There was some strong criticism in the questioning. John Lehman said that with regard to the FAA's failure to act on pre-9/11 intelligence about terrorist warnings, "[I]t is the failure of the performance of the headquarters of FAA that is very identifiable." This spoke, in part, to the criticism that hardening or locking cockpit doors—either before 9/11 or after the first hijacking—would have prevented the attacks. Lehman said, "Until you made the decision after all of the crashes to lock down everybody . . . it was a black hole."

The toughest criticism came from Bob Kerrey. Referring to the fact that the FAA put somebody on a teleconference initiated by the National Military Command Center who had no experience with hijacking situations, Kerrey asked, "How in God's name could you put somebody on the telephone who joined the call with no familiarity or responsibility for hijack situations, had no access to decision-makers, and had none of the information available to senior FAA officials? What the hell is going on that you would do such a thing?" Belger's response was "I don't know."

Kerrey also pressed on the issue of the FAA's slow notifications to NORAD about the hijackings. Referring to the long delay in notification about United 93, Kerrey asked why "a plane was headed to Washington, D.C., FAA headquarters knew it and didn't let the military know." Belger said that he was not responsible because "[t]here was an FAA security person running the hijack net. I had confidence that they were doing the right things."

It was a frustrating review of the government's immediate response to the attacks. The U.S. military—the last line of defense against the hijacked aircraft—had nine minutes' notice that American Airlines Flight 11 had been hijacked, two minutes' notice that an unidentified aircraft, American 77, was headed toward Washington, and no notice at all about United Airlines 175 or 93. The chain of command did not function effectively, and the president of the United States was often unable to communicate with his top commanders.

The only air defense that the American people received on the morning of September 11, 2001, was the heroism of the passengers on United 93. Amazingly, the phone calls placed to and from passengers of United 93 and their loved ones were more effective in foiling an attack than the communications between the FAA and NORAD, or among the seniormost officials in the U.S. government. The extraordinary feat undertaken by the passengers of United 93 to confront the hijackers instead of allowing the plane to crash into the hijackers' target was the boldest action taken that morning to update the existing protocols to a post-9/11 world.

Tom concluded the hearing with a statement, saying, "We hope that these hearings have enhanced the public's understanding of the 9/11 attacks, and the fact that we are still facing continuous threats." In a press conference afterward, he was asked if the commission was satisfied with the answers the FAA gave about its failure to notify the military of the hijackings, and failure to notify pilots to lock their cockpit doors. Tom replied, "No." We both acknowledged that the FAA and NORAD were unprepared for the types of attacks that occurred, but when asked whether they should have been better prepared, Tom responded, "I think they should have."

There were further questions, however, from the families. In the lead-up to our hearing, we had encountered much skepticism from the 9/11 families. After our hearing in New York City, they had complained about our questioning, particularly of Mayor Giuliani. One member of the Family Steering Committee, Patty Casazza, voiced the feelings of many when she said, "The Commission failed in its duty to learn all the lessons of 9/11 and squandered the opportunity to protect our country, our children, from terrorist harm." Another, Mindy Kleinberg, said, "The hearings in New York were such an extreme disappointment. No real questions were addressed." Referring to our June 16–17 hearings in Washington, she said, "People won't travel four hours to be frustrated and disappointed again."

Those words rang true. We had less of a turnout at our final hearing than we had hoped. Several buses that had been chartered to bring family members down from the New York area were canceled because people did not want to make the trip. Even at the hearing, the detailed hour-and-fifteen-minute staff statement did not answer all of the families' questions about the story in the skies on September 11, 2001, so we scheduled a meeting in our New York City offices several days after the hearing for our staff to brief interested family members. In a spirited exchange, the staff answered all of the families' questions, and walked the families through the timeline of the day. We still did not know whether or not they would embrace our report, but we had answered many of the specific questions they wanted answered, and also demonstrated a willingness to point out the falsehoods in official accounts of the day.

As for conspiracy theorists, it is hard to say how many minds we changed. At our two days of hearings at the NTSB, the greenroom for commissioners was located behind the seating in the auditorium, so we frequently had to walk back and forth through the audience to get from the dais to the greenroom. Without fail, we were approached by people handing out books or pamphlets that argued on behalf of one theory or another. Through our staff statements and hearings, we had cleared up inconsistencies in the FAA and NORAD accounts of 9/11—inconsistencies that had fed so many bizarre theories. Those who chose to continue believing conspiracy theories now had to rely solely on imagination, their theories having been disproved by facts.

With the final hearing behind us, we had to complete our most important tasks. Throughout the spring, we had been working steadily on drafting our report and considering recommendations. With just over a month to go until our reporting date of July 22, we faced a sprint to the finish.

13

MANY VOICES

Tuesday, September 11, 2001, dawned temperate and nearly cloud-less in the eastern United States.

— First sentence of chapter 1 of *The 9/11 Commission Report*

W HO WROTE THE REPORT? The two of us have heard that question as much as any other since we completed our work on the 9/11 Commission. When asked, though, we have no easy answer to offer. The report is the product of many voices.

By the spring, we had gone through many distractions, large and small. Yet through all of the bumps in the commission's road—the arguments over access to documents and people; the creation of interim reports and staff statements; public hearings and partisan bickering; peaks and valleys with the families—we knew that the ultimate success or failure of the commission depended upon our report and recommendations, and our ability to achieve a unanimous result. The public spotlight may shine brightly on this or that controversy, but over time the image of Condoleezza Rice testifying or the commission demanding access to the president's daily intelligence briefings would surely fade, as would the countless twenty-four-hour news cycle arguments that the commission had generated. History would judge us on our report.

The starting point for our report was that it would focus on the facts. We were not setting out to advocate one theory or interpretation of 9/11 versus another. Our purpose was to fulfill our statutory mandate, gathering and presenting all of the available and relevant information within the areas specified by our mandate, and that was the direction to our staff throughout our inquiry. The other direction dealt with tone and style. We wanted the report to be written in plain language: short sentences, simple words, and as few bureaucratic acronyms as possible. We did not want a policy briefing, nor did we want an extended academic paper. If there was a model for the report, it would be journalism: this happened, then this happened, then this happened.

At the outset of our work, Philip Zelikow and Ernest May prepared an outline along these lines, and they presented it to the two of us in July 2003. May is an academic with long experience, a courtly manner, and the slight hint of a native Texas drawl. He and Zelikow had collaborated on books in the past and had a strong mutual regard. Throughout the life of the commission, May stayed at Harvard while communicating with Zelikow, and flying on occasion to Washington. Unlike other staff members, he did not have responsibilities within the investigation. His primary role was advising Zelikow and occasionally weighing in on debates within the staff.

The outline envisioned a prologue followed by eleven chapters progressing roughly in chronological order. The starting point would be Usama Bin Ladin's February 1998 fatwa instructing his followers to kill Americans, military and civilian; the story would then progress to the day of 9/11, culminating in the emergency response and the initial decisions taken in the days after September 11, 2001. There were five additional chapters proposed for different topics for recommendations— "Intelligence," "National Leadership," International Policy," "National Defense," and "Homeland Security."

The outline was not immediately circulated. As the commission was just commencing its fact-finding, it was premature to consider the actual drafting of the report, though we did have frequent conversations with Zelikow and Chris Kojm, our deputy director, to discuss how material being gathered might fit into the report.

We also considered a format for publication. Usually, the Government Printing Office (GPO) prints and distributes government reports. However, the GPO lacked the capability to print the number of copies we wanted to release on our reporting date, nor could it widely distribute those copies. Within our mandate was a clause permitting the commission to "enter into contracts to enable the Commission to discharge its duties." In accordance with that allowance, Zelikow wrote to three trade publishers in October 2003, inviting them to submit proposals for publishing the report.

We wanted a publisher who could turn a draft manuscript into a book quickly—in a matter of days—to allow us the maximum amount of time to draft the report. We also wanted a publisher that could commit to printing several hundred thousand copies, distributing them to bookstores around the country, and keeping the report in print over time. Finally, as the commission would not be receiving any royalties for the book, we wanted the report to be provided at a low price in paperback form. For us, the bottom line was that on the day we issued our report, we wanted Americans across the country to be able to purchase a copy of it at their local bookstore, at an affordable price.

The best proposal came back from W. W. Norton & Company. Norton agreed to print and distribute the book in only six days, and to run at least 200,000 copies, priced no higher than ten dollars per copy. Norton also pledged to distribute complimentary copies to a representative of each 9/11 family, and suggested that it would make a donation to charity with portions of profits from the report. Other publishers were welcome to publish the report, as it would be in the public domain on the day of its release. But in spring 2004 we agreed that Norton's would be the "authorized version," as Norton's proposal allowed for the lowest-priced paperback, quick turnaround, and nationwide distribution.

Of course, before the report could be published, it had to be written. The question was how the fact-finding being done by our staff teams could feed into the chronological format envisioned for the report. Originally, there was a suspicion among staff that Zelikow and May would attempt to draft the entire report, which was a point of some tension, particularly because the prospective outline was not circulated to the staff teams. But clearly, no two people could process the results of a review of more than two million pages of documents and interviews with more than 1,000 witnesses; and the staff as a whole had a wealth of expertise and ability to offer. What transpired from the end of 2003 through 2004 was thus an ever-widening process in which different people contributed to the report.

For the staff teams, the first task was organizing their fact-finding. Originally, there were plans for each team to prepare an extended monograph on their topic. These monographs would be drafted with specific audiences in mind—experts or people who worked in the area covered by the monograph. In addition to having an independent value, these monographs could inform the drafting of the final report, by serving as primary sources.

For a variety of reasons, the process of drafting the monographs converged with the planning for the final report. First, several of the staff

WITHOUT PRECEDENT / 272

teams, with our encouragement, began to put their work into a chrono-logical timeline at the end of 2003. By preparing for monographs in this manner, the teams had a device for compiling and synthesizing informa-tion in language that could transfer easily to the drafting of a report that told a chronological story. So, as we discussed in chapter 5, the team on counterterrorism policy created a timeline in which it could detail what the United States government was doing to counter al Qaeda from early 1998 through the 9/11 attacks.

Second, the staff teams started drafting statements for our 2004 hear-ings. These statements—written in the simple style and tone that we insisted upon, and edited by our staff "front office" of Zelikow, Kojm, Dan Marcus, and Steve Dunne—presented the results of our factual investiga-tion in an understandable and generally nonjudgmental manner. Because the statements had to be short, they were invaluable in identify-ing the most important points to make in telling the story of 9/11. Because the statements were written in a common journalistic style and edited by the front office, they suggested a blueprint for how a final report drafted by many could sound as if it had been drafted by one.

The statements also helped build trust. Commissioners could trust in the quality of the staff's work. The staff could trust one another—the front office trusting the staff teams to do excellent work, the staff trusting that they were being included in the process. There were disagreements—the contents of the staff statements were sometimes debated line by line—yet those discussions had the benefit of ensuring that many voices and perspectives were brought to bear.

It did not hurt that the statements were widely praised. Journalists were happy that they contained a wealth of substantive information, much of it previously unknown. Politicians across the partisan divide appreciated the statements' nonpartisan nature, even if they were wary of some of the partisanship on display at the commission's hearings. The general public responded to the statements with intense curiosity—thousands of copies were downloaded from our Web site, and the first twelve staff statements were published along with key witness testimony from our hearings in a book entitled *The 9/11 Investigations,* which appeared in bookstores around the country in May 2004.

It was a long way, however, from seventeen statements drafted by the staff to a homogenous book, reviewed, edited, and approved by the com-mission. The first step was figuring out how to fold the staff material into the eleven-chapter story outlined by Zelikow and May. In April 2004, this process began when Zelikow presented the latest draft of the outline to the staff and assigned different sections and subsections of it to individual staff members. In assigning sections, the front office was seeking staff members who were particularly good writers; sections and subsections could not just be stapled together to make a report—they had to function as pieces of a puzzle that would fit together to tell the story of 9/11.

At this point, some teams were drawn deeply into the process of drafting the final report, and others continued to pursue individual monographs. The teams working on terrorist financing, border security, and aviation security did not have to do extensive drafting for the report, and were thus able to focus their attention on producing book-length monographs that explored their topics in detail. Other teams—such as the counterterrorism policy team or the team working on emergency response—had to focus all of their attention on the final report.

Fortunately, we had excellent writers on staff. For the chapters on emergency response in New York City and the 9/11 story in the sky, John Farmer took the lead in drafting what became—along with sections on what took place within the four flights by aviation security team members John Raidt and Bill Johnstone—some of the most gripping material in the report. For the chapters on al Qaeda, Doug MacEachin took the lead in producing first-draft material on the history of the organization, and Dietrich Snell took the lead on the two chapters outlining the 9/11 plot, which succeeded in placing the reader in the shoes of the enemy.

For the two chapters on how the Clinton and Bush administrations confronted terrorism, our staff team on counterterrorism policy, led by Mike Hurley, provided much of the first draft. This material—which covered sensitive political ground, including the accounts of Condoleezza Rice and Richard Clarke and the actions of the two presidents—contained some of the most closely read and edited portions of the book. Barbara Grewe drafted much of the chapter on the summer of 2001. Ernest May drafted some material for the chapter providing background on America's various national security agencies, and Philip Zelikow drafted chapters on the response in the days after 9/11, and the recommendations—what became the last four chapters of the report.

All draft material was funneled up to the front office and then to the full commission. Each member of the front office was able to make a unique contribution—Zelikow had an overarching vision for how the report should flow; Kojm is a gifted editor who enforced a crisp, clean style; Marcus and Dunne are able editors who brought a sharp eye for accuracy. Ultimately, responsibility for final staff edits of the respective chapters was divided up among Zelikow, Kojm, and Marcus.

In late May 2004, the initial drafts of the report were circulated to the two of us, and then to the full commission. After the staff statements began to come out, there was some commissioner concern that we not end up with a "staff report"—commissioners were determined to review every word, and supply their own comments, corrections, and language for the report. While we did expect there to be a good deal of commissioner editing, we did not anticipate the extent of back-and-forth that took place through June and the first part of July. Commissioners went through the text of the report six or seven times, word by word, and comments flowed through e-mails, memos, phone calls, and several marathon editing sessions.

Some of the comments were structural. For instance, several commissioners suggested moving up the chapter about the story of the four flights in the air on 9/11 to begin the book, thus bumping back the chapter on the history of al Qaeda. So the report begins with the sentence "Tuesday, September 11, 2001, dawned temperate and nearly cloudless in the eastern United States," grounding the reader immediately in the drama of the day. By the time the report reaches the beginning of chapter 2—which opens with the publication of Bin Ladin's 1998 fatwa—the reader is well aware of the reverberations of that fatwa.

Other comments delved into the specifics. For instance, the first round of comments from Jamie Gorelick, who was one of our most careful editors, ran twenty-five pages long, covering everything from the manner in which a passage was phrased, to areas that demanded more clarification, to substantive disagreements that had to be hashed out at commission meetings. Similar comments came from all of the commissioners, some of whom wrote extended memos with comments on individual chapters.

Different commissioners homed in on different sections. Slade Gorton, for instance, was very interested in the question of how we characterized al Qaeda—the extent to which the group was motivated by politics or religion—so those chapters became a focus for him. Richard Ben-Veniste was interested throughout our inquiry in the FAA/NORAD story, so he took a close look at that chapter.

By late June and early July, we were having eight-hour commissioner editing sessions in our conference room, occasionally meeting until after midnight. Sometimes we spent thirty minutes on a single sentence, trying to get wording acceptable to all of the commissioners. Time and again, our mantra was to go to the facts. In this manner we worked through some of the more difficult issues. The two of us were wary of shutting down debate while any commissioner was unhappy—everyone had to feel invested in the language of the report to achieve a consensus result. In both our experiences, the only way to build consensus was to talk, talk, and then talk some more.

When there was a disagreement on the facts, we sometimes asked Zelikow and Kojm to bring in whichever staff members had drafted the section we were debating. Then we could ask them directly: What are the facts? What is the context for this section? Why did you write it this way? What else could have been written? What document or interview transcript is this based upon? Is there another document that we can look at to make an assessment? On several occasions, we asked the responsible staff to draft a memo outlining the facts of a particular topic. Indeed, the term "go to the facts" became something of a joke within the commission—the phrase that could break any logjam. Facts, as John Adams said, are stubborn things. We could agree on facts, even if we could not all agree on what those facts meant.

This rule held true for the more controversial sections of the report. One example is the section dealing with Condoleezza Rice's and Richard Clarke's accounts of the first eight months of the Bush administration. We could have argued indefinitely about whether Rice and the incoming Bush administration treated the threat of terrorism as "urgent," as Rice said, or as "important, but not urgent," as Clarke said. Instead, what we did was lay out all of the facts of what took place between President Bush's election and 9/11.

Where there was disagreement on the interpretation of those facts, we acknowledge it. So on the question of whether the Bush administration crafted a "comprehensive new strategy" to deal with al Qaeda by September 10, 2001, or simply reiterated the strategy suggested by Clarke in January 2001, we wrote:

> Rice viewed this draft directive as the embodiment of a comprehensive new strategy employing all instruments of national power to eliminate the al Qaeda threat. Clarke, however, regarded the new draft as essentially similar to the proposal he had developed in December 2000 and put forward to the new administration in January 2001. In May or June, Clarke asked to be moved from his counterterrorism portfolio to a new set of responsibilities for cybersecurity. He told us that he was frustrated with his role and with an administration that he considered not "serious about al Qaeda." If Clarke was frustrated, he never expressed it to her, Rice told us.

The facts of Clarke's proposal of December 2000 and Rice's draft directive are contained in the report. The reader can draw from those facts and make their own decision about whose interpretation they agree with—Clarke's or Rice's. Our task was to provide those facts for the reader, not to make that judgment for them.

There were also detailed discussions about thematic questions. One prominent issue was accountability. Many of the families were intent that individuals be held to account for 9/11. This could mean that mid-level officials—such as border guards or air traffic controllers or FBI analysts—be singled out for some kind of rebuke in the report. On a broader level, it could mean passing judgment on senior officials: Who did more to combat terror, Bush or Clinton?

We did not think this kind of approach would be helpful. First, 9/11 was not the fault of any one individual. Singling out individuals—saying Joe Smith or Mary Johnson failed in their duty—and thus assigning culpability for the deaths of nearly 3,000 Americans, would have drawn a disproportionate amount of attention. The story of 9/11 is not a story of how a handful of government employees made mistakes; it is the story of how an entire government—across two administrations and many bureaucracies—failed to understand and adjust to the growing threat from al Qaeda, and was poorly organized to combat terrorism. We could not draw a straight line of causation from a mistake or decision by one official to the events of 9/11; this event was much too complex for that kind of analysis. In the report, we refer to the problem as "systemic" because it was.

Conversely, it is inaccurate to say our report holds nobody accountable, particularly at the senior levels of government. The names of all the top officials involved in counterterrorism are in the report—we make very clear the actions, decisions, and even deliberations of various officials. Once again, the reader is capable of making a judgment about who he or she feels performed well, and who could have done better.

Another difficult task regarding accountability was distinguishing between effort and results. These issues are not black and white. For instance, the CIA can argue convincingly that it did more than any other agency to fight terrorism before 9/11. So did they fail? Or did they fail to get the resources and support they needed? An individual such as Richard Clarke can argue that—as the official responsible for counterterrorism—he was trying to get faster and more robust action against al Qaeda. So did he fail? Or did people fail to listen to him? Again, our approach was to present the facts. Some people might assess those facts and find that the CIA or Clarke performed admirably. Others might draw different conclusions.

In writing the history of 9/11, we decided, you address the issue of accountability. You detail the actions. You name the responsible senior officials. You describe what was going on in the various agencies and within the two administrations. You characterize the deliberations. In doing so, you put the reader back into the pre-9/11 context, rather than simply dispensing sweeping judgments in hindsight. On the contrary, our most important judgments had to be forward-looking—what, based on the history of 9/11, were the recommendations that needed to be made to keep the American people safer and more secure?

A related question was: Could we have prevented 9/11? We were asked this question over and over again, particularly after Tom's December 2003 interview with CBS. Lurking in the background was the notion of accountability and politics: Should President Clinton or President Bush have prevented 9/11? But once again, the issue was not that clear-cut. The attacks of 9/11 were preventable in the sense that they did not have to happen, but the government lacked precise intelligence about the plot; the commission could not point to one presidential decision and say that it failed to prevent 9/11. Both President Clinton and President Bush could have done more to fight al Qaeda, but they were not going to personally stop hijackers at the border or track intelligence leads.

We approached the question of preventability by looking at missed opportunities: When did we miss a chance to foil the plot? We identified ten "operational opportunities" when we missed a chance to disrupt the 9/11 plot. Among those opportunities were: the failure to share information about the two hijackers Hazmi and Midhar, who were known to the CIA and living under their own names in San Diego; the FBI's failure to link the arrest of Moussaoui—described as interested in flight training for the purposes of carrying out a terrorist attack—to the increased warning of an attack in the summer of 2001; the failure to detect fraudulent passports or false statements on hijackers' visas; and the failure to take action in aviation security, such as hardening cockpit doors, in response to warnings of an attack. These opportunities are listed in the report.

More broadly, we agreed on four overarching failures. A "failure of imagination" characterized our inability, at all levels of government and society, to appreciate the magnitude of the threat from al Qaeda and Islamist terrorism. A "failure of capabilities" was a failure that limited the effectiveness of the actions we were taking to combat terrorism before 9/11. A "failure of management" was inherent in the inability of national security leaders to get their agencies to share information and work together. And a "failure of policy" was evident in the inability of the leadership of two administrations to make policies that reflected how great a priority counterterrorism should have been before 9/11.

What these four failures do is tie together the facts within our report. A reader can assess which individuals should be tied to these failures. For instance, through the two PDBs that were declassified—one to President Clinton, one to President Bush—we provide the reader with the most urgent reporting that both presidents received about the possibility of al Qaeda attacks within the United States. The reader can judge whether, provided that information, the presidents should have acted, or were simply let down by their intelligence community and top advisors.

We also had debates about the question of how to characterize the enemy. In particular, there was vigorous discussion about whether al Qaeda was motivated by political grievances or religion or both. Some commissioners stressed al Qaeda's fundamentalist strain of Islam and the group's desire to reestablish an Islamic caliphate. Others, including Lee, indicated al Qaeda's clearly stated grievances with American policies as a key motivating factor in its decision to attack America—a point that was made repeatedly in Usama Bin Ladin's fatwas and public statements. On this issue, we agreed that strands of both politics and religion fed into Bin Ladin's murderous ideology. This also became a matter for debate as we considered our recommendations.

As we moved into early July, it became apparent that these debates were not going to preclude us from reaching a unanimous agreement on the facts of the 9/11 story. We could all agree to tell the story straight and let the facts speak for themselves. We decided that whatever extra point a commissioner wanted to make could be developed within a note without sending the text of the report off on a tangent. With our use of a straightforward, factual writing style, we would not be derailed by debates over adjectives and adverbs passing judgment on individuals or individual administrations. And because we had extended deliberations—with staff and commissioners—over the contents of the report, everyone could feel confidence and investment in the product of our investigation.

What we were producing was a foundational narrative for 9/11 based on facts available to us before July 26, 2004. We knew that readers would draw a variety of interpretations from those facts. We knew that countless other books would be written evaluating the events detailed within our report. We knew that more facts would become available in the years to come. But if we wrote the report as clearly and comprehensively as possible, drawing on the full expertise of our staff and commissioners and the evidence we had gathered, those future interpretations and books and facts would build upon a solid and authoritative foundation of the story. Our corresponding task, however, was to make recommendations based upon those facts.

CONSIDERING RECOMMENDATIONS

IF OUR DIRECTION ON DRAFTING the report was to focus on the facts, our direction on making recommendations was to find solutions that emerged from those facts: Based on the story of 9/11, what changes did the United States need to make to better protect the American people? We also stressed the need for pragmatism: we wanted a set of recommendations that stood a chance of being passed into law.

To that end, we had to look both at the pre-9/11 failings and at the steps taken to correct those failings since 9/11. From the beginning of our inquiry, we were aware of questions people would be looking to us to answer: Do we need a new domestic intelligence agency to replace the FBI? Do we need to reform our intelligence agencies? How should we approach our relationships with Saudi Arabia, Pakistan, Afghanistan, and the broader Islamic world?

From early 2003 through our final deliberations in the spring of 2004, commissioners met with a wide variety of experts and current and former officials to discuss possible recommendations. These meetings began in the summer of 2003, when we met informally with groups from prominent think tanks in Washington, including a group from the Center for Strategic and International Studies, led by former Senator Sam Nunn, and a group from the Brookings Institution, led by former Deputy National Security Advisor James Steinberg. We also held private commission meetings with individual experts, including former National Security Advisor Brent Scowcroft; former Secretary of Defense William Perry; former House Speaker Newt Gingrich; former Senators Warren Rudman and Gary Hart, who had chaired the U.S. Commission on National Security in the 21st Century; and former diplomats such as Richard Holbrooke, Richard Murphy, and Richard Haas.

On the specific issue of a possible domestic intelligence agency, the commission received a variety of views. At commission meetings, we hosted Dennis Richardson, the director-general of the Australian Security Intelligence Organisation, and Elizabeth Manningham-Buller, the director-general of the United Kingdom's MI5, to learn more about how domestic intelligence gathering was conducted in foreign countries. We also heard from, among others, a prominent group of former U.S. national security officials led by former intelligence official John Mac-Gaffin, named the MacGaffin Group, which had worked on the issue of FBI reform for more than a year.

Several points of consensus emerged. Nearly every expert whom we spoke with anticipated that Islamist terrorists would attack the United States again. Many identified the possibility of terrorists armed with weapons of mass destruction as the most dangerous threat facing America in the years to come. Several people commented that the United States needed a better framework for improving its relations with the Islamic world—winning hearts and minds in addition to killing or capturing terrorists. As one expert said to us, "We still don't have an approach for dealing with the Islamic world."

Regarding U.S. counterterrorism, many voiced concern with the organization of our intelligence agencies: that they don't share information effectively or work together in a "joint" manner. Many spoke of the "foreign-domestic division"—the CIA collects intelligence abroad; the FBI collects at home—that hindered CIA-FBI cooperation before 9/11. Despite the legal changes of the PATRIOT Act, people felt that information still was not being pooled, analyzed, or acted upon across this foreign-domestic divide or, for that matter, across the other agencies of the intelligence community.

Most people voiced strong concerns about the FBI's ability to be the lead counterterrorism agency in the United States, yet they also spoke favorably of the post-9/11 reforms undertaken by FBI Director Robert Mueller. Nearly everyone highlighted the legal, bureaucratic, and civil liberties difficulties of creating a new domestic intelligence agency. Several people said bluntly that a domestic intelligence agency fashioned on the UK's MI5 would not work in the United States.

Commissioners had many other meetings. For instance, through 2003 and 2004, Lee met with a variety of current and former officials to discuss possible recommendations: former Secretary of Defense William Cohen; former National Security Advisor Sandy Berger; former Director of Central Intelligence Stansfield Turner; Secretary of Defense Donald Rumsfeld; Director of Central Intelligence George Tenet; and Director Mueller. Nearly everyone agreed that the United States was at a pivotal moment: our national security organization had been designed in the late 1940s to deal with the threat of communism; the United States was now attempting to adjust this organization to face the nimble and lethal threats of the twenty-first century.

One thing that Lee heard time and again from his former colleagues in Congress was that congressional oversight of national security was dysfunctional. For homeland security, for instance, eighty-eight committees and subcommittees in the Congress had oversight authority over the

Department of Homeland Security (DHS). This meant that there was no single point in either the House or the Senate where oversight of this hugely important new Cabinet department was focused, and that leading DHS officials—including former Secretary Tom Ridge—spent much of their time tramping around to different meetings on Capitol Hill, rather than receiving the informed guidance of a single committee with real authority and expertise.

There were also problems with the oversight of the intelligence community. In both the House and the Senate, the Intelligence Committees lacked authority over the budget of U.S. intelligence agencies—most of that authority fell to the armed services and appropriations committees, where the reportedly $40 billion intelligence community budget was a relative blip within the annual defense budget of nearly $500 billion.

At one meeting, a senator said to Lee, "Do you know how much time we spent debating the budget of the intelligence community last year? Ten minutes!" Lee repeated that anecdote at another meeting a few days later. This time, a senator stood up and said, "Lee, you're wrong! I was involved in the budget process last year. We spent five minutes on it."

To look at the problems of both intelligence reform and congressional oversight, Lee met with most members of the House and Senate Intelligence Committees, as did Tim Roemer. Within these committees, many said that the agencies of the intelligence community did not work effectively together—*balkanized* was a word that came up time and again—and many members advocated better information sharing and more empowered leadership of the intelligence community. Nearly all of the members also favored strengthened congressional Intelligence Committees—for instance, some suggested merging authorization and appropriation responsibility for the intelligence budget into a single committee, but doubted that this could be accomplished. Congressional committees are notorious for protecting their "turf"—it was unlikely that the armed services or appropriations committees would yield any budget authority.

Other commissioners focused on areas of particular interest. For instance, John Lehman spent a great deal of time on the issue of intelligence reform. It was particularly useful that—as a former secretary of the navy—he kept in close touch with the Pentagon. Lehman understood the difference, and the overlap, between the "national" intelligence that must be collected for the policy maker and the "tactical" intelligence that is collected for military commanders and troops in the field. Any recommendation for reorganizing the intelligence community had to be sure that both of these needs were effectively met.

As one former leading national security official expressed to us, when it came to intelligence, the Department of Defense was the "800-pound gorilla in the room." The Pentagon, not the CIA, controls more than 80 percent of intelligence budgets and several intelligence agencies. For this reason, Pentagon officials are often wary of plans for intelligence reform that might weaken this authority. The fact that Lehman could, on various occasions, go see Secretary Rumsfeld, Deputy Secretary Paul Wolfowitz, or Under Secretary of Defense for Intelligence Steve Cambone helped us maintain an exchange of views with the Pentagon.

All of these meetings were useful, as were our policy hearings of 2003. The determining factor in what we recommended, however, would be our understanding of the facts of our investigation. In the fall of 2003, Lee held lunch meetings with each of the staff teams to discuss how their investigations could lead to recommendations. His direction was to focus on a few key recommendations and to prioritize them. Instead of suggesting ten to twenty recommendations, Lee wanted the teams to identify the one, two, or three most important reforms that could be taken to correct the problems uncovered in the team's investigation. The commission could expect to get the attention of Congress, the president, and the general public on only a handful of reforms. The key was identifying areas where we could make the most important difference.

A wealth of lessons emerged in our public hearings of 2004. Our January hearing on how the hijackers got into the country demonstrated the importance of being able to ensure that people are who they say they are—on visa applications, passports, and other identification—so that you can check their identity against terrorist watch lists. Our March hearing on counterterrorism policy showed the importance of developing an integrated national strategy: diplomacy to obtain the cooperation of other countries; a variety of military options to strike at the terrorists; so-called actionable intelligence so that policy makers have information that can lead to timely and effective action; and policy coordination so that all of these tools of U.S. power work in unison.

Our April hearing on law enforcement and intelligence was instructive. Time and again, nobody could answer the question "Who is in charge?"—who directs the budget, personnel, and priorities of these fifteen intelligence agencies, spread across the government? It was a question we asked many people at all levels throughout our inquiry—from the soldiers and spies pursuing Usama Bin Ladin in Afghanistan, to the analysts and agents tracking terrorism in northern Virginia. Nobody had a satisfactory answer. Nominally, the director of central intelligence was in charge, but he controlled only about 20 percent of the intelligence budget, and had direct authority over only the CIA and foreign intelligence. The hearing also catalogued the FBI's crippling inability to analyze threats and pursue terrorists before 9/11, and Director Mueller's efforts to address these shortcomings.

Our May hearing on emergency response detailed the need for stronger communications and command and control for emergency responders at the scene of an attack, and our June hearing on the FAA and NORAD raised similar issues for crisis management at the national level. Our June hearing on al Qaeda portrayed the characteristics of the enemy that we had to reform our government to combat—creative and nimble, and blending a core of hardened operatives with a hateful ideology with wider support in the Islamic world. Any counterterrorism strategy had to be designed to defeat this twofold enemy.

There were some recommendations that would be largely staff-generated. For instance, technical assessments on a variety of issues: how you use biometric technologies on passports, how you develop communications equipment for first responders that is interoperable, how you track terrorist funds within financial markets, or how you develop a technological infrastructure for intelligence agencies to share information. On these types of questions, commissioners were basically supportive of recommendations generated by the experts among our staff.

Other recommendations were going to demand more deliberation at the commissioner level. Through the spring, the staff teams funneled their recommendations up to the front office. In April and May, Zelikow and Kojm each drafted documents to serve as starting points for commission deliberation. At the beginning of June, a fifteen-page summary of "possible policy recommendations" was circulated to the commission.

When we stepped back to consider these recommendations, we found the enormity of the task striking. Drawing on the breadth of our mandate and investigation, we would be assessing everything from how the United States should reach out to the Islamic world, to how the government should apportion funding for homeland security, to how we should organize our intelligence community. Some of these topics proved more difficult than others.

The commission embraced a definition of the enemy as two-pronged: "al Qaeda, a stateless network of terrorists that struck us on 9/11; and a radical ideological movement in the Islamic world, inspired in part by al Qaeda, which has spawned terrorist groups and violence across the globe." We made a conscious decision to refer to the enemy as "Islamist terrorism"—not as "terrorism" the tactic, or "Islam" the religion.

For our recommendations for relations with key countries in the struggle against al Qaeda—Afghanistan, Pakistan, and Saudi Arabia—there was also broad consensus. For Pakistan and Saudi Arabia, commissioners agreed that the United States needed to deepen its relationships. The oil-for-security deal with Saudi Arabia, and the agreement with Pakistan regarding cooperation on terror in exchange for support for President Pervez Musharraf, were not sufficient; dialogue between our countries needed to be deeper, and to involve more issues, including pragmatic political reform. For Afghanistan, commissioners applauded the progress made since 9/11, and agreed with the plea heard from many Afghans throughout our inquiry: "Don't leave us again." We outlined several steps for sustaining the U.S. commitment to Afghanistan's future.

We did, however, have some disagreement over foreign policy issues. Much of it revolved around the question of al Qaeda's motivation. For instance, Lee felt that there had to be an acknowledgment that a settlement of the Israeli-Palestinian conflict was vital to America's long-term relationship with the Islamic world, and that the presence of American forces in the Middle East was a major motivating factor in al Qaeda's actions. Similarly, several commissioners pointed out that we had to acknowledge that the American presence in Iraq had become the dominant issue in the way the world's Muslims viewed the United States.

This was sensitive ground. Commissioners who argued that al Qaeda was motivated primarily by a religious ideology—and not by opposition to American policies—rejected mentioning the Israeli-Palestinian conflict in the report. In their view, listing U.S. support for Israel as a root cause of al Qaeda's opposition to the United States indicated that the United States should reassess that policy. To Lee, though, it was not a question of altering support for Israel but of merely stating a fact that the Israeli-Palestinian conflict was central to the relations between the Islamic world and the United States—and to Bin Ladin's ideology and the support he gained throughout the Islamic world for his jihad against America.

Since neither U.S. policy in the Israeli-Palestinian conflict nor U.S. policy in Iraq was covered in our mandate, we were not required to discuss the issues at length. Had that been the case, reaching consensus would have been difficult. We ended up agreeing on language that acknowledged the importance of the two issues, without passing judgment:

> America's policy choices have consequences. Right or wrong, it is simply a fact that American policy regarding the Israeli-Palestinian conflict and American actions in Iraq are dominant staples of popular commentary across the Arab and Muslim world. That does not

mean U.S. choices have been wrong. It means those choices must be integrated with America's message of opportunity to the Arab and Muslim world. Neither Israel nor the new Iraq will be safer if worldwide Islamic terrorism grows stronger.

Surprisingly, though, we were able to reach agreement rather easily on our foreign policy recommendations. For instance, there was broad agreement within the commission that the United States needed to engage more aggressively in the "battle of ideas" within the Islamic world, to combat the ideology of radical Islam—through outreach, public diplomacy, support for pragmatic reform, and educational and economic assistance. We outlined a series of steps that would serve this purpose, calling it an "agenda of opportunity" for the Arab and Islamic world, contrasted with the violent and regressive agenda of the terrorists.

On perhaps the two most anticipated recommendations—our assessment of the FBI, and our assessment of the organization of the intelligence community—the commission's view had evolved throughout our inquiry, as we looked at the facts of 9/11 and the changes made in its wake. If you had asked us at the beginning of 2003 what our recommendation for intelligence reform would be, we probably would have said that it was likely that the commission would recommend the creation of a new domestic intelligence agency—an American MI5; and we would have said it was unlikely that we would recommend the creation of a new office to oversee America's intelligence agencies—a director of national intelligence, or DNI. Through the course of our inquiry, this perspective flipped.

On the question of a DNI, we knew that commission after commission had recommended the creation of such an office—including the congressional Joint Inquiry into 9/11. To all of these observers, it was apparent that the existing director of central intelligence (DCI) lacked authority over the fifteen agencies of the intelligence community, and could not possibly run both the CIA and all of these other agencies. However, change had proven impossible, with the Department of Defense resisting challenges to its authority over several intelligence agencies and budgets; other agencies, including the CIA, resisting change; and Congress declining to restructure entrenched bureaucracies.

But the facts of the 9/11 story—and our analysis of post-9/11 reforms—cried out for stronger leadership at the top of the intelligence community. It was unacceptable that a DCI could issue a directive in 1998 stating, "We are at war" with al Qaeda, with no discernible effect. The U.S. intelligence community collects millions of bytes of data every hour; it is an extraordinary task to manage all of this information and to ensure that it is shared and that people act on management's priorities. To force information sharing between intelligence agencies, set clear priorities, and coordinate the various intelligence collection and analytical capabilities, we needed a single official who was in charge and accountable. It was not apparent that this could be accomplished without sweeping reform.

Within the commission, John Lehman and Tim Roemer made strong arguments for a DNI. Lehman's support was important, due to his experience at the Pentagon. Roemer had embraced the DNI concept since his stint on the Joint Inquiry. Lee had advocated the creation of a DNI for decades, and testified on behalf of the idea before the Joint Inquiry. Yet initially he thought that recommending a DNI was not likely to gain approval. Over the course of our inquiry, though, we both came to believe that it was the only solution to the crippling status quo.

Commissioners realized that implementing the DNI recommendation would be difficult; several people said that it would push the limits of what we could expect to have enacted into legislation. But the environment was ripe for reform. That spring and early summer, the Senate Intelligence Committee issued a damning report on the intelligence community's performance in the run-up to the Iraq war; the chairman and ranking member of the House Intelligence Committee—Porter Goss and Jane Harman—had introduced their own intelligence reform bills; and George Tenet had announced his resignation as DCI. Based on our overwhelming finding that systemic problems had contributed to 9/11 and remained inadequately addressed, we decided to seize the opportunity to recommend a DNI.

Another difficult intelligence issue was the recommendation for a National Counterterrorism Center, or NCTC. The idea, strongly advocated from the staff level by Zelikow, was that there should be one center in the government where all intelligence on terrorism was pooled and analyzed, and where counterterrorism operations were planned—thus addressing the pre-9/11 problems of incomplete intelligence assessments, poor coordination among agencies, and a lack of "actionable intelligence" that translated into counterterrorism operations. This proposal went beyond the government's initial post-9/11 solution—the creation of a Terrorist Threat Integration Center, which fell short of being the analytical and operational counterterrorism hub that the NCTC could be.

Lee was wary of the NCTC recommendation. He liked the idea of integrating information and different tools of American power, but he was wary of combining intelligence and operational planning. In part because of his experience heading the House Iran-Contra investigation, he was reluctant to consolidate so much power within one center of the government. In order to agree to the concept, Lee insisted that it be made clear that policy would not be made within the NCTC; on the contrary, the NCTC would follow the direction of the president and the National Security Council. To ensure this, Lee insisted that the head of the NCTC report to the president and be confirmed by the Senate, that the NCTC be located in the Executive Office of the President, and that there be a separation between the intelligence and operations functions within the NCTC. Lee and Zelikow worked out these details in a meeting at the commission's offices, and the recommendation was embraced by the full commission.

On the FBI, the consensus within the commission was that Director Mueller's reforms needed more time to be given a chance to work: he was headed in the right direction and should be given time to try to succeed. There were questions, however, about how to ensure that those reforms became institutionalized. Some commissioners advocated creating a more clearly identified "national security" unit within the FBI, which would report to a prospective DNI. Others objected. Ultimately, we agreed to recommend the establishment of a "national security workforce" of analysts and agents at the FBI, but stopped short of having that workforce report to a DNI.

The other difficult intelligence recommendation was congressional oversight. In retrospect, we probably should have spent more time building consensus on a practical solution to the problem. There was no staff team or hearing on congressional oversight. Instead, commissioners—several of whom had served on the House or Senate Intelligence Committee—brought their own experience to bear, talking to many members of the House and Senate.

Based on what we had heard from members of Congress, we had no problem declaring oversight on intelligence and counterterrorism "dysfunctional"; nor did we have much trouble in agreeing that both the House and Senate needed a single committee with responsibility for "oversight and review" of homeland security. For intelligence, however, we could not agree with precision, and ended up listing two alternatives for empowering Intelligence Committees—one was to create a joint House-Senate committee; the other was to unify authorization and appropriations for the intelligence budget in the existing Intelligence Committees. We realized that these were ambitious recommendations and that they would be difficult to implement.

Our dialogue and debates on recommendations continued through June and into the first part of July. Often, discussions in commission meetings spilled over into dinners. Tom sought to coax people into agreement. Usually, commissioners' intent was similar; it was only a matter of making slight adjustments to different recommendations in order to achieve consensus. Tom would point out to commissioners the common ground between their positions, and urge them to chip away at their differences. Repeatedly, he would say that gaps between commissioners could be bridged.

Late in this process, Bob Kerrey introduced the phrase "unity of effort," which helped conceptualize both our recommendations and what the commission hoped to achieve. "Unity of effort" referred to the performance we wanted out of America's government—a DNI that enforced "unity of effort" among intelligence agencies; an NCTC that achieved "unity of effort" in counterterrorism analysis and operations; and a Congress that encouraged "unity of effort" through oversight committees that could contribute to the efficacy of the government's counterterrorism policies.

Unity of effort was also what was needed in the country—a sense of national unification and resolve that could cut across partisan lines. This was also what we needed within the commission. Many of the misgivings about some of the language in our report and about our recommendations were tied to entrenched ideological attitudes. The commission had to articulate the absolute urgency of putting aside those attitudes to get the job done, by drawing upon the kind of unity that the American people—and American politicians—had demonstrated spontaneously in the wake of 9/11.

The other question was how to draft the section of the report on recommendations. We did not hold to the plan from the original outline to have five chapters; this was neither feasible nor necessary. Instead, Zelikow distilled the recommendations into two chapters. The first chapter addressed the question of "what to do"—what steps did the United States have to take to forge a global strategy to combat terrorism? The second chapter dealt with the question of "how to do it"—what structural changes did the U.S. government need to make in order to carry out an effective global strategy?

These two chapters received the most careful review from commissioners of any part of the report. As we began to crystallize our recommendations in early July 2004, we also looked ahead to a strategy for working on behalf of their implementation. Through the spring, the two of us had met with the Republican and Democratic congressional leadership, with a good number of other members of Congress, and with the White House. Other commissioners had performed similar outreach. It was a delicate balancing act—we did not want to tip our hand as to what, exactly, we were going to recommend, but we did want to give an indication that we intended to press for significant change. Meanwhile, commission meetings focused on how we could seize the political momentum for change, educate the American people about our recommendations, and press for reforms in the months, even years, ahead.

As the calendar moved through the July 4 weekend, the fact that we were discussing implementation strategies suggested that we had turned a corner. Given the partisan atmosphere in the country, we knew that anything less than a unanimous report signed with confidence by all ten commissioners would be chalked up as another occasion for partisan division, and the report would be quickly assigned to the wastebasket. This would be doubly tragic because it would splinter the national unity exhibited by the American people in the wake of September 11, 2001, and undercut the opportunity to enact reform. As we drew nearer to July 22, the date we planned to roll out our report, there remained an incredible amount of last-minute work and planning to do. But after a whirlwind of drafting, editing, and debating through the spring and early summer, it appeared that the commission was going to achieve what at the outset of our work had seemed improbable, if not impossible: unanimity.

14

UNANIMOUS

We file no additional views. . . . We have no dissents. We have each
decided that we will play no active role in the fall presidential campaign. We will instead . . . work together in support of the recommendations in this report. [W]e believe that acting together . . . we
can make a difference.

> — Tom Kean, speaking at the rollout of *The 9/11*
> *Commission Report,* July 22, 2004

U NANIMITY DID NOT COME EASILY. Each commissioner was a proud
member of his or her respective political party, with strongly held
views. Throughout our inquiry, we had strong disagreements within the
commission over hiring staff, how aggressive we should be in negotiating
for documents, and how commissioners should speak to the media. Commissioners split roughly down partisan lines regarding the public disputes
between Condoleezza Rice and Richard Clarke, and commissioners
themselves became targets for politicians and pundits from both sides of
the partisan divide. Almost certainly, five of us planned to vote for George
W. Bush in November, and five of us planned to vote for John F. Kerry.

Yet through May and June of 2004, the two of us could sense momentum building within the commission for a unanimous result. Over a year
and a half, commissioners had learned a tremendous amount, and had
come to know and respect one another very well. It was a relief to finally
be able to put behind us questions about commission process and access
to documents and people. After the partisan attacks on Jamie Gorelick,

we had rallied together. After the clamor over the questions about Iraq and al Qaeda, we had taken our private mantras—"Go to the facts" and "Stay within the mandate"—and deferred to them as our public posture. Behind closed doors, the two of us could look around the conference room table and see people with genuine affection for one another making compromises that would have been hard to envision at the beginning of 2003. Even in our most vigorous debates, there was no personal acrimony.

As the commission worked through the language of the report and our recommendations, it became clear to us that a dissenting opinion, even on a single recommendation, was unlikely. We were still concerned, though, about the possibility of commissioners drafting their own addenda to the report or recommendations—the kinds of concurring opinions that are common for commissions and task forces, in which commissioners opt out of endorsing parts of the report by inserting independent opinions. Even these kinds of separately issued individual opinions could crack the veneer of nonpartisanship and unity that was so important for us to project to the nation. After all, if we were going to ask Congress to come together behind our report and recommendations, we would have to do so ourselves.

The two of us began to pull commissioners aside privately at breaks during meetings, or before or after a commission editing session, to discuss any problems they were having with the report. If two commissioners were arguing over a particular recommendation, we suggested that they talk on their own to hash things out. If someone was raising a particular objection to the language of a certain paragraph in the report, we suggested a compromise. If a commissioner was adamant about making an additional point not contained within the draft of the report, we encouraged him or her to do so by inserting a passage in the notes, rather than issuing an independent opinion.

The more we talked about achieving a unanimous result, the more commissioners seemed to like the idea. The point we made time and again was that if the report was going to have any impact, it had to be unanimous. And as unanimity appeared possible, commissioners became more determined to make it happen. We liked one another and wanted to come together. We recognized and respected the place of 9/11 in the national consciousness. We wanted to see our recommendations implemented, and understood that unanimity would be a huge boost to that effort.

All ten commissioners had been in and around politics for decades, and nearly all of us commented that the atmosphere in Washington was currently as partisan as we had ever seen it. We were disappointed in the poisoned political rhetoric in the country—the personal attacks, negative advertisements, and nonstop media echo chambers. We were disappointed in the partisanship in Congress: the trench warfare within congressional committees, the brutal rhetoric, and the failure to build consensus on the key issues of the day. When it became apparent that we could reach agreement on the facts of 9/11 and on our recommendations, we saw that we had a chance to make a point about how politics could still work in a bipartisan manner. We could show that more could be achieved by working together than by standing apart.

We also could trust in the quality and thoroughness of the work that had been done. None of us felt that we were pulling any punches in signing off on the report. On the contrary, there were sections that offered harsh criticisms of two administrations, and recommendations that went against or beyond the existing platforms of both parties. Meanwhile, our knowledge of the facts of the 9/11 story also made us realize how superficial the political posturing about 9/11 was.

At a commission meeting the first week in July, we were working out the details of some of our final policy recommendations. At the end of the meeting, we moved for the commission to support the contents of the report unanimously—without dissenting or assenting opinion. Everyone agreed. For a moment, a remarkable feeling of achievement came over the room. We knew we had realized what we had set out to do nearly twenty months ago in Lee's office, when we decided to allow no daylight between us; now, all ten of us were inalterably bound together. We could not yet enjoy the feeling or the achievement, though, and no one expressed a triumphal word. It was two weeks to the scheduled rollout of our final report. In order to distribute the report on July 22, it had to be completed, declassified, and in the hands of the book printer by Saturday, July 17. To meet that deadline, an extraordinary amount of last-minute effort would have to be made.

We decided to draft text boxes—highlighted passages within the text of our report—to answer a number of specific questions. Originally, we envisioned a good deal of these boxes, but due to time constraints and space limitations, we ended up with a total of five: one explaining the way in which the commission received detainee information; one offering a "case study" in terrorist travel; one detailing the unlikelihood that Mohammed Atta traveled to Prague to meet with Iraqi intelligence; one providing answers to the questions about the Saudi flights that left the

United States after 9/11; and one listing the ten missed "operational opportunities" to disrupt the 9/11 plot.

We also included two additional boxes that provided the contents of the most specific PDB information received by both presidents pertaining to Bin Ladin, to attacks within the United States, and to possible hijackings. For President Bush, the PDB item was from August 6, 2001, and had been declassified in the wake of our hearing with Condoleezza Rice. For President Clinton, the PDB item was from December 4, 1998, and was entitled "Bin Ladin Preparing to Hijack US Aircraft and Other Attacks." The PDB indicated Bin Ladin's plans to hijack airplanes in order to secure the release of Islamist extremists held in the United States:

> Reporting [. . .] suggests Bin Ladin and his allies are preparing for attacks in the US, including an aircraft hijacking to obtain the release of Shaykh 'Umar 'Abd al-Rahman, Ramzi Yousef, and Muhammad Sadiq 'Awda. . . . Some members of the Bin Ladin network have received hijack training, according to various sources, but no group directly tied to Bin Ladin's al-Qa'ida organization has ever carried out an aircraft hijacking.

We had been pressing Judge Alberto Gonzales and the White House (which controlled the Clinton papers) for weeks to declassify the Clinton PDB, but they had resisted. Abruptly, they reversed their position shortly before the release of our report, and we were able to print the PDB in a box.

Reviewing our notes was another area that demanded a great deal of tedious work. The report contained more than 1,700 notes, which ran over one hundred pages. Some of these notes were simple and straightforward—citing a particular interview or document. Others were much longer—explaining an issue in greater detail, providing context for a portion of the report, or conveying the viewpoint of an individual commissioner. Our deputy general counsel, Steve Dunne, headed a "cite check" team of six staffers, who checked every single note in the report—pulling up the source to double-check its accuracy, cutting down lengthy notes, and rewriting notes in standard form. Dunne's team comprised some of our younger staff members, who were more recently accustomed to long and detailed work at law firms and in academia.

To illustrate the extent to which the commission was working up until the reporting date, the latest cited documents in our notes are dated "July 16, 2004," less than twenty-four hours before our report went to the printer. These notes reference interrogation reports from Khalid Sheikh

Mohammed (KSM) and Ramzi Binalshibh. Our staff had uncovered disturbing evidence about connections between al Qaeda, Iran, and the 9/11 hijackers, suggesting that between October 2000 and February 2001, eight to ten of the so-called Saudi muscle hijackers traveled in or out of Iran en route to Afghanistan. Iranian government officials apparently facilitated this travel—for instance, by not stamping the Saudi passports, which would enable the hijackers to draw less attention during future travels. (An Iranian passport stamp would, for instance, draw scrutiny from a U.S. border or visa official.) Our staff had responded to this intelligence reporting by submitting questions for U.S. interrogators to ask KSM and Binalshibh. Those intelligence reports came back to us just in time for inclusion in the report.

These revelations of Iranian contacts with al Qaeda and the 9/11 hijackers were deeply troubling. In one of the last drafted passages of our report, we summarize our findings:

> [T]here is strong evidence that Iran facilitated the transit of al Qaeda members into and out of Afghanistan before 9/11, and that some of these were future 9/11 hijackers. There also is circumstantial evidence that senior Hezbollah operatives were closely tracking the travel of some of these future muscle hijackers into Iran in November 2000. . . . We have found no evidence that Iran or Hezbollah was aware of the planning for what later became the 9/11 attack.

The issue surfaced in the media a few days before our reporting date, and was highlighted in part because the commission had just emerged from the controversy over our finding of no collaborative, operational relationship between al Qaeda and Iraq. Now our staff had uncovered evidence of closer ties between al Qaeda and another member of the so-called axis of evil. No inquiry with a fixed end date can answer every question completely; commissioners believed that the issue merited further investigation, and a sentence was included in the report saying, "We believe this topic requires further investigation by the U.S. government."

Another item that resurfaced in early July was the "Able Danger" Department of Defense surveillance program that our staff had been briefed on in Afghanistan. On July 12, Dietrich Snell interviewed Captain Scott Phillpott, who requested the meeting. At that point, our staff had received all of the Department of Defense documents on Able Danger and had found no mention of Atta, though there had been mention of the al Qaeda operative Mohammed Atef.

Phillpott told Snell he recalled seeing the name and photo of

Mohammed Atta on an "analyst's notebook chart" involved in Able Danger before 9/11—in other words, Able Danger had managed to get Mohammed Atta under surveillance. Phillpott said he saw this chart only briefly, and that it dated from the period February–April 2000.

There was no documentary evidence whatsoever to back up Phillpott's sensational claim. Phillpott himself had not performed the analysis, nor could he explain what information had led to this supposed identification of Atta by Able Danger. In addition to the lack of documentary evidence from Able Danger, there was no corroboration of Phillpott's account by any information from within the U.S. government, or by German government sources that had tracked the Hamburg cell. Phillpott's account also failed to match up with detailed evidence compiled by our staff documenting Atta's travels, activities, and entry into the United States, including from INS and State Department records. Snell concluded that the officer's account was not sufficiently reliable to warrant inclusion in the report or further investigation. This conclusion was not a challenge to Captain Phillpott's good intentions; the tip he provided just did not check out.

At the same time that we were dealing with these last-minute substantive questions, our staff had a heart-stopping phone call of a different sort. Our contract with Norton stipulated that the report be a certain number of words and a certain number of words per page, yet we had a misunderstanding as to what that word limit was. Only a few days before the report was due to go to press, Stephanie Kaplan, the commission's special assistant and managing editor of the report, who was keeping track of the word count, received a call from Norton—they had reviewed the text of the drafts, and the report was 90,000 words over the limit.

Since we had already edited the text many times, we knew we could not possibly cut another 90,000 words without sacrificing the quality of the report. We set about making it work in other ways. We had already obtained a security clearance for a copy editor and hired our own graphic designer to work on the book. Now we had to sit down and figure out clever ways to make the report work without cutting the additional words: by shifting margins, adjusting the spacing between lines, and adjusting the font. The biggest casualty of this process was the notes section, which is best read in the printed report with a magnifying glass.

We also had to draft an executive summary. In the hours and days immediately after the rollout of our report, members of the media, members of Congress, and congressional staff would not have time to read and digest a several-hundred-page report. In writing, commenting, and acting upon our report, they would depend on a clearly written summary of our findings and recommendations. Because of the word limit imposed on our report, we had to condense all of our work into a digestible thirty-page executive summary that could stand on its own as a separately published document. This document would prove essential in the days and weeks after our report came out, as it was often the reference point for members of Congress and their staff during hearings on our recommendations.

The last nights were increasingly frenzied as our staff pored over the report, notes, and executive summary in last-minute editing sessions. Calls and e-mails flowed at all hours of the night. On Friday, June 16, Philip Zelikow, Chris Kojm, Dan Marcus, and Steve Dunne assembled in Kojm's office, where they stayed all night and into the following evening, hardly taking breaks, going through the report one final time.

Meanwhile, the White House lawyers responsible for clearing the report for publication had also been staying up all night for several days, performing a "classification review" on the report. White House chief of staff Andrew Card and the lawyers in Judge Gonzales's office deserve credit for the efficiency of this process. What could have been laborious and contentious ended up yielding an extraordinary level of declassification. Through a direction from Card, the normal process of declassification—which can get stuck at the middle levels of the bureaucracies—was bypassed, and our report was sent immediately to designated senior officials at the various agencies. We wanted to avoid the kinds of problems the congressional Joint Inquiry had encountered—notably the twenty-eight "redacted pages" in the middle of their report—and we did.

Our recommendations chapters presented another difficult matter. We did not want our recommendations to be viewed by the White House—or anyone else—in advance of our rollout because we wanted the opportunity to explain them to the American people ourselves. The White House argued that they needed to review the recommendations chapters for declassification. Dan Marcus worked out a compromise whereby one of the National Security Council's declassification experts would review the chapters, keeping them strictly confidential and from the rest of the administration.

On Saturday evening, July 17, the final draft of the report went off to the printing presses. At five-thirty, Zelikow sent an e-mail to notify the commission and staff, with a short accompanying statement: "There is much more to be said, and there will be a time to say it." Already, we had a sense of the enormity of the public interest. Norton had scheduled a first printing of 500,000 copies, nearly all of which had been ordered in advance by booksellers.

The growing interest was evident in political debate as well. It is the nature of the current dialogue in this country that people are eager to comment on things before they happen in order to steer public opinion about them. The Monday before our report was released, the Bush and Kerry campaigns each started sending long e-mails to reporters, detailing how the report would cast blame on either the Bush or Clinton administration. The Bush campaign argued that one needed to approach our report looking at "the posture of the United States from the time of the 1993 World Trade Center bombing," and the Kerry campaign countered that the White House was using our report to "spin the nation's intelligence failures as the fault of the Clinton Administration." Liberal and conservative commentators took to the airwaves, the print media, and the Internet to write preliminary responses, echoing these thoughts, about a report they had not yet read.

The Tuesday before our report was released, another controversy erupted when it was made public that former Clinton national security advisor Sandy Berger was under investigation for removing classified documents from the National Archives while preparing his testimony before the commission. As we noted in chapter 6, the two of us had been aware of the story for months; when it broke, it unleashed bitter partisan comments. House Majority Leader Tom DeLay said, "I think it's gravely, gravely serious what he did, if he did it. It could be a national security crisis." Republicans prepared to hold hearings on the matter in Congress. Democrats, including President Clinton, countered that Republicans had leaked the news of the charges to distract from our upcoming report. Berger resigned his position as a top foreign policy advisor to the Kerry campaign. We were left explaining to the media that the commission had seen all of the documents Berger had removed because several copies had been made beforehand.

Some of our findings and recommendations began to leak out, which was inevitable given the number of people with access to our report. *The Washington Post* reported on Monday that we were planning to recommend sweeping intelligence reform, including the creation of a director of national intelligence (DNI). *The New York Times* reported on the same day about the Iran–al Qaeda links uncovered in the final days of our investigation. We refused to comment on any of these reports, preferring to address them on our own terms on the day of our rollout.

Congressional leaders continually asked to be briefed on our recommendations. We were eager to work with Congress, but were wary; usually, once a report is delivered to Congress, it is almost guaranteed to leak out to the press, with the leaks inevitably designed to support a particular agenda. Fortunately, we literally did not have a copy of the report to offer—because of the last-minute nature of our work, Norton did not deliver the printed report to us until Wednesday evening, the night before our rollout.

Tuesday and Wednesday, the two of us were on Capitol Hill, meeting with the Republican and Democratic leadership, as well as other key members of Congress. Our goal was to prepare people for our findings and recommendations, without disclosing them entirely. People were generally laudatory, but there was a distinct wariness. Less than twenty-four hours before our rollout, the Senate Select Committee on Intelligence held a hearing on intelligence reform. One witness at the hearing, former Deputy Defense Secretary John Hamre, argued, "We already have too much groupthink in a fractured intelligence community. I fear bringing it all under one chief would seriously threaten what little competition for ideas we have." Senators of both parties criticized our idea of a DNI, which had not even been made public yet. It was indicative of how much of an uphill climb intelligence reform would be in the Congress.

Our allies were also preparing for our rollout. Weeks before our report came out, Senators John McCain and Joe Lieberman agreed to introduce legislation to implement our recommendations. Since they did not know what our recommendations were, they reserved the right to amend them, but were committed to starting congressional action immediately. Several days before the rollout, the two of us scheduled a news conference on Capitol Hill with Senators McCain, Lieberman, Evan Bayh, and Arlen Specter to follow the commission's press conference. Yet even our congressional allies were not fully aware of the contents of our report. Senator Lieberman's office, for instance, had been preparing for our rollout on the assumption that our report would contain ten recommendations. The night before the rollout, Zelikow and Kojm briefed Lieberman and Specter's staff on the report and our forty-one recommendations.

The political environment was extremely charged. The Democratic Party was set to start its convention on July 26. Much of the commentary swirled around how our report would affect the election. Our intent was to take the report as far outside of politics as possible. All ten of us agreed to sit out the presidential campaign on issues related to the work of the commission. Instead, we would commit ourselves to getting our recommendations implemented into law. As a part of that commitment, each of us agreed to travel around the country to talk to the American people. We also initiated plans to raise money for a privately funded entity to continue our work after the commission officially shut its doors in August.

Our first task, though, would be to seize the momentum at our rollout. Thursday, July 22, would be both an ending and a beginning. On that day, we would reach the end of a long road; we also knew we had to start a push to pressure both parties to take action. We felt it was urgent in order to make the American people safer. To make that point, for one day, the commission had to use its moment of maximum attention to stress the necessity of action, and the country's desperate need to move beyond partisan politics.

ROLLING OUT THE REPORT

How you roll out a report is enormously important. You get only one chance to present your findings and recommendations on your own terms. After that, you are constantly answering questions, responding to criticism, or adjusting to changing circumstances. If you fail to make a good first impression, you risk having your work defined by your critics. Ultimately, of course, we would be judged by the contents of the report. But in order to focus attention accurately on what was in the report—and generate momentum to implement our recommendations—we had to make good use of our day in the spotlight.

We had a long checklist of things to accomplish on the day of our rollout: meet with President Bush to present him with a copy of the report; speak with Senator John Kerry, the Democratic nominee for president; meet with members of Congress; meet with the 9/11 families; and hold a public event where the two of us would make a statement and the full commission would take questions from the press. We also planned a busy two days of media interviews, meetings with the editorial boards of major newspapers, and briefings for key opinion leaders in the country—columnists, think tanks, academics, and others.

The press operation within the commission—which consisted of Al Felzenberg and his able deputy, Jonathan Stull—was simply not big enough to handle a public event of this size and scope, and with this many logistical demands. In the spring of 2004, we put Chris Kojm in charge of planning our rollout, and our staff's front office began talking quietly to some public relations firms around Washington.

One decision to make was the date for the rollout. Under our revised statute, we were required to report by July 26, 2004. However, there were obvious reasons to avoid releasing our report on the same day as the opening of the Democratic National Convention—most notably, that we would be competing for attention with another major news event, and our work would be more likely to be immediately politicized. Moving the rollout date up by a week or two weeks might have been preferable, but we needed that time to get the job done. So we settled on Thursday, July 22, allowing a small cushion between the release of our report and the Democratic Convention.

People in various quarters advised us to split our rollout in two—with one day to feature key recommendations, and one day, a week or so later, to put out the report. The idea behind this proposal was to maximize attention on our recommendations, while also ensuring that the commission stayed in the news for a longer period of time. But we were uncomfortable with such a division. The report and recommendations could not be separated; the power of the suggested reforms came from their connection to the failings detailed in the report. Better, we thought, to put everything out at once. To assist us with planning, we hired the Edelman Group, a public relations firm based in Washington, D.C. Edelman was able to lend its expertise to the huge task of scheduling media interviews for all of the commissioners on July 22, and to our efforts to publicize our report in the days and weeks afterward.

Another question was location. Initially, we considered doing the roll-out in New York City, but that presented enormous logistical challenges, and would have prevented us from holding meetings with President Bush and members of Congress. We scouted several locations in Washington, settling upon the Andrew W. Mellon Auditorium, located just across from the National Mall on Thirteenth Street and Constitution Avenue. The Mellon Auditorium provided the ideal setting. Its magnificent classical interior had served as the venue for a number of momentous events, including the signing of the North Atlantic Treaty in 1949, which created the North Atlantic Treaty Organization (NATO).

There were many last-minute preparations. We worked with the White House to schedule a time for the two of us to present a copy of the report to President Bush before our eleven-thirty event at the Mellon Auditorium. Our staff family liaisons worked with representatives of the 9/11 families to ensure that all who wanted to come would have seats. Commissioners planned to fan out in bipartisan pairs to do interviews throughout the day. Working with Lee's aide, Ben Rhodes, who was helpful to us throughout our tenure on the commission, we put together a fifteen-minute public statement to read at the rollout. Meanwhile, Norton and the Government Printing Office delivered copies of the report to us on July 21, and we prepared to release an electronic version on our Web site so that people all over the world could access it free.

July 22 was a warm and muggy day in Washington. The first stop for the two of us was Capitol Hill, for a briefing with members of Congress. We then moved on to the White House for a meeting with President Bush shortly after 9:00 a.m., in the Oval Office. We met for a few minutes with the president, and with Andy Card and Alberto Gonzales. We chatted informally, as more substantive discussions about our recommendations would come later, after the president and his advisors had had a chance to review the report. Bush thanked each of us for our public service.

Then the president surprised us by saying that he wanted to move to the Rose Garden, where he made a brief statement thanking us for our work on the commission. He also pledged action on our recommendations, saying, "I look forward to studying their recommendations, and look forward to working with responsible parties within my administration to move forward on those recommendations." With that, we shook hands with the president, presented him with a hardcover copy of our report, posed for photographs, and left the White House grounds. The Rose Garden appearance had not been on our schedule, but it was an important event for the commission. The president's positive comments—and statements about moving forward on our recommendations—sent an important signal to the country and the Congress, particularly Republicans.

After our meeting with the president, we had a phone call with Senator Kerry, who had been sent a copy of our report. Kerry was in Denver, preparing a trip east across the country to Boston, where he would accept the Democratic Party nomination for president in one week. He was enthusiastic about the report, and gracious about our work. Some of the recommendations—including the proposal for a DNI—were things he had already come out in support of. From our conversation, it was apparent that he had decided to fully embrace our report.

After speaking to Senator Kerry, we spoke on the phone with his running mate, Senator John Edwards, who was also very positive. Lee was talking with Edwards when our car pulled up to the Mellon Auditorium, where an extremely important meeting was already under way: because of our commitments on Capitol Hill and at the White House, the two of us could not lead the meeting with the 9/11 families, who were scheduled to receive an hour briefing by commissioners on the contents of our report. Tim Roemer and Jim Thompson were leading the meeting in our place.

For the families, it was sure to be an emotional day. For many of them, their engagement with a "9/11 Commission" predated ours, going back to their advocacy over the summer of 2002. They had invested so much of their grief and emotion into seeing their questions about 9/11 addressed. Now, the day had finally come when they were going to get answers.

We were not certain how the families were going to respond to the report. We had tried our best to meet their expectations. Throughout our inquiry, staff team leaders worked with all of the questions submitted by the families; we instructed them to answer those questions as best they could—affirmatively, negatively, or by saying we didn't know, in the cases where we could not find answers. In the final days of the report drafting and editing, Chris Kojm led a group that put together a concordance for the families, which indicated where in the report they could find the answers to specific questions. Still, given our up-and-down relations with them, we did not know if they would be satisfied.

Roemer, Thompson, and the other commissioners were briefing the family members in a room backstage of the auditorium. Roemer had been preparing them for several weeks—for instance, by explaining how we were approaching the issue of accountability, which was so important to them. Roemer also explained how important the support of the families would be to the implementation of our recommendations. Just as it would take all ten commissioners solidly working on behalf of implementation, strong support from the prominent 9/11 family members would also make a tremendous difference. Conversely, if the families criticized our work, it would cloud our efforts.

When we arrived, the meeting had already been going well. After an extended briefing, the first question from a number of families near the front of the room was "Can you sign my copy of the report?" The meeting became very emotional, for families and for commissioners. These were the people who had lobbied on behalf of our creation, and on our behalf at key junctures. We had gone through valleys together, but on our reporting day they were joining with us once again as partners. It was another indication that the day ahead would be special, and that the commission had real momentum.

All ten commissioners took seats on the dais at the front of the Mellon Auditorium. The two of us stood at the lectern, where we would take turns reading our opening statement, as we had taken turns speaking at all our public events. Once again, the commission's proceedings were being carried live on television by several stations. This time, though, the occasion was not a hearing—we were finally prepared to speak with one voice about our findings and recommendations. Looking out at the audience of several hundred, we saw assembled the faces of so many people who had helped us through our work—the 9/11 families sitting up front, our own families and friends, nearly all of our extraordinary staff, and the reporters who had been covering the commission as a beat for the previous nineteen months.

Tom opened the statement by referring to the place of 9/11 in each of our lives: "We ask each of you to remember how you felt that day—the grief, the enormous sense of loss. We also came together that day as a nation—young and old, rich and poor, Republicans and Democrats. We all had a deep sense of hurt. We also had a deep sense of purpose." The implication was clear: the nation had to recall and retain some of the unity that it had achieved in the days after 9/11.

Tom then read a summary of our findings. To the question of whether 9/11 was preventable, he read a list of some of the missed opportunities to foil the plot. He then detailed the broader policy failures—of diplomacy; military and covert action; intelligence and law enforcement; border and immigration protection; aviation security; and immediate response on 9/11. On the issue of accountability, Tom said, "Our failure took place over many years and administrations. There is no single individual who is responsible for this failure. Yet individuals and institutions are not absolved of responsibility. Any person in a senior position within our government during this time bears some element of responsibility for the government's actions."

To illustrate the necessity of action and reform, Tom then turned to an assessment of the threat, passing on a frightening truth that emerged in our interviews: "Every expert with whom we spoke told us that an attack of even greater magnitude is now possible—even probable. We do not have the luxury of time. . . . We believe we are safer today than we were on 9/11—but we are not safe." Tom also spoke about an enemy that is both al Qaeda, and a broader ideology. Because of that duality, Tom said, "we should not expect the danger to recede for years to come. No matter whom we kill or capture—including Usama Bin Ladin—there will be those who plot against us."

Lee then provided an overview of our recommendations. He began with the question of "what to do"—our recommendations for a global counterterrorism strategy—saying, "There is no silver bullet or decisive blow that can defeat Islamist terrorism." Instead, it would take every tool of counterterrorism that the government possessed. Lee went through each of those tools, detailing what needed to be done to pursue terrorists;

prevent terrorist sanctuaries; work with Afghanistan, Pakistan, and Saudi Arabia; sustain a broad counterterrorism coalition; extend an "agenda of opportunity" to the Arab and Islamic world; protect infrastructure at home; secure borders; and respond to the attacks that might come. He stressed, as well, the need to engage in the "battle of ideas within the Islamic world" so that the United States offered "progress in place of persecution, life instead of death."

On the question of "how to do it," Lee went through our most important recommendations for government reform. He began by saying, "A critical theme that emerged throughout our inquiry was the difficulty of answering the question: 'Who is in charge?' . . . Too often the answer is: 'No one.' " Lee then briefly described our recommendations to correct this and other systemic flaws: a National Counterterrorism Center, a national intelligence director, reformed congressional oversight of national security, reform in the FBI, more robust information sharing in the government, and smoother transitions between presidential administrations. Lee concluded, "We stress that these measures need to be accompanied by a commitment to our open society and the principle of review—safeguards that are built into the process, and vigorous oversight. We must, after all is said and done, preserve the liberties we are fighting for."

Tom concluded the opening statement by returning to the place of 9/11 in the country's history. He referenced the presidential election and bitter partisan divide in the country, saying, "Our two great parties will disagree, and that is right and proper. But at the same time we must unite to make our country safer. Republicans and Democrats must unite in this cause. . . . This is the challenge of our generation." After thanking the other commissioners, our staff, and the 9/11 families, Tom concluded by referencing the commission's unanimity: "We file no additional views. . . . We have no dissents. We have each decided that we will play no active role in the fall presidential campaign. We will instead . . . work together in support of the recommendations in this report. [W]e believe that acting together . . . we can make a difference. We can make our nation safer and more secure."

In the question-and-answer session that followed, each commissioner made a strong statement on behalf of the recommendations. The most dramatic comment, though, came from Jim Thompson, who said:

> Our reform recommendations are urgent. We have come together
> with the families to agree on that. If these reforms are not the best

that can be done for the American people, then the Congress and the president need to tell us what's better. But if there is nothing better, they need to be enacted and enacted speedily. If something bad happens while these recommendations are sitting there, the American people will fix political responsibility for failure—and that responsibility may last for generations.

Thompson's voice filled with emotion. When he was done, applause rang out from the 9/11 families in the audience, as it often had throughout our hearings. Coming from a Republican commissioner who was close to Speaker Dennis Hastert and a strong supporter of President Bush, the comments had a special resonance: here was a Republican speaking about the necessity of his own party taking action.

When the press conference was over, commissioners moved out into the crowd, preparing for a busy afternoon of meetings and media appearances. We shook hands with many of the families, signing some books on our way out of the auditorium. Outside, the television vans and cameras crowded Constitution Avenue. The two of us got into a car, and were driven back up to Capitol Hill, where we were going to hold our press conference along with Senators McCain, Lieberman, Bayh, and Specter. As we had come together, it was notable to appear with four senators— two Republicans, two Democrats—who could represent a bipartisan consensus for action in the Senate. In the House, we had similar bipartisan support from a number of members.

The senators were generous in their praise of the commission, and announced their intention to introduce a bill to implement our recommendations. By chance of timing, Congress was scheduled to enter its August recess the following day, which did not reflect the kind of urgency for action we were stressing. McCain and Lieberman raised the possibility of calling an unusual special session in August to consider our recommendations. We both thanked the senators—who had supported us throughout our work—and pledged to work with them to implement our recommendations. All of us also had words of praise for the 9/11 families, some of whom made it to the press conference after leaving the Mellon Auditorium.

The rest of the day was spent in one media interview after another. The Edelman Group had all ten commissioners booked for television, radio, or print media interviews for every hour. In Washington, many of the television news stations share studio space on Capitol Hill. As the night wore on, the two of us could sit in one studio and look through sets of windows to see two of our fellow commissioners speaking in another room to another interviewer. We could not hear their words through the glass, but we knew what they were saying.

In the coming days the report was widely well received. In the media, the commentary was exceedingly positive. Nearly every editorial had praise for the thoroughness of the report, and urged the government to act on our recommendations. Even those who had been heavily critical of the commission had kind words—*The Wall Street Journal* editorial page referenced this sentiment, saying, "Its unanimous final report seems on our first reading to be better than the process that produced it."

Perhaps because the contrast to the current political environment was so stark, everyone noted our bipartisanship and unanimity. As we waited for television and radio interviews, commentators remarked to us on how refreshing it was. Wherever we went, ordinary people thanked us for coming together across party lines. There were some immediate attempts to take partisan advantage from our report, with Republicans predictably using it to bash the Clinton administration, and Democrats using it to bash the Bush administration, often in statements that sounded like they had been prepared before our report was even released. But it quickly became apparent that the trend in the country was to embrace the bipartisanship of our efforts, and return to the kind of unity that characterized the country after 9/11.

This unity was bolstered by the continuing support of the 9/11 families. In a statement that went well beyond what we could have hoped for, the Family Steering Committee strongly embraced our report, saying, "The Commission has brought us together again—truly committed in a mission to make our homeland safer. . . . The American people are demanding action in response to the 9/11 Commission's recommendations. They will not accept the fate of past Commissions, whose reforms were never implemented." The families also embraced bipartisanship, saying, "The tone of bipartisan cooperation set by this commission is a model that we would like to see adopted by all of our government representatives."

The support of the general public was perhaps best indicated by the interest in the report. In the first day that it was out, the report sold more than 100,000 copies, and hit number one on the best-seller lists of online booksellers such as Amazon and Barnes & Noble. By Sunday, 350,000 copies had been sold, and Norton had ordered 200,000 extra copies for printing. In the first day that we posted our report online, the commission's Web site recorded more than 50 million hits. From our perspective, we were heartened that our account of this singular event in American history was breaking through to mass distribution to the American people. We were also pleased at the prospect that Americans might ask their representatives and senators, home for August recess, what action they were taking on our recommendations.

John Kerry and his campaign supported our recommendations as vigorously in public as Kerry had expressed to us over the phone. Speaking on the day of our rollout, Kerry said, "We have to act now. If I am elected president and there still has not been sufficient progress rapidly in these next months on these issues, then I will lead." In a separate interview, he said, "If I were president today, or yesterday, I'd be appointing one person in the White House responsible for liaison with the Congress and the agencies immediately to implement the vast majority of the recommendations of the 9/11 Commission." The Bush administration responded as well. President Bush, though still circumspect about whether or not he would fully embrace our suggested reforms, appointed Andy Card to lead a Cabinet-level review of our recommendations, to report back to the president in August.

The day after our report was released—as we continued to make the rounds of talk shows and interviews—Congress announced that it would, indeed, take action. In the House, Speaker Hastert and Majority Leader Tom DeLay announced that they would hold committee hearings on our report through August, and that committee leaders should produce legislative recommendations by the fall. Minority Leader Nancy Pelosi echoed John Kerry's enthusiastic embrace of our recommendations, and a bipartisan "9/11 Commission Caucus" emerged, led by Congressman Chris Shays and Congresswoman Carolyn Maloney.

In the Senate, Majority Leader Bill Frist and Minority Leader Tom Daschle announced similar plans for August action, making the Senate Governmental Affairs Committee, led by Chairwoman Susan Collins and Ranking Member Joe Lieberman, the lead committee in considering our recommendations for institutional reform of the government. Meanwhile, on a separate track, Senators McCain and Lieberman pressed ahead with a bill addressing all of our recommendations.

As the Democrats began their convention on the following Monday, it was a welcome respite for commissioners, who had been through an exhausting period. We suspended public comment during the convention, as we did not want our work to be too politicized, and did not want to interfere with the Democratic Party's claim to the national stage. In his acceptance speech on Thursday night, Senator Kerry again cited the commission, saying, "The 9/11 Commission has given us a path to follow, endorsed by Democrats, Republicans, and the 9/11 families. As president, I will not evade or equivocate; I will immediately implement the recommendations of that commission."

The same day, we faced an unexpected show of support from Senator Kerry, when he called for an eighteen-month extension of the commission for the purpose of helping to implement our recommendations. As currently mandated, the commission was set to expire at the end of August. Kerry's proposal was not a likely one—that kind of extension would have required quick statutory approval from Congress, and commissioners and staff had planned to move on to other endeavors. But we were in the process of raising private funds for a follow-on project, led by all ten commissioners, to be called the 9/11 Public Discourse Project. We were not planning to go away. Each of us was now deeply invested in educating the American people about our report, with speaking engagements planned around the country for the month of August.

Friday, July 30—the day after the Democratic Convention—was a day for the commission to look back and to look forward. That evening, commissioners pitched in to hold an event for our staff at the Metropolitan Club in Washington. It was the perfect occasion for commissioners to sign copies of the report and express our gratitude for the hard work done by our staff. We had all worked long and hard on a deeply emotional subject, and had enjoyed both a wonderful professional opportunity, and a chance to forge personal bonds that would last for years to come. Finally, people could relax and embrace one another. For Lee, it was a moment when the emotions of the achievement sunk in. Every commissioner gave a toast. Tom expressed appreciation when he looked at everyone around the room and told them they should be honored to have "made history."

Meanwhile, that morning, we had begun the process of looking forward. The two of us were called to testify at the first hearing of the Senate Governmental Affairs Committee. Ahead of us, in August and September, were well over twenty-five congressional hearings on our report and recommendations. The commission had generated its own perfect storm: by issuing a bipartisan report on the most urgent security matter of the day in the midst of the most intense political season imaginable, we had put the onus on Congress and the president to come together across partisan lines, and to act.

The location of the hearing that morning was the same room in the Hart Senate Office Building that had provided a venue for so many of our most memorable public hearings. Once again, the seats were filled with many 9/11 families, the walls were lined with members of the press, and flashbulbs lit up to record the proceedings. Behind the dais, members of the panel reviewed submitted testimony and awaited the witnesses. Only, this time, the two of us took our seats at the witness table, our finished report and prepared testimony in front of us, ready to make our case for reform to elected representatives of the American people.

LOOKING BACK TO LOOK FORWARD

In a few minutes, I will sign into law the most dramatic reform of our nation's intelligence capabilities since President Harry S. Truman signed the National Security Act of 1947.

> — President George W. Bush, at the signing of
> the Intelligence Reform and Terrorism
> Prevention Act, December 17, 2004

LAWS ENACTED AND LESSONS LEARNED

The timing could not have been better. The deferrals and delays that greet many commission reports were impossible, given the public's focus on our work and the prominence of terrorism and national security in the 2004 election. Politicians had to take positions on our recommendations. As Tom said shortly after the rollout, the American people could watch how their elected representatives responded, "and vote on it."

The week after the rollout, the two of us met in the White House with Andy Card; Condoleezza Rice; Stephen Hadley; Scooter Libby, the vice-president's chief of staff; and Alberto Gonzales. At that time, much of the talk around Washington centered on the wariness toward our recommendations regarding the Department of Defense and the CIA. We answered many questions about our plan for reorganizing the intelligence community, and left the meeting confident that the key people in the White House were increasingly knowledgeable about and supportive of our ideas.

On Friday, August 2, President Bush appeared in the Rose Garden along with the secretaries of defense, state, and homeland security, the acting director of central intelligence, the director of the FBI, and the attorney general. The president announced that he was issuing several executive orders in response to our report, notably creating a director of national intelligence (DNI) and a National Counterterrorism Center. The two of us put out a statement calling the president's action "an important first step." We were pleased he was embracing the need for reform, and the outline of two of our key recommendations. However, his proposals did not give the DNI the authority we had proposed, notably control over the budgets of U.S. intelligence agencies; nor did his orders address all of our forty-one recommendations. Furthermore, the kind of institutional reform of the federal government that we had proposed depended upon legislation.

Congress did act. Both the Senate and the House took the extraordinary step of scheduling hearings on our recommendations through the August congressional recess. For us, it meant a busy summer. Between July 30 and mid-September, the two of us testified together at seven separate congressional hearings, appearing before the House Intelligence, Armed Services, Homeland Security, and International Relations committees, and the Senate Governmental Affairs, Intelligence, and Commerce committees. Lee ended up testifying a total of eleven times. Commissioners altogether made more than twenty appearances in front of congressional committees and subcommittees.

Congressional testimony is tedious. Each appearance took hours of preparation, and this was done without most of our staff, who had been dismissed at the end of July, when their contracts ran out. Because of the breadth of issues covered in our report, we would discuss intelligence one day, and then have to turn around and prepare to discuss international finance the next. Some of the issues were quite technical—for instance, the use of biometric identifiers such as fingerprints on passports; others were broad—for instance, how the United States interacts with the Islamic world. After each hearing, we received streams of follow-up questions from individual members of Congress, either in writing or over the phone. Lee spent nearly all of August 2004 on Capitol Hill.

In the Congress and in the country, there was a clear consensus and momentum for reform. The executive summary of our report was widely read by members of Congress, and many began to take the time to work through our full report. Through August, Senators Susan Collins and Joe Lieberman drafted a bipartisan intelligence reform bill in the Senate, and Senators McCain and Lieberman worked on a bill encompassing all of our recommendations. In the House, the Republican leadership was drafting a bill, and a bipartisan "9/11 Commission Caucus," headed by Congressman Chris Shays and Congresswoman Carolyn Maloney, was calling for legislative action.

The greatest resistance to intelligence reform came from supporters of the Department of Defense. In the House and Senate, the toughest questioning was from the chairmen of the Armed Services Committee, Congressman Duncan Hunter and Senator John Warner, and from Senator Carl Levin, the ranking member of the Senate Armed Services Committee. Our reforms, after all, reapportioned power—control over budgets and personnel appointments—moving some of that power from the Pentagon to the DNI. Hunter and several others insisted that our reforms would upset the chain of command, denying support for American soldiers on the ground. We countered that our reforms did not affect "tactical intelligence"—the information that reaches our troops. But we faced a formidable adversary: with a budget of nearly $500 billion, the Pentagon is one of the most powerful bureaucratic players in Washington.

Meanwhile, commissioners traveled to New York City, Los Angeles, Chicago, Seattle, Atlanta, Boston, Indianapolis, and many other destinations to speak directly to the general public. All of us were surprised by the positive reception we received. The report continued to sit atop the best-seller lists. Time and again, in airports, on the street, and in shopping malls, we were approached by people thanking us for working in a bipartisan manner, who lamented that the tone in the country and the campaign was so divisive.

August 21 was, by statute, the formal end date for the 9/11 Commission. As we shuttled from congressional hearing to congressional hearing, our remaining staff was busy closing down our offices. All of our records were transferred to the National Archives, with an agreement that they would be made public at the beginning of 2009. Our staff teams on terrorist financing, borders and immigration, and aviation security completed monographs; two were released before our end date, but the monograph on aviation security was kept classified for several months—a decision that we disputed, as much of the classified information had already been made public at our hearings and in our report.

As the commission closed down, a new organization opened. Each commissioner had agreed to push for the implementation of our recommendations while educating the public about our findings. To facilitate that work, we raised money from several foundations to start a "9/11 Public Discourse Project," or "9/11 PDP." The ten former commissioners served as the PDP's board; Chris Kojm headed the organization, which had an office in downtown Washington, and several staffers assisted us with public outreach and responded to the many congressional inquiries. Through the summer, as most of our staff took well-deserved vacations or moved on to other pursuits, Kojm worked long hours coordinating our extensive testimony on Capitol Hill, and explaining our recommendations to congressional staff.

As summer turned to fall, the situation was extremely fluid. President Bush appointed the House Intelligence Committee chairman, Porter Goss, to become the new CIA director. Several proposals for intelligence reform circulated in Congress, including a plan by Senator Pat Roberts, the chairman of the Intelligence Committee, to dismantle the CIA. The Republican Convention was held in New York City at the beginning of September, and 9/11 and terrorism were featured prominently at it.

Out of their summer deliberations, Susan Collins and Joe Lieberman succeeded in producing a very effective bill known as "Collins-Lieberman." Collins-Lieberman took a giant step toward getting our recommendations implemented. It passed by an overwhelming bipartisan majority of 96–2 on October 5 in the Senate. The only senators who did not vote were John Kerry and John Edwards, who were on the campaign trail, but they were strong public supporters as well.

In the House, the process did not go as smoothly. Unlike in the Senate, there was not a bipartisan bill. On October 7, the "9/11 Recommendations Implementation Act," which had been drafted by the Republican leadership, passed 282–134, with House Democrats attempting to substitute the language of the Collins-Lieberman bill as an alternative. The House bill significantly reduced the powers of the DNI, in accordance with Duncan Hunter's concerns, and included a series of controversial provisions on illegal immigration and driver's licenses that went beyond our recommendations.

The House and Senate then went into a conference committee to resolve the differences between the two bills. We pressed hard for a resolution in advance of Election Day, fearing that the Congress might revert back to complacency once the election had passed. We placed countless phone calls and pressed members of the conference committee to act; the main point of difference was the powers of the DNI. On several occasions we thought we were close to a resolution, but the differences, and the distraction of the presidential campaign, proved too great; on October 27 the conferees announced that they would not succeed in reaching an agreement before the November 2 election.

Commissioners stayed out of the presidential campaign, but the 9/11 families split three ways. The majority of the more engaged family members stayed neutral, working alongside us to press Congress to act. The "Jersey Girls"—the four prominent New Jersey widows—split from the rest of the Family Steering Committee by coming out in support of John

Kerry, traveling with Kerry and Edwards in the final days of the campaign. Other families supported President Bush, touting his leadership in a number of television advertisements.

Meanwhile, terrorism was a looming presence. Repeated terror alerts from the Department of Homeland Security warned about the probability of an al Qaeda attack before the election. On September 4, hundreds of Russians—including many schoolchildren—were killed in a horrific showdown between terrorists and Russian security forces in Beslan. In the final week of the presidential campaign, Usama Bin Ladin appeared in a videotape boasting that Americans would not be safe with either a President Bush or a President Kerry.

On November 2, Americans concluded a campaign of unprecedented expense and unusual divisiveness by reelecting President Bush. On November 3, the reelected president held a news conference during which he cited his newly minted "political capital," and called on Congress "to pass an effective intelligence reform bill that I can pass into law." We joined with our supporters in the Congress and the 9/11 families for a final push to get the legislation passed before Congress disbanded in December. Otherwise, the incoming 109th Congress would have to start from scratch in January 2005.

The conference of House and Senate lawmakers resumed on November 16. After four days of around-the-clock negotiation, we thought an agreement had been reached on November 20, and we even prepared and issued a statement commending the conferees for their work. However, a last-minute meeting of the House Republican leaders derailed the process. Speaker Hastert decided to hold up the agreed-upon bill, declining to bring it before the full House for a vote.

There were clearly enough votes to pass the bill, but there were not enough Republican votes for the bill to pass with a majority of the Republican caucus. The Speaker wanted to win not just a majority of House votes but a "majority of the majority," meaning a majority of Republican members of the House. The House Republican caucus had put forth the most intense opposition to the 9/11 Commission dating back to before our creation, and the Speaker made it clear to us that he needed more time to win the support of more of his caucus, and that he would work to get it.

We were confident that Hastert supported the bill, but the two biggest obstacles were two powerful House committee chairmen. Armed Services Chairman Duncan Hunter objected to the creation of a strong DNI with any budget authority over intelligence agencies within the Pentagon;

Judiciary Chairman James Sensenbrenner insisted on provisions outlaw-
ing the issuance of driver's licenses to illegal immigrants, as well as other
provisions that would crack down on illegal immigration. We had taken
no position on these questions, and felt that such divisive issues were best
handled separately.

At this point, our attention turned to the White House. President Bush
had stated his support for the bill, but it was being blocked by members of
his own party. The two of us met with Vice-President Cheney, who is
widely respected in the House Republican caucus, and Scooter Libby. We
asked for the vice-president's support, and he pledged to give it to us, saying, "You won't hear anything about what I'm doing, but that's when I'm
most effective."

On November 30 we held a press conference at the Wilson Center—
the scene of our two interim reports of 2003—to urge that the bill receive
a vote. In our opening statement, Tom said:

> The bill has the support of the President. It has the support of Con-
> gressional leaders in the House and Senate, on both sides of the
> aisle. It has the support of majorities in both chambers and the sup-
> port of the vast majority of the American people. Our request to our
> nation's leaders is simply: Give this bill a vote. Pass this bill.

Over the weekend, Vice-President Cheney made good on his word to
personally oversee negotiations to move the bill forward. On Monday,
December 3, President Bush sent a letter to congressional leaders declaring his support for the bill, saying, "We are very close to a significant
achievement that will better protect our country for generations to come.
Now is the time to finish the job for the good of our national security."

On December 6, an agreement was reached. Language was inserted
into the bill that satisfied Duncan Hunter's concerns, stating that the new
DNI would not "abrogate the responsibilities" of the Department of
Defense, while maintaining strong budgetary authority for the DNI. The
Speaker promised Sensenbrenner that he would bring up his immigration provisions in the next Congress, but Sensenbrenner maintained
his opposition. Yet with the support of Hunter, other Republicans followed, and there were thus enough Republicans to achieve the Speaker's
"majority of the majority." On December 7, the anniversary of Pearl Harbor, the Intelligence Reform and Terrorism Prevention Act passed the
House by a vote of 336–75; the following day, it passed the Senate by a
vote of 89–2.

A week later, on December 17, the full 9/11 Commission found itself back at the site of our rollout, the stately Mellon Auditorium. Less than five months after the release of our report, President Bush was going to sign the bill implementing many of our key recommendations into law. The president opened his brief remarks by saying:

> In a few minutes, I will sign into law the most dramatic reform of our nation's intelligence capabilities since President Harry S. Truman signed the National Security Act of 1947. Under this new law, our vast intelligence enterprise will become more unified, coordinated, and effective. It will enable us to better do our duty, which is to protect the American people.

As President Bush sat at the table to sign the legislation, the two of us stood behind him along with the congressional leaders who had worked over the previous months to turn our recommendations into law. It was a moment of great satisfaction and a significant milestone, though there was still much left to do. The audience included the other eight commissioners, many of our former staff, and many of the 9/11 families. With a stroke of a pen, America's cold war national security apparatus was reorganized to confront new dangers. The lessons of one terrible day had become law.

REFLECTIONS ON THE COMMISSION

OFTEN, WHEN A PROCESS reaches a positive conclusion, it appears that success was preordained. With the 9/11 Commission, this certainly was not the case. As we said at the opening of this story, it appeared to both of us that the commission was set up to fail, and there were any number of occasions throughout the process when it felt as if we were, for one reason or another, being pulled apart. Our mandate was exceedingly broad, the issues were inherently difficult, the partisan atmosphere was extraordinarily polarized, and commissioners were affected by constant outside pressure. In this case, though, the center held. How did that happen?

To begin with, we had a clear idea of what we wanted our report to look like. We set out to write a foundational story of 9/11—the most comprehensive account of the facts possible. We did not set out to endorse one particular theory, or to single out one particular agency or individual. We sought a level of access to the facts that was absolute, and we related those facts to the public with as little editorial comment as possible. Our two mantras—"Go to the facts" and "Stick to the mandate"—kept us on a straight and steady course. We knew we could not turn up every fact or resolve every dispute, but we resolved to do the best possible job.

We also had the benefit of a clear mandate. The statute creating the 9/11 Commission was clear in specifying areas of inquiry, to the point that we were able to structure our staff around these specifications (e.g., "aviation security," "intelligence"). We resisted the calls from some quarters to expand our investigation beyond the scope of our statute—for instance, by assessing the questions of whether or not to go to war in Iraq; but we were relentless in asserting our right to review all of the facts that pertained to our charge to examine "the facts and causes relating to the terrorist attacks of September 11, 2001."

Some people were disappointed that we did not issue harsher judgments of different people or administrations. Others might have focused more on one particular aspect of the story. That is fine. We did not expect ours to be the final word. There will likely be scores of books—investigative or opinionated—about 9/11; that is all part of the dialogue of democracy in this country and around the world. Our responsibility, given our mandate, resources, and unique level of access, was to provide the foundation for that dialogue.

The arguments about 9/11 did not end with the publication of our report. For instance, over the summer of 2005, Congressman Curt Weldon repeatedly accused us of overlooking the importance of Able Danger, the Department of Defense open-source data-mining program. We dispute the facts of Congressman Weldon's charge—that Able Danger identified Mohammed Atta before 9/11 and that he gave then Deputy National Security Advisor Stephen Hadley an Able Danger chart with Atta's name on it on September 25, 2001, a chart developed in 1999 (Weldon made the charge in his June 2005 book, *Countdown to Terror*). Hadley has no recollection of such a chart and no such chart has been found in the records of the National Security Council. To date, despite extensive reviews by the Department of Defense and the Senate Intelligence Committee, no chart—or any other Able Danger document that had been created before 9/11—has been found that includes Atta's name or any other hijacker's name.

The absence of any documents supporting the charge, the manifold contradictions in the statements made about Able Danger by Weldon and others, the improbability—if not impossibility—of the program's ability to identify Atta, and the simple fact that people can have faulty memories about what took place years in the past, led us to the conclusion that Able Danger just did not do what Weldon said it did. Yet there will be other

"Able Dangers" in the years to come; it is always possible for new information to emerge. That information should be reviewed on its merits, and we are happy to welcome that information into the dialogue on 9/11.

We discovered real defects within the United States government. Our recommendations arose out of serious concern. We found national security institutions built to fight and win the cold war, yet poorly designed to combat the stateless and shadowy enemy of al Qaeda and Islamist terrorism. We found a lack of counterterrorism capabilities across the government—from our border protection, to our military and covert action capacity, to the communications capabilities of our emergency responders. We found a disturbing lack of unity of effort in the way government shares, analyzes, and acts on information.

Our recommendations were designed to address these defects. With the Intelligence Reform and Terrorism Prevention Act, some of those defects were addressed—notably, the structure of our national security agencies. Yet no law is self-executing. And people, not organizational charts, will win the fight against Islamist terrorism. It will take years to see if our recommendations are implemented effectively to correct the defects they were intended to address.

Some of our recommendations do not lend themselves to legislation, chief among them our foreign policy recommendations. The United States must enhance its outreach and communication with the Arab and Islamic worlds, and deepen its relationships with Saudi Arabia, Pakistan, and Afghanistan. This will take many years, and cannot be accomplished by an act of Congress.

Yet the lessons we took away from the 9/11 Commission went beyond even the substantive results of our work. We learned a great deal about 9/11 and terrorism, and much of that is shared in our report and within these pages. We also learned from the process of our inquiry. Through those twenty months, we learned a great deal about American democracy—above all, how much it works, but also how it could work better.

We learned that the United States Congress needs help. Too often, Congress cannot deal with the toughest questions facing the nation. Because of the divisiveness in the country, the dizzying twenty-four-hour news cycle, the constant need to raise funds and travel back and forth to a home district, the complexity of some bills, and the pressure on members to be partisan team players, it is harder for Congress to take the time to work through issues and build consensus. So many tough issues now get foisted off on commissions. One commentator put it well during our public hearings by saying that our public form of inquiry was important, but why couldn't it take place in Congress?

Many times throughout our inquiry, we were struck by how much our government does not look back—either within the executive branch, or within Congress. As we grappled with question after question related to 9/11, people within the commission, and sometimes people we were interviewing, said, "Why hasn't anybody done this?" There are good reasons, of course. Government is a forward-looking business. The in-box for policy makers is always overflowing, as people deal with immediate responsibilities and crises, and planning for the future. But sometimes you need to look back and learn the lessons of the past in order to move forward effectively. That was part of what went wrong before 9/11: nobody had taken the time to look back, to gather the facts from across government about a growing threat, and to draw the right lessons from those facts.

We learned that there is a thirst for accountability in this country. Americans expect their government to work, and are disappointed when it does not. The events of 9/11 raised many questions about how our government could fail to protect its people. When we began to put out information in the form of our staff reports, we were astonished by the hunger for facts among the American people. The same was true for our report— the simple reason that it was a bestseller is that it answered people's questions. Many people were traumatized by 9/11. After 9/11, they wanted to know how this had happened, and the government had a responsibility to tell them.

Among politicians, though, there was an ever-present and understandable fear that a full accounting would lead to blame, perhaps at the ballot box. This fear must not and need not preclude transparency and accountability in government. Someone needs to guard the guardians. Almost any public official whom you encounter is doing his or her best on behalf of the American people, and certainly trying to protect them from harm. But human beings are not infallible. That is why there must always be mechanisms for review and accounting built into our system of governance. And government would do well to heed people's desire for accountability. Often, the appearance of a cover-up is far more damaging to public perception than the consequences of full revelation of the truth.

We learned the power of openness and transparency. Given the importance of 9/11 and the increasing assignment of tough issues to commissions, we had to pursue our inquiry in an open manner. We could not retreat behind closed doors in Washington, meeting periodically, reading documents, and emerging at our reporting date to issue a report to be filed on the shelves of the Library of Congress. We had to bring the public along throughout our inquiry, keep the American people alerted to our pitfalls and our progress, and use our commission to educate the American people and their representatives in Congress about 9/11 and the need for reform.

Our public hearings were sometimes a difficult exercise. We did not always tread precisely the line between fact-finding and finger-pointing, and it was painful to revisit 9/11 in such a public manner. Yet, overwhelmingly, people thanked us for holding those hearings. We received our share of public criticism—these days, when you are in the public eye, you are also a bull's-eye. But American democracy is strong enough to have these conversations out in the open. When the government fails to do its work in the open, questions go unanswered, and public doubts erode the foundation of our government's legitimacy.

We learned the value of collective effort. Often, commissions or committees are driven almost entirely by the chair and vice-chair. On our commission, every single commissioner participated actively throughout the process. Certainly, that made things unwieldy at times. Yet at different junctures of our work, every single commissioner had at least one moment when he or she made an indispensable contribution—through a suggestion about how to solve a problem, or through an important act of outreach. This allowed the commission to succeed, and gave commissioners confidence in the process and substance of our report.

That effort went beyond the commissioners. We would not have achieved what we did without an extraordinary staff. These people of immense talent were asked to do far more than could be expected—the workload was unrelenting, the topics covered were varied, and the emotions were raw. In assessing public service, many Americans overlook the people who work out of sight, in support of their elected or appointed officials. Starting at the top, with our staff front office, and working down through each of our staff teams, we were able to expect work of remarkable quality, and trusted that work throughout our inquiry.

We also had the support of an extraordinary outside group: the 9/11 families. They were our most immediate and human connections to the events of 9/11, and made both the commission itself and whatever success we had possible. Our relations were up and down, and sometimes very difficult. Yet at every key moment—at the commission's creation; when we needed more money, more access, or more time; and when we needed to press the president and the Congress to act—the families made the difference. Their public voice did not waver, nor did their determination to learn the full truth about 9/11, and to see this nation made safer from future attacks.

Both the commission and the families took criticism at times for their prominent roles. That criticism misunderstood the nature of each group's contribution, and offered a cynical view of American democracy. On a basic level, our inquiry was answering the question Why did these people's loved ones have to die? The ability of the 9/11 families to come together, educate themselves about national security and national politics, and raise their voices to demand action is in the best tradition of grassroots democracy in this country.

We learned the necessity of pursuing consensus. We could have taken a more rigid approach. With regard to the White House, we received a lot of advice to be confrontational, notably through the issuance of blanket subpoenas for documents and witnesses. Instead, we negotiated with executive branch officials, and then negotiated some more. When we reached a point where we needed to take a firm stance, we did so—by issuing a subpoena or a public statement. Yet by staying in touch with the White House (particularly Alberto Gonzales and Andy Card), keeping the lines of communication open, and seeking a full understanding of our respective positions, we prevented misunderstandings from derailing the process; we were always moving forward.

The same was true within the commission. How did we reach a unanimous result? We talked. And talked. And then talked some more. Because every commissioner had his or her voice heard, every commissioner was invested in the process, and felt comfortable signing off on the report. If we had cut off debate, such unanimity might not have been possible. Because we spent so much time together, we came to respect one another as individuals, rather than viewing one another simply as partisans. And because every commissioner represented a different viewpoint across the country's ideological spectrum—from liberal to conservative—the broad majority of the American people could accept our report because they saw their own perspective represented on the commission.

We learned the power of facts. We have repeated this several times because it was so fundamental to our approach. Why? Think of the alternative. When people of opposing viewpoints begin their debate by simply stating their opposing views, you get nowhere. In public discourse, much of the debate shortly after 9/11 started like this: Clinton was too weak on terrorism. Bush ignored terrorism. The events of 9/11 happened because of illegal immigration. The attacks happened because the CIA meddles too much abroad. They happened because the CIA does not do enough abroad. They happened because of Saudi Arabian, Pakistani, Iranian, or Iraqi involvement. And on and on. Often people made these statements because they believed them to be true, not because they knew them to be true based on the facts.

If we had begun our deliberations from entrenched ideological positions, or partisan political theories, we would have gotten nowhere. Instead, we began with the facts, which are neither Republican nor Democratic. We could identify facts, and agree upon them. Out of those facts, we could identify what was wrong with the government, and offer recommendations to fix those deficiencies. Through the debate over our recommendations, many in the Congress and the government reverted to their ideological or bureaucratic bases, and put up stiff resistance to reform. We could counter by pointing out the facts—that the status quo they were protecting was unacceptable, and that the reforms we recommended were urgent and based on their merits. As Abraham Lincoln said, "I am a firm believer in the people. If given the truth, they can be depended upon to meet any national crises. The great point is to bring them the real facts."

We learned more than we cared to about the crisis of division within this country. Even though we were an independent commission investigating a singular national crisis, nearly everything we did was cast into Washington's cauldron of partisanship. Nearly all of our public statements were used in some venue by some outside party to gain partisan advantage. Media stories dealing with the commission often skipped past the substance of our work to focus on which political party or presidential candidate had gained an "edge" in the context of the twenty-four-hour-news-cycle wrestling match that is Washington's reality.

This divisive partisan atmosphere was our greatest obstacle. It surfaced in the questioning at our public hearings, and undoubtedly in pressure on commissioners from various quarters. It led to constant wariness of the commission in politicians who feared that we would cause them political harm. And it led to attacks on the commission, most notably from Attorney General Ashcroft—attacks that, ironically, only served to bring the commission closer together.

The divisiveness is at its most acute on the political fringes—the so-called radical right and loony left. On these extreme flanks of American political discourse, people have no interest in any evidence that does not adhere to their views. It is interesting that the 9/11 Commission was held in equal derision by these two opposing poles of thought—on the far right, because we dared to ask questions about the war on terror and failed to draw a straight line from 9/11 to this or that Clinton administration policy; and on the far left, because we did not endorse heinous conspiracy theories assigning culpability for 9/11 to the Bush administration. Indeed, in their dogmatic adherence to a partisan worldview and disdain for open and informed debate, the extremes in American politics have more in common with each other than they would imagine.

We learned, above all, that 9/11 exists in a place within the American consciousness that must transcend the partisan divide of our times. The events of that day were simply too important—to the American people, the 9/11 families, the staff, and the commissioners—for us to fail. Of course, over the years, "9/11" has been used in countless ways, and the term has been twisted in all directions. But when you return to the day itself, the experience retains its searing impact, and all of the accumulated political and emotional baggage falls by the wayside.

We had ample reminders of the day: meeting with widows and widowers, and parents who had outlived their children; hearing the recording of the calm voice of flight attendant Betty Ong reporting from American Airlines Flight 11 before it crashed into the World Trade Center; learning of the incidental heroism of an Orlando border inspector named Jose Melendez-Perez doing his daily job, or the dramatic actions of the passengers on United Airlines Flight 93, who saved the U.S. Capitol or White House from destruction; watching a fire department chief who took command in the lobby of the World Trade Center on that day view a tape of his brother climbing the steps of the burning tower to rescue civilians, never to come back down.

As we traveled around the country speaking to audiences about our work, it was striking the things people thanked us for. We were pleased to hear that many people bought our report and had words of praise for it. We were, of course, heartened that Congress and the president implemented many of our recommendations. But overwhelmingly the comment we received the most from ordinary Americans was that they appreciated our having come together, across partisan lines, to tell the story of 9/11 in a detailed, nonjudgmental way. In the long summer of 2004—filled with the rhetoric of a bitterly contested and at times nasty presidential election—they had found within the commission a brief respite, and perhaps a memory of how the country had come together in grief and resolve in the days after September 11, 2001.

As two people who have spent decades in public life, we found serving on the 9/11 Commission to provide a fascinating vantage point on American democracy. We were, at times, frustrated. But we emerged with more faith than we had when we started out. Democracy is a civil religion in this country, and it should be. With all of its imperfections, life in this country's political culture is far better than it would be under kings, oligarchs, or theocrats. Our system is not always efficient, effective, or wise, and it can stand improvement, but it is a system worth defending abroad, and advancing here at home. Where else could ten independent citizens probe the inner workings of government, question everybody up to a sitting president of the United States, and engage in a national dialogue on the key question of the day?

The threat of terrorism will be with us for years, likely decades, to come. The United States will be attacked again. Americans will die abroad pursuing terrorists. Americans will die at home going about their daily lives. In short, life—for at least one generation of Americans—will in part be shaped by the forces that struck us on 9/11, and by our ongoing response to that day.

Given that reality, our political divisions must and will inevitably fade against the larger responsibility to come together anew. There is a place— indeed, an obligation—for dissent and debate in a democratic society. But that dissent and debate pale in comparison to our shared interests, shared experience, and shared values. The day of 9/11 will, with time, become yet another moment in our nation's history, albeit a singular one. The cause of the 9/11 Commission was to capture that moment, make its story known to the American people, and make recommendations to prevent future 9/11s. The opportunity of the 9/11 Commission was to respond to a brutal attack on our democratic society with a demonstration of the value of democracy itself.

AFTERWORD

The struggle against Islamist terrorism has known several names. One phrase that has become popular among military officers is simply "the long war." While this refers chiefly to only one aspect of the struggle—its length—it correctly identifies the time frame: Americans will confront the challenge of terrorism for decades.

The recommendations of the 9/11 Commission were issued to reflect and respond to that reality. Many of our recommendations correct urgent problems—restructuring the intelligence community or giving first responders the ability to communicate with one another. Of these, many have been passed into law, and the Speaker of the House of Representatives, Nancy Pelosi, pledged during the 2006 campaign to legislate our pending recommendations after a Democratic takeover of Congress. As the new Congress moves ahead, the two of us look forward to working with Speaker Pelosi and members of Congress on both sides of the aisle to implement our remaining recommendations.

However, as we have said time and again, no law is self-executing. The key to success is the effectiveness of implementation. Today, we have a director of national intelligence, but it still is not clear that he has full control over the various agencies of the intelligence community. We have new mechanisms to share information among and within our intelligence agencies, but old habits of stovepiping and closely guarding information have proven hard to break. The Federal Bureau of Investigation is reforming itself to better counter terrorism, but serious problems continue: inadequate information technology, deficiencies in analytical capabilities, too much turnover in the workforce and leadership, and insufficient investment in human capital and training.

We have taken a special interest in the Privacy and Civil Liberties Oversight Board within the executive branch, which we recommended and the Congress created. The government needs strong powers to protect us, but there also needs to be a strong voice on behalf of individual and civil liberties. This board is up and running, but it needs to flex its muscles and demonstrate that it is a vigorous advocate for the rights and liberties of the American people. Whether it is wiretapping telephone conversations or monitoring financial transactions, the United States is still grappling with the balance between security and liberty. The board should be an important part of striking that balance.

We still feel that more can and must be done to prevent nuclear terrorism. In our report, we called for a "maximum effort" against this threat, including stepped-up efforts to secure loose nuclear materials abroad— particularly in the former Soviet Union. Often, this is simply a question of applying more resources and greater priority, while removing some cumbersome restrictions on U.S. action. Given the terrorists' determination to acquire a nuclear weapon—and the devastation that could be wrought by an attack—we must act with a greater sense of urgency.

The most important long-term recommendations in our report address issues that cannot be legislated: the way in which America engages the Islamic world. The problem goes well beyond Usama Bin Ladin and his cohorts in al Qaeda—though they must be pursued and captured or killed. Terrorism cannot be defeated by rounding up a list of people, or even destroying a terrorist organization like al Qaeda. From the mountains of Pakistan to apartment buildings in London, the United States is confronted by the deeper crisis of the radicalization of too many of the world's Muslims.

Terrorist recruiters prey upon Muslims who are angry. Sometimes they are without jobs, education, or hope. Sometimes they do not like the Western culture that is moving into their communities. And often they flat-out do not like American foreign policy: the war in Iraq, U.S. support for Israel, or U.S. backing for certain repressive regimes in the Islamic world. That does not mean that all of our foreign policy is wrong, or that it must be tailored to the satisfaction of others. It does mean that we need to do a better job of understanding the consequences of our policies around the world. And we must do far better—and far more—to reach out to the world's Muslims.

That begins with robust public diplomacy. This must be more than an advertising campaign—it has to be a sustained program of dialogue and outreach. In the cold war, the United States used every tool it could to reach beyond the Iron Curtain. We recommend similar initiatives, including television broadcasting, radio broadcasting, scholarship programs for young Muslims, educational exchanges, and an increase in American libraries and cultural centers around the world. These may seem like small things, but if a young person in a far-off land has his first experience with America in a welcoming library paid for by U.S. taxpayers, it makes a critical and potentially lasting first impression.

We also recommend "an agenda of opportunity" for the Islamic world. While the principal responsibility for progress lies with the governments of Muslim nations, the United States can send an important signal by helping Muslims help themselves. This should include support for pragmatic reform toward greater freedom and political participation in Muslim countries; economic initiatives to increase trade and investment; funding for educational reform in Muslim countries; and other creative foreign assistance.

The United States has spent roughly $6 billion on military assistance for Pakistan since 9/11; we could get a greater return on our investment if we provided more resources to give Pakistani kids alternatives to radical madrasahs. In Indonesia, when the U.S. military delivered aid and support for tsunami survivors, support for the U.S. in the country skyrocketed—and support for Bin Ladin plummeted. That's a lot cheaper than war.

Finally, the United States must offer moral leadership. We should treat all people—including those whom we detain—with respect for the rule of law and human decency, and take a strong stand against torture. We can and must be vigilant in pursuing our enemies and protecting our people. But as we do so, we can set a clear example to the world—and draw a clear distinction between America and the terrorists—by safeguarding our cherished values as closely as our security.

As the United States goes forward, we hope our nation can heal the internal divisions that have emerged since September 11, 2001. Partisanship is part of our political process, and it should be. But the American people do not want their political leaders to remain divided on the most important security issues confronting our nation. The United States cannot succeed in this great struggle—this long war—unless we move forward with united effort as a government, and as a nation.

Thomas H. Kean and Lee H. Hamilton

ACKNOWLEDGMENTS

This book, like the 9/11 Commission, depended upon the hard work of an extraordinary number of people. We would once again like to thank President George W. Bush and the members of Congress and the executive branch who made our service on the 9/11 Commission possible.

It was an honor to serve alongside our fellow commissioners, and we are extremely grateful that they took the time to cooperate with this project; their recollections and insights were essential. Many members of the 9/11 Commission's excellent staff also shared recollections of the commission through interviews and responses to queries, and their cooperation has made this a far richer book. In particular, Chris Kojm was diligent in reviewing drafts of the book's chapters, as were Dan Marcus, Steve Dunn, and Stephanie Kaplan.

Ben Rhodes was invaluable to us throughout the commission's work, and in helping us to research, prepare, and draft this book. We are also grateful to our talented and hard-working research assistant, Amanda Murphy. James Morris was generous in reviewing early drafts. The extraordinary photographs inside the book were taken by the very talented David Coleman; those who are interested in seeing more of David's work—including more photographs of the 9/11 Commission—should visit www.pxlar8.com. Our agent, Flip Brophy, provided exceptional guidance and support throughout the publication process. At Alfred A. Knopf, Dan Frank has been an exemplary and patient editor.

This book is dedicated to the memory of those who died on September 11, 2001. It is also dedicated to their families, who were inspirational partners to us throughout our work, and who once again helped us as we put this book together. We will never forget those who were lost on that terrible day. We can, however, draw on the example of their families, who turned an incomprehensible loss into a lasting service to their nation.

THE REPORT CARD

And all 10 of us have decided to keep in touch, to work to implement these recommendations, do everything we can . . . to let the American people know about these recommendations, know how important they are, our belief that they can save lives, and [we will] continue to work as a group long after our charter goes out of existence. And we agreed to meet in a year to determine our progress.

— Thomas Kean, July 22, 2004

WHY THE PUBLIC DISCOURSE PROJECT?

Many commissions preceded the 9/11 Commission. Many made excellent recommendations on intelligence, terrorism, and what would become known as homeland security. As we reflected on their efforts, we realized that these panels did superb work, but their recommendations were not implemented. A news column would be written about their reports, and then memory of them would fade away, forgotten by the general public and policy maker alike.

How to avoid this fate preoccupied us throughout the life of the 9/11 Commission. Every public event we held, every hearing and interim report, had as its purpose to engage the attention of the American public. We wanted to bring our fellow citizens along, so that they would understand our work and support our recommendations.

We soon realized that a press conference held on the day of our final report would not be enough to achieve our purpose. We would need ongoing work, performed by an organization dedicated to achieving our goal. That became apparent as we were flooded with requests for testimony—just as we were letting most of our staff go because the mandate of the commission was expiring. In those final, frenzied weeks, we decided to create a small private, nonprofit foundation, the 9/11 Public Discourse Project, to carry on and support our work. In the fall of 2004, the PDP staff helped commissioners prepare testimony for some twenty appearances before congressional panels.

Tom, Jamie Gorelick, and John Lehman took the lead in raising money, and Jim Thompson provided us with the legal help to set up a new organization. We quickly raised close to $1 million—enough to carry out our project for the next sixteen months with a small staff, including five veterans from the commission (Chris Kojm, Al Felzenberg, Dianna Campagna, Mike Hurley, and Alexis Albion) and two talented young people (Adam Klein and Erin Smith). Throughout 2005, the PDP was a platform from which to educate the American people about our recommendations.

SPEAKING NATIONWIDE

Throughout the project, we placed strong emphasis on public speaking and outreach. That emphasis never wavered. Commissioners received many, many speaking invitations. We tried to accept each one. If commissioners could not meet a request, the small PDP staff would try to do so, or would call on their former colleagues from the commission staff. Over its life span, the Public Discourse Project had more than five hundred speaking engagements—an average of more than one a day. In each case, the speakers' central theme was the commission's recommendations and their goal: stressing both the necessity and the urgency of action.

The speaking venues were as diverse as the country itself. At one end of the media spectrum, Tom and Lee and other commissioners would appear on the Sunday morning news talk shows. (During the life of the PDP, Tom and Lee both appeared three times on NBC's *Meet the Press*.) At the other end of the spectrum, former staff did local drive-time radio talk shows. And commissioners and staff appeared on almost every electronic media variant in between.

Commissioners spoke to editorial boards, at college commencements, with scout leaders, port officials, and model UN students, at the Hadassah, Rotary, and Kiwanis clubs, and at chambers of commerce, law schools, and scores of colleges and high schools. We participated in chat room discussions, and spoke in classrooms to a dozen people and in large halls to more than a thousand. Our staff went to Minnesota in mid-winter, and Mike Hurley drove three hours from the nearest airport, Sault Ste. Marie, to answer the invitation of a small school in Michigan's Upper

Peninsula. We spoke to military, intelligence, and foreign service officers; we spoke to trade associations, real estate agents, and doctors. We spoke in thirty-seven states and five countries.

We talked frequently to young people. For them, the war on terrorism was concrete. Their classmates and siblings were serving on the front line. We spoke to them not only of the mistakes our government had made, but of the importance of national service and of staying aware of what was happening in the world. Not paying enough attention to terrorism before 9/11 had hurt us; we wanted young people to understand that their involvement made a difference.

We found that we could always connect to our audiences, whatever age or walk of life. Everyone remembered where they were and what they were doing when they heard of the attacks. When we spoke of our recommendations, our audiences did not consider them abstract or bureaucratic. The story of 9/11 led directly to a discussion about the safety and security of their loved ones. We knew that making that connection with our fellow citizens was essential in order to get action on our recommendations from our elected leaders.

Throughout our work, we always got the question: "How did you get five Republicans and five Democrats to agree?" The question itself usually brought applause. Tom Brokaw, the former *NBC News* anchor, said that the real resonance of the report was that "for once, there was agreement in Washington without partisan bickering."

WASHINGTON, D.C.

In addition to public speaking nationwide, our focus was Washington. The epilogue already recounts the intense period from the report rollout in July, to December 2004, when we succeeded, after many twists and turns and near failures, in getting major intelligence reform legislation signed into law. Support from the 9/11 families and the staff of the Public Discourse Project was crticial to our success. After the president's bill-signing ceremony on December 17, we celebrated. With the family members present at that event, we were also keenly mindful of the loss that had brought about our work. We closed out the year with a sense of accomplishment tempered by the knowledge that much work was still ahead.

The new year brought us challenges right at the outset. The 109th Congress organized itself, as the Constitution requires, on the third of January. Lee knew from long experience that it was only in the run-up to votes on the very first day of a new Congress that you had the ability to influence how the Congress organized itself. We wanted the new Congress to adopt the reforms we had recommended for improving oversight of homeland security and intelligence. We had limited success. The Speaker, to his considerable credit, took on powerful committee chairmen and worked to strengthen the Homeland Security Committee, which became a permanent standing committee of Congress, with enhanced jurisdiction.

On intelligence oversight, we were less successful. As we had recommended, the House created an oversight subcommittee of the Intelligence Committee. It did not, however, act on far-reaching commission recommendations to strengthen the authorities of the Intelligence Committee and its ability to perform oversight. In some respects, reform actually went backward. In October 2004 the Senate had agreed to establish a separate appropriations subcommittee to handle intelligence funding. While this was not precisely what we had recommended, we had supported it as a step in the right direction. It was far better, we thought, to have one subcommittee giving careful attention to the annual intelligence appropriations than to have intelligence funding buried as a small fraction of the defense appropriations bill, where it could receive only scant attention from the committee. But even this modest reform was rolled back when the House refused to go along with the creation of a new appropriations subcommittee. As members of Congress described it to us, oversight of intelligence remains "dysfunctional."

We also spent the first weeks of 2005 carefully analyzing the bill that had been signed into law. Without question, the reforms of the intelligence community mandated in the new law were significant. The legislation addressed many aspects of our recommendations: the creation of a National Counterterrorism Center, the creation of a Privacy and Civil Liberties Oversight Board, reforms at the FBI, national standards for ID documents, and far greater attention to information sharing across the government.

We were certainly heartened by the many positive reforms in the new law, but we knew that passage of a law was only the first step. As Woodrow Wilson said, "Quite as important as legislation is vigilant oversight of administration." The long road of implementation of reform would be a hard slog. We realized that the Public Discourse Project would need to perform its own oversight, to monitor carefully what the government was doing to execute faithfully the new law of the land.

Our analysis of the new law also found that several significant recommendations from the commission had been left unaddressed. The new law did not change the formula for homeland security funding, which was to provide dollars strictly on an assessment of risks and vulnerabilities: for example, New York still receives less funding per capita for homeland security than the state of Wyoming. The new law also did not provide the broadcast spectrum long promised to first responders, so they could communicate reliably in a crisis. The new law did not strengthen the Incident Command System for emergency response. The new law was silent on the question of weapons of mass destruction, except for increasing criminal penalties for possessing them. The new law had many "sense of Congress" provisions on foreign policy that supported our recommendations, but without the necessary funding to achieve them.

So it was clear to us, as we moved into 2005, that a lot of work remained to be done—both in terms of oversight of the law that had been passed, and regarding advocacy on behalf of the commission recommendations that had been left undone.

OVERSIGHT WORK

It is difficult for an organization outside the government to conduct oversight, especially in areas that involve significant amounts of classified material. Our security clearances had disappeared with the end of the commission, and unlike congressional committees, we did not have legal authority to compel testimony or the production of documents. We could compensate for this with the excellent contacts we had throughout Washington—and with the credibility we had established. Moreover, we had the advantage of knowing exactly where we wanted to focus our efforts and attention. Congressional committees are so often preoccupied with budget matters and the crisis of the moment that they fall short in their ability to perform systematic oversight.

So, in the spring of 2005, we put together a detailed plan for oversight hearings to be held by the Public Discourse Project, to cover key aspects of our recommendations and to evaluate how much progress had been made. We asked each commissioner to chair a session, and we invited the best experts we could find to comment in detail on what had been accomplished and what remained to be done. To inform and supplement the hearings, we sent out a dozen letters to the Bush administration, including the responsible Cabinet departments, asking the same questions.

We spent the spring preparing, and then held the hearings throughout the summer. Jamie Gorelick kicked off our panels on June 6, with the topic of "Reform at the FBI and CIA"; John Lehman followed a week later with a session on the new "Director of National Intelligence." We rounded out the month with a session chaired by Tim Roemer on terrorism and the proliferation of weapons of mass destruction, and a session chaired by Bob Kerrey on several of our homeland security recommendations.

July was a busy month, with a session chaired by Slade Gorton on the reform of congressional oversight, followed by one co-chaired by Richard Ben-Veniste and Fred Fielding on the balance between civil liberties and national security. Lee finished off in August with a session on foreign policy in the Middle East and South Asia.

In each case, we were able to gain the enthusiastic participation by members of Congress, former senior officials, and nationally known experts. We had strong interest from the media, and in several cases we even asked journalists to join our panels. Our sessions were covered by C-SPAN and rebroadcast repeatedly. Time permitting, we took questions from the audience. As with the 9/11 Commission, we believed that opening our work to the public was the best way to inform and engage public opinion on behalf of the commission's recommendations.

The role of the administration was disappointing. White House chief of staff Andy Card made clear that the administration would treat the 9/11 Public Discourse Project no differently than it treated any other nonprofit organization: we were accorded no special status. The White House did not consult with us at all on its progress or lack of progress in implementing our recommendations. Of the dozen letters we sent to the White House, the intelligence community, and Cabinet departments, only three were answered: those from the Departments of State, Energy, and Homeland Security.

In each letter we also made clear our interest in meeting with senior administration officials, whether in public or private. No administration official participated in our public panels. Tom and Lee benefited on three occasions from meeting with the director and deputy director of National Intelligence, but the DNI's office declined to schedule a meeting with a broader group of former commissioners. The commission staff did meet with Admiral John Scott Redd, the director of the National Counterterrorism Center.

The spring and summer were our seasons to gather information. As late summer turned to fall, our plan was to start the evaluation process. We had originally intended to hold one session, around the anniversary of September 11, to present a full report on the commission's forty-one recommendations. Then Hurricane Katrina hit.

HOMELAND SECURITY

The disastrous response to Hurricane Katrina by all levels of government reminded us immediately of the response to 9/11. Poor communications, poor command and control, and poor emergency preparedness were huge problems on the Gulf Coast, as they had been on 9/11. As we gathered with our fellow commissioners in September, we decided to concentrate on these critical homeland security topics. We felt that the government had learned little, and that performance had fallen far short.

First, better communications could have saved many lives, both on 9/11 and during Hurricane Katrina and its aftermath. Emergency responders in New Orleans and the nearby parishes all used different radio systems, operating on different spectrum bands, and therefore had problems talking to one another, and to state and federal authorities. It is scandalous that four years after 9/11, police, firefighters, and emergency medical technicians still could not communicate reliably.

Second, disarray in command structures hurt emergency response to both 9/11 and Hurricane Katrina. There was confusion at all levels of government. No agency was clearly in charge. Search-and-rescue operations—both in the Twin Towers and on the flooded streets of New Orleans—were duplicative and not coordinated. Poor command structures cost lives.

When multiple agencies or multiple jurisdictions are involved in an emergency response, they must designate one agency to lead that response. They must have a plan—not just on paper; it must be exercised regularly. All agencies must know to whom they should report and what they are expected to do.

Third, whether for terrorism or natural disasters, the federal government must allocate homeland security grants strictly on the basis of risk and vulnerability, not politics. The 9/11 Commission recommended that federal funds for emergency preparedness not be distributed as political pork. It is up to Congress to write these principles into law. Congress still has not done so. As Jim Thompson asked, "Are we crazy? Have we learned nothing?"

REFORM OF THE INSTITUTIONS OF GOVERNMENT

In October, we turned to a public evaluation of the institutions of government—both the new institutions created by the reform statute and those undergoing significant reforms mandated by the statute. We found that the new institutions of the director of National Intelligence and the National Counterterrorism Center were up and running, but both had a long way to go in addressing critical issues such as information sharing and building a unified community.

Several of our fellow commissioners, especially Slade Gorton and Tim Roemer, joined us in expressing our deep disappointment in the pace of reform within the FBI. The trend on FBI reform has been in the right direction, but reform has been far too slow. Numerous problems still impede the Bureau's ability to carry out its new counterterrorism function: significant deficiencies in the FBI's analytic capabilities and in information sharing with other agencies and with local law enforcement; high turnover in the workforce and in top-level counterterrorism and intelligence leadership; and insufficient investment in human capital and training. To date, initiatives to improve the FBI's inadequate information technology capabilities have failed. As we write this, the Bureau has failed to make intelligence its dominant mission.

We also found that little progress had been made in implementing the Privacy and Civil Liberties Oversight Board recommended by the commission and created by the Congress. The board's purpose is an essential one. To fight terrorism and to protect the American people we need strong institutions and robust governmental powers. We also need checks and balances for those powers. The commission had deliberately recommended a board within the executive branch to play that role.

The President did not appoint members to this board until June 2005, and did not send up his nominations for chair and vice-chair to the Senate until September. As of February 2006, these nominations have yet to be confirmed. No meetings of the board have been held. No staff has been named. No work plan has been outlined. No work has begun. No office has been established. No funds have been spent. The board shows few signs of life.

FOREIGN POLICY, PUBLIC DIPLOMACY, AND NONPROLIFERATION

In November 2005, as commissioners, we took up a third evaluation session, looking at the international aspects of our recommendations. We placed our most intense focus on securing nuclear materials. The president has stated correctly that the gravest danger our nation faces is at the crossroads of radicalism and technology. As the commission recommended, preventing terrorist access to weapons of mass destruction "warrants a maximum effort" by our government.

We found that the administration is taking useful steps, but what struck us is that the size of the problem still dwarfs the level of effort being made. The Nunn-Lugar Cooperative Threat Reduction Program to secure nuclear materials in the former Soviet Union is fourteen years old. About half of the nuclear materials in Russia still have no security upgrades. At the current rate of effort, it may take another fourteen years to complete the mission. This is unacceptable. The terrorists will not wait. We still do not have a maximum effort against the most urgent threat to the American people. With proper leadership, we believe the mission can be completed in three years.

In Afghanistan, we found signs of progress—an elected government in place, schools open, infrastructure improving. But profound problems remain. The drug trade is booming, and a low-level Taliban insurgency is growing.

As the commission stated, the challenge for the United States and the international community is to stay engaged, to keep attention focused. We need to accept the fact that reform in Afghanistan will take many years. The road is long, and it will be bumpy. But our commitment must be consistent and steadfast. If we are to defeat al Qaeda, Afghanistan must never again become a terrorist sanctuary.

Regarding Pakistan, we expressed our concern that President Musharraf had not done more to combat terrorism or promote reform. Taliban still pass freely across the Pakistan-Afghanistan border and operate in Pakistani tribal areas. Full cooperation with the United States in hunting down Bin Ladin and his supporters has not been forthcoming. Madrasahs with known links to terrorist groups have not been closed down. Promised democratic reforms are not in evidence, yet Musharraf remains our best ally. Without reform, Pakistan, with its nuclear weapons, could become the most dangerous country in the world.

With respect to Saudi Arabia, we found progress to be mixed. Since the 2003 Riyadh bombings, Saudi security forces have been acting forcefully against domestic al Qaeda cells, but practical reform in the kingdom is lagging. The United States has not yet taken up, as the commission recommended, building a relationship with Saudi Arabia on a new basis, going beyond the exchange of oil for security. We called for broader U.S.-Saudi dialogue, to increase people-to-people exchanges and promote pragmatic reform.

On public diplomacy, we commended the president for appointing his trusted adviser Karen Hughes as his point person for outreach, but we also noted that all the key challenges are ahead of her. Public diplomacy is not a one-way street. It is not merely delivering a message—it is communication. At its heart, public diplomacy is a process of engagement and developing relationships. We still need to reach out to young people, combat misinformation, and communicate our ideals with force and eloquence. We have a long way to go.

DECIDING ON LETTER GRADES

In the fall of 2005, the reports of the Public Discourse Project gained some attention. Terrorism and homeland security experts and the attentive public understood our views. Still, we had not grabbed the attention of the general public in the way we thought necessary. As a method of engaging the public, commissioners had discussed on and off the idea of issuing letter "grades" on the progress made on each of our recommendations.

We had initially held back from expressing a strong view on letter grades, but by the fall, Tom was pressing hard for them as a means of connecting with the press and the general public at our final event. Letter grades were something that everyone had experienced, and they were self-explanatory: everyone understood what it meant to get an A or an F. As Tom saw it, letter grades were a powerful public communications tool. Would our letter grades be fair? Certainly not everyone would think so, but the point of using them was to focus attention on problem areas, and thereby on improved performance.

We had some worries about finding common ground among the commissioners on the letter grades. For example, John Lehman had written—and later published—an article highly critical of the new Office of the Director of National Intelligence. Lehman saw complex "layering" and "bureaucracy" taking hold within the office—both antithetical to his strongly held views about how the office should be structured. Other commissioners had strong views about the progress on reform at the FBI, and about reform inside Saudi Arabia.

Our usual practice, during the life both of the commission and of the Public Discourse Project, was to talk out our views, and then talk some more. Staff would circulate drafts, and long trains of e-mailed comments would follow. We reflected on each of these comments and then tried to come to a consensus in a conference call. By late 2005, we knew one another very well, and had been around these issues a long time. There was no disagreement among us as to the facts, as we had all participated in assembling them, so we were able to come to closure on report card grades with little difficulty.

On Sunday night, December 4, the 9/11 commissioners gathered together for a last social event. Tim Roemer graciously opened his home to us, and he and his lovely wife, Sally, hosted a dinner. Tim's son Patrick, age twelve, asked several of the commissioners questions about a report he was doing for school. We had finished our work; we enjoyed one another's company before our final event the next day.

To wrap up the party, we made remarks, thanking our fellow commissioners and staff, and took note not only of our twenty months' work as a commission, but also of the ensuing sixteen months as the Public Discourse Project—working as best we knew how to implement the ideas we had recommended to make our country safer and more secure. Whatever road each of us later pursued, we knew that service on the commission would be a high point in our careers.

THE REPORT CARD

Monday, December 5, was cold and cloudy; later that day it would snow. We gathered that morning in the Ronald Reagan Building to present our report card before the assembled press and public. The grades matched December's chill.

We had seen some positive steps toward carrying out the recommendations of the 9/11 Commission, but still found so much to be done. Of the forty-one letter grades we issued, nine were Cs, ten were Ds, and five were Fs. As Jamie Gorelick put it, this was not a report card a child would be proud to take home to his parents.

Tom spoke to some of our frustration in his opening remarks:

> Many obvious steps that the American people assume have been completed, have not been. Our leadership is distracted. Some of these failures are shocking. Four years after 9/11: It is scandalous that police and firefighters in large cities *still* cannot communicate reliably in a major crisis. It is scandalous that airline passengers are still not screened against all names on the terrorist watch list. It is scandalous that we still allocate scarce homeland security dollars on

the basis of pork barrel spending, not risk. . . . We believe that the terrorists will strike again. If they do, and these reforms have not been implemented, what will our excuses be? While the terrorists are learning and adapting, our government is still moving at a crawl.

Despite our frustration, we wanted to be as constructive as possible in the report we presented. We spotlighted those areas where attention and improvement were especially still needed. Tom highlighted the importance of risk-based allocation of homeland security funding. The House had passed an excellent bill on the subject, but the Senate had refused to take it up in conference committee. Lee highlighted problems in information sharing. Despite the creation, in the new law, of a program manager to improve information sharing across the government, progress there was minimal.

All of us felt strongly about reform at the FBI. Director Mueller has the right goals, but progress has been far too slow, and he cannot do it alone: the president needs to lead, and Congress needs to provide careful oversight. Unless there is improvement in a reasonable period of time, Congress will have to look at alternatives.

THE MOST DIFFICULT AND THE MOST IMPORTANT

We closed our presentation of the Report Card by focusing on our most difficult recommendation, and the most important one.

The most *difficult* recommendation surely is the one regarding enacting reform within the Congress. Redistributing power within an institution is never easy, yet it is clear to us that, now more than ever, Congress needs powerful oversight committees for intelligence and homeland security. Why? Because Congress has provided powerful authority to the executive branch in order to protect us. It has created a director of National Intelligence, a National Counterterrorism Center. It has given the executive branch strong powers to investigate citizens and inspect their documents.

Congress now needs to act as an effective check on the executive branch in carrying out the counterterrorism policies of the United States. Because so much information is classified, Congress is the only source of independent oversight on the full breadth of intelligence and homeland security issues before our country.

During our investigation, the word we heard most often on Capitol Hill describing this oversight was *dysfunctional.* The oversight committees need stronger powers over the budget and exclusive jurisdiction. When too many committees are responsible for something, nobody is responsible. So far, Congress's efforts to reform intelligence oversight merit no higher than a D.

If its oversight committees are weak, Congress cannot play its proper role under the Constitution to provide checks and balances on the actions of the executive. Strong oversight by Congress protects our liberties and makes our policies better. Our freedom and safety depend on robust, bipartisan oversight by Congress. This is not happening.

Our most *important* recommendation was surely the one regarding preventing terrorists from gaining access to nuclear weapons. These are the weapons Usama bin Laden has promised to obtain and use. This would be not the most *likely* terrorist scenario but the most *consequential,* putting millions of lives at risk. Such a possibility must be elevated above all other problems of national security, because it represents the greatest threat to the American people, and would be devastating to our economy and our way of life. We felt that efforts to prevent such a scenario merited no better than a D.

The president should request the personnel and resources, and provide the domestic and international leadership, to secure all weapons-grade nuclear material as soon as possible. There is simply no higher priority on the national security agenda.

On the day we issued our report card, Tom received one final call from the White House. Like so many of the calls during the life of the commission, this one, too, was a complaint. "The grades are unfair," said Chief of Staff Andy Card, but he did not explain how or why. The administration told the press later that day that it had implemented nearly all of our recommendations. We disagreed.

WHAT DID WE ACCOMPLISH?

As we look back at this past year and the work of the Public Discourse Project, we ask ourselves: What did we accomplish?

We caught the attention of Congress and of the American people, both with our recommendations and with our bipartisan approach. We played a role in bringing about, as President Bush put it, "the most dramatic reform of our nation's intelligence capabilities . . . since 1947." That same law enacted about half of our recommendations. Yet the challenge of implementing the new law remains, as our Report Card amply makes clear.

People asked us: Why did you end the Public Discourse Project when there was so much work left to be done?

Our view is a simple one: Congress and the president gave the ten of us a mandate. We carried it out to the best of our ability. We made our recommendations. As ten private citizens, we then worked on behalf of those recommendations, as best we knew how. After a year of effort, we felt strongly that it was time to take the responsibility we had been given and give it back.

To whom?

First, to the citizens of this country. What we learned this past year is that change and reform don't happen in this country unless the American people demand them. There is no substitute for an engaged and attentive public watching what its elected leaders do. The 9/11 families are an example for every student of government: citizen involvement makes a huge and positive difference. As individual citizens, we will continue to speak out.

Second, to organizations. We hope that from the seeds of our work of this past year other efforts will grow. Every government institution benefits from the informed attention of outside watchdog groups. The intelligence community, above all, needs the interest and attention of those outside of government who care deeply about its success.

Finally, to our elected leaders. The first purpose of government, as stated in the preamble of our Constitution, is to "provide for the common defense." We have made clear, time and again, what we believe needs to be done to make our country safer and more secure: the responsibility for action, and leadership, rests with Congress and the president.

September 11, 2001, was a day of unbearable suffering. It was also a day when we were united as Americans. We came together as citizens with a sense of urgency and of purpose.

We now call upon our elected leaders to come together again, with that same sense of urgency and purpose. We call upon Republicans and Democrats to work together to make our country safer and more secure. The American people deserve no less.

Final Report on 9/11 Commission Recommendations

December 5, 2005

Thomas H. Kean, Chair
Lee H. Hamilton, Vice Chair
Richard Ben-Veniste
Fred F. Fielding
Jamie S. Gorelick
Slade Gorton
Bob Kerrey
John F. Lehman
Timothy J. Roemer
James R. Thompson

www.9-11pdp.org

Part I: Homeland Security, Emergency Preparedness and Response

RECOMMENDATION	GRADE

EMERGENCY PREPAREDNESS AND RESPONSE

Provide adequate radio spectrum for first responders   F (C if bill passes)
The pending Fiscal Year 2006 budget reconciliation bill would compel the return of the analog TV broadcast (700 Mhz) spectrum, and reserve some for public safety purposes. Both the House and Senate bills contain a 2009 handover date—too distant given the urgency of the threat. A 2007 handover date would make the American people safer sooner.

Establish a unified Incident Command System   C
Although there is awareness of and some training in the ICS, hurricane Katrina demonstrated the absence of full compliance during a multi-jurisdictional/statewide catastrophe—and its resulting costs.

Allocate homeland security funds based on risk   F (A if House provision passes)
Congress has still not changed the underlying statutory authority for homeland security grants, or benchmarks to insure that funds are used wisely. As a result, homeland security funds continue to be distributed without regard for risk, vulnerability, or the consequences of an attack, diluting the national security benefits of this important program.

Critical infrastructure risks and vulnerabilities assessment   D
A draft National Infrastructure Protection Plan (November 2005) spells out a methodology and process for critical infrastructure assessments. No risk and vulnerability assessments actually made; no national priorities established; no recommendations made on allocation of scarce resources. All key decisions are at least a year away. It is time that we stop talking about setting priorities, and actually set some.

Private sector preparedness   C
National preparedness standards are only beginning to find their way into private sector business practices. Private sector preparedness needs to be a higher priority for DHS and for American businesses.

TRANSPORTATION SECURITY

National Strategy for Transportation Security   C-
DHS has transmitted its National Strategy for Transportation Security to the Congress. While the strategy reportedly outlines broad objectives, this first version lacks the necessary detail to make it an effective management tool.

Improve airline passenger pre-screening   F
Few improvements have been made to the existing passenger screening system since right after 9/11. The completion of the testing phase of TSA's pre-screening program for airline passengers has been delayed. A new system, utilizing all names on the consolidated terrorist watch list, is therefore not yet in operation.

Improve airline screening checkpoints to detect explosives   C
While more advanced screening technology is being developed, Congress needs to provide the funding for, and TSA needs to move as expeditiously as possible with, the appropriate installation of explosives detection trace portals at more of the nation's commercial airports.

Checked bag and cargo screening   **D**

Improvements here have not been made a priority by the Congress or the administration. Progress on implementation of in-line screening has been slow. The main impediment is inadequate funding.

BORDER SECURITY

Better terrorist travel strategy   **Incomplete**

The first Terrorist Travel Strategy is in development, due to be delivered by December 17, 2005 as required by PL 108-458.

Comprehensive screening system   **C**

We still do not have a comprehensive screening system. Although agencies are moving ahead on individual screening projects, there is lack of progress on coordination between agencies. DHS' new Screening Coordination Office still needs to establish and implement goals for resolving differences in biometric and traveler systems, credentialing and identification standards.

Biometric entry-exit screening system   **B**

The US-VISIT system is running at 115 airports and 15 seaports, and is performing secondary screening at the 50 busiest land borders. But border screening systems are not yet employed at all land borders, nor are these systems interoperable. The exit component of the US-VISIT system has not been widely deployed.

International collaboration on borders and document security   **D**

There has been some good collaboration between US-VISIT and Interpol, but little progress elsewhere. There has been no systematic diplomatic effort to share terrorist watchlists, nor has Congress taken a leadership role in passport security.

Standardize secure identifications   **B-**

The REAL ID Act has established by statute standards for state-issued IDs acceptable for federal purposes, though states' compliance needs to be closely monitored. New standards for issuing birth certificates (required by law by December 17, 2005) are delayed until at least spring 2006, probably longer. Without movement on the birth certificate issue, state-issued IDs are still not secure.

Part II: Reforming the Institutions of Government

RECOMMENDATION	GRADE

THE INTELLIGENCE COMMUNITY

Director of National Intelligence   **B**

The framework for the DNI and his authorities are in place. Now his challenge is to exercise his authorities boldly to smash stovepipes, drive reform, and create a unity of effort—and act soon. He must avoid layering of the bureaucracy and focus on transformation of the Intelligence Community. The success of this office will require decisive leadership from the DNI and the president, and active oversight by the Congress.

National Counterterrorism Center   **B**

Shared analysis and evaluation of threat information is in progress; joint operational planning is beginning. But the NCTC does not yet have sufficient resources or personnel to fulfill its intelligence and planning role.

Create FBI national security workforce   C

Progress is being made—but it is too slow. The FBI's shift to a counterterrorism posture is far from institutionalized, and significant deficiencies remain. Reforms are at risk from inertia and complacency; they must be accelerated, or they will fail. Unless there is improvement in a reasonable period of time, Congress will have to look at alternatives.

New missions for CIA Director   Incomplete

Reforms are underway at the CIA, especially of human intelligence operations. But their outcome is yet to be seen. If the CIA is to remain an effective arm of national power, Congress and CIA leadership need to be committed to accelerating the pace of reforms, and must address morale and personnel issues.

Incentives for information sharing   D

Changes in incentives, in favor of information sharing, have been minimal. The office of the program manager for information sharing is still a start-up, and is not getting the support it needs from the highest levels of government. There remain many complaints about lack of information sharing between federal authorities and state and local level officials.

Government-wide information sharing   D

Designating individuals to be in charge of information sharing is not enough. They need resources, active presidential backing, policies and procedures in place that compel sharing, and systems of performance evaluation that appraise personnel on how they carry out information sharing.

Homeland airspace defense   B-

Situational awareness and sharing of information has improved. But it is not routine or comprehensive, no single agency currently leads the interagency response to airspace violations, and there is no overarching plan to secure airspace outside the National Capital region.

CIVIL LIBERTIES AND EXECUTIVE POWER

Balance between security and civil liberties   B

The debate surrounding reauthorization of the PATRIOT Act has been strong, and concern for civil liberties has been at the heart of it. Robust and continuing oversight, both within the Executive and by the Congress, will be essential.

Privacy and Civil Liberties Oversight Board   D

We see little urgency in the creation of this Board. The President nominated a Chair and Vice Chair in June 2005, and sent their names to the Senate in late September. To date, the Senate has not confirmed them. Funding is insufficient, no meetings have been held, no staff named, no work plan outlined, no work begun, no office established.

Guidelines for government sharing of personal information   D

The Privacy and Civil Liberties Oversight Board has not yet begun its work. The DNI just named a Civil Liberties Protection Officer (November 2005).

CONGRESSIONAL AND ADMINISTRATIVE REFORM

Intelligence oversight reform   D

The House and Senate have taken limited positive steps, including the creation of oversight subcommittees. However, the ability of the intelligence committees to perform oversight of the intelligence agencies and account for their performance is still undermined by the power of the Defense Appropriations subcommittees and Armed Services committees.

Homeland Security committees   **B**

The House and Senate have taken positive steps, but Secretary Chertoff and his team still report to too many bosses. The House and Senate homeland security committees should have exclusive jurisdiction over all counterterrorism functions of the Department of Homeland Security.

Declassify overall intelligence budget   **F**

No action has been taken. The Congress cannot do robust intelligence oversight when funding for intelligence programs is buried within the defense budget. Declassifying the overall intelligence budget would allow for a separate annual intelligence appropriations bill, so that the Congress can judge better how intelligence funds are being spent.

Standardize security clearances   **B**

The President put the Office of Management and Budget (OMB) in charge of standardizing security clearances. OMB issued a plan to improve the personnel security clearance process in November 2005. The Deputy Director of OMB is committed to its success. All the hard work is ahead.

Part III: Foreign Policy, Public Diplomacy, and Nonproliferation

RECOMMENDATION	GRADE

NONPROLIFERATION

Maximum effort by U.S. government to secure WMD   **D**

Countering the greatest threat to America's security is still not the top national security priority of the President and the Congress.

FOREIGN POLICY

Long-term commitment to Afghanistan   **B**

Progress has been made, but attacks by Taliban and other extremists continue and the drug situation has worsened. The U.S. and its partners must commit to a long-term economic plan in order to ensure the country's stability.

Support Pakistan against extremists   **C+**

U.S. assistance to Pakistan has not moved sufficiently beyond security assistance to include significant funding for education efforts. Musharraf has made efforts to take on the threat from extremism, but has not shut down extremist-linked madrassas or terrorist camps. Taliban forces still pass freely across the Pakistan-Afghanistan border and operate in Pakistani tribal areas.

Support reform in Saudi Arabia   **D**

Saudi authorities have taken initial steps but need to do much more to regulate charities and control the flow of funds to extremist groups, and to promote tolerance and moderation. A U.S.-Saudi strategic dialogue to address topics including reform and exchange programs has just started; there are no results to report.

Identify and prioritize terrorist sanctuaries   **B**

Strategies have been articulated to address and eliminate terrorist sanctuaries, but they do not include a useful metric to gauge progress. There is little sign of long-term efforts in place to reduce the conditions that allow the formation of terrorist sanctuaries.

Coalition strategy against Islamist terrorism   C
Components of a common strategy are evident on a bilateral basis, and multilateral policies exist in some areas. But no permanent contact group of leading governments has yet been established to coordinate a coalition counterterrorism strategy.

Coalition standards for terrorist detention   F
The U.S. has not engaged in a common coalition approach to developing standards for detention and prosecution of captured terrorists. Indeed, U.S. treatment of detainees has elicited broad criticism, and makes it harder to build the necessary alliances to cooperate effectively with partners in a global war on terror.

Economic policies   B+
There has been measurable progress in reaching agreements on economic reform in the Middle East, including a free trade agreement with Bahrain and the likely admission of Saudi Arabia to the WTO before long. However, it is too early to judge whether these agreements will lead to genuine economic reform.

Vigorous effort against terrorist financing   A-
The U.S. has won the support of key countries in tackling terrorism finance—though there is still much to do in the Gulf States and in South Asia. The government has made significant strides in using terrorism finance as an intelligence tool. However, the State Department and Treasury Department are engaged in unhelpful turf battles, and the overall effort lacks leadership.

Public Diplomacy

Define the U.S. message   C
Despite efforts to offer a vision for U.S. leadership in the world based on the expansion of democratic governance, public opinion approval ratings for the U.S. throughout the Middle East remain at or near historic lows. Public diplomacy initiatives need to communicate our values, way of life, and vision for the world without lecturing or condescension.

International broadcasting   B
Budgets for international broadcasting to the Arab and Muslim world and U.S.-sponsored broadcasting hours have increased dramatically, and audience shares are growing. But we need to move beyond audience size, expose listeners to new ideas and accurate information about the U.S. and its policies, and measure the impact and influence of these ideas.

Scholarship, exchange, and library programs   D
Funding for educational and cultural exchange programs has increased. But more American libraries (Pakistan, for example) are closing rather than opening. The number of young people coming to study in the U.S. from the Middle East continues to decline (down 2% this year, following declines of 9% and 10% in the previous two years).

Support secular education in Muslim countries   D
An International Youth Opportunity Fund has been authorized, but has received no funding; secular education programs have been initiated across the Arab world, but are not integrated into a broader counterterrorism strategy. The U.S. has no overarching strategy for educational assistance, and the current level of education reform funding is inadequate.

9/11 COMMISSION TIMELINE

2002

NOVEMBER 27 President Bush signs 9/11 Commission into law, appoints Henry Kissinger chairman; Democratic leadership appoints George Mitchell vice-chair

DECEMBER 11 Mitchell resigns; Hamilton appointed vice-chair; remaining Democrats and Slade Gorton appointed

DECEMBER 13 Kissinger resigns

DECEMBER 16 Kean appointed chair; Speaker Hastert appoints Thompson and Fielding

DECEMBER 19 First Kean-Hamilton meeting held at Wilson Center

2003

JANUARY 26 Commissioner dinner held at Wilson Center

JANUARY 27 First meeting of commission held (at Wilson Center); Philip Zelikow announced as executive director

JANUARY 28 *President Bush delivers State of the Union Address*

JANUARY 31 Commission acquires office space in downtown Washington, D.C.

FEBRUARY 1 *Space shuttle* Columbia *falls to pieces during descent; seven astronauts die*

MARCH 17 Dan Marcus hired as general counsel

MARCH 19 *President Bush announces beginning of military operations to disarm Iraq*

MARCH 28 Congress approves commission budget increase, to $14 million

MARCH 31–APRIL 1 First public hearing held, in New York City

APRIL 16 All ten commissioners are granted security clearances

MAY 1 *President Bush lands aboard USS Abraham Lincoln, declares major combat over in Iraq*

MAY 1 Commission staff team work plans presented

MAY 22–23 Second public hearing held, "Congressional Oversight and Civil Aviation Security"

JUNE 16 New York office opens

JULY 8 Commission issues first interim report

JULY 9 Third public hearing held, "Al Qaeda and Terrorism"

JULY 11 Agreement reached on access to Moussaoui materials; Max Cleland appointed to Ex-Im Bank (awaiting confirmation)

AUGUST 8 *Truck bomb attack on UN headquarters in Baghdad kills seventeen, including top UN envoy*

SEPTEMBER 23 Commission issues second interim report

OCTOBER 7 *California voters recall Governor Gray Davis, elect Arnold Schwarzenegger as new governor*

OCTOBER 14 Fourth public hearing held, "Intelligence and War on Terror"; White House briefing held on PDBs

OCTOBER 15 Commission issues subpoena to FAA

OCTOBER 15–28 Commission staff travel to Saudi Arabia, Pakistan, Afghanistan, and United Kingdom

OCTOBER 27 President Bush addresses PDB issue for first time in news conference

NOVEMBER 6 Commission issues subpoena to Department of Defense

NOVEMBER 12 Agreement with White House on PDBs is announced

NOVEMBER 19 Fifth public hearing held, at Drew University, "Emergency Preparedness"; commission agrees on PDB "review team"; commission issues subpoena to New York City

DECEMBER 3 Agreement reached with New York City on access to 911 tapes, other remaining materials

DECEMBER 8 Sixth public hearing held, "Security and Liberty"

DECEMBER 9 Bob Kerrey replaces Max Cleland on commission upon Cleland's confirmation to the board of the Ex-Im Bank

2004

JANUARY 25 *NASA's Mars Rover beams back images from surface of Mars*

JANUARY 26–27 Seventh public hearing held, "Borders, Transportation, and Managing Risk"; decision announced to seek two-month extension of commission's deadline

JANUARY 27 *Senator John Kerry wins New Hampshire Democratic Primary*

FEBRUARY 4 White House announces support for extension of commission's reporting date

FEBRUARY 7 Commission interviews Condoleezza Rice at White House

FEBRUARY 10 Agreement on implementation of PDB agreement

FEBRUARY 13 Letters sent to Presidents Clinton and Bush, Vice-Presidents Gore and Cheney, requesting interviews

FEBRUARY 23 Gonzales letter sent refusing Rice public testimony

MARCH 2 Chair, vice-chair, and Thompson meet with Speaker Hastert; formal announcement made of extension

MARCH 2 *Senator John Kerry sweeps "Super Tuesday" primaries, locking up Democratic presidential nomination*

MARCH 11 *Madrid train bombing takes place*

MARCH 20 FSC calls for Zelikow resignation

MARCH 21 *Richard Clarke appears on CBS's* 60 Minutes

MARCH 22 *Richard Clarke's book* Against All Enemies *is published*

MARCH 23-24 Eighth public hearing held, "Counterterrorism Policy"

MARCH 30 White House agrees to Rice testimony, and Bush and Cheney meet with all ten commissioners; commission meeting, Zelikow distributes final report outline

APRIL 8 Ninth public hearing held; Condoleezza Rice testifies before commission; commission interviews former President Clinton

APRIL 9 Commission interviews former Vice-President Gore

APRIL 10 August 6, 2001, PDB declassified, released

APRIL 13-14 Tenth public hearing held, "Law Enforcement and the Intelligence Community"; John Ashcroft accuses Jamie Gorelick of having constructed "the wall"

APRIL 29 Commission interviews President Bush and Vice-President Cheney in Oval Office

MAY 18-19 Eleventh public hearing held, at New School in New York City, "Emergency Response"

JUNE 3 *George Tenet resigns as director of Central Intelligence Agency*

JUNE 5 *Ronald Reagan dies in California at age ninety-three*

JUNE 16-17 Twelfth public hearing held, "9/11 Plot and National Crisis Management"

JUNE 28 *United States transfers sovereignty to transitional government in Iraq*

JULY 6 Statement on Iraq–al Qaeda ties and having access to same information as Vice-President Cheney is made

JULY 21 *Sandy Berger resigns as foreign policy advisor to Kerry campaign*

JULY 22 Final report released

JULY 26–29 *Democratic National Convention held in Boston, Massachusetts*

JULY 30 Chairs testify before Senate Governmental Affairs Committee

AUGUST 2 President Bush announces executive orders based on commission recommendations

AUGUST 21 Commission closes down; releases staff monographs on terrorist financing, terrorist travel

AUGUST 30–SEPTEMBER 2 *Republican National Convention held in New York City*

SEPTEMBER 4 *More than three hundred killed in attack on Russian school in Beslan*

OCTOBER 6 Collins-Lieberman passes Senate 96–2

OCTOBER 8 House 9/11 Recommendations Implementation Act passes 282–134

OCTOBER 12 *The 9/11 Commission Report* nominated for National Book Award

OCTOBER 27 House-Senate conference committee on implementing recommendations fails

NOVEMBER 3 *George W. Bush wins reelection*

NOVEMBER 20 House-Senate conference committee fails again

NOVEMBER 30 Commission holds press conference urging a vote on bill implementing recommendations

DECEMBER 3 Bush issues letter in support of bill

DECEMBER 6 House approves legislation

DECEMBER 7 Senate approves legislation

DECEMBER 17 Bush signs Intelligence Reform and Terrorism Prevention Act of 2004

INDEX

INDEX / 373